Advanced Database Marketing

Advanced Database Marketing

Innovative Methodologies and Applications
for Managing Customer Relationships

Edited by

KRISTOF COUSSEMENT
KOEN W. DE BOCK
and

SCOTT A. NESLIN

Routledge
Taylor & Francis Group

LONDON AND NEW YORK

First published in paperback 2024

First published 2013 by Gower Publishing

Published 2016 by Routledge
4 Park Square, Milton Park, Abingdon, Oxon OX14 4RN

and by Routledge
605 Third Avenue, New York, NY 10158

Routledge is an imprint of the Taylor & Francis Group, an informa business

Gower Applied Business Research
Our programme provides leaders, practitioners, scholars and researchers with thought provoking, cutting edge books that combine conceptual insights, interdisciplinary rigour and practical relevance in key areas of business and management.

British Library Cataloguing in Publication Data
Advanced database marketing : innovative methodologies and
  applications for managing customer relationships.
  1. Database marketing. 2. Consumer profiling.
  I. Coussement, Kristof. II. Bock, Koen W. de. III. Neslin,
  Scott A., 1952-
  658.8'34-dc23

Library of Congress Cataloging-in-Publication Data
Advanced database marketing : innovative methodologies and applications for managing customer relationships / [edited] by Kristof Coussement, Koen W. De Bock, and Scott A. Neslin.
    p. cm.
  Includes bibliographical references and index.
  ISBN 978-1-4094-4461-9 (hbk) -- ISBN 978-1-4094-4462-6 (ebk)
  1. Database marketing. 2. Consumer profiling. 3. Customer
  relations. I. Coussement, Kristof. II. Bock, Koen W. de. III. Neslin, Scott
  A., 1952-
    HF5415.126.A377 2013
    658.8'120285574--dc23
                                                                2012032138

ISBN: 978-1-4094-4461-9 (hbk)
ISBN: 978-1-03-283719-2 (pbk)
ISBN: 978-1-315-56568-2 (ebk)

DOI: 10.4324/9781315565682

Contents

List of Figures	*ix*
List of Tables	*xi*
About the Editors	*xiii*
List of Contributors	*xv*
Preface	*xvii*

Introduction		1
1	The Brave New World of Database Marketing	1
2	Book Contents	2
	References	7

PART I   **METHODS**

Chapter 1   **Data Preprocessing in Database Marketing: Tasks, Techniques, and Why They Matter**   **11**
Stefan Lessmann

1	Introduction	11
2	The Process of Knowledge Discovery from Databases	13
3	The Tasks and Techniques of Data Preprocessing	14
4	Predicting Households' Income Level: The Effect of Data Projection on Forecasting Accuracy	29
5	Conclusions	34
	References	35

Chapter 2   **Textual Customer Data Handling for Quantitative Marketing Analytics**   **41**
Kristof Coussement and Koen W. De Bock

1	Introduction	41
2	The Unpopularity of Textual Data Analysis	42
3	Text Mining: The Process	42
4	Software	58
5	Conclusion and Directions for Further Research	58
	Appendix 1: 10 Hotel Le Palais in Prague Reviews Randomly Scraped from TripAdvisor	59
	Appendix 2: Term-by-document Matrix	61
	References	64

Chapter 3   **Bayesian Networks and Applications in Direct Marketing**   **67**
Yuan Yuan Guo and Man Leung Wong

1   Introduction   67
2   Bayesian Networks   69
3   Bayesian Network Classifiers   74
4   Learning Bayesian Networks from Incomplete Databases   80
5   Direct Marketing Modeling   82
6   The Evolutionary Bayesian Network (EBN) Algorithm   84
7   Application in Direct Marketing Modeling   84
8   Conclusion   92
    Acknowledgments   92
    References   92

Chapter 4   **Quantile Regression for Database Marketing: Methods
and Applications**   **97**
Dries F. Benoit and Dirk Van den Poel

1   Introduction   97
2   Methodological Background   98
3   Case Studies   103
4   Summary   114
    References   114

Chapter 5   **Ensemble Learning in Database Marketing**   **117**
Koen W. De Bock and Kristof Coussement

1   Introduction   117
2   Basics of Ensemble Learning   119
3   Algorithms   124
4   Applications in Database Marketing   131
5   Advanced Topics   134
6   Software   139
7   Summary   139
    References   140

Chapter 6   **Advanced Rule-based Learning: Active Learning, Rule
Extraction, and Incorporating Domain Knowledge**   **145**
*Thomas Verbraken, Véronique Van Vlasselaer, Wouter Verbeke,
David Martens, and Bart Baesens*

1   Introduction   145
2   Rule Extraction   146
3   Decompositional Rule Extraction from Artificial Neural Networks   148
4   Decompositional Rule Extraction from Support Vector Machines   153
5   Pedagogical Rule Extraction Algorithms   156
6   Visualizing the Extracted Rule Sets Using Decision Tables   158

7   Case Study: Rule Extraction for Customer Churn Prediction   160
8   Conclusion   162
    References   162

PART II   APPLICATIONS

Chapter 7   Hybrid Models for Recommender Systems   167
               Asim Ansari

               1   Introduction   167
               2   Hybrid Latent Factor Models   172
               3   Model Extensions   177
               4   Estimation Methodologies and Issues   182
               5   Item Selection Model   183
               6   Conclusions   184
                   References   185

Chapter 8   Marketing in the New Mobile Economy   189
               Anindya Ghose and Sang-Pil Han

               1   Introduction   189
               2   Mobile Web and Apps   191
               3   Mobile Social Media and Social Network   195
               4   Location-based Services: The Impact of Real-time Geography
                   on User Browsing and Purchase Behaviors   198
               5   Mobile Commerce   199
               6   Conclusion   202
                   References   203

Chapter 9   Targeting Display Advertising   209
               Wendy W. Moe

               1   Introduction   209
               2   Measuring the Effectiveness of Online Display Advertising   210
               3   Targeting Strategies   216
               4   Risks of Targeting Display Ads   224
               5   Future Research   225
                   References   226

Chapter 10   Paid Search Advertising   229
               Oliver J. Rutz and Randolph E. Bucklin

               1   Introduction   229
               2   A Short-term Perspective – Paid Search as a Direct Marketing Tool   232
               3   A Long-term Perspective – Indirect Effects of Paid Search   236
               4   Beyond Keywords   240
               5   Emerging Topics   241

6   Conclusion   242
References   243

Chapter 11   Social Media Management   247
Dina Mayzlin

1   Introduction   247
2   The "Why" and "What?" of Social Media   248
3   Social Media Metrics and Data Collection   250
4   The Firm's Management of Social Interactions (and Social Media)   253
References   262

Chapter 12   Dynamic Customer Optimization Models   265
Scott A. Neslin

1   Introduction   265
2   The Impetus for Dynamic Customer Optimization   265
3   The Elements of Dynamic Customer Optimization   268
4   The Development of the Dynamic Customer Optimization Field   271
5   Applications   274
6   Summary, Key Challenges, and Future Research   283
References   284

Chapter 13   Direct Marketing in the Non-profit Sector   287
Griet Verhaert

1   Introduction   287
2   Different Aspects of the Donor Lifecycle   288
3   Multi-channel Approach   291
4   Database and Methods to Optimize Direct Marketing in
Fundraising   293
5   Campaign Evaluation   298
6   Conclusion, Challenges, and Opportunities for the Future   300
References   300

Index   *303*

List of Figures

P1.1	Book structure and chapter overview	xix
1.1	Effect of a log-transformation for numeric attributes	23
1.2	Lift distribution for different prediction methods and category coding procedures	32
2.1	Different steps in the text mining process	43
3.1	A Bayesian network example	69
3.2	The structure of the naïve Bayesian classifiers	76
3.3	The structure of the semi-naïve Bayesian classifiers	78
3.4	The TAN learning procedure	79
3.5	EBN algorithm	85
4.1	The asymmetric Laplace distribution	101
4.2	Quantile regression plots	107
4.3	Ordered predictive performance	110
4.4	Lift curves	113
5.1	Increasing classification performance as a result of creating an ensemble of CART classifiers	118
5.2	Generic ensemble classifier structure	120
5.3	Graphical representation of Dietterich's three reasons for ensemble learning performance	123
5.4	Kappa-error and correlation-AUC diagram for the UCI churn data set comparing AdaBoost, the Random Subspace Method, Rotation Forest, and Bagging	135
5.5	Original permutation accuracy-based Random Forest variable importance scores for the UCI churn data set	137
5.6	Random Forest partial dependence plots for a selection of four variables in the UCI churn data set	138
6.1	Pedagogical (a) and decompositional (b) rule extraction techniques	147
6.2	Architecture of a multilayer perceptron	148
6.3	Example of Nefclass network	152
6.4	Decision table quadrants	159
6.5	Decision table for customer churn prediction	161
7.1	Components of a recommender system	168
8.1	Framework for strategic goals, tactics, and research issues on mobile marketing	190
9.1	Online advertising expenditures	209
9.2	Illustration of clickstream-based behavioral targeting across an ad network	221
9.3	Illustration of how ad exposures affect advertising goodwill	223
10.1	Direct versus indirect effects of paid search	230

11.1   The roles the firm can play in managing social interactions   248
12.1   Wear-in, wear-out, and forgetting   266
12.2   The need for dynamic customer optimization – optimal mailing in the
       presence of wear-in   267
12.3   The three components of dynamic customer optimization   268
13.1   The donor lifecycle with marketing actions   288

List of Tables

1.1	Summary of the data mining process for knowledge discovery from databases	13
1.2	Standard data mining table for a direct marketing example	15
1.3	Projection of categorical attributes by means of recoding and dummy-encoding	19
1.4	Discretization of numeric attributes	24
1.5	Summary of the US Census data set	30
1.6	Experimental setup	30
1.7	Results of mixed-mode ANOVA on top-decile-lift for the within-subject factor prediction method and its factor interactions	34
1.8	Results of mixed-mode ANOVA on top-decile-lift for between-subject factors and their factor interactions	35
2.1	The unprocessed hotel review	43
2.2	Hotel review after raw text cleaning and tokenization	44
2.3	Hotel review after part-of-speech tagging	44
2.4	Hotel review after removing infrequent terms during term filtering	45
2.5	Hotel review after removing the stopwords during term filtering	46
2.6	Hotel review after stemming	46
2.7	The concept-term similarity matrix with rank 5	50
2.8	Singular values of the diagonal singular values matrix	51
2.9	The concept-document similarity matrix with rank 5	52
2.10	W matrix	54
2.11	H matrix	56
3.1	Gains table of the EBN models for the ten test sets of the data set with 1 percent missing values	88
3.2	Cumulative lifts of the networks learned by different methods for the real-world data sets with 1 percent missing values	89
3.3	Cumulative lifts of the networks learned by different methods for the real-world data sets with 5 percent missing values	90
3.4	Cumulative lifts of the networks learned by different methods for the real-world data sets with 10 percent missing values	91
4.1	Overview of the variables in the analysis	106
4.2	Description of variables	111
4.3	Parameter estimates of the different methods	112
4.4	Confusion matrices	113
5.1	Data mining contests won using ensemble learning algorithms	119
5.2	Configurations of basic ensemble learner algorithms: Bagging, the Random Subspace Method, Random Forest and AdaBoost	124
5.3	Configurations of advanced ensemble learner algorithms: Stochastic Gradient Boosting, Rotation Forest, and RotBoost	128
5.4	Ensemble learning applications in database marketing	132

6.1	The thermometer encoding procedure for ordinal variables	150
6.2	Variables of the churn data set	161
6.3	Performance of the classification algorithms	161
7.1	Ratings matrix for four users and nine movies	169
7.2	Ratings matrix with unary data	179
9.1	Online advertising performance metrics	211
9.2	Summary of online display ad effects	215
9.3	Overview of targeting approaches	216
9.4	Expected visits for various ad impression histories	223
9.5	Expected conversion for various ad impression histories	224
10.1	Sample statistics for a hotel campaign on Google	234
12.1	Examples of dynamic customer optimization model	272

About the Editors

Kristof Coussement is Associate Professor of Marketing at IÉSEG School of Management (LEM-CNRS) of the Catholic University of Lille in France and co-director of the Expertise Center for Database Marketing. He has served as a Visiting Scholar at EMLyon Business School (2011).

Professor Coussement teaches several marketing-related courses including *Customer Relationship Management, Database Marketing* and *Strategic Marketing Research* in which students are taught the theoretical principles of all aspects in operational and analytical customer relationship management (CRM), the methodological foundations of predictive marketing modeling, and marketing research.

Professor's Coussement's main research interests are all aspects in customer intelligence, B-to-B (business to business) intelligence, direct marketing, and analytical CRM. Improving his "practical" experience over the years by doing several real-life research projects in a different number of industries, his main focus lies on doing profound academic research with a high added value to business. He publishes in international peer-reviewed journals such as *Decision Support Systems, Information & Management, European Journal of Operational Research, European Journal of Marketing, Journal of Business Research, Computational Statistics & Data Analysis* and *Expert Systems with Applications*. These works have been presented at various conferences around the world. Moreover, he is co-author of the book *Marketing Research With SAS Enterprise Guide*.

Professor Coussement is founder and committee member of BAQMaR, the largest online European Association for Quantitative & Qualitative Marketing Research. More information about his work can be found at www.kristofcoussement.com

Koen W. De Bock is Assistant Professor of Marketing at the IÉSEG School of Management (LEM-CNRS) with campuses in Lille and Paris in France. He is a co-director of the Expertise Center for Database Marketing. In November 2011, Professor De Bock taught at the MBA program at the University of Stellenbosch Business School (USB), Cape Town, South Africa as visiting faculty.

In the Master in Management, he teaches the Internet marketing-related courses Digital Marketing, Web Analytics, Web Advertising, Social Media Marketing, and Search Engine Marketing. Moreover, he conducts research in database marketing and Internet marketing and is especially passionate about big-data machine learning methodologies for predictive modeling in marketing that generate true business value. He has published in international journals such as

Journal of Business Research, Computational Statistics & Data Analysis, and *Expert Systems with Applications* and has presented his work at various international academic and industrial conferences. More information can be found at www.koendebock.be

Scott A. Neslin is Albert Wesley Frey Professor of Marketing at the Tuck School of Business, Dartmouth College. He has been at the Tuck School since completing his PhD in 1978 at the Sloan School of Management, MIT. He has served as a Visiting Scholar at the School of Management, Yale University (1989–1990), the Teradata/Duke CRM Center located at the Fuqua School of Management, Duke University (2002), and the Graduate School of Business, Columbia University (2009–2010). Professor Neslin's expertise includes database marketing, sales promotion, and marketing mix models. He has researched the application of predictive modeling for cross-selling and identifying customer "churners," evaluated the effectiveness of loyalty programs, and examined the determinants of customer channel migration and "research shopping." He has investigated the impact of promotion on consumer stockpiling, brand loyalty, and consumption, as well as the role of advertising in reinforcing brand loyalty. He has published several articles on these topics in journals such as *Marketing Science, Journal of Marketing Research, Journal of Marketing*, and *Journal of Interactive Marketing*. He is co-author, with Professor Robert C. Blattberg, of *Sales Promotion: Concepts, Methods, and Strategies*; co-author, with Robert C. Blattberg and Byung-Do Kim, of *Database Marketing: Analyzing and Managing Customers*, and author of the monograph *Sales Promotion*. He is Associate Editor of *Marketing Science*, and on the editorial boards of the *Journal of Marketing Research, Journal of Marketing, Journal of Interactive Marketing, Journal of the Academy of Marketing Science*, and *Marketing Letters*. He serves as Senior Advisor for Resource Systems Group, Inc.

List of Contributors

Asim Ansari, Columbia Business School, Columbia University, New York, USA

Bart Baesens, Katholieke Universiteit Leuven, Belgium

Dries F. Benoit, Universiteit Gent, Belgium

Randolph E. Bucklin, Anderson School of Management, University of California, Los Angeles, USA

Kristof Coussement, IÉSEG School of Management, Université Catholique de Lille (LEM, UMR CNRS 8179), France

Koen W. De Bock, IÉSEG School of Management, Université Catholique de Lille (LEM, UMR CNRS 8179), France

Anindya Ghose, New York University's Leonard N. Stern School of Business, USA

Yuan Yuan Guo, Lingnan University, Tuen Mun, Hong Kong

Sang-Pil Han, City University of Hong Kong, College of Business, Hong Kong

Stefan Lessmann, Universität Hamburg, Germany

David Martens, Universiteit Antwerpen, Belgium

Dina Mayzlin, Yale School of Management, USA

Wendy W. Moe, Robert H. Smith School of Business, University of Maryland, USA

Scott A. Neslin, Tuck School of Business, Dartmouth College, USA

Oliver J. Rutz, Michael G. Foster School of Business at the University of Washington, USA

Dirk Van den Poel, Universiteit Gent, Belgium

Wouter Verbeke, Edinburgh Business School, United Kingdom

Thomas Verbraken, Katholieke Universiteit Leuven, Belgium

Griet Verhaert, Direct Social Communication, Belgium

Véronique Van Vlasselaer, Katholieke Universiteit Leuven, Belgium

Man Leung Wong, Lingnan University, Tuen Mun, Hong Kong

Preface

1   Book Rationale

Marketing analytics – and database marketing in particular – is recognized as an important business discipline, and its popularity and adoption is still growing. According to the 2012 CMO Survey, partnered by Duke University's Fuqua School of Business, the American Marketing Association and McKinsey & Company, spending on marketing analytics is expected to increase by 60 percent over the next three years from 5.7 percent to 9.1 percent of the marketing budget, and the size of customer analytic teams is expected to grow by nearly 20 percent (The CMO Survey, 2012). Analytical applications and performance management software's revenue reached $12.2 billion in 2011, representing a 16.4 percent increase in comparison to 2010 (Aquino, 2012). Furthermore, database marketing is a well-researched academic discipline. The popularity of the database marketing field in terms of the amount of scholarly journal publications is growing, especially during the last decade.

Moreover, database marketing thrives on the cross-fertilization of ideas and approaches. First, academics and corporations exchange best practices with one another. Academic research in database marketing is strongly business-driven. Many novel methodologies and applications are inspired by actual business problems, and researchers often seek collaborations with businesses which inspire them and give them access to unique customer data. For instance the reputed Customer Analytics Initiative at the Wharton School of the University of Pennsylvania focuses on the development and application of customer analytic methods with the idea to connect leading academic research institutions with the business world. For business professionals, academic research is often seen as the origin of innovative approaches to handle data and analyze customers' behavior in the continuing effort to create competitive advantage. Second, cross-fertilization exists not only between academia and the professional world, but also among various (academic) disciplines. Database marketing draws on the interplay among fields such as marketing, statistics, operations research, management information systems, and computer science.

A crucial recent trend in database marketing is the veritable explosion of techniques, capabilities, and applications. Advances in machine learning, econometrics, and optimization, combined with more powerful computing resources for applying these techniques, have created new opportunities for database marketers. Nowhere is this more apparent than in the field of internet marketing, where digital advertising, recommendation systems, social media, and mobile marketing are in the exponential phases of growth.

The rationale of this book is the following. We want to popularize and review recent advances in the field of database marketing. We see this book as a complement to previously published database marketing books as we assembled chapters that represent the most up-to-date methodologies to analyze customer data and deliver insights into the fastest emerging applications wherein database marketing plays a crucial role.

2   Target Audience

This book is of interest to both academics and professionals by offering an overview of innovative methodologies and applications in the database marketing field. The target audience includes:

- *MSc/Masters students* in marketing analytics;
- *academics* and *PhD students* who are interested in researching and teaching in the field of database marketing; and
- *marketing analysts* in business with at least a medium understanding of the basic principles in database marketing.

The unique selling proposition of this book is to offer the above audiences an integrated set of methods and applications that go a step further than introductory books on database marketing. We hope to offer masters students an appreciation for the capabilities of modern database marketing, triggering their interest in novel areas. Academics and PhD students should consider this a valuable reference work and a cutting-edge overview of what is currently "hot" in academia and business. Finally, we are convinced that due to saturated markets and fierce competition, analysts in business search for innovative ways of creating unique *customer intelligence*, something that is found in this book.

3   Structure of the Book

This book describes recent advances in database marketing. The chapters are organized in terms of Methods and Applications, as shown in Figure P1.1.

Part I describes the recent advances in the *methods* used in the database marketing domain. The structure of Part I follows the database marketing analysis process with:

1. assembling data (Chapters 1–2);
2. modeling the data (Chapters 3–5); and
3. implementing model results (Chapter 6).

Part II illustrates innovative *applications* in the database marketing field. The majority of them are situated in the field of Internet marketing. Chapter 7 explores the field of the recommender systems for generating one-to-one personalized offers. Chapter 8 investigates the new field of mobile marketing, spawned by the increased popularity of smartphones that allow customers to create, interact, and share content. Furthermore, firms are exposed to new opportunities and challenges to optimize their online advertising strategies (Chapters 9–10), while various strategies are discussed in Chapter 11 about how firms can manage online social interactions. Chapter 12 details customer management approaches for maximizing customer lifetime value (CLV) by combining the power of predictive models and dynamic programming, while the last chapter reveals the best practices of applying traditional direct marketing activities in the non-profit sector.

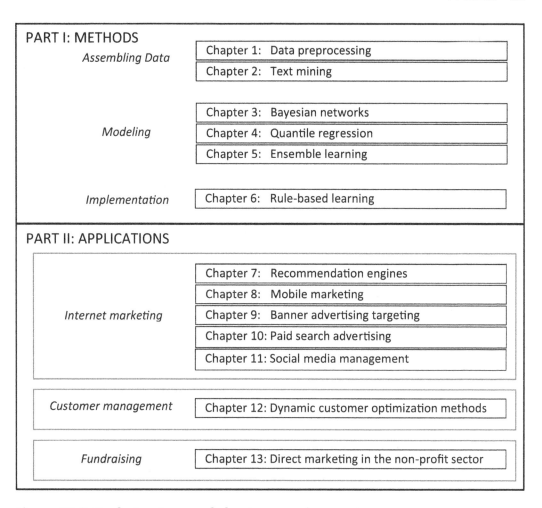

Figure P1.1 Book structure and chapter overview

4 Acknowledgments

First, the editors would like to thank all contributing authors for sharing their expertise. We greatly appreciate the contributors' motivation throughout this book project. Furthermore, we thank all database marketing researchers who built the foundations of and who contributed to our domain. Next, database marketing is a management discipline and its study is irrelevant in the absence of the practical relevance for business. Therefore, we would like to thank all marketing analysts working in firms around the globe who daily inspire our research, and who act as ambassadors of our domain on a day-to-day basis. We thank our home institutions, the IÉSEG School of Management and the Tuck School of Business, Dartmouth College, for providing the resources and research support that make possible an undertaking such as this. Lastly, we extend special thanks to Jonathan Norman and his team at Gower/Ashgate Publishing for well-receiving the book idea and providing us with all the necessary support.

References

Aquino, J. (2012). Business intelligence and analytics are getting hotter. *CRM Magazine*, June 2012, 15.

The CMO Survey (2012). Highlights and Insights February 2012. Available at: http://www.cmosurvey. org [accessed October 15, 2012].

Reviews for

Advanced Database Marketing: Innovative Methodologies and Applications for Managing Customer Relationships

This is a great book for masters or doctoral students, academics and practitioners interested in learning the cutting-edge knowledge in database marketing. It provides a comprehensive coverage on the recent advances in the methods and applications in the area. The topics are interesting, relevant and managerially useful.

Shibo Li, Indiana University, USA

This is an excellent contribution to current knowledge on database marketing, an essential dynamic field that demands continuous learning from marketers. The book covers state-of-the-art approaches in classical database marketing areas, yet also in emerging areas such as mobile, social media and Internet advertising. It is highly recommend for quantitative consultants, market researchers and managers as well as academic researchers in this field.

Barak Libai, Arison School of Business, Interdisciplinary Center (IDC), Israel

Database marketing has a long history, but it is rapidly evolving in new directions. This book has all the important new content: Internet and web, mobile, social, etc. It's a fantastic source of up-to-date knowledge for both students and practitioners.

Thomas H. Davenport, Harvard Business School, USA and co-founder and Director of Research, International Institute for Analytics

In a time where Big Data – the analysis of large datasets – has been frequently named as the main source of competitive advantage in future, this book is essential reading for researchers and managers alike. It provides an excellent in-depth overview of methods and exemplary applications illustrating the potential of generating insights from large-scale databases.

Michael Haenlein, Professor of Marketing, ESCP Europe

WOW! As a 20-year practitioner of database marketing, I found this book to be packed full of practical applications on a wide range of topics within a theoretical framework. An astonishingly rich resource for anyone with intentions to increase lifetime value of the customer, not just measure it.

Peter Liberatore, Senior Manager of Customer Analytics, L.L.Bean

Advanced Database Marketing introduces state-of-the-art methods in marketing and business analytics that firms can use to extract meaningful information from the wide range of available data. Contributions by leading researchers create an easy-to-read collection of chapters that cover data analytics (such as text mining, Bayesian networks, and quartile regression) as well as comprehensive reviews of most timely applications (such as recommendation systems, mobile marketing, online advertising, and online social interaction management). This book is particularly valuable to managers in any firm that uses the Internet for e-commerce or social media work and/or has access to individual customer-level data and, further, an indispensable asset to academics interested in a comprehensive introduction to the field of database marketing and an inventory of its current state-of-the-art.

Prof. dr. Jacob Goldenberg, Hebrew University of Jerusalem, Israel and
co-editor of the *International Journal of Research in Marketing*

Introduction

The aim of marketing is to know and understand the customer so well the product or service fits him and sells itself.

(Peter F. Drucker, 1973)

1   The Brave New World of Database Marketing

The origins of database marketing can be traced to the fields of direct marketing and relationship marketing. Direct marketing brought to the forefront the importance of customer data, concepts such as recency, frequency, and monetary value (RFM), predictive modeling, and the need for accountability in marketing efforts. Relationship marketing, introduced by Leonard Berry (Berry, 1983), broadened the scope of database marketing to consider the customer relationship, exemplified by concepts such as customer acquisition, retention, and development, and the unifying theme of customer lifetime value. The result of this fusion between direct marketing and relationship marketing is what we know as customer relationship management (CRM). Database marketing can be seen as the analytical side of CRM, and is sometimes called analytical CRM.

Blattberg et al. (2008: 4) considered these developments in developing a definition of database marketing, namely:

Database marketing is the use of customer databases to enhance marketing productivity through more effective acquisition, retention, and development of customers.

This definition indeed captures the importance of analyzing customer data, making the analysis accountable (*enhance marketing productivity*) while focusing on the the importance of the customer relationship (*acquisition, retention, and development*).

This definition still applies today. However, there are four recent trends that substantially amplify this definition. These trends are:

1.   the greater variety of data available;
2.   the availability of a broader set of methodologies beyond standard statistical tools;
3.   the desire to develop not only actions but *insights* from the data; and
4.   the ability to implement these targeted actions quickly and in real time.

The proliferation of data available today is due in part to advances in data processing, collection, and management, but perhaps most strikingly due to the diffusion and harnessing of the Internet. The Internet provides traditional transactional data such as customer purchases, but much more, including product search behavior, the formulation as well as use of recommendations, participation in social media, exposure to advertising, and the modern form of direct mail, namely email. Even more important is that companies are starting to merge these data with offline data, creating a "360-degree view" of the customer. Indeed the proliferation of Internet data is why we find ourselves with five chapters strongly related to database applications involving the Internet.

The "tried and true" methodologies of simple RFM analysis and regression are still widely used in database marketing. But new, more powerful methods are making their way into modern database marketing. The distinction of these methods is they draw on several disciplines, including computer science, operations research, computational linguistics, sociology, economics, as well as statistics. This is why methods such as machine learning, dynamic programming, text mining, Bayesian analysis, and consumer choice models make their way into this book.

One criticism of database marketing is that it has been "black-box;" it prescribes actions that work in the sense of increased response rates and profits, but in today's world of database marketing there is more emphasis on insight. The de-mystification of database marketing has become important for two key reasons. First, as database marketing has become a more significant investment, senior marketing management pays more attention to it, and marketing managers want to understand *why* they are contacting customer A but not customer B, and why they are recommending certain products to certain customers. They want to make sure the activities of the database marketing group are consistent with the positioning and target group strategy of the brand. Second, new tools are becoming available for deriving insights. This is particularly evident in the rules-based learning chapter.

Finally, database marketing's emphasis on implementation and accountability has been enhanced by modern-day capabilities. Companies can now implement the recommendations prescribed by statistical models. They can do so in real time on the Internet. They can conduct field tests of recommendation engines, search advertising copy, and banner advertising. In general, companies' ability to implement and evaluate the actions prescribed by sophisticated models can be tested more easily today than ever before.

In summary, the definition of database marketing hasn't changed – it's still about analyzing customer data and using it to improve marketing productivity by managing the customer relationship. But the *meaning* of the definition has become more vivid and more exciting due to the greater variety of data, the increasingly multidisciplinary analytical "toolkit," the drive for insights in addition to financial performance, and the capability to implement and evaluate more effectively. The reader will see these themes emerge in the chapters we have assembled for this book.

2   Book Contents

The contributions within this book are structured along the two dimensions – methodology and application. Part I describes the methodological advances, while Part II summarizes innovative applications areas in the database marketing field. Below you will find a detailed overview of the different chapters in the book.

2.1   PART I: METHODS

During the last few decades, methods for tracking consumer behavior became more sophisticated, and there has been a move from describing historical customer information to predicting consumers' future behavior. Predictive modeling has established itself as a popular tool in database marketing. The true utility of a predictive model depends on the decisions made in:

1. assembling data;
2. modeling; and
3. implementation.

Part I is structured along these three stages of the predictive modeling process. Chapter 1 addresses data preprocessing, a necessary and vital step that has to take place before any modeling activity can be initiated. Data preprocessing greatly influences the degree to which pattern extraction is feasible and successful. The chapter strives to increase the awareness that data preprocessing is an important part of predictive analytics and a potential leverage to increase performance. Core preprocessing tasks and techniques are reviewed and some guidelines are provided on how to choose among alternative procedures. Furthermore, an empirical case study is undertaken to explore the relationship between prediction method, preprocessing, and forecasting accuracy. The results confirm a significant accuracy impact for certain preprocessing techniques and evidence that their effectiveness differs across prediction methods.

Chapter 2 zooms in upon text mining, a technique for assembling data when the data are in text format. The increasing amount of textual customer information that is stored in customer data warehouses leads to increased challenges and opportunities for marketing managers to better grasp the underlying customer behavior. However, marketing analytics often neglect this valuable type of information as it requires additional knowledge and effort to convert the text into a numeric representation suitable for subsequent processing. This chapter discusses the text mining process, and zooms into:

1. the text preprocessing phase that convert the textual consumer data into a high dimensional term-by-document matrix;
2. the dimension reduction techniques singular value decomposition and non-negative matrix factorization that group together related terms and projects them into a semantic space of lower dimensionality that could be used in traditional marketing analysis; and
3. the text mining applications published in top-tier marketing journals.

Chapter 3 shifts the focus to the actual model building process. Bayesian networks are popular within the fields of artificial intelligence and data mining due to their ability to support probabilistic reasoning from data with uncertainty. They can represent the co-related relationships among random variables and the conditional probabilities of each variable from a given data set. With a network structure at hand, people can conduct probabilistic inference to predict the outcome of some variables based on the values of other observed ones. The objective of the direct marketing modeling problem is to predict and rank potential buyers from the buying records of previous customers. The customer list will be ranked according to each customer's likelihood of purchase. Bayesian networks can estimate the probability of a customer belonging to certain class(es) and are therefore suitable for many database marketing applications. For example, by assuming the estimated probability to be equal to the likelihood of purchase or response, they are suitable to handle the direct marketing problem. However, the databases containing the buying records of customers may contain missing values. This chapter gives an introduction to Bayesian networks and proposes a system for discovering Bayesian networks from incomplete databases in the presence of missing values. The authors apply it to a real-world direct marketing modeling problem, and compare the performance of the discovered Bayesian networks with other models obtained by other methods. In the comparison, the Bayesian networks learned by the proposed system outperform other models.

Chapter 4 discusses quantile regression and its relevance for database marketing. The simple yet well-performing and easily interpretable statistical methods such as linear and logistic regression account as gold standard methods in predictive modeling for marketing in both academic literature and business usage. In regression, an equation is sought describing the relationship between a number of independent variables and the mean of the dependent variable conditional upon the independent variables' values. Unfortunately, a mean is a strong simplification of reality as it is unable to unveil other characteristics of the underlying data distribution and might lead to incomplete or flawed conclusions when the conditional distribution is for instance highly skewed or contains outliers. Quantile regression is a generic approach that extends the mean regression model to a model specifying the relationship between covariates and any conditional quantile of the response variable of interest.

This chapter introduces the topic of quantile regression. A distinction is made between the frequentist and the Bayesian approach to estimate such models. Further, special attention is given to a recent development within this family of methods: binary quantile regression. Then, an elaborate section discusses the potential usage and advantages of quantile regression for database marketing through two case studies on customer lifetime value and customer churn prediction.

Chapter 5 sheds light upon the advantages of letting predictive models in database marketing join forces, whereby several models are combined into new, more flexible, and more powerful models. These so-called ensemble learners or multiple classifier systems have consistently emerged as winning entries in data mining contests, such as the Teradata/Duke CRM competition, KDD Cup or the Netflix Prize since many years. However, despite their strength and intuitive nature, their applications in real-life business are still scarce. This chapter untangles the topic of ensemble learning by first explaining their common structure, shared by the numerous algorithms that have been proposed within this category of statistical learners over recent years. Three intuitive arguments are presented to explain the potential of these methods to predict more accurately. The chapter continues with an elaborate overview of a selection of the most prominent and relevant ensemble learning algorithms for classification. Subsequently, it provides an overview and discussion of the academic literature on real-life database marketing applications in which ensemble learning was deployed, while a practical example is used to illustrate several concepts throughout the chapter. Special attention is given to two more advanced topics: (1) diversity, a key ingredient of any successful ensemble learner, and how it can be measured and assured; and (2) model interpretability.

The final chapter of the first part of this book (Chapter 6) shifts the focus to implementation by focusing on interpreting and operationalizing predictive models. Various different data mining techniques for marketing purposes are recently discussed in literature and have proven their excellence performance in a day-to-day business setting. Besides the search for optimal prediction performance, classification models should be intuitively correct and in accordance with the experts' knowledge. This chapter focuses on rule-based methods, that is, techniques which supplement the superior performance of black-box models with a set of insightful and comprehensible rules. These techniques open up these black-box models. The chapter summarizes the state-of-the-art rule-based models, describes the use of decision tables to visualize the extracted rules and concludes with an application in a churn prediction setting.

2.2   PART II: APPLICATIONS

Part II describes new applications in which the principles of database marketing can be applied in companies. Chapter 7 presents an integrated, comprehensive discussion of recommender systems. Recommender systems are software systems and statistical procedures used by firms to suggest ("recommend") products to their customers. A recommender system consists of data, a user model, and a selection model. A recommender system utilizes customer and product data to predict what product the customer is likely to prefer or purchase, and uses this prediction to select the product to be recommended to the customer. The data used to compute these predictions can pertain to the user, the product, or the user/product dyad. The chapter builds a general structure that shows how all three types of predictor data can be integrated into a "hybrid latent factor model." The model incorporates observed as well as unobserved user, product, and dyad data. It combines content-type user models that rely on observed predictors and collaborative filtering models that rely just on observed preferences or purchases. The chapter shows how the general model can be extended to binary preferences, missing data, unary data, buying context, and preference evolution. It then includes a discussion of estimation and selection models and closes with an overview of future research topics.

Chapter 8 examines strategic goals, tactics, and research issues related to marketing via mobile devices. The strategic goals examined include advertising and promotion, targeting, branding, and sales. The tactics that help achieve these goals include mobile web and applications ("apps"), mobile social media and social networks, location-based services, and mobile commerce. Mobile devices enhance the potential of companies to market to customers in real time more so than ever before. The chapter discusses these marketing tactics and reviews academic research relevant to them. This research provides key insights on how consumers use mobile devices, how consumers generate and consume user-generated content, how consumers select and use apps, how consumers use mobile devices as social media, the relevance of geography, and complementarity/substitution between mobile and non-mobile channels. While there is much more that needs to be learned, and the mobile platform is evolving, research to-date reveals the tremendous potential of mobile devices to enhance marketing effectiveness.

In Chapter 9, online display advertising and its targeting strategies are addressed. Online display advertising, or banner advertising, while being one of the earliest forms of advertising on the Internet, is still highly relevant today as expenditures have been consistently on the rise. Simultaneously however, this form of online advertising has been troubled by steadily decreasing effectiveness in terms of click-through rates, a phenomenon often described as banner blindness. However, over the years, as strategies have been developed to gather increasing amounts of data and establish better metrics and analytics, online marketers have developed and refined their ability to target display ads to the most promising prospects. This chapter first provides an overview of metrics that are commonly used to evaluate the effectiveness of online display ads. Thereby, initially, a distinction is made between metrics that measure short-term and long-term effects. Further, the chapter discusses models that take into account immediate and long-term response simultaneously, and models that formally incorporate the multi-channel effect of online advertising. Finally, targeting strategies are discussed that deploy individual information to match ads and their most likely responders. Subsequently, targeting based upon user characteristics, geographical targeting, contextual targeting, and behavioral targeting are discussed.

Chapter 10 discusses paid search advertising, where Internet advertisers reach customers in the midst of their product search process. The chapter addresses the direct and indirect impacts of paid search. The direct effect is the immediate impact of a paid search ad, whereas indirect effects are longer term. The chapter reviews the history of paid search advertising and institutional issues such as the bidding process for ad placement. It then turns to a summary of empirical studies and models pertaining to direct effects, including the determinants of click-through rates and conversion. The chapter next discusses indirect effects including the impact of generic search on future branded search, the impact of click-through visits on future visits, the value of search advertising as a customer acquisition channel, and search ad copy design. The chapter concludes with a discussion of emerging topics such as the long tail in paid search, and the relationship between organic search and paid search click-throughs.

Chapter 11 summarizes how the firm can manage online social interactions. First, it describes the why and what of social interactions. That is, the chapter discusses what motivates consumers to share product recommendations and what product characteristics result in more word of mouth. The chapter then discusses issues related to social media metrics and data collection. It next proceeds to summarize existing research on the three roles that the firm can play in the management of social interactions:

1. observer;
2. influencer; and
3. participant.

Existing research suggests that the firm can measure the impact of social media interactions and successfully influence these interactions. While there is growing literature related to the role of the firm as observer and as influencer, the role of the firm as participant has not been studied extensively. Hence, the opportunities for impactful new research are greatest in this area.

Dynamic customer optimization models, discussed in Chapter 12, combine customer response models and optimization to determine what types of marketing to target to which customers at what time in order to maximize customer lifetime value. The fundamental premise of dynamic customer optimization is that marketing activities targeted in the current period should take into account the implications of these actions for marketing in subsequent periods. This chapter reviews the dynamic elements of customer response models that come to play in dynamic customer optimization, and then discusses the fundamentals of dynamic optimization techniques. The chapter next reviews the evolution of the customer optimization field, starting with its roots in sales force management, proceeding to modern applications in catalogs, to more recent applications involving marketing tactics such as emails, sampling, and coupons, and free shipping. The last section of the chapter reviews several research papers, discussing the customer response model, the optimization, and the application. We conclude with a discussion of the promise and challenges of dynamic customer optimization models.

Chapter 13 focuses on how direct marketing practices in the non-profit sector differ from traditional direct marketing activities in the public and private sector. Using real-life case studies throughout the chapter, the author illustrates several direct marketing activities along the customer lifecycle, that is, donor acquisition, retention, and reactivation. Understanding charitable giving in its stage of the customer lifecycle is of crucial importance to optimize the donor database. More specifically, three questions are crucial: "To whom should the non-profit organizations send a donor invitation?"; "How to optimize or personalize the content of the mailing campaign?" and "Via which channels should the direct marketer target its donors?" This chapter concludes with an explanation of numerous campaign evaluation keywords.

References

Berry, L.L. (1983). *Relationship Marketing*. American Marketing Association, Chicago.
Blattberg, R.C., Kim B.-D. and Neslin, S.A. (2008). *Database Marketing: Analyzing and Managing Customers*. Springer, New York.

Methods

Data Preprocessing in Database Marketing: Tasks, Techniques, and Why They Matter

STEFAN LESSMANN

1 Introduction

The marketing domain has a long tradition of employing quantitative models to elicit and support decision making. For example, the well-known RFM (recency, frequency, monetary value) model has been used for decades by mail-order companies and charity organizations for targeting purposes (for example, Bauer, 1988). Nowadays, companies have access to vast amounts of customer-centric data. The data is gathered internally through a holistic use of information systems to support core business operations, and externally through partnering and exchanging data with suppliers, logistic service providers, and so on to improve efficiency and effectiveness of the overall supply chain. Finally, rich sets of data are collected from direct interactions with customers through various channels. The availability of such data has led to data-driven decision aids becoming ever more prominent in marketing.

Forecasting plays an important role in database marketing. Predictive models help marketers to anticipate future customer behavior and are routinely employed in a variety of applications including estimating customer lifetime value (for example, Bemmaor and Glady, 2011; Kumar, et al., 2006; Kumar, et al., 2008), fighting attrition through proactively identifying likely churners (for example, Glady, et al., 2009; Neslin, et al., 2006; Verbeke, et al., 2012), predicting customers' share of wallet (for example, Du, et al., 2007; Reichheld, 1996; Rosset, et al., 2007), or modeling customers' likelihood of responding to direct mail (for example, Bose and Xi, 2009; G. Cui, et al., 2006; O'Brien, 1994).

The vast majority of marketing prediction models ground on the principles of supervised learning. To estimate customers' likelihood of reacting to direct mail, for example, a functional relationship (that is, a model) between a set of independent variables, usually associated with the recency, frequency and monetary value of customers' past purchases as well as demographic customer information, and a zero-one dependent variable indicating whether or not a customer has responded to a past campaign, is inferred (for example, Banslaben, 1992; Deichmann, et al., 2002; Malthouse, 2001).[1] In supervised learning, models are estimated (*learnt*) from past observations where attribute values *and* actual values of the target variable have been observed (for example, Hastie, et al., 2009). The resulting model facilitates predicting the target variable when only the attribute values are observable; for example, estimating how likely it is that customers (with known attribute values) respond to a future mailing if they are solicited.

Much research has concentrated on examining the effectiveness of alternative prediction methods such as logit models, neural networks, or tree-based ensemble learners for different marketing tasks (for example, Coussement, et al., 2010; Coussement and Van den Poel, 2008; Cui and Curry, 2005; Curry and Moutinho, 1993; De Bock and Van den Poel, 2011; Ghosh, et al., 1984; Kim, et al., 2005; Lemmens and Croux, 2006; Neslin, et al., 2006; West, et al., 1997). From a practitioner's point of view, devising a prediction model might not be the biggest challenge since many powerful techniques are readily available in standard software packages. Instead, the task of collecting and integrating the data needed for any modeling activity is often the most time-consuming and costly step within industrial data mining projects (for example, Berry and Linoff, 2011). In this sense, data collection/integration and model building[2]/development can be regarded as particularly well explored and understood from a practical and academic perspective, respectively.

This chapter deals with data preprocessing, a modeling phase in between data collection/integration and model building, which has received much less attention in both academia and industry. The objective of data preprocessing is to convert raw data into a format that facilitates the application of quantitative prediction methods *and* aids the model building algorithm in extracting predictive information from the independent variables. In particular, the choices made within data preprocessing have a significant influence upon the accuracy of prediction models (Crone, et al., 2006; Neslin, et al., 2006).

The chapter gives an overview of data preprocessing for database marketing and illustrates the choices that need to be made in this modeling stage. This is to increase awareness for data preprocessing as an integral part of predictive modeling and a potential opportunity to increase forecasting accuracy. In addition, the exposition shall equip readers with a sound understanding of alternative preprocessing techniques and their respective merits and demerits. Finally, a case study is undertaken to:

1.   demonstrate empirically the impact of preprocessing on predictive accuracy;
2.   explore the intricate relationship between prediction and preprocessing methods in some detail; and
3.   provide some guidance on when a specific form of preprocessing is effective.

The remainder of the chapter is organized as follows: Section 2 briefly reviews the overall data mining process, to give a context for data preprocessing activities and techniques. These are elaborated in Section 3. The results of the empirical case study are presented in Section 4, before conclusions are drawn in Section 5.

---

1   The dependent and independent variables are known by many names in the literature. In this chapter, the dependent variable is referred to as the target variable. Independent variables are synonymously referred to as attributes or features.

2   Also termed model estimation in the statistics literature.

2   The Process of Knowledge Discovery from Databases

Knowledge discovery from databases (KDD) is defined as "the nontrivial process of identifying valid, novel, potentially useful, and ultimately understandable patterns in data" (Fayyad, et al., 1996). According to the authors, data mining is a single step within the overall process concerned with the selection and application of a specific learning algorithm. Nowadays, the distinction between data mining and KDD has vanished and both terms are often used interchangeably.

The KDD process aims at solving some analytic problem and comprises eight main steps. These steps are traversed in a linear or cyclic fashion, possibly going back to a previous stage to improve some measure of modeling quality. The individual tasks and their results are summarized in Table 1.1 (Fayyad, et al., 1996):

Table 1.1   Summary of the data mining process for knowledge discovery from databases

Step	Description	Outcome
1.	Task definition – Specifying the decision problem and developing an understanding for the particular application domain.	Project plan.
2.	Data selection – Identifying data sources that could be relevant for the analytical task at hand. – Creating a documentation of available data sources and how they can be accessed.	Selection of candidate data.
3.	Data cleaning and preparation – Gathering and integrating potentially useful data from identified sources to form an analytic data set. – Accounting for noise and obvious errors. – Deciding upon strategies to deal with missing values.	Cleaned analytic data set in raw format.
4.	Data preprocessing – Selecting informative candidate features or creating novel features. – Sampling to decrease the amount of data to a manageable level. – Encoding variables so as to increase their value for the modeling procedure.	Preprocessed data set ready for analysis.
5.	Selection of data mining task – Mapping the analytic problem to a category of data mining methods such as regression, segmentation, or association (for example, Berry and Linoff, 2011).	Family of candidate algorithms.
6.	Selection of data mining method – Choosing an appropriate data mining method from the previously defined category (for example, neural networks, K-means, and so on). – Deciding upon the parameterization of the method. – Explanatory data analysis to aid the above tasks.	Data mining method.

Table 1.1   Continued

Step	Description	Outcome
7.	Model creation – Applying the selected method to the data. – Building a predictive or descriptive model. – Searching for patterns in the data.	Data mining model.
8.	Interpretation of results – Visualizing mining results. – Appraising discovered patterns. – Verifying results' compliance with available domain knowledge. – Possibly going back to a previous step to improve the model's fit for the focal problem.	Insight into previously unknown patterns/ Verification of prior hypothesis.

3   The Tasks and Techniques of Data Preprocessing

Data preprocessing activities can be categorized into two main streams, data projection and data reduction (Fayyad, et al., 1996). Approaches of the former category convert raw attribute values into another format, which may be essential to comply with the input requirements of certain prediction methods. Furthermore, the creation of novel, more predictive features from the available attributes also belongs to the field of data projection. Data reduction concentrates on removing less informative variables (that is, feature selection) as well as sampling. An additional task often encountered in database marketing relates to the treatment of missing or extreme attribute values in a data set. However, before exploring specific preprocessing steps in detail, we first introduce the standard data mining table (for example, Berry and Linoff, 2011), which represents the input for any data preprocessing operation.

3.1   THE STANDARD DATA MINING TABLE

A standard data mining table is a two-dimensional grid where rows represent cases, often customers in database marketing, and columns represent attributes that describe the cases. More specifically, each case is characterized by its particular combination of attribute values.

In direct marketing, for example, predictive modeling is employed to select customers for mail solicitations. In this case, the standard data mining table could refer to a catalog mailing. The cases correspond to customers who were targeted in a past campaign. For each customer, the company has collected some data associated with, for example, demographic (age, gender, marital status, household size, and so on) and transactional (number of past purchases, amount spent, days since last purchase, and so on) information. These are the customer attributes. If the table relates to a past campaign, the customers who actually responded are also known to the company. The table includes this piece of information in form of a special attribute, a binary indicator variable with values of zero for customers who did not respond and values of one for those who did. Table 1.2 gives an example of this standard data mining table.

Table 1.2   Standard data mining table for a direct marketing example

Target variable	Transactional variables				Demographic variables			External data (for example, credit worthiness, census-based neighborhood characteristics, and so on		
Accepted last offer	*Days since last purchase*	*No. of orders*	*Amount spent*	...	*House-hold size*	*City*	...	*Credit Score*	*Avg. household income*	...
0	25	12	$725		1	LA		535	$45,000	
0	100	5	$375		4	Boston		790	$75,000	
1	4	19	$2501		1	New York		505	$65,000	
0	67	7	$945		2	San Diego		498	$51,000	
1	15	1	$75		3	New York		425	$53,000	

A large number of supervised learning methods are available to derive a prediction model from a data set such as the one above. The statistical principles underlying these methods are described in detail in textbooks like Izenman (2008) or Hastie et al. (2009), and are beyond the scope of this chapter. In general, approaches for supervised learning can be categorized into regression and classification methods, depending on whether the target variable is continuous or discrete, respectively. The point central to this work is that the particular way in which real-world data is represented in the standard data mining table affects the model building process. It may be that some attribute values are missing for some customers, so that imputation strategies need to be defined. Prediction methods may benefit from encoding categorical attributes like *city* in a particular way. Some methods may require the values of numeric attributes such as *amount spent* to lie in a specific value range; yet others are sensitive to the overall number of attributes and may require a prior reduction to operate reliably. Addressing these issues is the subject of data preprocessing.

3.2   MISSING VALUES, DATA ERRORS AND OUTLIERS

Missing values are a common problem in database marketing. Customers may have omitted answering questions in surveys, customer data may have been entered incorrectly into a database in the first place, there are many reasons why marketing data sets may be incomplete and suffer from missing or erroneous values. These two problems are closely related because obvious data errors – say a value of 1800 for an attribute *year of birth* – are usually treated as if the attribute value were missing. Specifically, this is the only feasible approach when additional information to correct the erroneous value is lacking. A more difficult case concerns the treatment of outliers. Outliers are unusual values, often defined as being more than three standard deviations away from an attribute's mean value (for example, Anderson, et al., 2010). Say a customer's *year of birth* suggests that he or she is 105 years old. This is highly unlikely but not impossible. In other words, the value is not obviously wrong. There is no standard approach or general guideline how to deal with outliers. The marketing analyst has to decide on a case-by-case basis whether to keep an outlier in the data set or to take some corrective action. In the latter case, the viable strategies are the same as if the value was missing. This is why strategies to handle missing values play such an important role in preprocessing for database marketing.[3]

The problem of missing data has been covered in great detail in the statistics literature (for example, Little and Rubin, 1987; Rubin, 1976, 1978). When approaching the problem from a statistical angle, one usually begins with examining whether data is missing completely at random, missing at random, or not missing at random (for example, Lakshminarayan, et al., 1999). This categorization is important because the estimation of statistical models in the presence of missing values depends on the particular type of missing data mechanism (for example, Dempster, et al., 1977).

Without questioning the value of clarifying the nature of missing data, it is debatable whether the above classification is useful for database marketing. For example, the theory that links model estimation to missing data mechanism grounds on particular types of models and model estimation procedures such as maximum likelihood in particular. Today, the marketing analyst has access to a rich set of alternative prediction methods, which employ various different estimation principles and may ground on fundamentally different paradigms for learning from data. General theory, how the type of missing data mechanism can and should be accounted for when working with arbitrary prediction methods, is missing. Consequently, there is no obvious way to make use of the knowledge that data for some attributes is, for example, missing at random during model building. Due to these difficulties, it is common practice in data mining to decouple the treatment of missing values from model building. This has led to the development of standard imputation procedures that work independently from the data mining method.

The by far easiest way to deal with missing data is to delete from the data mining table all cases where values for one or multiple attributes are missing. The disadvantage of this approach is that potentially useful data is dropped from further analysis. Specifically, less data is available for subsequent data mining steps and the model building step in particular. Moreover, deleting cases might change some characteristics of the data (that is, the underlying distributions when data is not missing at random) and thus impede model building. The severity of these risks depends on the overall amount of available data. If the absolute number of cases without missing values is sufficiently large, then discarding cases with missing values from the data set can indeed be a feasible and efficient approach.

A slightly more elaborate approach involves replacing missing values with the attribute's mean value, or mode in case the attribute is categorical. The replacement approach is simple, fast, and avoids loss of data. However, it may unduly alter the distribution of attribute values and thereby bias subsequent modeling activities. This risk is especially large when an attribute exhibits many missing values.

The mean replacement approach can be considered *univariate* in the sense that it only uses information from the focal attribute (that is, the mean/mode over the focal

---

3   Note that strategies for handling missing/erroneous attribute values do not belong to the data preprocessing stage in Fayyad's et al. (1996) original KDD process. However, as will become clear in the following, missing value imputation is related to data projection of categorical attributes, which motivates our choice to cover the topic in this chapter on data preprocessing.

attribute's values). It is plausible that exploiting the information contained within other attributes can help to find more appropriate replacements for missing values. Assume for example that two customers, A and B, have similar values for many attributes and that A exhibits a missing value for an attribute *days since last purchase*. Given the similarity between A and B, B's attribute value is maybe a more appropriate replacement than the mean *number of days since last purchase* over all, similar and dissimilar, customers. More generally, accounting for similarity between customers during missing value replacement is likely to improve over simple strategies such as mean/mode replacement. In this context, appraising *similarity* involves comparing the values of many/all attributes. Consequently, respective replacement approaches can be considered *multivariate*.

A multivariate replacement of missing values can be implemented in different ways. One approach is to first cluster customers into homogenous subgroups by means of some standard procedure like k-means (for example, Berry and Linoff, 2011). Subsequently, a cluster-wise mean/mode replacement can be carried out. That is, the mean/mode is computed per cluster and used to replace missing values for customers within this cluster. Employing similarity information to perform a weighting mean/mode replacement is also possible. A more direct approach is to estimate missing values with a dedicated prediction model. Considering once more the example of an attribute *days since last purchase*, one can infer a functional relationship between this attribute and all others by means of regression and then use the resulting model for missing value imputation (for example, Gheyas and Smith, 2010). Finally, it should be noted that some prediction methods like C4.5 decision trees or random forest incorporate strategies for handling missing values and can work directly with incomplete data (Breiman, 2001; Quinlan, 1986).

Some studies have investigated the question of how different treatments of missing values affect the predictive performance of classification or regression models. For example, Schmid, et al. (2001) compared the omission of records suffering from missing values with mean replacement and regression-based imputation on artificial data sets where data was missing completely at random. They found that the imputation approach is often superior. In addition, their study showed that simpler prediction methods are generally less affected by missing values than more complex learners. The effectiveness of model-based imputation has also been confirmed by Batista and Monard (2003). Specifically, they showed that missing data imputation by means of the k-nearest neighbor algorithm can outperform the internal methods used by C4.5 as well as mean/mode replacement strategies. The largest empirical comparison including 15 data sets, five imputation strategies, different degrees of missingness, and six classification methods was made by Farhangfar, et al. (2008). Their findings were mixed; the effectiveness of an imputation approach differs across classifiers. Their main general conclusion is that imputation improves predictive accuracy over using the raw data in most cases. They also demonstrate the robustness of some methods (Naïve Bayes and C4.5) toward missing values. Other comparative studies concentrate on specific modeling challenges like imbalanced data or specific prediction methods such as classification trees (for example, Ding and Simonoff, 2010; Pendharkar, 2008; Twala, et al., 2008; Zarate, et al., 2006).

Given that previous studies differ notably in terms of data sets, employed prediction methods, considered missing value treatments, and other experimental conditions, it is difficult to draw general conclusions as to which approach works best, or excels under which circumstances. Model-based mechanisms have the important advantage that they make better use of the available information (that is, work in a multivariate manner). Their drawback is complexity. An individual imputation model is required for all attributes that suffer from missing values. Creating these models may be computationally demanding and it is an open question which prediction method should be used for this purpose. One general recommendation is that the fact that an attribute value is missing may contain predictive information in itself. Consequently, it is a good idea to flag missing, replaced, or imputed values with a binary dummy variable (Lemmens and Croux, 2006). This way, a prediction method is given a chance to account for the anomaly of the corresponding observation.

Finally, it should be noted that the above discussion focuses on missing value imputation in preprocessing; that is, prior to building a prediction model. Some specific problems may arise when attribute values are missing for test cases, for example, when applying a model to score novel customers according to their probability of accepting an offer. Interested readers are referred to Saar-Tsechansky and Provost (2007) for an overview and empirical comparisons of imputation strategies for this situation.

3.3   DATA PROJECTION

Data projection aims at transforming raw data into a representation that is feasible and beneficial for predictive modeling (Crone, et al., 2006). Here, the term raw data refers to a standard data mining table where attributes appear in their original version (for example, actual city names, actual income values, and so on). The transformations needed to convert this data into an appropriate format depend on attributes' measurement scale and differ between categorical and numeric attributes.

3.3.1   Treatment of categorical attributes

Categorical attributes take a value that is one of several possible categories. Examples include variables such as marital status, place of birth, and so on, where there is no ordering among distinct categories. These attributes are called nominal or, in the special case that there are only two categories, binary. Ordinal variables also belong to the family of categorical data. Unlike nominal variables, ordinal variables possess an intrinsic ordering that allows sorting operations. Credit ratings are a good example. Clearly, a rating of AAA is better than, for example, A (that is, the values can be ordered), but it is impossible to tell how much better. The problem with categorical data is that mathematical operations such as addition, subtraction, and so on are inapplicable. Many methods rely on these operations when building a prediction model. Consider for example the attribute *city* from Table 1.2. Methods such as logit or probit, neural networks, and many others are all unable to process this textual variable directly.

Recoding is an easy solution to the problem of textual data. It involves mapping all categories to distinct real numbers (see Table 1.3). However, recoding suppresses the categorical nature of the attribute, which may impede model building. Specifically, a prediction method would process the recoded variable just as if it were numeric, which bears the risk of introducing artificial relationships. For example, employing the recoded *city* variable together with, for example, a nearest neighbor classifier, customers from LA would be viewed as "more similar" to customers from Boston than to customers from San Diego, simply because the mathematical difference between the codes is smaller (1 for LA and Boston c.f. 3 for LA and San Diego).

Table 1.3   Projection of categorical attributes by means of recoding and dummy-encoding

Target variable	Original variable	After recoding	After dummy-encoding			
Accepted last offer	City	City recoded	City=LA	City=Boston	City=NY	City=SanDiego
0	LA	1	1	0	0	0
0	Boston	2	0	1	0	0
1	New York	3	0	0	1	0
0	San Diego	4	0	0	0	1
1	New York	3	0	0	1	0

An approach which avoids introducing artificial relationships when projecting categorical variables is dummy-encoding (for example, Pyle, 1999). Let c be the cardinality of a categorical attribute. Dummy-encoding replaces the original attribute with c binary variables, each of which encodes one distinct category. [4] Table 1.3 illustrates that dummy-encoding overcomes the problem of textual data while preserving the information level of the original variable. Consider once more a distance-based learner that strives to classify customers on the basis of the *city* attribute. Employing the four new variables *City=LA, ..., City=SanDiego* the distance of different customers in terms of this attribute is always two for *customers from different cities* and zero for *customers from the same city*.[5] The categorical nature of the original attribute is sustained; attribute values can be equal or different, but one cannot tell how much they differ.

Table 1.3 also depicts the main disadvantage of dummy-encoding. Introducing one new variable for each category, dummy-encoding multiplies the total number of attributes. Working with a large number of attributes is well-known to complicate predictive modeling (for example, Hastie, et al., 2009; see also the following chapter on data reduction). Therefore, dummy-encoding can be inappropriate for database marking where real-world data sets commonly involve several categorical attributes and/or attributes with many distinct categories (for example, zip codes). In such situations, a possible solution is to reduce the number of categories by means of clustering prior to dummy-encoding (for example, Verbeke, et al., 2012). This hybrid approach effectively circumvents the main problem of dummy-encoding. However, clustering is a non-trivial data mining task in its own right and future research is needed to understand how the various choices to be made in this step (for example, which type of clustering procedure to use, whether to consider only the focal variable or using information from other variables in a multivariate setting, whether or not to make use of the target variable) affect the performance of data projection.

---

4   In fact, the number of novel attributes could be c-1, if one category is encoded by all dummy variables being zero. An advantage of this approach is that it (slightly) reduces the number of new variables. A disadvantage is that an implicit coding of one category makes it impossible for some learners to capture an interaction of this category with some other attribute. However, Crone et al. (2006) observe no performance differences between c and c-1 dummy-encoding in their preprocessing study.

5   Assuming Euclidian distance.

Weight of evidence (WOE) coding is another projection method for categorical attributes. It has gained some popularity in credit scoring (for example, Thomas, et al., 2002) but is rarely known elsewhere. An appealing feature of WOE coding is that it preserves the number of attributes in the data set. One categorical attribute is mapped to one new numerical attribute. To achieve this without taking the risk of introducing artificial relationships, WOE coding makes use of the target variable. In particular, the WOE represents a measure of a category's predictive value. It is estimated for of every distinct category and governs the data transformation. In the case of two classes (accept/reject last offer), the WOE for category i of attribute j is defined as:

$$WOE_j^i = \ln\left(\frac{P(i\,|\,accept)_j}{P(i\,|\,reject)_j}\right) \tag{1}$$

where $P(i|accept)_j$ denotes the conditional probability of observing a customer of the i'th category (for example, City=Boston) who accepted the last offer made by the company; and the meaning of $P(i|reject)_j$ is analogous.[6] Both probabilities are approximated by their relative frequencies in the data set. The WOE will be positive if the category i customers who accepted the offer outnumber the ones who rejected the offer, and negative in the opposite case. Therefore, the numeric values created through WOE coding are monotonically related to the target variable with higher WOE implying a higher likelihood of accept (Martens, et al., 2009). Computing a distance between two customers for a WOE encoded categorical attribute, results in a distance measure that captures the extent to which the attribute values of the two customers differ in terms of predictiveness. Consequently, distance computations are meaningful and not spurious as in the recoding example. In other words, although categorical – more precisely nominal – attributes do not carry ordering information by themselves, an ordering can be defined on the basis of the categories' predictiveness. This is exactly what WOE coding does.

As any other approach, WOE coding has some disadvantages. First, it is less general than the previous techniques. Making use of the target variable, WOE is restricted to supervised learning. More specifically, WOE is feasible only if the target variable is binary. Future research is needed to develop a general WOE coding framework for arbitrary supervised learning tasks.

A fourth projection technique for categorical attributes involves a tree-based transformation. This idea shares similarities with WOE coding in that the target variable is used to guide the mapping of categories to numeric values. Tree-based methods like CART, C4.5 or their ensemble extensions (for example, Hastie, et al., 2009) are well prepared to deal with categorical data because they rely on frequency comparisons when building a prediction model and avoid mathematical operations that are prohibited for categorical data. This implies that tree-based methods can work directly with the original attributes and do not require any projection. It also implies that they can be employed as a means of projection mechanisms for other data mining methods. Considering once more the example of Table 1.3, one can derive a decision tree from the univariate data

---

6   Note that the probability estimates require an additional modification whenever a category occurs only in conjunction with a single class. In this case, smoothing techniques can be employed to ensure that the conditional probability of the category given the other class is defined (for example, Provost and Domingos, 2003).

set including only the target variable and the categorical attribute *city*. The induction algorithm will then create a set of rules that capture the relationship between categories – or category combinations – with the target variable. These rules, maybe pruned to the top two or three tree levels, can be employed to convert categories into probabilities that estimate a customer's likelihood of belonging to a particular class. Specifically, each category of the original attribute is replaced with the output of the (pruned) decision tree for this category. Niculescu-Mizil et al. (2009) have employed this approach in their winning entry of the KDD-Cup 2009. In fact, they further extend the procedure and employ not only univariate trees to translate categorical attributes individually, but also construct multivariate trees from several categorical attributes to create new variables that capture possible variable interactions.

The tree-based approach is feasible whenever a target variable is available, be it discrete as in classification or continuous as in regression. Therefore, it is more general than WOE coding. The opportunity to create novel features from multiple (categorical and/or numeric) attributes is unique to this approach and has been reported to boost predictive performance (Niculescu-Mizil, et al., 2009). A minor disadvantage is associated with its implementation. A first question is whether the data to derive the tree should differ from the data to which it is applied for category translation. An in-sample approach benefits from using all available data but may be prone to overfitting. Alternatively, one can partition the data into two disjoint sets. This, is associated with the reverse advantages/disadvantages. A second issue concerns tree pruning. The analyst has to decide upon an appropriate pruning level as well as other parameters of tree learning. Employing sparse trees with only a few levels reduces the risk of overfitting and may thus facilitate an in-sample translation of categories. Overall, some experience and/or experimentation are needed for tree-based translation to unfold its full potential.

3.3.2 Treatment of numeric attributes

Most data mining methods can work directly with numerical attributes such as *days since last purchase* or *number of orders* (see Table 1.2). However, preprocessing is advisable because it can improve of the performance of prediction models and avoids numerical problems during model building (for example, Hsu, et al., 2003). Nearest neighbor classifiers, for example, rely on distance computations to discriminate between customers that accept direct-mail orders and customers who do not. That is, a customer is assigned to the class prevalent among k neighboring customers, whereby vicinity is measured in terms of some distance measure such as the Euclidian metric (for example, Berry and Linoff, 2011). The distance computations are affected by the value range of attributes. Without preprocessing, a distance-based classifier overemphasizes attributes with large values (for example, *amount spent*), whereas differences between customers along attributes like *household size*, which have much smaller values, receive less attention. To ensure that differences are equally weighted across attributes, the values of all attributes should be projected to a common scale.[7]

---

7   This is true unless domain knowledge suggests that certain attributes are indeed more important for classifying customers. In this case, however, one should strive to incorporate such prior knowledge in an explicit fashion (for example, Feelders, 2000; Heckerman, 1997; Sinha and Zhao, 2008) and still put all attributes on a common scale.

The predominant approaches for scaling numerical attributes are the z-transformation and linear scaling (for example, Crone, et al., 2006). The former converts attribute values into z-scores as follows:

$$z_j = \frac{x_j - \overline{x}_j}{s_j} \tag{2}$$

where z_j represents the standardized value of the original attribute x_j, and $\overline{x}_j$ and s_j denote the mean and standard deviation of attribute j, respectively. If attribute j follows a normal distribution, the z_j's can be expected to lie in the interval $[-1;+1]$ with 68 percent probability and $[-2;+2]$ with 95 percent probability. Almost all values (99.7 percent) will lie in the interval $[-3;+3]$ (for example, Duda, et al., 2001). Alternatively, linear scaling ensures that all values of the projected attribute lie in a specific, predefined interval. Let l and u denote the lower and upper bound of this interval. Then, with Min_j and Max_j denoting the minimal and maximal values of attribute j, respectively, linear scaling is performed as follows (for example, Haykin, 2009):

$$x_j^{scaled} = l + (u - l) \frac{x_j - Min_j}{Max_j - Min_j} \tag{3}$$

Given that the interval boundaries of the z-transformation cannot be chosen by the modeler but depend on the data, linear scaling is preferable for prediction methods of the neural network family that require all attribute values to lie in a specific value range.[8] On the other hand, the z-transformation is more robust toward noisy data. Employing an attribute's minimal and maximal values, linear scaling is heavily affected by extreme values. The z-transformation is less affected because extreme values influence both the mean and the standard deviation, which dampens their overall effect. This suggests that the z-transformation is preferable in general, unless the specific requirements of the prediction method call for a different approach.

The log-transformation (for example, Pyle, 1999) is an approach orthogonal to the previous two projection methods. Replacing the values of an attribute with their natural logarithm produces a distribution that is closer to normal. An example is shown in Figure 1.1. The left histogram depicts the raw values of an attribute *credit amount* taken from a well-known data set (German Credit) of the UCI Machine Learning Repository (Asuncion and Newman, 2010). The distribution of raw values (panel a) is heavily skewed and this skew is removed through the log-transformation shown in panel (b). The distribution of the projected attribute is close to normal. The approach is orthogonal to the z-transformation and linear scaling because the range of the resulting values will still differ across multiple attributes and thus require additional scaling.

---

8   Neural networks employ sigmoid activation functions to capture non-linear patterns in data. The output of such functions differs only for a specific range of input value, whereas input values outside the range are mapped to (almost) the same output value. Consequently, the network is unable to distinguish between attribute values outside the admitted range and cannot learn their relationship with the target variable. Enforcing a specific range of attribute values avoids this detrimental effect and is therefore the recommended preprocessing approach (for example, Haykin, 2009).

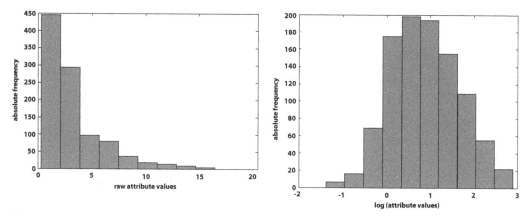

Figure 1.1   Effect of a log-transformation for numeric attributes

A log-transformation can be beneficial if an attribute exhibits a skewed distribution and if this skew impedes learning. Consider a univariate prediction task where some classifier is employed to infer a relationship between the above attribute *credit amount* and a binary target variable indicating whether the customer paid back a loan. The attribute's distribution is skewed because some borrowers were granted very large loans. Correcting for this skew, the log-transformation's influence on the learning task is twofold. On the one hand, it magnifies the differences among the "ordinary" debtors and thereby increases heterogeneity among the average customers.[9] On the other hand, the few customers with very big loans become more similar to the rest. The net impact on the classification task can be positive or negative. Specifically, relationships between the target variable and typical attribute values are easier to learn from the transformed data. This is beneficial if the corresponding customers differ in their repaying behavior. However, if the main differences in credit risk are between customers with large loans and other customers (that is, if the fact that an attribute value is extremely large has predictive value), the log-transformation will blur this information and thus complicate the prediction task.

A fundamentally different approach toward preprocessing numeric attributes is discretization (for example, Liu, et al., 2004). It maps an attribute's values to bins, which cover a specific range of values and are represented by a symbol in the transformed data set. This way, a numeric attribute is replaced by an artificially created ordinal attribute. Consider for example the attribute *amount spent* in Table . One could define three disjoint bins with value ranges $0 < x_j £ 250$, $250 < x_j £ 750$, and $750 < x_j £ ¥$ and symbols 1, 2, and 3, respectively. Afterwards, the original values can be replaced with their corresponding symbol as shown in Table 1.4 on the next page.

An important advantage of discretization is that it suppresses noise in the data and removes extreme values (for example, Pyle, 1999). Another important motivation for discretization is that it can be used to capture non-linear patterns in data (that is, attributes which are related to the target variable in a non-linear fashion). In particular, discretization allows identifying intervals of the attribute's range wherein the relationship with the target is monotonously (quasi) linear. If, for example, the relationship looks like (one cycle of) a cosine, one can identify three intervals and map the original variable's

---

9   This is also apparent from the absolute frequencies shown in Figure 1.1.

Table 1.4   Discretization of numeric attributes

Target variable	Original variable	Transformed variable
Accepted last offer	Amount spent	Amount spent binned
0	$725	2
0	$375	2
1	$2501	3
0	$945	3
1	$75	1

value to a symbol representing the corresponding interval. Linear prediction methods would be unable to capture the relationship in the original data but are able to do so after the transformation.

A disadvantage of discretization is that it may decrease an attribute's informational value. For example, customers three and four differ in terms of their acceptance behavior (that is, target variable). The attribute *amount spent* facilitates discriminating between the two customers but this opportunity is lost after discretization.

In general, the amount of retained information depends on the number of bins. A higher quantity of symbols captures more details of the original attribute but also increases the risk of sustaining noise. A larger number of symbols may also complicate category encoding, as discussed in the previous chapter. This exemplifies that the number of bins and their specific value ranges are critical parameters of discretization. Different discretization procedures can be categorized according to their strategy toward determining these parameters. An important distinction is the one between supervised methods, which make use of the target variable[10] to guide the discretization process, and unsupervised methods, which are generally applicable but vulnerable to non-uniform distributions and outliers in particular (for example, Catlett, 1991). Equal-width-binning and equal-frequency-binning are classical forms of unsupervised procedures, whereas the method of Fayyad and Irani (1992) is a popular choice when opting for a supervised approach. Only a few attempts (for example, Cerquides and Màntaras, 1997; Dougherty, et al., 1995) have been made to systematically compare alternative discretization procedures. A comprehensive hierarchical framework for discretization methods as well as empirical comparisons is due to (Liu, et al., 2004).

3.3   FEATURE EXTRACTION

The preprocessing of numerical or categorical attributes represents a form of univariate projection. The representation of attributes is altered one by one; every column of the standard data mining table is processed individually. Multivariate attribute transformations are also possible and are typically encountered in the form of feature extraction. Feature extraction aims at increasing the performance of a prediction model through creating novel attributes with higher predictive value. To that end, the original attributes undergo some mathematical transformation. Principal component analysis

---

10   Note that the vast majority of papers are rooted in classification.

(PCA), for example, performs an orthogonal transformation of the standard data mining table to reduce correlation among attributes (for example, Haykin, 2009). The resulting features, called principal components, are constructed in a way so as to ensure that every principal component captures more variance of the original data set than the following components while being uncorrelated with preceding components.

Due to the particular way in which principle components are constructed, PCA is often employed as an approach for both feature extraction and selection (see below). Specifically, every principle component captures less variance than the previous one and can therefore be considered less informative. Therefore, an intuitive feature selection strategy involves building a prediction model from a data set containing only the first n principal components (for example, Kim, et al., 2005). The parameter n needs to be specified by the user or can be tuned empirically within a model selection stage (for example, Guyon, et al., 2010).

A downside of PCA and related techniques such as kernel PCA, independent component analysis or factor analysis (for example, Hastie, et al., 2009) is that the models estimated from the transformed data set are not directly interpretable. More specifically, the artificial features created by PCA are not interpretable. Whereas customer attributes such as *age, amount spent, days since last purchase*, and so on have meaning to the marketing analyst, interpreting a principal component resulting from an orthogonal transformation of these variables is not straightforward. Comprehensibility is a key concern in database marketing and other business prediction tasks (Shmueli and Koppius, 2011), which explains why PCA-based feature extraction is employed sparsely in marketing.

3.4   DATA REDUCTION

Data reduction techniques fall into two main categories: feature selection and sampling. The former decreases the size of a data set by discarding less informative attributes, whereas the latter removes some observations. So referring to the standard data mining table (Table 1.2), feature selection and sampling are column-centric and row-centric reduction approaches, respectively.

3.4.1   Sampling

Sampling is simply a necessity whenever the amount of available data is too large to be processed and analyzed in reasonable time. It is typically performed by means of random sampling from the whole data set.[11] More advanced sampling schemes concentrate largely on the classification setting and involve, for example, drawing stratified random samples to ensure that the class frequencies in the sample and the original data set are identical (for example, Han and Kamber, 2004). Furthermore, special-purpose sampling schemes have been developed to circumvent modeling problems associated with skewed class distributions. More specifically, the class imbalance problem (for example, Japkowicz and

---

11   While not being part of data reduction, (re-)sampling regimes such as cross-validation or bootstrapping have received considerable attention in the literature. These techniques are useful for (1) assessing forecast accuracy (for example, Cooil, et al., 1987; Stone, 1974); (2) conducting statistical comparisons of alternative models (for example, Dietterich, 1998; Francois, et al., 2007); and (3) constructing ensemble classifiers from collections of models (for example, Breiman, 1996; Freund and Schapire, 1997).

Stephen, 2002) is associated with classification tasks where one class heavily outnumbers the alternative class. Imbalance complicates predictive modeling because most classifiers have a tendency to overemphasize the majority class while neglecting accuracy on minority class examples. This is due to the fact that constructing a classifier involves maximizing some measure of fit between the classification model and the actual target variable such as error rate or likelihood (for example, Hastie, et al., 2009). These measures are sensitive toward class distributions and bias the model building mechanism toward majority class examples. For example, a data set resulting from a past catalog-mailing may exhibit a response rate of 2 percent. That is, only 2 percent of the solicited customers purchased an item from the catalog. If this data is used to build a targeting model for an upcoming campaign, a naïve classifier which always predicts the majority class will achieve an almost perfect error rate of 2 percent. This exemplifies that standard accuracy indicators and thus model building mechanisms optimizing these indicators are not well prepared to cope with imbalanced data.

Database marketing applications as well as related marketing applications such as churn modeling commonly suffer from skewed class distributions. In fact, the customers most interesting from a business perspective (respondents of a catalog-mailing, actual churners, and so on) typically represent minorities. This, emphasizes the importance of preprocessing approaches to deal with class imbalance. Oversampling and undersampling are two such approaches (for example, Weiss, 2004) and have gained some popularity in marketing (for example, Burez and Van den Poel, 2009; Ling and Li, 1998). The former involves duplicating randomly selected minority class observations until class skew is removed or some predefined class ratio is achieved. Alternatively, undersampling balances class distributions by randomly discarding majority class examples. Lemmens and Croux (2006) and Verbeke, et al. (2012) confirm that oversampling improves the predictive accuracy of their churn models. Overall, findings regarding the relative superiority of oversampling versus undersampling are somewhat contradictory (for example, Batista, et al., 2005; Drummond and Holte, 2003; Hulse and Khoshgoftaar, 2009; Hulse, et al., 2007) so that clear guidance which approach is better is lacking. Undersampling always goes hand in hand with a loss of data, which may be detrimental. Oversampling, on the other hand, increases the amount of data and thus the computational burden of building a prediction model. More sophisticated versions of under-/oversampling have also been proposed in the literature and concern, for example, constructing synthetic minority class examples rather than simply duplicating observed ones (Chawla, et al., 2002). In general, an important determinant how to treat class imbalance appears to be the absolute number of minority class examples (for example, Jo and Japkowicz, 2004; Weiss, 2010). Finally, it should be noted that sampling mechanisms as a means of preprocessing are not the only strategy to deal with class imbalance. Several predictions methods incorporate mechanisms to deal with the problem in an internal manner (for example, Chen, et al., 2004; Veropoulos, et al., 1999).

3.4.2 Feature selection

Feature selection also decreases the amount of data and thus accelerates the task of building a prediction model. But this merit is not central to feature selection. Instead, it aims at:

1. reducing the cost of data gathering;
2. enhancing model comprehensibility;
3. increasing the speed with which forecasts are generated (for example, in online settings); and
4. improving predictive accuracy (Guyon and Elisseeff, 2003).

The relative importance of these objectives differs between tasks. For example, a direct marketing company could be interested in augmenting a repeat-purchase modeling data set with external customer information offered by list brokers or specialized service companies. Such information would enter a modeling data set in the form of novel features. Feature selection techniques can then help to assess whether the external data is worth buying (for example, Ji and Carin, 2007). Objectives number two and three are best explained in the context of linear regression. Consider the following regression equation which computes a forecast, $\hat{y}$, from the value of n attributes, x_j, and their corresponding coefficients, β_i, as determined during model estimation.

$$\hat{y} = \beta_0 + \sum_{j=1}^{n} \beta_j \cdot x_j \qquad (4)$$

It is clear that the speed with which this equation can be computed and thus the speed of forecast generation depends on the number of terms in the summation. While this effect is negligible for regression models, a large number of attributes can severely reduce forecasting speed for other types of models. A prior selection of attributes also simplifies understanding the mechanisms of the final model and its valuation of attributes in particular. It is widely accepted that parsimonious models are easier to interpret (for example, Kim, et al., 2005; Lessmann and Voß, 2009; Orsenigo and Vercellis, 2003). Finally, accuracy is always pivotal in predictive modeling. Accordingly, the goal to improve accuracy through removing irrelevant features is often pursued in feature selection research and gave rise to forecasting competitions dedicated to the task of feature selection (Guyon, et al., 2006; Guyon, et al., 2007). The rational is that attributes which are either not related with the target variable or are redundant, because of being heavily correlated with other variables, complicate and possibly impede predictive modeling (for example, Hastie, et al., 2009). For example, the model building algorithm may capture a false relationship between the attribute and the target variable that, exists only in the training sample but does not generalize to novel data (overfitting).

Feature selection techniques are traditionally grouped into wrappers and filters (John, et al., 1994). Guyon and Elisseeff (2003) extend this list by a third category, embedded methods, which are tightly coupled with a particular prediction method and implicitly perform feature selection as part of model building. Examples include Breiman's (2001) random forest procedure or gradient boosting (Friedman, 2001).

Wrappers use the learning method that will eventually be employed for the prediction task to score attributes. To that end, the learning algorithm is executed repetitively with varying feature subsets and the predictive performance of the resulting model is traced on validation data. Subsequently, the feature subset resulting in maximal accuracy is retained. Given that the number of possible feature subsets grows exponentially with the number of attributes, a fully enumerative evaluation of alternative feature sets is infeasible. Therefore, heuristics are employed, with forward selection and backward elimination being popular choices (for example, Ratner, 2001). More advanced and efficient approaches have been proposed in the literature (for example, Guyon and Elisseeff, 2003), especially in the context of regression modeling (for example, Efron, et al., 2004).

Filter methods examine intrinsic properties of the data to score attributes prior to applying the prediction method (for example, Hall, 2000; He, et al., 2006; Huan and Lei, 2005). Most filter methods evaluate attributes on a one-by-one basis and make use of the target variable to measure an attribute's predictive value. The stronger the relationship of an attribute with the target variable the higher its relevance score. Popular scoring criteria for classification settings include the Fisher Score for numeric attributes or information-theoretic criteria like mutual information or the Gini-coefficient for categorical attributes (for example, Arauzo-Azofra, et al., 2011; Verbeke, et al., 2012). Statistical hypothesis tests such as the F-test, the χ^2-test or the Kolmogorov-Smirnov test are also applicable (for example, Hastie, et al., 2009).

An important advantage of the wrapper approach is that it accounts for the interactions between the data and the prediction method (Kohavi and John, 1997). However, it entails constructing and assessing a large number of models, which is computationally demanding and possibly infeasible for large data sets. Due to their method-independent attribute assessment, filter methods are usually more efficient. Computing a relevance score is less costly than constructing a prediction model. On the other hand, filters face difficulties in dismissing redundant attributes that are perfectly correlated with other variables because attributes are assessed one by one. For the same reason, identifying interacting attributes that jointly affect the target variable is a problem for many filters. Such attributes can easily be dismissed because their isolated influence on the target variable is insufficient. More advanced filters (for example, Gu, et al., 2011; Hanchuan, et al., 2005; He, et al., 2006) overcome these limitations but lose some of their computational advantage over the wrapper approach. Furthermore, once the relevance scores have been obtained, filter methods require an auxiliary model selection criterion to decide upon the number of features to be discarded. A significance level of five or 1 percent is an intuitive choice for approaches that ground on statistical hypothesis tests. Under the wrapper regime, one can simply choose the feature subset with maximal accuracy. However, assessing accuracy requires additional (hold-out) validation data and in this sense complicates the modeling process (for example, Lessmann and Voß, 2009).

3.5   SOFTWARE SUPPORT FOR DATA PREPROCESSING

In order to exploit the potential of data preprocessing and make use of the techniques described above, it is crucial that database marketers have access to powerful software systems that feature preprocessing methods in an easy-to-use manner. Nowadays, the market for data mining software offers a rich set of alternative solutions for various purposes, ranging from high-end general-purpose systems such as SAS Enterprise Miner[12] or IBM SPSS Modeler[13] to specialized modeling packages like Salford Systems' Predictive

---

12   See http://www.sas.com/technologies/analytics/datamining/miner/
13   See http://www.ibm.com/software/analytics/spss/products/modeler/

Modeling Suite[14] or InfiniteInsight,[15] which offer cutting-edge technology for the large-scale enterprise and SME segment. In addition, open-source software such as the WEKA workbench,[16] RapidMiner[17] or Orange[18] implement a rich set of different data mining algorithms and offer sophisticated functionality at low cost.

All data mining packages routinely incorporate basic routines for data preprocessing including missing value replacement/imputation, binning, scaling, or dummy-encoding. The degree of sophistication may vary between tools, so that more specialized procedures (for example, WOE-coding) are not supported by all systems. However, it is often the case that a data mining package comes with a scripting environment that enables extending the software's basic functionality with self-made add-on programs. Clearly, implementing preprocessing routines in such an environment can be a non-trivial endeavor and the associated development effort is surely non-negligible.

Finally, the requirement to preprocess analytic data in some fashion is by no means specific to data mining but occurs in any data-intensive application. Therefore, classical statistical software packages also support many of the above-mentioned techniques.

4   Predicting Households' Income Level: The Effect of Data Projection on Forecasting Accuracy

Previous sections have argued that alternative preprocessing techniques influence accuracy. This is the main reason why data preprocessing is considered an important part of predictive modeling. In this section, an empirical case study is undertaken to emphasize this view.

4.1   EXPERIMENTAL DESIGN

The case study employs a public data set related to the prediction of households' income level has been selected as testbed. The *US Census* data set (Asuncion and Newman, 2010) comprises data of 48,842 US households, which are characterized by six numeric and eight categorical attributes. The target variable is binary and indicates whether household income exceeds $50,000. Such a modeling task could occur in database marketing when selecting a target group for a campaign aiming at selling some luxury product. Some characteristics of the data are summarized in Table 1.5, on the following page, to give an idea about the attributes and their distributions.[19]

The empirical study combines different procedures for preprocessing numeric and categorical attributes as well as different types of prediction methods in a factorial setup. The specific factors and corresponding factor levels are summarized in Table 1.6.

The study employs three popular prediction methods (the binary logit model, a multi-layer perceptron neural network, and a random forest classifier; for example,

---

14   See http://www.salford-systems.com/salford-predictive-miner.html

15   See http://www.kxen.com/Products

16   See http://www.cs.waikato.ac.nz/ml/weka/

17   See http://rapid-i.com/

18   See http://orange.biolab.si/

19   For a detailed description of all attributes, see http://archive.ics.uci.edu/ml/data sets/Census+Income

Table 1.5   Summary of the US Census data set

Variable	Measurement scale	Descriptive statistics*
Household income above $50,000 (target variable)	Binary	<= $50K: 24,720 > $50K: 7,841
Age	Numeric	Mean: 38.6 Standard deviation: 13.7
Work class	Categorical	Private: 34,869 Never-worked: 10
Final weight	Numeric	Mean: 189,664 Standard deviation: 105,604
Educational degree	Categorical	HS-grad: 15,784 Pre-school: 83
Years of education	Numeric	Mean: 10,1 Standard deviation: 2,6
Marital status	Categorical	Married-civ-spouse: 22,379 Married-AF-spouse: 37
Occupation	Categorical	Prof-specialty: 7,138 Armed-forces: 15 Husband: 19,716
Race	Categorical	White: 41,762 Other: 406
Gender	Categorical	Male: 32,650 Female: 16,192
Capital-gain	Numeric	Mean: 1,079.1 Standard deviation: 7,452.0
Capital-loss	Numeric	Mean: 87,502 Standard deviation: 403,005
Working hours/week	Numeric	Mean: 40.4 Standard deviation: 12.4
Country of origin	Categorical	United States: 44,106 Netherlands: 1

Note: * The column depicts the mean and standard deviation for numerical and the most and least frequent categories for categorical variables.

Table 1.6   Experimental setup

Factor	Factor level	Applies to
Correction of skewness	No correction Log-transformation	All numeric attributes
Scaling	z-transformation interval scaling to [-1;+1]	All numeric attributes
Category coding	Recoding Dummy-encoding WOE coding Tree-based transformation (TBT)	All categorical attributes
Prediction method	Binary logit model Multi-layer perceptron neural network Random forest	All attributes

Hastie, et al., 2009) to construct classification models for each of the eight data sets resulting from the 2*2*4 combinations of preprocessing factors. The methods are run with default parameter settings and predictive accuracy is assessed in terms of top-decile lift. Lift is a well-established performance indicator in database marketing and captures the degree to which a prediction model improves over a random model (for example, Ling and Li, 1998; Shin and Cho, 2006). Therefore, higher values indicate better performance. All performance statistics are assessed on a hold-out sample resulting from randomly splitting the original data into an in-sample (60 percent) and out-of-sample (40 percent) set. The random partitioning is repeated ten times to collect a sufficient amount of data for subsequent analysis.

4.2   EMPIRICAL RESULTS

The empirical results are first analyzed by means of ANOVA. ANOVA comprises a family of statistical tools to test the significance of differences between population means (for example, Doncaster and Davey, 2007). Here, it allows answering the question which of the experimental factors affect predictive accuracy significantly and which factors interact with each other. The key results of the analysis are as follows.[20]

The factor prediction method has a significant main effect (F-value: 213; p-value 0.000). This confirms that predictive performance differs significantly between the three classifiers. Specifically, random forest gives the best performance, followed by the neural network and the logit model (average top-decile-lift: 3.77 cf. 3.57 cf. 3.42). Pairwise comparison procedures (for example, Doncaster and Davey, 2007) suggest that these differences are significant at the 1 percent level.

The factor category coding has a significant main effect (F-value: 20.195; p-value<0.000). Overall, WOE coding and TBT perform best and are significantly better than dummy-encoding and recoding. Dummy-encoding and recoding do not differ significantly; neither do WOE coding and TBT.

A significant interaction between the factors prediction method and category coding exists (F-value: 8.837; p-value<0.000). This confirms that the suitability of a data preprocessing technique – here, a projection technique for categorical attributes – depends on the prediction method employed. This issue is explored in more detail below.

None of the projection methods for numeric attributes possess a significant main effect. Similarly, all interaction effects including one or more of these factors are insignificant. Two conclusions emerge from this result. First, both scaling methods work equally well for the data and methods considered here. The neural network learner should be the one most sensitive toward scaling. The average top-decile-lift over all networks trained on interval scaled data is 3.56, compared to 3.58 for network models derived from z-transformed data. The difference between these figures is not large enough to cast doubt on the null-hypothesis of equal performance. Second, correcting for skewness by means of the log-transformation increases predictive accuracy marginally (3.60 c.f. 3.58), but the effect cannot be considered significant (F-value: 1.002; p-value: 0.319).

The significant interaction between category coding and prediction method is explored in more detail in Figure 1.2. Each individual box depicts the distribution of lift scores for a particular combination of prediction method and category encoding. The

---

20   Detailed results in form of standard ANOVA tables are provided in the Appendix.

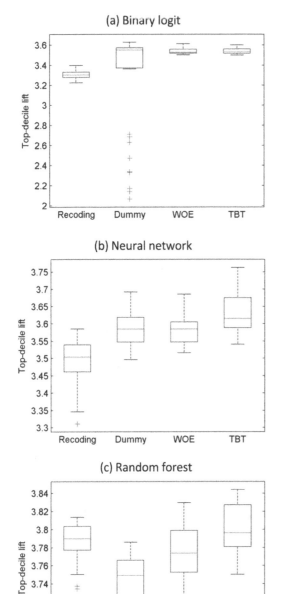

Figure 1.2 Lift distribution for different prediction methods and category coding procedures

horizontal red lines identify the median of the lift distribution and crosses mark extreme values that can be considered outliers.

Four main conclusions emerge from Figure 1.2. First, the condensed boxes for the logit model evidence stable performance. Variations in predictive accuracy under different treatments of numerical attributes and random sampling[21] are negligible in general. However, performance may be unstable under dummy-encoding so that this approach should be avoided. Second, panel (b) confirms the inappropriateness of simply recoding categorical attributes for neural network models. This approach produces the lowest lift values (worst performance) and is inferior to the other three. Dummy-encoding can be considered the standard approach for neural networks and works well. However, WOE and TBT perform as good as dummy-encoding, while avoiding an increase in dimensionality. Therefore, they should be preferred. Third, dummy-encoding should also be avoided when working with random forest. This is plausible because random forest samples from the attribute space as part of the model building process (Ho, 1998). Dummy-encoding results in a space with more attributes of lesser predictive value. While methods like neural networks that principally employ all attributes work well with this approach, it renders the attribute sampling mechanism within random forest ineffective, which, in turn, decreases the accuracy of the final model. On the contrary, WOE and TBT work well for random forest but can be considered dispensable. Being a tree-based learning algorithm, random forest does not require special treatment of categorical attributes, as evident from the

---

21   Recall that Figure 1.2 includes accuracy estimates resulting from ten randomly selected hold-out sets.

competitive performance of recoding. Finally, Figure 1.2 demonstrates that the variations in predictive performance can be substantial across different preprocessing procedures, especially for more sophisticated prediction methods from the neural network or ensemble family.

4.3 DISCUSSION

The case study results further support and extend previous findings regarding the impact of preprocessing choices on predictive performance (Crone, et al., 2006). Numerical attributes are of particular importance in database marketing because RFM-type variables typically belong to this group. With respect to preprocessing such attributes, this study and Crone et al. (2006) evidence that the z-transformation and interval scaling result in similar performance. Therefore, choosing between the two is of lesser importance.

Crone et al. (2006) did not consider techniques for correcting skewed attribute distributions. Again, database marketing data sets are likely to exhibit long-tailed value distributions for several attributes, for example, because a few customers may make purchases at very high frequency, spend unusually large amounts, and so on. The results observed in this study do not suggest that corrective preprocessing by means of the log-transformation is needed. However, this finding should be interpreted with care. The numerical attributes contained in the *US Census* data set relate to customers' financial activity (for example, capital gain and loss, see also Table 1.5) and are very valuable for predicting whether customers' income exceeds/is below $50,000. More specifically, large values for these variables are particularly informative for estimating customers' class memberships. This pattern should in theory diminish the suitability of the log-transformation. Therefore, the observed results can be considered a conservative estimate of the log-transformation's utility. Although the case study data is somewhat improper for this preprocessing method, it has not (significantly) hurt predictive performance. This suggests that the log-transformation is unlikely to decrease accuracy. Other data sets with different attributes and attribute-target-relationships may well benefit from correcting skewness. In summary, the log-transformation appears to be a safe choice and can be recommended for other database marketing applications.

This study also advances the results of Crone et al. (2006) in terms of preprocessing categorical attributes. Specifically, both studies confirm the inappropriateness of simply recoding categories. However, whereas Crone et al. (2006) argue in favor of dummy-encoding the results observed here indicate the more sophisticated techniques in form of WOE- or TBT-coding[22] have the potential to (significantly) improve modeling performance compared to dummy-encoding. Especially TBT-coding seems well-prepared to solve the problem of preprocessing categories in practical database marketing applications. It avoids an increase of dimensionality, is applicable in classification and regression settings, is able to account for interactions among categorical variables, and is relatively easy to implement.[23]

Finally, this study as well as Crone et al. (2006) confirms the importance of data preprocessing. Predictive performance differs significantly across alternative preprocessing

---

22   Note that Crone et al. (2006) did not consider these methods in their study.

23   Basically, TBT-coding requires nothing but a simple tree-building algorithm, which is available in any data mining software system.

methods. Depending upon the specific prediction task, the magnitude of lift differences observed here can well be managerial meaningful (Neslin, et al., 2006). Consequently, marketing analysts are well-advised to stay alert of data preprocessing as a potential leverage to boost the accuracy of their prediction models.

5   Conclusions

Forecasting is an integral part of decision making, not only in marketing but all areas of the business world. Accordingly, predictive modeling enjoys ongoing popularity in both academia and industry. This chapter has concentrated on data preprocessing, the stage of the modeling process which often receives the least attention. Therefore, examining the extent to which choices made within this step influence forecasting accuracy and how this influence differs across alternative preprocessing and prediction methods provides valuable insight for marketing professionals concerned with predictive analytics and sets the path for the development of general guidelines for data preprocessing in database marketing. This chapter made a first step toward this goal. Future research is needed to extend the results observed here along each of the key dimensions prediction method, preprocessing method and data. Large-scale benchmarking studies in supervised learning have contributed greatly toward the development of the field, but have largely concentrated on the modeling step (for example, Baesens, et al., 2003; Lessmann and Voß, 2010; Verbeke, et al., 2012). It is the author's firm belief that conducting corresponding experiments within a data preprocessing context is a fruitful area for future research to shed light on the intricate relationship between prediction method and data representation, and, more generally, advance the body of knowledge in predictive analytics.

Appendix

Table 1.7   Results of mixed-mode ANOVA on top-decile-lift for the within-subject factor prediction method and its factor interactions

Source of variation*	Sum of squares	Degrees of freedom	Mean squares	F-statistic	p-value
PM	10.059	1.057	9.513	212.969	0.000
PM*CoS	0.025	1.057	0.024	0.537	0.474
PM*S	0.065	1.057	0.062	1.387	0.243
PM*CC	1.252	3.172	0.395	8.837	0.000
PM*CoS*S	0.008	1.057	0.008	0.176	0.689
PM*CoS*CC	0.062	3.172	0.020	0.439	0.736
PM*S*CC	0.082	3.172	0.026	0.576	0.641
PM*CoS*S*CC	0.011	3.172	0.003	0.076	0.977
Error(PM)	6.801	152.270	0.045		

Note: * Factor abbreviations: PM = prediction method, CoS = correction of skewness, S = scaling, CC = category.

Table 1.8   Results of mixed-mode ANOVA on top-decile-lift for between-subject factors and their factor interactions

Source of variation*	Sum of squares	Degrees of freedom	Mean squares	F-statistic	p-value
Constant term	6183.890	1	6183.890	250662.356	0.000
CoS	0.025	1	0.025	1.002	0.319
S	0.002	1	0.002	0.099	0.754
CC	1.495	3	0.498	20.195	0.000
CoS*S	0.002	1	0.002	0.064	0.800
CoS*CC	0.032	3	0.011	0.438	0.726
S*CC	0.021	3	0.007	0.289	0.833
CoS*S*CC	0.003	3	0.001	0.046	0.987
Error	3.553	144	0.025		

Note: * Factor abbreviations: PM = prediction method, CoS = correction of skewness, S = scaling, CC = category coding.

References

Anderson, D.R., Sweeney, D.J., Williams, T.A., Freeman, J. and Shoesmith, E. (2010). *Statistics for Business and Economics* (2nd ed.). Andover: Cengage.

Arauzo-Azofra, A., Aznarte, J.L., and Benítez, J.M. (2011). Empirical study of feature selection methods based on individual feature evaluation for classification problems. *Expert Systems with Applications, 38,* 8170–77.

Asuncion, A. and Newman, D.J. (2010). *UCI Machine Learning Repository.* School of Information and Computer Science, University of California, Irvine, CA.

Baesens, B., Van Gestel, T., Viaene, S., Stepanova, M., Suykens, J. and Vanthienen, J. (2003). Benchmarking state-of-the-art classification algorithms for credit scoring. *Journal of the Operational Research Society, 54,* 627–35.

Banslaben, J. (1992). Predictive Modelling. In E.L. Nash (Ed.), *The Direct Marketing Handbook* (2nd ed.). New York, NY: McGraw-Hill, 620–36.

Batista, G. and Monard, M. (2003). An analysis of four missing data treatment methods for supervised learning. *Applied Artificial Intelligence, 17,* 519–33.

Batista, G., Prati, R.C. and Monard, M.C. (2005). Balancing strategies and class overlapping. In A.F. Famili, J.N. Kok and J.M. Peña (Eds), *Proceedings of the 6th International Symposium on Intelligent Data Analysis* (Vol. 3646, 24–35). Berlin: Springer.

Bauer, C.L. (1988). A direct mail customer purchase model. *Journal of Direct Marketing, 2,* 16–24.

Bemmaor, A.C. and Glady, N. (2011). Modeling purchasing behavior with sudden "death": A flexible customer lifetime model. *Management Science, 58* (5), 1012–21.

Berry, M.J.A. and Linoff, G. (2011). *Data Mining Techniques: For Marketing, Sales and Customer Relationship Management* (3rd ed.). Indianapolis, IN: Wiley.

Bose, I. and Xi, C. (2009). Quantitative models for direct marketing: A review from systems perspective. *European Journal of Operational Research, 195,* 1–16.

Breiman, L. (1996). Bagging predictors. *Machine Learning, 24,* 123–40.

Breiman, L. (2001). Random forests. *Machine Learning, 45,* 5–32.

Burez, J. and Van den Poel, D. (2009). Handling class imbalance in customer churn prediction. *Expert Systems with Applications, 36*, 4626–36.

Catlett, J. (1991). On changing continuous attributes into ordered discrete attributes. In Y. Kodratoff (Ed.), *Proceedings of the 8th European Working Session on Learning* (Vol. 482, 164–78). Berlin: Springer.

Cerquides, J. and Màntaras, R.L. d. (1997). Proposal and empirical comparison of a parallelizable distance-based discretization method. In D. Heckerman, H. Mannila, D. Pregibon and R. Uthurusamy (Eds), *Proceedings of the 3rd International Conference on Knowledge Discovery and Data Mining* (139–42). Newport Beach, CA: AAAI Press.

Chawla, N.V., Bowyer, K.W., Hall, L.O. and Kegelmeyer, W.P. (2002). SMOTE: Synthetic minority over-sampling technique. *Journal of Artificial Intelligence Research, 16*, 321–57.

Chen, C., Liaw, A. and Breiman, L. (2004). *Using Random Forest to Learn Imbalanced Data*. Working Paper, Statistics Department, University of California at Berkeley.

Cooil, B., Winer, R.S. and Rados, D.L. (1987). Cross-validation for prediction. *Journal of Marketing Research, 24*, 271–9.

Coussement, K., Benoit, D.F. and Van den Poel, D. (2010). Improved marketing decision making in a customer churn prediction context using generalized additive models. *Expert Systems with Applications, 37*, 2132–43.

Coussement, K. and Van den Poel, D. (2008). Churn prediction in subscription services: An application of support vector machines while comparing two parameter-selection techniques. *Expert Systems with Applications, 34*, 313–27.

Crone, S.F., Lessmann, S. and Stahlbock, R. (2006). The impact of preprocessing on data mining: An evaluation of classifier sensitivity in direct marketing. *European Journal of Operational Research, 173*, 781–800.

Cui, D. and Curry, D. (2005). Prediction in marketing using the support vector machine. *Marketing Science, 24*, 595–615.

Cui, G., Wong, M.L. and Lui, H.-K. (2006). Machine learning for direct marketing response models: Bayesian networks with evolutionary programming. *Management Sciences, 52*, 597–612.

Curry, B. and Moutinho, L. (1993). Neural networks in marketing: Modelling consumer responses to advertising stimuli. *European Journal of Marketing, 27*, 5–20.

De Bock, K.W. and Van den Poel, D. (2011). An empirical evaluation of rotation-based ensemble classifiers for customer churn prediction. *Expert Systems with Applications, 38*, 12293–301.

Deichmann, J., Eshghi, A., Haughton, D., Sayek, S. and Teebagy, N. (2002). Application of multiple adaptive regression splines (MARS) in direct response modeling. *Journal of Interactive Marketing, 16*, 15–27.

Dempster, A.P., Laird, N.M. and Rubin, D.B. (1977). Maximum likelihood from incomplete data via the EM algorithm (with discussion). *Journal of the Royal Statistical Society: Series B (Statistical Methodology), 39*, 1–38.

Dietterich, T.G. (1998). Approximate statistical tests for comparing supervised classification learning. *Neural Computation, 10*, 1895–923.

Ding, Y. and Simonoff, J.S. (2010). An investigation of missing data methods for classification trees applied to binary response data. *Journal of Machine Learning Research, 11*, 131–70.

Doncaster, C.P., and Davey, A.J.H. (2007). *Analysis of Variance and Covariance: How to Choose and Construct Models for the Life Sciences*. Cambridge: Cambridge University Press.

Dougherty, J., Kohavi, R. and Sahami, M. (1995). Supervised and unsupervised discretization of continuous features. In A. Prieditis and S.J. Russell (Eds), *Proceedings of the 12th International Conference on Machine Learning* (194–202). Tahoe City, CA: Morgan Kaufmann.

Drummond, C. and Holte, R.C. (2003). C4.5, class imbalance, and cost sensitivity: Why under-sampling beats over-sampling. In N. Chawla, N. Japkowicz and A. Kolcz (Eds), *ICML Workshop on Learning from Imbalanced Data Sets*. Washington, DC.

Du, R.Y., Kamakura, W.A. and Mela, C.F. (2007). Size and share of customer wallet. *Journal of Marketing, 71*, 94–113.

Duda, R.O., Hart, P.E. and Stork, D.G. (2001). *Pattern Classification* (2nd ed.). New York, NY: Wiley.

Efron, B., Hastie, T., Johnstone, I. and Tibshirani, R. (2004). Least angle regression. *Annals of Statistics, 32*, 407–99.

Farhangfar, A., Kurgan, L. and Dy, J. (2008). Impact of imputation of missing values on classification error for discrete data. *Pattern Recognition, 41*, 3692–705.

Fayyad, U.M. and Irani, K.B. (1992). On the handling of continuous-valued attributes in decision tree generation. *Machine Learning, 8*, 87–102.

Fayyad, U.M., Piatetsky-Shapiro, G. and Smyth, P. (1996). From data mining to knowledge discovery in databases: An overview. *AI Magazine, 17*, 37–54.

Feelders, A.J. (2000). Prior knowledge in economic applications of data mining. In D.A. Zighed, H.J. Komorowski and J.M. Zytkow (Eds), *Proceedings of the 4th European Conference on Principles of Data Mining and Knowledge Discovery* (Vol. 1910, 395–400). Lyon: Springer.

Francois, D., Rossi, F., Wertz, V. and Verleysen, M. (2007). Resampling methods for parameter-free and robust feature selection with mutual information. *Neurocomputing, 70*, 1276–88.

Freund, Y. and Schapire, R.E. (1997). A decision-theoretic generalization of on-line learning and an application to boosting. *Journal of Computer and System Science, 55*, 119–39.

Friedman, J.H. (2001). Greedy function approximation: A gradient boosting machine. *The Annals of Statistics, 29*, 1189–232.

Gheyas, I.A. and Smith, L.S. (2010). A neural network-based framework for the reconstruction of incomplete data sets. *Neurocomputing, 73*, 3039–65.

Ghosh, A., Neslin, S. and Shoemaker, R. (1984). A comparison of market share models and estimation procedures. *Journal of Marketing Research, 21*, 202–10.

Glady, N., Baesens, B. and Croux, C. (2009). Modeling churn using customer lifetime value. *European Journal of Operational Research, 197*, 402–11.

Gu, Q., Li, Z. and Han, J. (2011). Generalized fisher score for feature selection. In *Proceedings of the 27th Annual Conference on Uncertainty in Artificial Intelligence*. Barcelona: AUAI Press, 266–73.

Guyon, I. and Elisseeff, A. (2003). An introduction to variable and feature selection. *Journal of Machine Learning Research, 3*, 1157–82.

Guyon, I., Gunn, S., Nikravesh, M. and Zadeh, L. A. (2006). Feature extraction: Foundations and applications. In J. Kacprzyk (Ed.), *Studies in Fuzzyness and Soft Computing*. Berlin: Springer.

Guyon, I., Li, J., Mader, T., Pletscher, P.A., Schneider, G. and Uhr, M. (2007). Competitive baseline methods set new standards for the NIPS 2003 feature selection benchmark. *Pattern Recognition Letters, 28*, 1438–44.

Guyon, I., Saffari, A., Dror, G., and Cawley, G. (2010). Model selection: Beyond the Bayesian/Frequentist divide. *Journal of Machine Learning Research, 11*, 61–87.

Hall, M. A. (2000). Correlation-based feature selection for discrete and numeric class machine learning. In P. Langley (Ed.), *Proceedings of the 17th International Conference on Machine Learning* (359–66). Stanford, CA: Morgan Kaufmann

Han, J. and Kamber, M. (2004). *Data Mining: Concepts and Techniques* (7th Dr ed.). San Francisco, CA: Morgan Kaufmann.

Hanchuan, P., Fuhui, L. and Ding, C. (2005). Feature selection based on mutual information criteria of max-dependency, max-relevance, and min-redundancy. *IEEE Transactions on Pattern Analysis and Machine Intelligence, 27*, 1226–38, New York, NY

Hastie, T., Tibshirani, R. and Friedman, J. H. (2009). *The Elements of Statistical Learning* (2nd ed.). New York, NY: Springer.

Haykin, S. S. (2009). *Neural Networks and Learning Machines* (3rd ed.). New York, NY: Prentice Hall.

He, X., Cai, D., and Niyogi, P. (2006). Laplacian Score for Feature Selection. In Y. Weiss, B. Schölkopf and J. Platt (Eds), *Advances in Neural Information Processing Systems 18* (507–14). Cambridge: MIT Press.

Heckerman, D. (1997). Bayesian networks for data mining. *Data Mining and Knowledge Discovery, 1*, 79–119.

Ho, T.K. (1998). The random subspace method for constructing decision forests. *IEEE Transactions on Pattern Analysis and Machine Intelligence, 20*, 832–44.

Hsu, C.-W., Chang, C.-C. and Lin, C.-J. (2003). *A Practical Guide to Support Vector Classification*. Taiwan: Department of Computer Science and Information Engineering, National Taiwan University.

Huan, L. and Lei, Y. (2005). Toward integrating feature selection algorithms for classification and clustering. *IEEE Transactions on Knowledge and Data Engineering, 17*, 491–502.

Hulse, J.V. and Khoshgoftaar, T. (2009). Knowledge discovery from imbalanced and noisy data. *Data and Knowledge Engineering, 68*, 1513–42.

Hulse, J.V., Khoshgoftaar, T.M. and Napolitano, A. (2007). Experimental perspectives on learning from imbalanced data. In Z. Ghahramani (Ed.), *Proceedings of the 24th International Conference on Machine Learning* (935–42). Corvallis, OR: ACM.

Izenman, A.J. (2008). *Modern Multivariate Statistical Techniques*. Berlin: Springer.

Japkowicz, N. and Stephen, S. (2002). The class imbalance problem: A systematic study. *Intelligent Data Analysis, 6*, 429–50.

Ji, S. and Carin, L. (2007). Cost-sensitive feature acquisition and classification. *Pattern Recognition, 40*, 1474–85.

Jo, T. and Japkowicz, N. (2004). Class imbalances versus small disjuncts. *ACM SIGKDD Explorations Newsletter, 6*, 40–49.

John, G.H., Kohavi, R. and Pfleger, K. (1994). Irrelevant features and the subset selection problem. In W.W. Cohen and H. Hirsh (Eds.), *Proceedings of the 11th International Conference on Machine Learning* (121–9). New Brunswick, NJ: Morgan Kaufman.

Kim, Y.S., Street, W.N., Russell, G.J. and Menczer, F. (2005). Customer targeting: A neural network approach guided by genetic algorithms. *Management Science, 51*, 264–76.

Kohavi, R. and John, G.H. (1997). Wrappers for feature subset selection. *Artificial Intelligence, 97*, 273–324.

Kumar, V., Lemon, K.N. and Parasuraman, A. (2006). Managing customers for value. *Journal of Service Research, 9*, 87–94.

Kumar, V., Venkatesan, R., Bohling, T. and Beckmann, D. (2008). The power of CLV: Managing customer lifetime value at IBM. *Marketing Science, 27*, 585–99.

Lakshminarayan, K., Harp, S.A. and Samad, T. (1999). Imputation of missing data in industrial databases. *Applied Intelligence, 11*, 259–75.

Lemmens, A. and Croux, C. (2006). Bagging and boosting classification trees to predict churn. *Journal of Marketing Research, 43*, 276–86.

Lessmann, S. and Voß, S. (2009). A reference model for customer-centric data mining with support vector machines. *European Journal of Operational Research, 199*, 520–30.

Lessmann, S. and Voß, S. (2010). Customer-centric decision support: A benchmarking study of novel versus established classification models. *Business and Information Systems Engineering*, *2*, 79–93.

Ling, C.X. and Li, C. (1998). Data mining for direct marketing: Problems and solutions. In R. Agrawal, P.E. Stolorz and G. Piatetsky-Shapiro (Eds), *Proceedings of the 4th International Conference on Knowledge Discovery and Data Mining* (73–9). New York, NY: AAAI Press.

Little, R.J. and Rubin, D.B. (1987). *Statistical Analysis with Missing Data*. New York, NY: John Wiley and Sons.

Liu, H., Hussain, F., Tan, C.L. and Dash, M. (2004). Discretization: An enabling technique. *Data Mining and Knowledge Discovery*, *6*, 393–423.

Malthouse, E.C. (2001). Assessing the performance of direct marketing scoring models. *Journal of Interactive Marketing*, *15*, 49–62.

Martens, D., Baesens, B. and Van Gestel, T. (2009). Decompositional rule extraction from support vector machines by active learning. *IEEE Transactions on Knowledge and Data Engineering*, *21*, 178–91.

Neslin, S.A., Gupta, S., Kamakura, W., Lu, J. and Mason, C.H. (2006). Defection detection: Measuring and understanding the predictive accuracy of customer churn models. *Journal of Marketing Research*, *43*, 204–11.

Niculescu-Mizil, A., Perlich, C., Swirszcz, G., Sindhwani, V., Liu, Y., Melville, P., Wang, D., Xiao, J., Hu, J., Singh, M., Shang, W.X. and Zhu, Y.F. (2009). Winning the KDD Cup Orange Challenge with ensemble selection. *Journal of Machine Learning Research: Workshop and Conference Proceedings*, *7*, 23–34.

O'Brien, T.V. (1994). Neural nets for direct marketers. *Marketing Research*, *6*, 47–9.

Orsenigo, C. and Vercellis, C. (2003). Multivariate classification trees based on minimum features discrete support vector machines. *IMA Journal of Management Mathematics*, *14*, 221–34.

Pendharkar, P.C. (2008). Maximum entropy and least square error minimizing procedures for estimating missing conditional probabilities in Bayesian networks. *Computational Statistics and Data Analysis*, *52*, 3583–602.

Provost, F. and Domingos, P. (2003). Tree induction for probability-based ranking. *Machine Learning*, *52*, 199–215.

Pyle, D. (1999). *Data Preparation for Data Mining*. San Francisco, CA: Morgan Kaufmann

Quinlan, J.R. (1986). Induction of decision trees. *Machine Learning*, *1*, 81–106.

Ratner, B. (2001). Finding the best variables for direct marketing models. *Journal of Targeting, Measurement and Analysis for Marketing*, *9*, 270–96.

Reichheld, F.F. (1996). Learning from customer defections. *Havard Business Review*, *74*, 56–69.

Rosset, S., Perlich, C., and Zadrozny, B. (2007). Ranking-based evaluation of regression models. *Knowledge and Information Systems*, *12*, 331–53.

Rubin, D.B. (1976). Inference and missing data. *Biometrika*, *63*, 581–92.

Rubin, D.B. (1978). Multiple imputations after 18+ years. *Journal of the American Statistical Association*, *91*, 473–89.

Saar-Tsechansky, M. and Provost, F. (2007). Handling missing values when applying classification models. *Journal of Machine Learning Research*, *8*, 1623–57.

Schmid, C.H., Terrin, N., Griffith, J.L., D'Agostino, R.B. and Selker, H.P. (2001). Predictive performance of missing data methods for logistic regression, classification trees and neural networks. *Journal of Statistical Computation and Simulation*, *71*, 115–40.

Shin, H. and Cho, S. (2006). Response modeling with support vector machines. *Expert Systems with Applications*, *30*, 746–60.

Shmueli, G. and Koppius, O.R. (2011). Predictive analytics in information systems research. *MIS Quarterly, 35*, 553–72.

Sinha, A.P. and Zhao, H. (2008). Incorporating domain knowledge into data mining classifiers: An application in indirect lending. *Decision Support Systems, 46*, 287–99.

Stone, M. (1974). Cross-validatory choice and assessment of statistical predictions. *Journal of the Royal Statistical Society: Series B (Statistical Methodology), 36*, 111–47.

Thomas, L.C., Edelman, D.B. and Crook, J.N. (2002). *Credit Scoring and its Applications*. Philadelphia, PA: Siam.

Twala, B.E.T.H., Jones, M.C. and Hand, D.J. (2008). Good methods for coping with missing data in decision trees. *Pattern Recognition Letters, 29*, 950–56.

Verbeke, W., Dejaeger, K., Martens, D., Hur, J. and Baesens, B. (2012). New insights into churn prediction in the telecommunication sector: A profit driven data mining approach. *European Journal of Operational Research, 218*, 211–29.

Veropoulos, K., Cristianini, N. and Campbell, C. (1999). Controlling the sensitivity of support vector machines. In T. Dean (Ed.), *Proceedings of the 16th International Joint Conference on Artificial Intelligence* (55–60). Stockholm: Morgan Kaufmann.

Weiss, G.M. (2004). Mining with rarity: a unifying framework. *ACM SIGKDD Explorations Newsletter, 6*, 7–19.

Weiss, G.M. (2010). The impact of small disjuncts on classifier learning. In R. Stahlbock, S.F. Crone and S. Lessmann (Eds), *Data Mining* (193–226). Berlin: Springer.

West, P.M., Brockett, P.L. and Golden, L.L. (1997). A comparative analysis of neural networks and statistical methods for predicting consumer choice. *Marketing Science, 16*, 370–91.

Zarate, L.E., Nogueira, B.M., Santos, T.R.A. and Song, M.A.J. (2006). Techniques for missing value recovering in imbalanced databases: Application in a narketing database with massive missing data. In *IEEE International Conference on Systems, Man and Cybernetics* (Vol. 3, 2658–64). Taipei: IEEE Computer Society.

2

Textual Customer Data Handling for Quantitative Marketing Analytics

KRISTOF COUSSEMENT AND KOEN W. DE BOCK

1   Introduction

Recently there has been a huge influx in the creation, storage, and accessibility of textual consumer information resulting in challenging opportunities for database marketing analysts in academia and business. Three main circumstances are identified in which textual customer information is produced and could help to deliver better customer knowledge and insights. First, companies are shifting from traditional consumer contact methods such as telephone or letters, to more advanced online ways of communicating and interacting with their customers such as emails, online helpdesks/question forms, third-party customer contact solutions (for example, feefo.com) or 24/7 chat boxes. This individual traceable *client/company interaction information* could help to deliver valuable insights in explaining customers' behavior. Second, the popularity of mass online user-generated content mechanisms in the form of *social media environments* like Twitter, Tripadvisor, Rottentomatoes, and so on, where consumers post their opinions and thoughts about the company's product or services, delivers new challenges to marketing managers nowadays. Third, traditional offline marketing research by paper and pen and face-2-face interviews shifted toward online surveying at the beginning of this century, after which it moved toward an online *(n)ethnography-based research* environment where customers are put together for a longer period in an online community in which different topics are discussed. Community-based research regularly results in a tremendous amount of textual information that has to be analyzed at the end of each research session.

A lot of marketing academics are contributing with interesting pieces of research in these three streams (*client/company interaction information – social media environments – (n)ethnography-based research*) in top-tier marketing journals. However, very few of these top-tier academic marketing papers use a quantitative text mining approach which is frequently researched in other domains like computer science, management science, and information systems. Text mining is a broad umbrella term for a range of technologies used to analyze unstructured and semi-structured information. The unifying theme behind all these methodologies is turning text into numbers. However, to date, marketing academics traditionally analyze textual information by applying qualitative and subjective content analysis.

This chapter intends to make a call to marketing academics to bridge the gap with other research domains and to cross-fertilize by introducing its readers to the elementary quantitative text mining process of converting unstructured textual consumer information to a structured, numeric format that can be used in other traditional database marketing analyses.

2   The Unpopularity of Textual Data Analysis

Although a lot of marketing analysts nowadays acknowledge the fact that textual customer information could drastically improve marketing decision making, few dare to use textual information in a day-to-day environment. There are multiple reasons why textual customer information scares marketers (Coussement and Van den Poel, 2008b). First, analyzing unstructured information requires an *additional data collection effort* because these data are very often not directly available to the marketing analyst. Indeed most databases are nowadays operationalized by collecting all customer information in a structured format. In most organizations, it is very difficult to find the textual information that is needed and to link it to individual customers in the customer base. Second, in most cases *no in-house knowledge* is available to analyze this type of data. In the past, a lot of people became interested in analyzing large streams of customer data which were accessible through traditional data mining. Moreover, statistical and data mining software vendors sold graphical user interfaces on top of the traditional programming syntax which opened the path for traditional non-quantitative minded marketers to mine huge amount of customer data. However, advanced text mining practices are still a difficult analysis domain where the main expertise lies in the hands of computer scientists. A third reason why marketers are lagging behind when it comes to analyzing data is because *no ready-to-use framework* is available to incorporate the information from, for instance, call center transcripts into a day-to-day business environment.

3   Text Mining: The Process

Textual customer information is highly unformatted by nature. So in order to use it for traditional marketing analysis, the data needs to be initially converted into a structured representation. Figure 2.1 visualizes the different steps of the text mining process to convert textual information to a numeric representation by means of a so called term-by-document matrix, and to prepare this information for day-to-day marketing practice.

3.1   TEXT PREPROCESSING

The most common way of representing textual information into a numeric format is by using the bag-of-words model (Feldman and Sanger, 2007). This means that all words are used as features to represent the content of the document without taking into account the order of the words in the sentence. The dimension of the total feature space is equal to the number of different words in the document collection or corpus. This is usually a very high-dimensional matrix. Usually, each document is represented using the vector-space approach (Salton, 1971). In detail, each document is represented as a vector in a

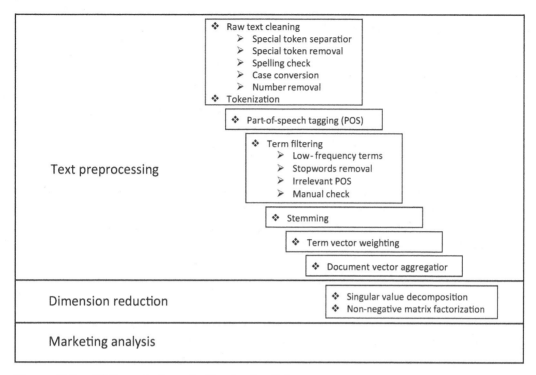

Figure 2.1   Different steps in the text mining process

feature space based on a particular weighting scheme, whereas each vector component is given a weight if the corresponding term is present in that document and zero otherwise. Therefore, in the text preprocessing step, the documents are converted into a manageable representation, called the term-by-document matrix.

The different steps of the text preprocessing are explained using a real-life example. Appendix 1 contains ten product reviews of hotel Le Palais in Prague scraped from Tripadvisor, and these examples are used throughout the remainder of this chapter. The first review (see Table 2.1) will be used to demonstrate the impact of the different preprocessing steps. Searching online for hotel accommodation is becoming a very important and popular consumer activity on the Internet, resulting in huge databases of online customer feedback. Thus, it delivers enormous opportunities to database marketers working within these online customer feedback platforms to use this consumer textual information to better grasp and communicate the importance of underlying hotel attribute perceptions.

Table 2.1   The unprocessed hotel review

My husband and I stayed at this hotel for 2 days and had a wonderful experience. Staff were very friendly, rooms were spacious with elegant decor and breakfast was served in a lovely room overlooking the city. The hotel even provides a town car to the main square. I recommend getting the refreshing facial at the spa! Great place to stay

3.1.1   Raw text cleaning and tokenization

The first step in the text preprocessing process is raw text cleaning. It consists of all activities that polish the original textual information into a format which is cleaner for subsequent processing. Traditional activities include separation of special characters and punctuations from words and their removal from the term corpus. Furthermore, spelling errors are handled by comparing the word in the document with a reference dictionary. The well-known Wordnet database could be used to execute a first quality check (Fellbaum, 1998). Wordnet is a lexical reference system that holds definitions and semantic relations between words of over 100,000 English terms. Typically during this stage, all words are converted to lower case to increase uniformity of the terms in order to guarantee success during the subsequent preprocessing steps, while numbers are often removed. After the raw text cleaning phase, the stream of characters in the document must be converted into a stream of words or tokens. During this phase the white space characters are used as the borders of words, and a redundant number of white spaces are removed. Table 2.2 shows the results of the raw text cleaning and tokenization step.

Table 2.2   Hotel review after raw text cleaning and tokenization

> my husband and i stayed at this hotel for days and had a wonderful experience staff were very friendly rooms were spacious with elegant decor and breakfast was served in a lovely room overlooking the city the hotel even provides a town car to the main square i recommend getting the refreshing facial at the spa great place to stay

3.1.2   Part-of-speech tagging

Part-of-speech tagging is the process of labeling each word in the document corpus with its syntactic category (Brill, 1995). The words obtained during the tokenization phase are labeled different part-of-speech. The most well-known part-of-speech word bank that is available to assign a word the correct part-of-speech is called the Penn TreeBank1 (Mitchell, et al., 1993).

Table 2.3   Hotel review after part-of-speech tagging

> my/PRP$ husband/NN and/CC i/NN stayed/VBD at/IN this/DT hotel/NN for/IN days/NNS and/CC had/VBD a/DT wonderful/JJ experience/NN staff/NN were/VBD very/RB friendly/JJ rooms/NNS were/VBD spacious/JJ with/IN elegant/JJ decor/NN and/CC breakfast/NN was/VBD served/VBN in/IN a/DT lovely/JJ room/NN overlooking/IN the/DT city/NN the/DT hotel/NN even/RB provides/VBZ a/DT town/NN car/NN to/TO the/DT main/JJ square/NN i/NNS recommend/VBP getting/VBG the/DT refreshing/NN facial/NN at/IN the/DT spa/NN great/JJ place/NN to/TO stay/VB

---

1   More information on the Penn TreeBank tags is found via http://bulba.sdsu.edu/jeanette/thesis/PennTags.html

It labels words in the corpus according to 36 different tags amongst which are determiner, adjective, noun, adverb, and so on. Some references classify part-of-speech into non-informative and informative parts of speech. Words can be part of an informative part of speech like nouns, verbs, adjectives, and adverbs, while the other parts of speech could be considered as non-informative because they are not considered as containing crucial information to discriminate content between documents. Table 2.3 shows the parsed review using the Penn Treebank terminology.

3.1.3   Term filtering

Considering all distinct words or terms as separate features to characterize the content of the document corpus results in a very high-dimensional term-by-document matrix. It is not unusual to find thousands of distinct terms at this stage of the text mining process. Several term filtering practices are considered to reduce the number of terms in that matrix. First, rare words are removed from the term list because these words do not help in future document description. In general, word frequencies typically follow a Zipf distribution (Zipf, 1949): the frequency of each word's occurrence is proportional to $1/rank^p$, where *rank* is its rank among words sorted by frequency, and p is a fitting index close to 1 (Miller and Newman, 1958). In a lot of settings, terms that appear more than once or twice (for example, Coussement and Van den Poel (2008b)) or are amongst the top 10 percent of the most frequent terms (for example, Feldman and Sanger (2007)) are kept and this shrinks the dimension of the term-by-document matrix considerably. Table 2.4 increases the quality of the word dictionary by removing all terms appearing less than two times on the overall document corpus, as they are not helping in discriminating one document from the other.

Table 2.4   Hotel review after removing infrequent terms during term filtering

my husband and i stayed at this hotel for and had a wonderful experience staff were very friendly rooms were with and breakfast was in a lovely room the city the hotel even a town to the i recommend the at the spa great place to stay

Furthermore, stopwords, that is, words that appear overly common, like "a," "the" and context-specific words which are used a lot, are eliminated. These words appear so frequently in the text that they do not have any discrimination power anymore. Typically, stopword lists start from an overall collection of terms and are adapted to the context in which they are applied. For instance, if you are text mining complaint emails for the car division of Mercedes-Benz, the term "car" will be so common that its information value in the text mining exercise is zero. Therefore, it is common to remove them before further analysis. In our hotel example, words such as "hotel," "prague," "le palais" and "czech republic" are removed. The results of the stopword removal are given in Table 2.5.

Table 2.5   Hotel review after removing the stopwords during term filtering

husband stayed wonderful experience staff friendly breakfast lovely city town recommend spa stay

Another filtering technique could rely on only retaining those terms that belong to an informative part-of-speech. The intuition behind this step is that non-informative part-of-speech terms belonging to, for instance, determiners, auxiliaries, prepositions, and so on, are not crucial in describing the content of a document. A last but time-consuming step in the term filtering phase is removing irrelevant terms by manually checking the temporary term dictionary. In the end, term filtering is performed most of the time in an aggressive way, reducing the feature base by 90 to 99 percent (Feldman and Sanger, 2007).

3.1.4   Stemming

In a next step, term variations are conflated into a single representative form, called the stem. An example of a stem could be the word "inspect" which is the stem for the variants "inspected," "inspecting," "inspection" and "inspections." Lemmatization, or finding the canonical form of the lexeme, reduces the number of terms considerably (Bell and Jones, 1979) and it increases the retrieval performance significantly (Kraaij and Pohlmann, 1996). Three types of stemming algorithms exist in literature, that is, the affix removal stemmers, the statistical stemmers, and the mixed stemming algorithms. Affix removal stemmers are trying to create the stem by systematically removing prefixes and suffixes by applying some prescribed transformation rules. The two most well-known affix removal stemmers are the Lovins algorithm (Lovins, 1968) and Porters algorithm (Porter, 1980, 2006), which eventually resulted in the Snowball framework (Porter, 2001). The latter framework is the framework in which new stemming algorithms are created nowadays. The major drawback of these affix removal algorithms is that they rely heavily on the prior knowledge established in the predefined transformation rules. As a solution to that, statistical stemmers such as N-gram stemming (Mayfield and McNamee, 2003), the HMM algorithm (Melucci and Orio, 2003), and the YASS algorithm (Majumder, et al., 2007) learn distributions of root elements in a corpus and assign each word the correct stem based on the learned rules. Mixed stemming algorithms combine several approaches. For instance, the performance of an affix removal stemmer can be boosted by dictionary lookups for irregular verbs or exceptional singular/plural forms like tooth/teeth. Mixed algorithms are highly beneficial with high declensional languages with a lot of morphological variants, such as Dutch. Table 2.6 stems the hotel review using the Snowball stemmer.

Table 2.6   Hotel review after stemming

husband stay wonder experi staff friend breakfast love citi town recommend spa stay

3.1.5   Term vector weighting

At this stage, a preliminary term-by-document matrix can be built where a cell in the matrix contains the raw frequency of appearance of a term in a document. During the term vector weighting stage, the analyst can choose to weigh each term according to its importance for the document and in relation to its uniqueness in the total document corpus. It was Sparck Jones (1988) who showed significant improvements in performance when using weighted-term vectors. Different weighting schemes for a document corpus are available and they are decomposed in two parts; term frequency (*tf*) and (inverse) document frequency ((*i*)*df*).

The *tf* measures the frequency of occurrence of an index term in the document text (Salton and Buckley, 1988). The more a term is present in a document, the more important this term is in characterizing the content of that document. As such the frequency of occurrence of a content word is used to indicate term importance for content representation.

Various *tf* weighting schemes as an alternative to using the raw frequencies are available to the analyst. Let $w_{t,d}$ equal to the weighting of term t in document d.

Binary frequency weighting converts the raw frequencies of occurrence into 0 and 1, as follows:

$$w_{t,d} = \begin{bmatrix} 0 & \text{if } tf_{t,d} = 0 \\ 1 & \text{if } tf_{t,d} > 0 \end{bmatrix} \tag{1}$$

with $tf_{t,d}$ equal to the term frequency of term t in document d. This results in a term-by-document matrix with dichotomous terms.

Augmented normalized weighting uses maximum normalization on term level to obtain a *tf* value that lies between 0.5 and 1. Hence, the formula:

$$w_{t,d} = 0.5 + 0.5 \frac{tf_{t,d}}{\max(tf_{t,d})} \tag{2}$$

Logarithmic *tf* weighting is used in situations with a varying document length. By taking the logarithm, the *tf* reduces the importance of the raw term frequency in those collections with widely varying document length. The *tf* formula looks like:

$$w_{t,d} = \ln(tf_{t,d} + 1) \tag{3}$$

Furthermore, analysts do not consider the importance of a given term in the document as the only weighting criterion. The discriminating power of a term in the total document corpus is as important. This is exactly what is meant with the inverse document frequency (*idf*). The *idf* takes into account the importance of the term in the total document corpus, in the sense that the more rarely a term occurs in a document collection, the more discriminating that term is and the higher the weight will be. In the end, term weighting is still done by determining the product of the term frequency (*tf*) and the inverse document frequency (*idf*) as recommended by reference works in the field (Salton, 1975, 1989; Salton and Buckley, 1988; Sparck Jones, 1988) and is still frequently used in the text mining discipline. Thus the weight of term t in document d is given by:

$$w_{t,d} = tf_{t,d} * idf_t \tag{4}$$

with idf_t equal to the inverse document frequency of term t and is defined as:

$$idf_t = ln\left(\frac{N}{df_t}\right) \tag{5}$$

with N equal to the total number of documents in the corpus and df_t equal to the number of documents where term t is present. The result is a high-dimensional, weighted term-by-document matrix.

The final term-by-document matrix using the logarithmic tf weighting multiplied by the inverse document frequency is found in Appendix 2.

3.1.6   Document vector aggregation

The purpose of converting textual customer information in a database marketing exercise is very often to link it back to individual customer information. For instance, customer X could have sent three complaint emails in a given period to the call center of the company. One way or another, the textual information of this customer must be aggregated in order to link it, for instance, to the customer base. Coussement and Van den Poel (2008b) propose the creation of an aggregated term-by-document matrix. The aim is to make an aggregation of the document vectors – that is, the columns in the term-by-document matrix – belonging to the same customer. They describe the aggregated weight of term t for all documents belonging to customer j ($Aw_{t,j}$) as:

$$Aw_{t,j} = \sum_{d=1}^{r} w_{t,d} \tag{6}$$

with r equal to the number of documents belonging to customer j.

The text preprocessing module outputs a high-dimensional term-by-document matrix (see Appendix 2). Two problems still occur when you would like to use such a matrix in further analysis:

1. at this stage, there are still too many terms (that is, features) as compared to the number of documents. Using all these features is unmanageable and not useful, and this problem is often called the "curse of dimensionality."
2. this matrix is a very sparse matrix, containing a lot of zeros on document level. This does not increase the analyzability of the matrix.

The next paragraph describes several dimension reduction techniques to reduce the dimensionality of the matrix.

3.2   DIMENSION REDUCTION

Low rank approximations replace the large, often sparse original term-by-document matrix by a related matrix of much lower rank. The high-dimensional matrix requires a tremendous amount of storage space, while the efficient representation of the relationship of the true trends of the data could disappear. The key intuition behind dimension reduction techniques is to group related terms and to project them into a new semantic feature space. This process is often referred to as latent semantic indexing (LSI). LSI assumes that there is some latent or underlying structure in the corpus initiated by the original word choice used in the document. Several commonly used dimension reduction techniques are at the disposal of the marketing analyst, such as principal component analysis (PCA), independent component analysis (ICA), vector quantization, factor analysis, QR decomposition, or CUR decomposition. This chapter digs into the most popular dimension reduction techniques in text mining, that is, singular value decomposition and non-negative matrix factorization (NMF), and compares their merits and drawbacks.

3.2.1   Singular value decomposition

This paragraph describes how the dimension of the term-by-document matrix is reduced by using singular value decomposition (SVD) to form semantic generalizations from documents (Deerwester, et al., 1990). SVD uses the fact that certain terms appear in similar documents to establish relationships between those terms. Consequently, SVD projects documents from the high-dimensional term space to an orthonormal, semantic, latent subspace by grouping together similar terms into distinct concepts. As such, each concept can be described using many different keywords and it has a high discriminatory power to other concepts in the reduced feature space.

A high-dimensional term-by-document matrix A with rank r is constructed such that location (i,j) indicates w_{ij} which is the weight of term i for document j. SVD factorizes A into three distinct matrices by:

$$A = U \Sigma V^t \tag{7}$$

with Σ equal to a diagonal matrix containing the singular values of matrix A, U equal to the term-concept similarity matrix, and V equal to the concept-document similarity matrix.

Mathematically, $\Sigma = \text{diag} (\lambda_1, \lambda_2, ..., \lambda_r)$ is the singular-values matrix where $\lambda_1 \geq \lambda_2 \geq \lambda_3 \geq ... \geq \lambda_r$. U and V are column-orthonormal matrices. The weights of the original matrix A depend on the latent concepts by:

$$w_{ij} = \sum_{x=1}^{r} U_{ix} \Sigma_x d_{jx} \tag{8}$$

LSI based on SVD allows a simple strategy to approximate the original matrix A with rank r by $\hat{A}$ with rank k where $k \leq r$. Therefore LSI ignores the smaller lambda values in Σ by retaining only the first predetermined singular values equal to or bigger than k, i.e. $\lambda_1 \geq \lambda_2 \geq \lambda_3 \geq ... \geq \lambda_k$, while only the first k columns of U and V are kept.

$$\hat{A}_k = U_k \Sigma_k V_k^t \tag{9}$$

with U_k, Σ_k and V_k equal to the k-rank approximation of respectively U, Σ and V.

Matrix V_k is the approximated k-rank concept-document similarity matrix. A cell in the matrix V_k represents the loading for a specific document on one of the k concepts. This matrix contains information on how well a certain document loads on the different k concepts. The concepts reflect the hidden patterns in the textual data. Consequently, these concepts could be used as explanatory variables in traditional marketing analysis because they represent the latent semantic patterns of the textual information.

A numerical example of the SVD procedure is given below. The original term-by-document matrix as found in Appendix 2 is decomposed in three matrices of rank 5. A rank 5 concept-term similarity matrix, indicating the importance of a specific term on a dimension is given in Table 2.7, with {C1,...,C5} the five concepts. The matrix shows the "loading" of a term on the concept. The higher the absolute value of the loading, the more the term typifies the concept. Table 2.8 represents the truncated singular values matrix containing the five highest singular values, while Table 2.9 represents the concept-document similarity matrix. The latter matrix is used to assign a document to a certain concept based on the level of the loading.

Table 2.7   The concept-term similarity matrix with rank 5

Term	C1	C2	C3	C4	C5
amaz	-0.07529	0.272383	0.049128	0.011737	-0.15225
bar	-0.19594	-0.10026	-0.05832	-0.01394	-0.00068
beauti	-0.09379	0.304906	0.063327	0.003202	0.062902
birthday	-0.38505	-0.20852	-0.14421	0.113712	0.000484
bit	-0.03822	-0.00062	0.019774	-0.15843	-0.00055
bmw	-0.09762	0.067048	-0.00486	0.023561	0.015292
book	-0.06493	-0.18553	0.822315	0.20902	-0.01659
breakfast	-0.06844	0.076668	0.018457	-0.02539	0.019241
center	-0.05182	-0.03716	0.14279	-0.25444	0.008682
chose	-0.10429	0.069466	0.00055	0.009342	0.028521
citi	-0.03764	0.071508	0.132592	0.034809	0.010215
comfort	-0.03463	0.115744	0.022278	-0.00735	-0.13721
cooki	-0.14974	0.549103	0.099672	0.057018	0.110494
day	-0.17374	-0.04833	-0.00996	-0.15317	0.040595
delici	-0.1975	0.128827	-0.00721	0.039099	0.047863
didnt	-0.19594	-0.10026	-0.05832	-0.01394	-0.00068
dine	-0.18781	-0.10513	-0.04665	-0.12288	0.01746
excel	-0.0754	-0.02449	-0.02073	-0.00476	-0.00302
experi	-0.02678	-0.06476	0.297716	0.069772	-0.01499
food	-0.08232	-0.01389	-0.01481	-0.01169	-0.14315
free	-0.03797	0.055124	0.03718	-0.19692	0.031371
friend	-0.01319	0.008083	0.020256	-0.12442	-0.11069
garnet	-0.38505	-0.20852	-0.14421	0.113712	0.000484

Table 2.7   Continued

Term	C1	C2	C3	C4	C5
high	-0.01916	-0.02252	0.125764	-0.11043	0.006673
histor	-0.03596	-0.03417	0.0882	-0.75481	0.07397
husband	-0.11857	0.07416	0.00049	-0.00236	-0.06983
librari	-0.0225	-0.0041	0.023524	-0.20001	0.013162
littl	-0.12372	0.162753	0.012509	0.033499	0.03455
locat	-0.11265	-0.08611	0.183025	-0.12205	0.016089
love	-0.25795	-0.06935	-0.06768	0.033364	0.007576
metro	-0.08668	-0.05049	0.090671	0.026727	0.007094
minut	-0.12275	-0.05478	-0.01584	-0.10737	-0.00171
morn	-0.13039	0.165171	0.017922	0.019279	0.047779
neighborhood	-0.07564	0.199197	0.049698	-0.05061	0.047014
nice	-0.0275	0.020799	0.016941	-0.07706	0.001024
night	-0.16177	0.347387	0.054452	0.023375	0.081056
quiet	-0.03602	0.079167	0.032396	-0.12208	0.032177
recommend	-0.06463	-0.05061	0.080259	-0.06611	0.002993
restaur	-0.0837	0.049264	0.001353	-0.02017	0.01112
return	-0.09734	0.071713	-0.00576	0.018662	-0.13307
servic	-0.17419	-0.07821	-0.03875	-0.07425	0.010177
spa	-0.01855	0.017847	0.018937	-0.02906	-0.00175
staff	-0.01849	0.027669	0.043148	-0.01509	-0.04325
stay	-0.02229	0.011748	0.013465	-0.01435	-0.00938
tabl	-0.21431	0.030769	-0.04397	0.066272	0.02597
time	-0.1538	-0.08683	0.065537	0.046546	0.007178
tour	-0.07537	-0.04019	0.07406	-0.01776	0.004881
town	-0.12623	-0.05563	-0.02112	-0.0619	-0.00542
transport	-0.02584	-0.0201	0.131178	-0.12465	0.019902
uniqu	-0.19077	-0.12959	0.076496	0.089512	-0.00267
visit	-0.07565	-0.0163	-0.02023	0.002528	-0.15638
walk	-0.11256	0.11766	0.018572	-0.05999	0.029065
week	-0.02367	0.070869	0.011515	-0.06366	-0.87447
wine	-0.21431	0.030769	-0.04397	0.066272	0.02597
wonder	-0.06966	0.054207	0.00727	-0.03227	-0.25645

Table 2.8   Singular values of the diagonal singular values matrix

C1	C2	C3	C4	C5
23.14353	16.23941	15.28594	11.7174	11.2306

Table 2.9   The concept-document similarity matrix with rank 5

Document	C1	C2	C3	C4	C5
1	-0.04072	0.000518	0.067998	-0.01654	-0.04446
2	-0.34773	0.894773	0.152881	0.06704	0.124518
3	-0.16463	-0.02166	0.058447	-0.33776	-0.0044
4	-0.89421	-0.33979	-0.22119	0.133698	0.000546
5	-0.05497	0.115483	0.017662	-0.07485	-0.98545
6	-0.11309	-0.22674	0.945976	0.184319	-0.01402
7	-0.05875	0.071865	0.025507	-0.0418	-0.02619
8	-0.08351	-0.05568	0.135285	-0.88748	0.083358
9	-0.14769	0.09447	0.073151	-0.13772	0.059341
10	-0.05164	0.038977	0.013286	-0.12399	0.006145

In a predictive modeling setting like document classification, it is very important that the concept loadings from the training vectors of the concept-document similarity matrix are comparable with these from the test vectors. In other words, the meaning of the concepts during testing should stay the same as during training. Consequently, documents of the test set are projected into the same semantic latent subspace as created during training.

In order to compare a test document d with the training documents, its term vector A_d is derived using the same preprocessing steps as described above. Deerwester et al. (1990) propose to project each new term vector into the same latent semantic subspace as created during training by:

$$V_d = A_d' U_k \Sigma_k^{-1} \qquad (10)$$

with U_k the k-rank concept-term similarity matrix and Σ_k the diagonal singular value matrix in rank k, both of the SVD. V_d is the new concept-document vector which is comparable to the concept-document vectors of the matrix V_k.

The advantage is that SVD (compared to other algorithms like NMF) has a unique solution, while there are two major drawbacks of the SVD approach (as other dimensionality reduction techniques like PCA or ICA). First, the loadings of the terms on the different concepts can be negative. This makes it very hard to interpret the different concepts because they could be subtractive parts to one another. Second, the output of a SVD is often very condensed, that is, not a lot of zeros are present in the new truncated matrices, which is, however, the case in, for instance, NMF.

3.2.2   Non-negative Matrix Factorization

NMF takes into account that non-negativity in the cells of the decomposed matrices is a useful constraint in order to increase interpretability. NMF, introduced by Paatero and Tapper (1994) and popularized by Lee and Seung (1999), consists of truncated non-negative concept matrices $W \in R^{mxk}$ and $H \in R^{kxn}$ with k the reduced factor rank that approximates a given non-negative data matrix $A \in R^{mxn}$, so that:

$$A \approx WH \tag{11}$$

with WH the NMF of A at rank k. Compared to SVD, the solution of NMF is not unique and the non-linear optimization problem is described as:

$$\min_{W,H} f(W,H) = \frac{1}{2} \| A - WH \|_F^2 \tag{12}$$

with $\|.\|_F$ the Frobenius norm. The two original NMF algorithms introduced by Lee and Seung (1999, 2001), that is, the multiplicative update (MU) algorithm and alternating least squares (ALS) algorithm (Berry, et al., 2007; Lee and Seung, 2001), are considered good baselines against newer types of algorithms, for example, the gradient descent algorithms; MU and ALS algorithms being the most popular NMF algorithms used.

Over the years, different variations of NMF algorithms are proposed, but the general structure stays the same and is given in Algorithm 1 below (Berry and Kogan, 2010).

Traditionally, NMF algorithms consist of three different steps: an initialization step, an update step, and the verification of the termination criterion. Most NMF algorithms, including the MU algorithm, need pre-initialized factors W and H, but some algorithms only need one pre-initialized factor. For instance, the standard implementation of the ALS algorithm employs a pre-initialized W factor. In the past, several random initialization algorithms were proposed with the goal to reach a faster convergence and faster error reduction. However, only a few non-random initializations for the NMF algorithm have been published so far, including spherical k-means clustering based on centroid decomposition to obtain structured initialization for W (Wild, et al., 2004); Langville et al. (2006), who proposed four new algorithms, of which the SVD-Centroid algorithm clearly reduces the approximation error; and Boutsidis and Gallopoulos (2008) who proposed the non-negative double singular value decomposition (NNDSVD), resulting in a better initialization with faster convergence and error reduction.

The second step in solving a NMF lies in the updating steps and two alternative algorithms, that is, MU and ALS algorithms, as briefly discussed below (Berry and Kogan, 2010).

3.2.2.1 Multiplicative Update

The update steps for the MU as described by Lee and Seung (2001) are fundamentally based on reducing the mean squared error objective function (see Algorithm 2). Note that the ε is added to the update function to avoid division by zero. Both H and W need to be initialized.

Algorithm 1

1: given matrix A $\in R^{mxn}$ with k $\ll$
   min {m,n} the reduced factor rank
2: for r = 1 to maxrepetition do
3: W = rand(m,k)
4: H = rand(k,n)
5: for i = 1 to maxiter do
6: execute NMF update steps
7: check termination criterion
8: end for
9: end for

Algorithm 2

1: H = H.*(W^{T}A)./W^{T}WH+ε
2: W = W.*(AH^T)./WHH^T+ε

Algorithm 3

1: solve for H: $W^TWH = W^TA$
2: set all negative elements in H to 0
3: solve for W: $HH^TW^T = HA^T$
4: set all negative elements in W to 0

3.2.2.2   Alternating Least Squares Algorithm

As the name explains, an alternating least squares is followed by another alternating least squares step. In each step the non-negative elements are set to zero to ensure non-negativity, and the factor W needs to be pre-initialized, while H is computed in the first iteration. The pseudo code of the update part of the ALS algorithm is given in Algorithm 3 (Berry and Kogan, 2010).

The final step in the execution of an NMF algorithm is the decision to stop the iterative process. Three criteria are usually taken into consideration. First, the analyst defines a predefined maximum number of iterations. Once the maximum number of iterations is reached, the algorithm stops. Second, a condition based on the required approximation error is often included. This means that if the error falls below a certain threshold, the procedure terminates. Finally, the third condition is based on the relative change of the factors W and H from one iteration to another. If this change is very small and falls below a certain threshold, this means that the algorithm is not improving anymore, and consequently the algorithm terminates.

A numerical example of the NMF procedure is given below. The NMF procedure outputs two matrices: the W and H matrix based on the MU algorithm (Lee and Seung, 2001). Table 2.10 outputs the W matrix and contains the loadings of each term on the concept, while Table 2.11 outputs the H matrix containing the concept-document loadings. As compared to SVD, the concept-term and concept-document similarity matrix contains only positive loadings and a lot of zeros, which facilitates the interpretation of the outputs.

Table 2.10   W matrix

Term	C1	C2	C3	C4	C5
amaz	0,0639	0,0000	0,0000	0,0857	0,0000
bar	0,0000	0,0001	0,0458	0,0006	0,0123
beauti	0,0776	0,0009	0,0006	0,0015	0,0020
birthday	0,0000	0,0000	0,0937	0,0000	0,0000
bit	0,0025	0,0016	0,0043	0,0028	0,0414
bmw	0,0256	0,0000	0,0164	0,0020	0,0000
book	0,0000	0,3419	0,0000	0,0000	0,0000
breakfast	0,0244	0,0026	0,0085	0,0023	0,0089
center	0,0000	0,0461	0,0037	0,0019	0,0764
chose	0,0271	0,0010	0,0172	0,0000	0,0018
citi	0,0242	0,0473	0,0000	0,0025	0,0000
comfort	0,0259	0,0000	0,0000	0,0670	0,0000
cooki	0,1375	0,0000	0,0000	0,0000	0,0000

Table 2.10   Continued

Term	C1	C2	C3	C4	C5
day	0,0088	0,0038	0,0351	0,0000	0,0498
delici	0,0507	0,0004	0,0333	0,0000	0,0000
didnt	0,0000	0,0001	0,0458	0,0006	0,0123
dine	0,0000	0,0000	0,0427	0,0000	0,0447
excel	0,0028	0,0000	0,0168	0,0027	0,0041
experi	0,0001	0,1235	0,0002	0,0034	0,0000
food	0,0030	0,0012	0,0174	0,0644	0,0031
free	0,0156	0,0004	0,0006	0,0000	0,0557
friend	0,0004	0,0017	0,0000	0,0515	0,0324
garnet	0,0000	0,0000	0,0937	0,0000	0,0000
high	0,0009	0,0444	0,0000	0,0018	0,0384
histor	0,0000	0,0000	0,0000	0,0000	0,2145
husband	0,0276	0,0013	0,0196	0,0389	0,0037
librari	0,0006	0,0000	0,0009	0,0007	0,0554
littl	0,0496	0,0000	0,0161	0,0017	0,0000
locat	0,0004	0,0776	0,0193	0,0000	0,0507
love	0,0137	0,0009	0,0576	0,0015	0,0030
metro	0,0029	0,0461	0,0173	0,0000	0,0029
minut	0,0005	0,0013	0,0260	0,0021	0,0325
morn	0,0511	0,0007	0,0169	0,0000	0,0002
neighborhood	0,0519	0,0016	0,0021	0,0001	0,0153
nice	0,0069	0,0021	0,0025	0,0047	0,0198
night	0,0946	0,0000	0,0125	0,0000	0,0001
quiet	0,0211	0,0005	0,0002	0,0000	0,0350
recommend	0,0000	0,0357	0,0120	0,0016	0,0272
restaur	0,0198	0,0002	0,0136	0,0022	0,0084
return	0,0234	0,0000	0,0160	0,0642	0,0000
servic	0,0020	0,0006	0,0389	0,0011	0,0286
spa	0,0059	0,0049	0,0016	0,0055	0,0076
staff	0,0082	0,0142	0,0006	0,0210	0,0052
stay	0,0051	0,0047	0,0032	0,0065	0,0051
tabl	0,0309	0,0000	0,0433	0,0000	0,0000
time	0,0026	0,0458	0,0337	0,0000	0,0009
tour	0,0025	0,0356	0,0144	0,0002	0,0122
town	0,0012	0,0028	0,0276	0,0036	0,0212
transport	0,0024	0,0458	0,0002	0,0000	0,0424
uniqu	0,0000	0,0590	0,0435	0,0000	0,0000
visit	0,0015	0,0000	0,0166	0,0671	0,0000

Table 2.10   Continued

Term	C1	C2	C3	C4	C5
walk	0,0377	0,0002	0,0145	0,0010	0,0196
week	0,0000	0,0000	0,0000	0,3716	0,0000
wine	0,0309	0,0000	0,0433	0,0000	0,0000
wonder	0,0139	0,0015	0,0103	0,1138	0,0054

Table 2.11   H matrix

		C1	C2	C3	C4	C5
	1	1,3899	2,6043	2,2078	1,2623	0,9462
	2	70,0393	0,0000	0,0000	0,0000	0,0000
	3	2,1579	0,7523	11,5203	0,4497	14,1942
	4	0,0000	0,0000	104,4230	0,0000	0,0000
Document	5	0,0000	0,0000	0,0000	26,7060	0,0000
	60	0,0000	38,6099	0,0000	0,0000	0,0000
	7	6,0740	0,3121	2,0737	1,0884	1,7155
	8	0,0000	0,0000	0,0000	0,0000	39,6912
	9	10,6605	1,5473	7,6992	0,0000	6,1399
	10	3,6138	0,0000	1,7880	0,1743	5,0823

However the choice of the reduced rank k is critical for optimal (predictive) performance. In the next section, an overview of this parameter-selection procedure is given.

3.2.3   Optimal dimension selection

Beforehand it is unknown which value of k will lead to an optimal solution when validating the marketing model. Consequently, a parameter-selection procedure is needed in order to decide which rank-k model is most appropriate. The intensity of dimension reduction is critical. Ideally, the value of k must be large enough to fit all the underlying, relevant concepts in the document collection, but small enough to prevent the model from fitting sampling errors and unimportant details. Moreover, the obtained optimal k must be workable from an analysis point of view. In the factor-analytic literature, such choices are still an unanswered question (Bradford, 2008; Haley, et al., 2007) and choosing the optimal k could rely on traditional approaches which are classified in four main categories (Jolliffe, 2002): the *percentage variance approach* which searches for the smallest number of dimensions to capture a certain percentage of the total variance; the *scree plot* approach, searching for the elbow in the eigenvalue plot; *sequential tests* which sequentially conduct a series of formal hypothesis tests to determine whether the small eigenvalues are equal; and *resampling methods* that take bootstrap samples of the data to decide whether or not keep a dimension. However, a lot of text mining studies choose the optimal dimension k subjectively or follow the suggestion of Deerwester et al. (1990) who propose to use an operational criterion, that is, a value of k which yields good performance. In detail, several rank-k models are constructed on a part of the dataset, that is, the training set. The most favorable rank-k model based on the cross-validated performance is retained for further analysis. As such, the optimal value of k is obtained by doing a c-fold cross-validation on the training set. Practically, the training set is divided into c subsets of equal size. Iteratively, each part is used for validation, while the other c-1 parts are used for training. So finally, each case in the training set is predicted once. The cross-validation performance better reflects the real performance when validating the classifier to the rest of the dataset, the unseen test data. In the end, it is possible to select the optimal value of k based on the most favorable cross-validated model.

3.3 MARKETING ANALYSIS

The literature on using textual customer information in marketing applications appearing in publications other than marketing journals is broad. This section briefly overviews the handfull of text mining applications published in top-tier marketing journals, and a couple of interesting text mining-related marketing applications published by the management science, information systems research, and computer science community (without any claim to be exhaustive). Lee and Bradlow (2011) untangle the market structure by automatically eliciting product attributes and the brand's position to its competitors from online customer reviews obtained from Epinions.com by means of a new text mining approach. Decker and Trusov (2010) estimate the relative effect of product attributes and brand names on the overall evaluation of the products by using a text mining approach, while Rutz and Trusov (2011) develop an original framework to analyze composition and design attributes of paid search ads using text mining-based methodologies. Furthermore, it was Coussement and Van den Poel (2008b) who introduced the voice of the customer by means of client emails sent to call centers of companies into a traditional churn prediction model. They found that incorporating this additional source of customer information increased the prediction power of discriminating churners from non-churners. Also, in the movie industry, the use of textual information is available to support marketing decisions. A database of ready-to-produce movie scripts is readily available and it is often hard to decide which will be the most successful. Eliashberg et al. (2007) combine statistical learners with natural-language processing methods to predict the return on investment for a movie based on text mining features extracted from these movie scripts. Furthermore, more and more customers are communicating with companies by email, and thus call center operators face huge challenges to handle and organize the big inflow of customer emails. Coussement and Van den Poel (2008a) propose a decision support system for automatic email classification that identifies incoming complaint-related emails from other email types using linguistic-style characteristics. Using this method, complaint emails could be prioritized during email handling, thereby improving complaint management. Ghose and Ipeirotis (2011) explore multiple facets of product reviews including lexical, grammatical, semantic, and stylistic levels to identify important text-based attributes, while studying their impact on helpfulness of the review and their economic influence.

4   Software

Nowadays various text mining solutions are available on the market. Commercial products include *Clearforest*, a text-driven business intelligence solution; *Copernic Summarizer*, a summarizing software extracting key concepts and relevant sentences; *dtSearch*, a document search tool and analysis of text package; *IBM SPSS Modeler* and *Statistica*, a data and text mining workbench; *SAS Text Miner*, a suite of tools for knowledge discovery and knowledge extraction in texts; *TEMIS*, a tool set for text extraction, text clustering, and text categorization; *WordStat*, a product for computer-assisted text analysis; and *Clarabridge*, a software package that collects a variety of textual sources, transforms it using natural-language processing techniques and offers a wide variety of analysis tools. Most commercial tools lack easy-to-use Application Programming Interface (API) integration and provide a relatively monolithic structure regarding extensibility since their source code is not freely available. Among well-known open source data mining tools offering text mining functionality is the *Weka* suite (Frank, et al., 2009), a collection of machine learning algorithms for data mining tasks also offering classification and clustering techniques with extension projects for text mining, like *KEA* for keyword extraction. It provides good API support and has a wide user base. Then there is *GATE* (Cunningham, et al., 2011). Other tools are *RapidMiner* (formerly Yale (Mierswa, et al., 2006)), a system for knowledge discovery and data mining, and the *R tm* package which delivers a flexible integration to primal statistical text mining methods in a modularized form (Feinerer, 2012).

5   Conclusion and Directions for Further Research

This chapter introduces the reader to the process of converting unstructured, textual information to a numeric format. Researchers and analysts should try to unlock the hidden potential of textual customer information more regularly. Various opportunities arise to make use of textual customer information in order to boost marketing analytics. Some future challenges arise for the marketing community. First, although a lot of firms are shifting toward on online collection of written customer data, other advanced opportunities appear to convert spoken communication or on paper-written client/company communication to an online textual format by means of speech recognition or OCR software. Second, Coussement and Van den Poel (2008b) deliver a framework to incorporate textual client/company information into a churn prediction framework. Further research is needed to incorporate other written forms of customer information into alternative marketing analyses, for example, one could incorporate online available company information into a response model for better targeting in the B-2-B setting. Third, the world is becoming very "social" and "emotionally-connected" due to popular applications such as Twitter, Facebook, and so on, in which people feel very much connected to one another, while sharing a lot of subjective, emotional content. Measuring the customers' connection strength, and investigating their language style, topics, and emotionality accordingly, could be very useful to untangle and tailor marketing actions toward different customer segments. Today, the online world is becoming heavily multilingual. Customer are reacting and giving their opinion on brands and services in different languages. From a text mining perspective, this is not an easy task. Much more effort could be put into trying to understand customer online language use between different cultures and languages, and how these differences are resulting in different marketing strategies.

Appendix 1: 10 Hotel Le Palais in Prague Reviews Randomly Scraped from TripAdvisor

Document ID	Hotel review
1	My husband and I stayed at this hotel for a weekend and had a wonderful experience. Staff were very friendly, rooms were spacious with elegant decor and breakfast was served in a lovely room overlooking the city. The hotel even provides a town car to the main square. I recommend getting the refreshing facial at the spa! Great place to stay
2	Look no further....I researched for months about Prague hotels. Both myself and husband are very picky and have stayed in some beautiful hotels – I wanted our 20 year Wedding Anniversary trip to be perfect and it was amazing!! Le Palais is in a lovely neighborhood just a short 15 min walk away from all the noise of the city – and if you dont want to walk, there is a BMW shuttle. Le Palais is beautiful, every little detail is cared for. The rooms are very well appointed and immaculate. The bedroom was very quiet with a comfortable bed and high quality linens, bathrooms with heated floors, deep soaking tub, separate shower and Molton Brown products. A free minibar and my favorite Nespresso machine were tucked away in a closet. Every night when we returned a beautiful orchid and a handmade Czech gift were by my pillow, and Christmas cookies were left on the dining room table with a bottle of wine. The cookies were so delicious, I would get up in the middle of the night to have a snack!I I really miss this little treat – no one bakes me cookies at home! Breakfast was delicious and open until late morning. We did not dine in their restaurant but it smelled wonderful – we chose to venture out into the neighborhood and had many great meals. The sauna, steamroom and whirlpool were immaculate – we went 4 out of our 5 night stay and saw only one other couple. We had a very early morning flight to Paris and we received a real person wake-up call and a breakfast box to go. We couldnt have asked for more, it truly was an amazing 5 nights at Le Palais. I wish I had booked another 3 nights at Le Palais and passed on Paris! All the staff from the front desk to the maids and servers in the dining room all spoke good English and they seemed happy and always had smiles on their faces. For years I've talked about how I love Prague and thank you so much Le Palais for making my husband fall in love with Prague too. We cannot wait to return Ali Caracuzzi
3	My husband and I have traveled the world and stayed at many luxury hotels. We're super picky. Hotel Le Palais was some of the best service I have ever experienced. We booked a package through luxury link, and everything was impeccable. The staff helped us figure out everything from how we could arrive via train from Salzburg to where to find a good bakery in the neighborhood. Breakfast was fantastic, there was a free minibar, a lovely library with a fire place, a wonderful bar and the restaurant was great. My only reason for giving it 4 and not 5 stars is that the location is definitely out from the center of town a good bit. I am very happy to walk and use the subway so this didn't bother me at all, but I would never send someone here who really would prefer to be in the center of the action. It is a 7 minute walk to the subway and then a 10–15 minute journey to the center of town... so all in, we needed to leave ourselves about 30 minutes to get anywhere (ie: the opera, dinner reservation, tour in mala strana). The area itself is quite nice, however, and we liked being out of the fray a bit. Lots of great restaurants in the hood, but they're geared towards locals (so you might have to figure out how to read the menu in Czech).

4	We have recently returned from a 3 night stay at Le Palais and are still commenting on what a lovely hotel it was. We thought the location was perfectly situated in what appeared to be an affluent residential area – lots of hairdresser salons and ladies in fur coats walking little dogs! Arriving in the evening I would definitely recommend booking the hotel's BMW pick up service from airport. On arrival the charming Receptionist gave us a brief guided tour of the Hotel and facilities in our lovely room. My husband had emailed in advance that it was my birthday and I believe we were upgraded and a complimentary bottle o² champagne on ice was awaiting us. Since it was fairly late we opted for a bar meal – I had the most delicious goats cheese quiche with a lovely crisp white wine. My husband had a beef burger which he said was homemade and very good but was more delighted to find a comprehensive selection of excellent quality whiskys! Saturday morning we were presented with a birthday glass of champagne at breakfast. Saturday evening our dining table was beautifully decorated with a red silk heart, red petals and candles. The fire in the dining room was lit and the table inbetween was moved to one side so we could appreciate it. The attentive service was second to none, the food and wine delicious. It was so good in fact we didn't bother to go and find another restaurant or bar, we preferred to stay put in this lovely hotel. Prague centre was easy to get to, the first day we walked a brisk downhill (realistic) 15–20 minutes. The second day we wanted to get straight to the Old Town, a 10 minute walk to the metro (located in a pretty square, which at the time had a Christmas market) then 3 stops on the train. I believe the hotel does a drop off and pick up service as well. Whilst looking for my birthday gift what we didn't appreciate is that there is a garnet mine about 2 hours from Prague so the jewellery shops sell mostly garnet set items. Not a problem! I chose a lovely pair of unique gold and garnet earrings from a shop in the old town Jewish area. All in all a wonderful visit to Prague made special by the hotel's unique service, thank you. ps. If you go in winter please don't under estimate the cold! You must must have good boots, coats, scarves, gloves and especially hats. If you dress accordingly you will have a lovely time
5	We have just returned from a week end in Prague. On reading reviews stayed at this hotel...it was wonderful. The staff are friendly & helpful, food was good...room comfortable. My husband & I had a wonderful weekend & next December we will return, so many amazing places to visit...& a hotel definitely worth returning to...Thank you Le Palais for a wonderful weekend.
6	Le Palais is the setting of a superb thriller, travel novel called The God Complex. My wife packed it in my carry on as a surprise for my flight from NYC. I finished it by the time the plane touched down. It was riveting, and I had no desire to sleep until I found out what happened to Steve Benson. It turned my stay into a unique experience by painting a complete picture of the city, right down to the cafe a stone's throw away from the hotel. I highly recommend it. At the end of the book, there was a link to view story line images – http://godcomplexbook.com. In addition to pictures, there was a map you can download and take a one-day tour based upon the book. If you are heading to Prague, definitely get the book and print out the map. Its worth the money, even if you plan to take a guided tour. Regarding the hotel, no expense was spared on the facilities. The view was magnificent, and the concierge staff was exceptionally helpful in recommending restaurants, planning transportation and meeting rooms, as well as catering. The location was not the most central, but its only a metro stop from the city center. However, I felt like I was getting a local flavor, which I enjoyed tremendously. I admit that my experience was partly influenced by having read a book set in the location. With that said, I would prefer this location again in the future
7	Stayed with another couple for 5 days towards the end of Nov. As previously mentioned by other reviewers it is a little way from the centre, but the hotel shuttle service (up market BMW cars!) is perfectly suited to take you into town. The advantage is that you stay in a nice suburb of Prague which is a nice change after the hubble and bubble of the centre. An extremely attractive hotel very friendly, excellent service, the rooms are very comfortable the cleaning staff very attentive and did a great job. Didnt actually eat in the main restaurant but the breakfast was great covered most peoples needs. The hotel has an excellent spa and a very well equipped (if very underused) gym. Prague is a beautiful city, dont go there for the gastronomy...but as a base to visit it I cannot recomend Le Palais highly enough.

8	This hotel is a treasure – beautifully decorated, spacious rooms, great dining room and library with WiFi. Although it is not located in the heart of the historic area, it offers free shuttle services several times per day to its sister property which is located in the historic center. You have the best of both worlds – a quiet residential setting for a great value and convenient and free transportation to the historic sites and shopping. I would highly recommend a stay in this fine hotel where they pay attention to detail and friendly service. My marble bathroom floor was even heated.
9	We stayed three nights at Le Palais and we have no really complaints. Pros: Beautiful architecture, situated in a real neighborhood with local people live next door. – Delicious breakfast – whole grain bread never tasted better. I'm quite pleased with the food at the hotel. Use of spa facility is free of charge for hotel guests. Gorgeous and huge Jacuzzi pool, sauna room and steam room are also very good. Very clean. The time we visited, which was usually mid morning after breakfast, we always had the whole place by ourselves, so it was nice and quiet. Good service, with welcome drinks and individual tour of the property, etc. Cons: Near zero storage space in the room. The room was quite small (at least the one we stayed in), but small was not the problem. The problem was the room design really did not provide sufficient space for us to take things out of the luggage. 2 metro stations all about 5 blocks away. There is a tram station that is even closer. Prague's public transportation is great, just buy a 1 day or 3 day unlimited ticket and you can go anywhere. But since we visited in November, 5-blocks is a lot in sub zero weather, especially coming back from a day of touring. I guess I wanted to say that the hotel location is still inconvenient compared with other hotels, even though the hotel does offer a shuttle. But overall, Im glad that I chose La Palais.
10	Rested here one night and loved it. Staff very friendly, rooms excellent with free mini bar. Dinner nice but on the heavy side as typical Czech. Library was a lovely place for a coffee. A bit of a walk to the centre of town but compensated by being quiet.

Appendix 2: Term-by-document Matrix

Term	Document									
	1	2	3	4	5	6	7	8	9	10
amaz	0	4.643856	0	0	2.321928	0	0	0	0	0
bar	0	0	2.321928	4.643856	0	0	0	0	0	0
beauti	0	5.210897	0	0	0	0	1.736966	0	1.736966	0
birthday	0	0	0	9.965784	0	0	0	0	0	0
bit	0	0	4.643856	0	0	0	0	0	0	2.321928
bmw	0	1.736966	0	1.736966	0	0	1.736966	0	0	0
book	0	0	0	0	0	13.28771	0	0	0	0
breakfast	0.736966	1.473931	0.736966	0.736966	0	0	0.736966	0	1.473931	0

					Document					
Term	**1**	**2**	**3**	**4**	**5**	**6**	**7**	**8**	**9**	**10**
center	0	0	5.210897	0	0	1.736966	0	1.736966	0	0
chose	0	1.736966	0	1.736966	0	0	0	0	1.736966	0
citi	1.736966	1.736966	0	0	0	1.736966	0	0	0	0
comfort	0	1.736966	0	0	1.736966	0	1.736966	0	0	0
cooki	0	9.965784	0	0	0	0	0	0	0	0
day	0	0	0	3.473931	0	0	0	1.736966	5.210897	0
delici	0	3.473931	0	3.473931	0	0	0	0	1.736966	0
didnt	0	0	2.321928	4.643856	0	0	0	0	0	0
dine	0	0	0	4.643856	0	0	0	2.321928	0	0
excel	0	0	0	1.736966	0	0	1.736966	0	0	1.736966
experi	2.321928	0	0	0	0	4.643856	0	0	0	0
food	0	0	0	1.736966	1.736966	0	0	0	1.736966	0
free	0	1	1	0	0	0	0	2	1	1
friend	1.321928	0	0	0	1.321928	0	0	1.321928	0	1.321928
garnet	0	0	0	9.965784	0	0	0	0	0	0
high	0	0	0	0	0	1.736966	1.736966	1.736966	0	0
histor	0	0	0	0	0	0	0	9.965784	0	0
husband	1	2	1	2	1	0	0	0	0	0
librari	0	0	1.736966	0	0	0	0	1.736966	0	1.736966
littl	0	3.473931	0	1.736966	0	0	1.736966	0	0	0
locat	0	0	1	2	0	3	0	2	0	0
love	1	1	1	6	0	0	0	0	1	1
metro	0	0	0	1.736966	0	1.736966	0	0	1.736966	0
minut	0	0	4.643856	2.321928	0	0	0	0	0	0

Term	Document									
	1	2	3	4	5	6	7	8	9	10
morn	0	3.473931	0	1.736966	0	0	0	0	1.736966	0
neighborhood	0	3.473931	1.736966	0	0	0	0	0	1.736966	0
nice	0	0	1.321928	0	0	0	2.643856	0	1.321928	1.321928
night	0	6.60964	0	1.321928	0	0	0	0	1.321928	1.321928
quiet	0	1.321928	0	0	0	0	0	1.321928	1.321928	1.321928
recommend	1.321928	0	0	1.321928	0	1.321928	0	1.321928	0	0
restaur	0	1.321928	1.321928	1.321928	0	0	1.321928	0	0	0
return	0	1.736966	0	1.736966	1.736966	0	0	0	0	0
servic	0	0	1	4	0	0	1	1	1	0
spa	1.736966	0	0	0	0	0	1.736966	0	1.736966	0
staff	0.514573	0.514573	0.514573	0	0.514573	0.514573	0.514573	0	0	0.514573
stay	0.304006	0.304006	0.152003	0.304006	0.152003	0.152003	0.304006	0.152003	0.304006	0
tabl	0	2.321928	0	4.643856	0	0	0	0	0	0
time	0	0	0	3.473931	0	1.736966	0	0	1.736966	0
tour	0	0	1.321928	1.321928	0	1.321928	0	0	1.321928	0
town	1.321928	0	2.643856	2.643856	0	0	0	0	0	1.321928
transport	0	0	0	0	0	1.736966	0	1.736966	1.736966	0
uniqu	0	0	0	4.643856	0	2.321928	0	0	0	0
visit	0	0	0	1.736966	1.736966	0	1.736966	0	0	0
walk	0	2.643856	2.643856	1.321928	0	0	0	0	0	1.321928
week	0	0	0	0	9.965784	0	0	0	0	0
wine	0	2.321928	0	4.643856	0	0	0	0	0	0
wonder	1	1	1	1	3	0	0	0	0	0

References

Bell, C. and Jones, K.P. (1979). Towards everyday language information retrieval systems via minicomputers. *Journal of the American Society for Information Science, 30*(6), 334–39.

Berry, M.W., Browne, M., Langville, A.N., Pauca, V.P. and Plemmons, R.J. (2007). Algorithms and applications for approximate nonnegative matrix factorization. *Computational Statistics & Data Analysis, 52*(1), 155–73.

Berry, M.W. and Kogan, J. (2010). *Text Mining: Applications and Theory*. Chichester: John Wiley & Sons.

Boutsidis, C. and Gallopoulos, E. (2008). SVD based initialization: A head start for nonnegative matrix factorization. *Pattern Recognition, 41*(4), 1350–62.

Bradford, R.B. (2008). *An Empirical Study of Required Dimensionality for Large-scale Latent Semantic Indexing Applications*. Paper presented at the Proceedings of the 17th ACM Conference on Information and Knowledge Management, Napa Valley, CA.

Brill, E. (1995). Transformation-based error-driven learning and natural language processing: A case study in part-of-speech tagging. *Computational Linguistics, 21*(4), 543–65.

Coussement, K. and Van den Poel, D. (2008a). Improving customer complaint management by automatic email classification using linguistic style features as predictors. *Decision Support Systems, 44*(4), 870–82.

Coussement, K. and Van den Poel, D. (2008b). Integrating the voice of customers through call center emails into a decision support system for chum prediction. *Information & Management, 45*(3), 164–74.

Cunningham, H., Maynard, D. and Bontcheva, K. (2011). *Text Processing with Gate (Version 6)*. Sheffield: Department of Computer Science, University of Sheffield, UK.

Decker, R. and Trusov, M. (2010). Estimating aggregate consumer preferences from online product reviews. *International Journal of Research in Marketing, 27*, 293–307.

Deerwester, S., Dumais, S.T., Furnas, G.W., Landauer, T.K. and Harshman, R. (1990). Indexing by latent semantic analysis. *Journal of the American Society for Information Science, 41*(6), 391–407.

Eliashberg, J., Hui, S.K. and Zhang, Z.J. (2007). From story line to box office: A new approach for green-lighting movie scripts. *Management Science, 53*(6), 881–93.

Feinerer, I. (2012). Tm: A text mining package.

Feldman, R. and Sanger, J. (2007). *The Text Mining Handbook: Advanced Approaches in Analyzing Unstructured Data*. Cambridge: Cambridge University Press.

Fellbaum, C. (1998). *WordNet: An Electronic Lexical Database*. Cambridge, MA: MIT Press.

Frank, E., Holmes, G., Pfahringer, B., Reutemann, P. and Witten, I.H. (2009). The WEKA data mining software: An update. *SIGKDD Explorations, 11*(1), 10–18.

Ghose, A. and Ipeirotis, P.G. (2011). Estimating the helpfulness and economic impact of product reviews: Mining text and reviewer characteristics. *IEEE Transactions on Knowledge & Data Engineering, 23*(10), 1498–512.

Haley, D.T., Thomas, P., De Roeck, A. and Petre, M. (2007). *Tuning an LSA-based Assessment System for Short Answers in the Domain of Computer Science: The Elusive Optimum Dimension*. Paper presented at the Latent Semantic Analysis in Technology Enhanced Learning, Heerlen, The Netherlands, March 29–30.

Jolliffe, I.T. (2002). *Principal Component Analysis*. New York: Springer-Verlag.

Kraaij, W. and Pohlmann, R. (1996). *Viewing Stemming as Recall Enhancement*. Paper presented at the Proceedings of the 19th annual international ACM SIGIR Conference on Research and Development in Information Retrieval, Zurich, Switzerland.

Langville, A.N., Meyer, C.D. and Albright, R. (2006). *Initializations for the Nonnegative Matrix Factorization*. Paper presented at the ACM SIGKDD International Conference on Knowledge Discovery and Data Mining, Philadelphia, PA.

Lee, D.D., and Seung, H.S. (1999). Learning the parts of objects by non-negative matrix factorization. *Nature, 401*(6755), 788–91.

Lee, D.D. and Seung, H.S. (2001). Algorithms for non-negative matrix factorization. *Advances in Neural Information Processing Systems, 13*, 556–62.

Lee, T.Y. and BradLow, E.T. (2011). Automated marketing research using online customer reviews. *Journal of Marketing Research, 48*(5), 881–94.

Lovins, J. (1968). Development of a stemming algorithm. *Mechanical Translation and Computational Linguistics, 11*(1–2), 22–31.

Majumder, P., Mitra, M., Parui, S.K., Kole, G., Mitra, P. and Datta, K. (2007). YASS: Yet another suffix stripper. *ACM Transactions on Information and System Security, 25*(4), 18.

Mayfield, J. and McNamee, P. (2003). *Single N-gram Stemming*. Paper presented at the Proceedings of the 26th annual international ACM SIGIR Conference on Research and Development in Informaion Retrieval, July 28–August 1, 2003.

Melucci, M. and Orio, N. (2003). *A Novel Method for Stemmer Generation Based on Hidden Markov Models*. Paper presented at the Proceedings of the 12th international conference on Information and Knowledge Management, New Orleans, LA.

Mierswa, I., Wurst, M., Klinkenberg, R., Scholz, M. and Euler, T. (2006). *YALE: Rapid Prototyping for Complex Data Mining Tasks*. Paper presented at the 12th ACM SIGKDD International Conference on Knowledge Discovery and Data Mining (KDD-06), August 20–23, Philadelphia, PA.

Miller, G.A. and Newman, E.B. (1958). Tests of a statistical explanation of the rank frequency relation for words in written English. *American Journal of Psychology, 71*(1), 209–18.

Mitchell, P.M., Marcinkiewicz, M.A. and Santorini, B. (1993). Building a large annotated corpus of English: The penn treebank. *Comput. Linguistics, 19*(2), 313–30.

Paatero, P. and Tapper, U. (1994). Positive matrix factorization – a nonnegative factor model with optimal utilization of error-estimates of data values. *Environmetrics, 5*(2), 111–26.

Porter, M.F. (1980). An algorithm for suffix stripping. *Program, 14*(3), 130–37.

Porter, M.F. (2001). Snowball: A language for stemming algorithms. Available at: http://snowball. tartarus.org/texts/introduction.html [accessed January 2, 2012].

Porter, M.F. (2006). The Porter stemming algorithm. Available at: http://tartarus.org/martin/ PorterStemmer/ [accessed October 15, 2012].

Rutz, O.J. and Trusov, M. (2011). Zooming in on paid search ads – a consumer-level model calibrated on aggregated data. *Marketing Science, 30*, 789–800.

Salton, G. (1971). *The SMART Retrieval System: Experiments in Automatic Document Processing*. Englewood Cliffs, NJ: Prentice Hall.

Salton, G. (1975). *A Theory of Indexing*. Society for Industrial and Applied Mathematics.

Salton, G. (1989). *Automatic Text Processing: The Transformation, Analysis, and Retrieval of Information By Computer*. Boston, MA: Addison-Wesley.

Salton, G. and Buckley, C. (1988). Term-weighting approaches in automatic text retrieval. *Information Processing and Management, 24*(5), 513–23.

Sparck Jones, K. (1988). A statistical interpretation of term specificity and its application. In *Document Retrieval Systems* (132–42). London: Taylor Graham Publishing.

Wild, S., Curry, J. and Dougherty, A. (2004). Improving non-negative matrix factorizations through structured initialization. *Pattern Recognition, 37*(11), 2217–32.

Zipf, G.K. (1949). *Human Behavior and the Principle of Least Effort: An Introduction to Human Ecology.* Boston, MA: Addison-Wesley Press.

3 Bayesian Networks and Applications in Direct Marketing

YUAN YUAN GUO AND MAN LEUNG WONG

1   Introduction

Bayesian networks are popular within the fields of artificial intelligence and data mining due to their ability to support probabilistic reasoning from data with uncertainty. They can represent the co-related relationships among random variables and the conditional probabilities of each variable from a given data set. With a network structure at hand, people can conduct probabilistic inference to predict the outcome of some variables based on the values of other observed ones. Hence, Bayesian networks are widely used in many areas, such as diagnostic and classification systems (Jensen, 1996; Andreassen, et al., 1987; Cheeseman, et al., 1988), direct marketing, and so on. They are also suitable for reasoning with incomplete information.

Many methods have been suggested to learn Bayesian network structures from complete databases without missing values, which can be classified into two main categories (Cheng, et al., 2002): the dependency analysis method (Spirtes, et al., 2000) and the score-and-search approach (Cooper and Herskovits, 1992; Heckerman, 1995; Lam and Bacchus, 1994).For the former approach, the results of dependency tests are employed to construct a Bayesian network conforming to the findings. For the latter one, a scoring metric is adopted to evaluate candidate network structures while a search strategy is used to find a network structure with the best score. Decomposable scoring metrics, such as Minimum Description Length (MDL) and Bayesian Information Criterion (BIC), are usually used to deal with the problem of time consuming score evaluation. When the network structure changes, we only need to re-evaluate the score of the corresponding nodes related to the changed edges, rather than the scores of the whole nodes. And stochastic search methods which employ evolutionary algorithms have been used in the latter approach for complete data, such as genetic algorithms (GA) (Larrañaga, et al., 1996a, 1996b), evolutionary programming (Wong, et al., 1999) and hybrid evolutionary algorithms (Wong and Leung, 2004).

Nevertheless, learning Bayesian networks from incomplete data is a difficult problem in real-world applications. The parameter values and the scores of networks cannot be computed directly on the records having missing values. Moreover, the scoring metric cannot be decomposed directly. Thus, a local change in the network structure will lead to the re-evaluation of the score of the whole network, which is time-consuming considering the number of all possible networks and the complexity of the network structures. Furthermore, the patterns of the missing values also affect the dealing methods. Missing values can appear in different situations: *Missing Completely At Random*, or *Not Ignorable* (Schafer and Graham, 2002). In the first situation, whether an observation is missing or not is independent of the actual states of the variables. So the incomplete databases may be representative samples of the complete databases. However, in the second situation, the observations are missing to some specific states for some variables. Different approaches should be adopted for different situations, which again complicates the problem.

Many researchers have been working on parameter learning and structure learning from incomplete data. For the former, several algorithms can be used to estimate or optimize the parameter values of the known Bayesian network structures, such as Gibbs sampling, Expectation Maximization (EM) (Heckerman, 1995), and Bound-and-Collapse (BC) method (Ramoni and Sebastinani 1997a, 1997b). For structure learning from incomplete data, the main issues are how to define a suitable scoring metric and how to search for Bayesian network structures efficiently and effectively. Concerning the score evaluation for structure learning, some researchers proposed to calculate the expected values of the statistics to approximate the score of candidate networks. Friedman proposed a Bayesian Structural Expectation-Maximization (SEM) algorithm which alternates between the parameter optimization process and the model search process (Friedman, 1997, 1998). The score of a Bayesian network is maximized by means of the maximization of the expected score. Peña et al. used the BC+EM method instead of the EM method in their *BS-BC+EM* algorithm for clustering (Peña, et al., 2000, 2002). However, the search strategies adopted in most existing SEM algorithms may not be effective and may make the algorithms find suboptimal solutions. Myers et al. employed a GA to learn Bayesian networks from incomplete databases (Myers, et al., 1999). Both network structures and the missing values are encoded and evolved. The incomplete databases are completed by specific genetic operators during evolution. Nevertheless, it has the efficiency and convergence problems because of the enlarged search space and the strong randomness of the genetic operators for completing the missing values.

In this chapter, we propose a new learning system that uses EM to handle incomplete databases with missing values and uses a Hybrid Evolutionary Algorithm (HEA) to search for good candidate Bayesian networks. The two procedures are iterated so that we can continue finding a better model while optimizing the parameters for a good model to complete the database with more accurate information. In order to reduce the time for statistics computation, the database is preprocessed into two parts: records with and without missing values. Instead of using the expected values of statistics as in most existing SEM algorithms, our system applies a data completing procedure to complete the database and thus decomposable scoring metrics can be used to evaluate the networks. The MDL scoring metric is employed in the search process to evaluate the fitness of the candidate networks.

The objective of the direct marketing modeling problem is to predict and rank potential buyers from the buying records of previous customers. The customer list will be ranked according to each customer's likelihood of purchase. The decision makers can then select the portion of customer list to roll out. An advertising campaign including mailing of catalogs or brochures is targeted on the most promising prospects. Hence, if the prediction is accurate, it can help to enhance the response rate of the advertising campaign and increase the return of investment.

In real-life applications, the databases containing the buying records of customers may contain missing values. Irrelevant records or trivial items with missing values can be simply discarded from the raw databases in the data preprocessing procedure. However, in most cases, the variables are related to each other and the deletion of incomplete records may lose important information. This will affect performance dramatically especially if we want to discover some knowledge "nuggets" from the databases and they happen to be contained in the incomplete records. People may alternatively replace the missing values with certain values, such as the mean or mode of the observed values of the same variable. Nevertheless, it may change the distribution of the original database.

We apply our system to a direct marketing modeling problem, which requires to rank the previous customers according to their probability of potential purchasing. The results show that the performance of the evolved Bayesian networks obtained by our system is better than the models learned by several other learning algorithms.

The rest of this chapter is organized as follows. In Sections 2, 3, 4, and 5, we will present the backgrounds of Bayesian networks, Bayesian network classifiers, the missing value problem, and direct marketing modeling. In Section 6, our new learning system for incomplete databases, Evolutionary Bayesian Network (EBN), will be described in detail. In Section 7, we use our system to discover Bayesian networks from a real-life direct marketing database. We will conclude the chapter in the last section.

2 Bayesian Networks

A Bayesian network, G, has a directed acyclic graph (DAG) structure. As shown in Figure 3.1, each node in the graph corresponds to a discrete random variable in the domain. An edge, $X \leftarrow Y$, on the graph, describes a parent and child relation in which X is the child and Y is the parent. All parents of X constitute the parent set of X which is denoted by Π_X. In addition to the graph, each node has a conditional probability table (CPT) specifying the probability of each possible state of the node given each possible combination of states of its parents. If a node contains no parent, the table gives the marginal probabilities of the node (Pearl, 1988).

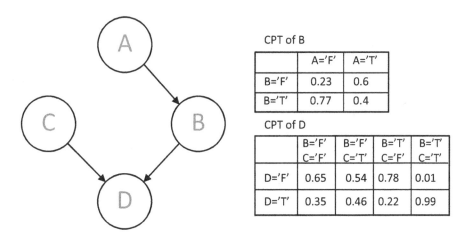

CPT of B

	A='F'	A='T'
B='F'	0.23	0.6
B='T'	0.77	0.4

CPT of D

	B='F' C='F'	B='F' C='T'	B='T' C='F'	B='T' C='T'
D='F'	0.65	0.54	0.78	0.01
D='T'	0.35	0.46	0.22	0.99

Figure 3.1   A Bayesian network example

Since Bayesian networks are founded on the idea of conditional independence (CI), it is necessary to give a brief description here. Let U be the set of variables in the domain and P be the joint probability distribution of U. Following Pearl's notation (Pearl, 1998), a CI relation is denoted by, $I(X,Z,Y)$ where X, Y, and Z are disjoint subsets of variables in U. Such notation says that X and Y are conditionally independent given the *conditioning set*, Z. Formally, a CI relation is defined as (Pearl, 1998):

$$P(x \mid y,z) = P(x \mid z) \quad whenever \quad P(y,z) > 0, \tag{1}$$

where x, y, and z are any value assignments to the set of variables X, Y, and Z respectively. A CI relation is characterized by its *order*, which is simply the number of variables in the conditioning set Z.

By definition, a Bayesian network encodes the joint probability distribution of the domain variables, $U = \{N_1,\ldots,N_n\}$:

$$P(N_1,\ldots,N_n) = \prod_i P(N_i \mid \Pi_{N_i}). \tag{2}$$

2.1   LEARNING BAYESIAN NETWORK FROM DATA

Suppose help is available from domain experts, we could construct a Bayesian network about the domain by consulting the experts. Such process is typical of building an expert system and is called *knowledge engineering* or *knowledge elicitation*. The advantage of using expert's knowledge is that the method is simple and direct. In general, the network structure as told by the experts will be a good approximation as they are knowledgeable about the domain. However, this approach has two disadvantages. First, reliability is a concern as the information obtained is largely from subjective judgments. Second, it is difficult, if not impossible, for people to estimate event probabilities precisely.

To avoid these problems, people resort to a machine learning approach, namely to learn a Bayesian network from collected data or past observations about the domain. Assume, for simplicity, that the data does not contain missing values and that there is no unobserved or hidden variable. In the literature of Bayesian network learning, we could roughly divide the works into two categories (Cheng, et al., 1997): the dependency analysis and the score-and-searching approaches.

The reason that there exist two distinctively different approaches follows from the fact that Bayesian networks can be viewed differently. On the one hand, Bayesian networks are considered as depicting the underlying dependency models. In this regard, it suggests the use of dependency information for the Bayesian network construction. On the other hand, Bayesian networks are considered as encoding a joint probability distribution (Equation 2). From this perspective, various kinds of measures are devised which evaluate the quality of a given network. Consequently, the learning problem can be formulated as a search problem in which the aim is to find the best network with respect to the given measure. Although there are two different approaches for Bayesian network learning, they have, in general, respective problems and difficulties remaining to be solved.

2.1.1   THE DEPENDENCY ANALYSIS APPROACH

The first approach is called the dependency analysis approach which includes the examples in Spirtes, et al., (2000), Fung and Crawford (1990), and Cheng, et al. (1997). Typically, it assumes the existence of a perfect map for a given distribution P. In other words, it is assumed that there exists a Bayesian network, G, that captures all the CI relations implied by P. Consequently, this suggests a general Bayesian network learning methodology: construct a network G by testing the validity of any independence assertions $I(X,Z,Y)$. In practice, we can use what is collectively called the CI test for testing. If the statement $I(X,Z,Y)$ is supported by the data, D, it follows that X should be d-separated with Y by Z in G; otherwise, X is not d-separated with Y by Z (Pearl, 1988).

As a digression from the ongoing discussion, we give a brief description of the CI test. A common approach is to use hypothesis testing procedure discussed in the statistical literature (Spirtes, et al., 2000; Spatz and Johnston, 1981; Agresti, 2002). To begin with, the CI assertion (that is, $I(X,Z,Y)$) is modeled as the *null hypothesis*. Suppose that we use the likelihood-ratio χ^2 test, the χ^2 statistics is calculated by:

$$G^2 = -2\sum observed * \log(observed / expected). \tag{3}$$

Simply put, the statistics calculate the discrepancies between the real occurrence, *observed*, and the expected count followed from the hypothesis, *expected* over every distinct events. In our case, because $I(X,Z,Y)$ implies:

$$P(X,Y,Z) = P(X\,|\,Y,Z)P(Y,Z)$$
$$= P(X\,|\,Y)P(Y,Z) \qquad (by\ equation\ )$$

The statistic is computed by:

$$G^2 = -2\sum_{x,y,z} P(x,y,z)\log\frac{P(x,y,z)}{P(y,z)P(x\,|\,z)}. \tag{4}$$

Suppose that the number of possible instantiations of the variables X, Y, and Z are respectively v_X, v_Y, and v_Z, G^2 follows a χ^2 distribution with $(v_X - 1)\times(v_Y - 1)\times v_Z$ degree of freedom. Checking our computed G^2 against the distribution, we obtain the p-value, which is "the smallest level of significance for which the data leads to the rejection of the null hypothesis" (Beaumont and Knowles, 1996). If the p-value is less than a predefined *cutoff value* α, the test shows strong evidence to reject the hypothesis; otherwise, the hypothesis cannot be rejected.

Take the SGS algorithm (Spirtes, et al., 2000) as an illustration. The algorithm begins with a completely connected undirected graph. In other words, dependence between every pair of variables is assumed. Then, CI tests between all pairs of connected nodes are conducted. When two nodes X and Y are found to be conditionally independent given Z, the undirected edge between them is removed so that $I(X,Z,Y)$ is not violated. When no more edges could be removed, the undirected edges in the graph are oriented according to some rules which conform to the CI relations discovered previously. This produces the final Bayesian network.

In general, there are three problems typical to the dependency analysis approach. First, it is difficult to determine whether two nodes are dependent. Quoting from Spirtes, et al. (2000): "In general, two variables X and Y may be conditionally dependent given a set Z while independent on the subset or superset of Z." In the worst case, like in SGS, every possible combination of the conditioning set needs to be examined which would require an exponential number of tests. Second, results from the CI test may not be reliable especially for high-order CI tests (when the size of the conditioning set is high) (Spirtes, et al., 2000; de Campos and Heute, 1999). Hence, for algorithms that require high-order CI tests, the results may be inaccurate. Third, because a network is constructed in a step-by-step manner, the construction algorithm may be *unstable* in the sense that an earlier mistake during construction is consequential (Spirtes, et al., 2000; Dash and Druzdzel, 1999). Moreover, this suggests that the order of testing the CI relations is important, which will be a concern when one pursues for the optimal performance.

2.1.2   The score-and-search approach

The second approach is called the score-and-search approach. Recalling that a Bayesian network encodes a joint probability distribution (Equation 2), we could derive a measure for assessing the goodness of such encoding. For instance, such measure could be derived from Bayesian statistics, information theory, or the MDL principle (Rissanen, 1978). Though their theoretical foundations are different, some studies show that different metrics are asymptotically equivalent under certain conditions (Bouckaert, 1995; Suzuki, 1999).

Since we employ the MDL metric (Lam and Bacchus, 1994) in our work, we take it as an example for illustration. Basically, the metric is derived from information theory and incorporates the idea of the MDL principle. The metric has two components: the network description length and the data description length. An optimal network is the one that minimizes both simultaneously.

Formally, let $U = \{N_1,\ldots,N_n\}$ be the set of discrete variables, Π_{N_i} denotes the parent set of a node N_i in the candidate network, and v_i denotes the number of possible states of the variable N_i. The network description length is given by:

$$\sum_{i=1}^{n}\left[\left|\Pi_{N_i}\right|\log_2(n)+d(v_i-1)\prod_{N_j\in\Pi_{N_i}}v_j\right]$$

where d is a constant denoting the number of bits used to store a numerical value. Intuitively, the network description length represents the structural complexity of the network which is evaluated by the number of bits required to encode the graphical structure and to store the conditional probability table at each node.

Meanwhile, the data description length is given by:

$$\sum_{i=1}^{n}\sum_{N_i,\Pi_{N_i}}M(N_i,\Pi_{N_i})\log_2\frac{M(\Pi_{N_i})}{M(N_i,\Pi_{N_i})}$$

where $M(.)$ is the count of the particular instantiation in the data set. In essence, the data description length evaluates the proximity of the distributions implied by the data and the candidate network, which is a measure of the accuracy of the candidate network.

Because the MDL metric is simply the sum of the two description lengths, it puts a balance between model complexity and model accuracy. In other words, the optimal network, with regard to the metric, should be simple while accurately representing the joint distribution.

As a property common to other metrics, the MDL metric is node-decomposable and could be written as in Equation 5. One can observe that the score is simply the summation of the independent evaluation on the parent set, Π_{N_i}, of every node N_i in the domain U.

$$\text{MDL}(G) = \sum_{N_i \in U} \text{MDL}(N_i, \Pi_{N_i})$$

(5)

With the metric defined, the network learning problem can be formulated as a search problem. The objective is to search for the network structure which has the optimal score. However, the problem does not become easier as the search space that contains all possible network structures is huge. As Chickering et al. have shown, the search problem is proved to be NP-hard with the use of a particular metric (1994). Some research works, therefore, resort to greedy search heuristics (Cooper and Herskovits, 1992; Lam and Bacchus, 1994) but the drawback is that the approach may yield suboptimal solutions. Some others use systematic and exhaustive searching, like branch-and-bound (Tian, 2000) to find the optimal solution. In the worst case, the time consumed would be considerable. Recently, there are attempts (Larrañaga, et al., 1996b; Wong, et al., 1999) to use evolutionary computation to tackle the problem, which provide a compromise between the computational cost and the quality of the solution obtained.

Although numerous algorithms are proposed to address the difficulties, it is our general impression that no concluding remarks could be readily given. Suffice it to say, different approaches have their strengths and weaknesses.

2.2   INFERENCE ON BAYESIAN NETWORKS

Since a Bayesian network encodes a joint probability distribution, it can be used to perform various kind of probabilistic inference in diagnosis or prediction. As discussed in Haddawy (1999), Bayesian networks are used for:

- computing the probability of the conjunction of a set of random variables;
- computing the most likely combination of values of variables in the network;
- computing the piece of evidence that most influenced or will have the most influence on a given hypothesis.

Unfortunately, to perform inference on a Bayesian network is a difficult problem. Theoretically speaking, it is NP-hard to compute the exact inference result (Heckerman and Wellman, 1995). Nevertheless, there exists an efficient algorithm for a special class of networks, called the singly-connected network (Haddawy, 1999).[1] Extending the

---

1   Also called polytree, in which there is only one adjacency path between any two nodes in the graph.

result, different algorithms have been developed to tackle the inference problem in most general cases.

Another approach to the inference problem is to perform *approximate* inference. In particular, cases are generated from the network and the desired probability is estimated by counting. For algorithms that perform approximate inference, they are further divided into a few major categories, including instantiation-based method, random sampling, structural approximation, and loopy-belief propagation (Koller and Murphy, 2012). However, since the exact inference problem is NP-hard, it follows that to perform approximate inference with which the error is bounded is also NP-hard (Koller and Murphy, 2012).

Although the inference problem remains difficult, different algorithms present practical methodologies or heuristics which help to tackle the problem more efficiently. After all, since the actual performance is what is noticeable, the theoretical limitation is merely a minor concern in real-world practice.

3   Bayesian Network Classifiers

3.1   THE CLASSIFICATION PROBLEM IN GENERAL

The classification problem is a well-known problem in the machine learning community. Simply put, it asks the question: "What is the *class* (or *label*) that a given *object instance* belongs to?" Indeed, classification has great practical significance as it is typical in human's reasoning. For example, in biology we classify living beings into different species; in chemistry, we discern different elements; and in daily life, we distinguish strawberry from cranberry. Besides that the classification result is useful, the problem itself is interesting because of the simple and readily comprehensible goal it sets.

An object instance (or instance for short) is described by a collection of *feature* or *attribute* values. A feature or an attribute stands for the extracted information that is relevant to the classification task and could either be continuous (such as height) or discrete (such as sex). Assume $A_1, \ldots, A_n$ denotes the set of features, an object instance is described by a feature vector $\{a_1, \ldots, a_n\}$ where a_i is the actual value that a feature A_i takes. As an illustration, suppose that we are classifying the type of an iris and the features $(A_1, \ldots, A_n)$ are the petal width, petal length, sepal width, and sepal length of the flower, $\{a_1, \ldots, a_n\}$ will be corresponding real measurements of the target. With the feature vector treated as input, the objective of classification is to output the correct class value $C = \{c_1, \ldots, c_k\}$ that the target object belongs to.

If an instance comes with the class information, it is called a labeled instance; otherwise, it is called an unlabeled instance. Typical in a classification problem, we are given a number of labeled instances in the first place, which may be considered as our previous observations. We call this set of data the *training set* or the *learning set* as they provide the information necessary for constructing a *classifier*. A classifier, once constructed, functions as the device that predicts the classes of unlabeled instances. Thus, in constructing the classifier, it is important that we aim at "get(ting) the most out of the data" (Weiss and Kulikowski, 1991). Since every classifier presumes a particular classification model (which depends on our approach taken), learning a classifier is equivalent to finding the *best* model that fits the data.

Often, it is necessary to evaluate the performance of the classifier so as to see how good it is or to make a comparison with other classifiers (Duda and Hart, 1973). Suppose that, for simplicity, the zero-or-one loss function is in use, the classifier is evaluated by the misclassification rate or the error rate on classifying unlabeled instances. In theory, the performance of the classifier is evaluated by the *true error rate* (Weiss and Kulikowski, 1991), which is the error rate on classifying *every* possible instance. Since it is likely to be computationally infeasible to compute the true error rate, various performance evaluation methods are proposed which approximate the estimation of the true error rate. In the simplest case, a separate set of data, called the *testing set*, is used to evaluate the performance of the classifier. In general, when the size of the testing set is large, evaluation on the testing set could give a good approximation to the true error rate. When the data set is small, it is common to use resampling techniques like cross-validation or bootstrapping in performance evaluation. Although we shall not delve into the details, suffice it to say, resampling techniques are reminiscent to the train-and-test methodology except that the training sets and the testing sets are selected in a particular manner.

In the classification literature, there are many different approaches to tackle the problem. For example, there are approaches that use decision trees, neural networks, and rule-based systems to perform classification. Also, there are works that begin with a probability point of view. We call the classifiers that fall into this category *Bayesian classifiers*.

3.2   BAYESIAN CLASSIFIERS

Theoretically, the Bayesian classifier, which follows the *Bayes decision rule*, is the best classifier in the sense that the probability of error is minimized (Duda and Hart, 1973). In particular, the Bayes decision rule estimates the conditional probability of the class variable for a given instance, and returns the class which yields the greatest value. Formally put, an instance $I = \{a_1,...,a_n\}$ is assigned to class c_i if:

$$P(C = c_i \mid I) > P(C = c_j \mid I) \quad \text{for all } j \neq i. \tag{6}$$

By Bayes rule, the class posterior probability could be expressed as:

$$P(C \mid A_1,...,A_n) = \frac{P(A_1,...,A_n \mid C)P(C)}{\sum P(A_1,...,A_n \mid C)P(C)}. \tag{7}$$

Because the denominator in Equation 7 is the same for every $P(C \mid A_1,...,A_n)$, the decision function can be rewritten as:

$$P(I \mid C = c_i)P(C = c_i) \geq P(I \mid C = c_j)P(C = c_j) \quad \text{for all } j \neq i. \tag{8}$$

Although the idea is theoretically sound, to represent $P(A_1,...,A_n \mid C)P(C)$ presents a problem. If the training set is very large, it is possible to store the entire distribution in a table (assuming all attributes are discrete). However, this is impractical for two reasons. First, it is difficult to represent or store the entire distribution. Second, in real-world practice, the training set often has limited size. Thus, it is almost impossible to learn the true distribution from the training data. With such limitations, people resort to make various assumptions so as to approximate the estimation of the true distribution (Weiss and Kulikowski, 1991). Bayesian network classifiers are one of the examples.

3.3   BAYESIAN NETWORK CLASSIFIERS

Since Bayesian networks can be used to represent a joint probability distribution, we can apply them to approximate the estimation of $P(A_1,\ldots,A_n,C)$. The classifier thus built is named a Bayesian network classifier. In retrospect, the naïve Bayesian classifier could be regarded as a forerunner of the Bayesian network classifiers despite that it is proposed long before Bayesian networks become formalized. Following the naïve Bayesian classifier, there are many exciting developments in the field which attempt to improve upon the naïve Bayesian classifier. Recently, Friedman et al. (1997) proposed the tree augmented classifier which is regarded as the state-of-the-art Bayesian network classifier (Keogh and Pazzani, 1999). Not only does their classifier attain outstanding performance, but their comprehensive study (Friedman, et al., 1997) also contributes by formalizing the *Bayesian network classifier* terminology, detailing its development, making both qualitative and quantitative comparisons among various classifiers, and discussing possible extensions. Although it would be a repeat of words to speak more of Bayesian network classifiers, we still give an overview along the line of development which constitutes the necessary background to put forward our Bayesian network classifier learning algorithm.

3.3.1   Naïve Bayesian classifiers

The naïve Bayesian classifier is an early attempt that follows the Bayesian classification principle. The classifier simplifies the estimation of the joint probability distribution by assuming that each attribute is conditionally independent of others given the class variable. Although the naïve Bayesian classifier existed long before Bayesian networks were formalized, its independence assumption could readily be depicted using a Bayesian network. As shown in Figure 3.2, the structure of the classifier is characterized by the fact that every attribute node would have the class node as its parent. Formally, such independence assumption enables the likelihood probability be represented as a product of $P(A_i \mid C)$:

$$P(A_1,\ldots A_n \mid C) = \div P(A_i \mid C) \qquad (9)$$

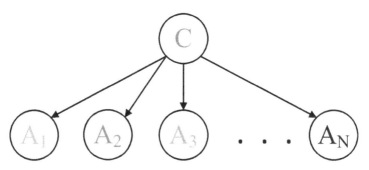

Figure 3.2   The structure of the naïve Bayesian classifiers

Because of the naïve assumption, it is trivial to learn the classifier from data (Langley and Sage, 1994). In particular, we only need to evaluate each of the n conditional probability distribution, that is, $P(A_i | C)$. If all the attributes are discrete, this amounts to filling in a two-way contingency-table by counting the occurrence of each distinct instantiation (c_i, a_i) in the training set. Not only is the learning efficient, but prediction is also a trivial matter. From Equation 9, to classify a new instance only requires multiplying the n product terms for k times.

As we would normally expect that attributes are intervened in an intricate manner, the assumption behind the naïve Bayesian classifier seems unrealistic (Friedman, et al., 1997). However, in many real-life problems, the classifier often exhibits surprisingly good and robust performance (Langley and Sage, 1994). Because the classifier is simple to construct and use, it has widespread applications in many domains. Although its robustness has been inexplicable,[2] the naïve Bayesian classifier initiates the development of many better classifier models. We discuss the approaches in the following text.

3.3.2   Two ways to improve the naïve Bayesian classifier

Following the success of the naïve Bayesian classifier, there are a number of works that attempt to make further improvements. In general, they would modify the basic assumption that is simply fallible in theory. Consider an example given by Langley and Sage, 1994. Supposethe problem domain contains three attributes A_1, A_2, A_3. By Equation 9, the naïve Bayesian classifier calculates the posterior probability by:

$$P(A_1, A_2, A_3 | C) = P(A_1 | C)P(A_2 | C)P(A_3 | C) \tag{10}$$

Suppose that we include a redundant attribute A_4 such that A_4 is perfectly correlated with A_1. In particular, we could imagine that A_4 copies the value of A_1 for each instance in the training set. Hence, the conditional probability distribution of A_4 equals that of A_1, that is, $P(A_4 | C) = P(A_1 | C)$. It turns out that the class posterior probability is given by:

$$P(A_1, A_2, A_3, A_4 | C) = P(A_1 | C)P(A_2 | C)P(A_3 | C)P(A_4 | C)$$
$$= P(A_1 | C)^2 P(A_2 | C)P(A_3 | C)$$

As can be observed, the influence of A_1 is now doubled because of the existence of the redundant attribute A_4. Meanwhile, the influence of the other attributes, A_2 and A_3, is diminished. Consequently, we say that the naïve Bayesian classifier produces a "biased prediction" (Langley and Sage, 1994). Although this example is imaginary and is unlikely to happen in real-world problems, it nevertheless demonstrates that dependency among attributes will aggravate the performance of the naïve Bayesian classifier.

Among the works that try to improve over the naïve Bayesian classifier, they are roughly divided into two categories (Friedman, et al., 1997):

---

2   Recently, there are also works (Domingos and Pazzani, 1997) that attempt to give reasons why the naïve Bayesian classifier is so good.

Feature Selection Approach

Because redundant attributes may have detrimental effect on the naïve Bayes classifier. One way to circumvent the problem is to use only a subset of features for building the classifier. A noteworthy work in this category is the *selective Bayesian classifier* which is proposed by Langley and Sage (1994). As the authors point out, their main contribution is in extending the feature selection methodology, which has been studied in the literature, into building a naïve Bayesian classifier. Nevertheless, they present a thoughtful analysis of the problem and the approach they have taken. As suggested by empirical results, they conclude that the selective Bayesian classifier retains the simplicity of the naïve Bayesian classifier yet overcomes the weakness mentioned.

Although not strictly related to the naïve Bayesian classifier, Singh and Provan also employ feature selection to learn Bayesian network classifier (Singh and Provan, 1998). They call their approach *selective Bayesian network*. In their work, they examine a number of feature selection approaches and make comparisons with the naïve Bayesian classifier, decision tree, and a Bayesian network classifier without feature selection. Experimental results show that the feature selection provides improvement on learning Bayesian network classifiers. Furthermore, the selective Bayesian network outperforms the naïve Bayesian classifier for most of the problems and has comparable performance to the decision tree. They observe that their approach excels on a large dataset but may have poor performance on small data sets that have many attributes.

Augmented Network Approach

Another approach to improve upon the naïve Bayesian classifier is to remove some of the independence assumptions. Equivalently, this amounts to adding *augmenting* edges to the naïve Bayesian classifier structure, and hence the name *augmented network approach*. For example, in the semi-naïve Bayesian classifier (Kononenko, 1991; Friedman, et al., 1997), in contrast to assuming that attributes are conditionally independent, it assumes that different attribute *groups* are conditionally independent while making no independence assumption on attributes within the same group. With regard to its structure, this is equivalent to having the augmenting edges to form a complete subgraph for attributes in the same group, which is illustrated in Figure 3.3.

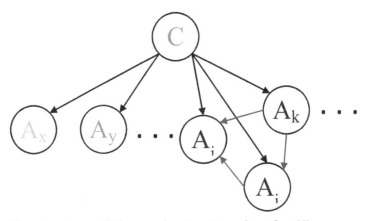

Figure 3.3   The structure of the semi-naïve Bayesian classifiers

Ezawa and Norton (1996) proposed the *Advanced Pattern Recognition and Identification* system (APRI) which constructs an augmented network based on results from mutual information tests. Since the APRI system targets on predicting uncollectible telecommunications account, they have special emphasis on minimizing the access to the large database and are more concerned with the misclassification result. Unlike other approaches where the naïve structure is assumed, APRI chooses depending on the mutual information between the class node C and each attribute variable A_i. Furthermore, augmented edges are added according to the class conditional mutual information (Equation 11) between every pair of attribute variables.

3.3.3   Tree-augmented naïve Bayesian network classifiers

Recently, Friedman et al. proposed the tree-augmented naïve Bayesian network classifier (TAN). In essence, the classifier structure contains augmented edges which form a spanning tree. By modifying Chow and Liu's work (1968), they develop an efficient learning algorithm which returns the maximum likelihood estimate of tree-augmented structures. In Figure 3.4, we show the learning algorithm from Friedman, et al., 1997.

---

1. Compute the conditional mutual information $I_p(A_i; A_j | C)$ between each pair of attributes, $i \neq j$.
2. Build a complete undirected graph in which the vertices are the attributes $A_1, \ldots, A_n$. Annotate the weight of an edge connecting A_i to A_j by $I_p(A_i; A_j | C)$.
3. Build a maximum weighted spanning tree.
4. Transform the resulting undirected tree to a directed one by choosing a root variable and setting the direction of all edges to be outward from it.
5. Construct the classifier network by adding the class node, labeled by C, and adding an edge from C to each A_i.

Figure 3.4   The TAN learning procedure

The conditional mutual information is defined by:

$$I_p(X;Y|Z) = \sum_{x,y,z} \log \frac{P(x,y|z)}{P(x|z)P(y|z)}$$

(11)

Intuitively, $I_p(X;Y|Z)$ measures the information that Y provides about X when Z is known. Let N be the size of the training set, calculating the *weights* of the edges has complexity of $O(n^2 N)$. Once the weights are obtained, the learning algorithm amounts to constructing the maximum weight spanning tree, which could be solved in $O(n^2 \log n)$. Since N is usually larger than $\log n$, the overall complexity of the learning algorithm is thus $O(n^2 N)$, which is computationally efficient.

In their work, they compare TAN with a number of existing classification algorithms, including the naïve Bayesian classifier, the selective naïve Bayesian classifier, C4.5, Chow-

and-Liu multinet classifier, and other Bayesian network classifiers. On evaluating across a number of data sets, TAN shows promising performance and is evidently superior to the naïve Bayesian classifier while being competitive with C4.5 and the selective naïve Bayesian classifier.

Because of its efficient learning algorithm and its remarkable performance, TAN is regarded as the state-of-the-art Bayesian network classifier (Keogh and Pazzani, 1999). In addition to TAN earning a high reputation, the comprehensive study by Friedman et al. also put forward research on the Bayesian network classifier. Since TAN, there have been a number of works which attempt to learn Bayesian network classifiers of various kinds and with different approaches (Keogh and Pazzani, 1999; Cheng and Greiner, 1999; Monti and Cooper, 1999; Meilà-Predoviciu, 1999).

Although its performance is satisfactory, a question naturally arises: "Why should the augmented edges exist as a spanning tree?" If we consider the tree-like structure as constraints, are the constraints simplistic (like in the naïve Bayesian classifier), or are the constraints stringent? In response to this, it is important to note that the adherence to learning a tree-like network in TAN is mainly due to computational consideration (Friedman, et al., 1997): while there is an efficient and theoretically sound algorithm to learn a tree-like network, there seems to be no efficient way to learn a classifier with a free structure (or more complicated than a tree). Hence, despite the fact that an unrestricted structure is more expressive and could possibly lead to a better performance; the question remains as to how to tackle the construction problem in the first place.

4   Learning Bayesian Networks from Incomplete Databases

In real-world applications, the databases may contain incomplete records which have missing values. People may simply discard incomplete records, but relevant information may be deleted. Alternatively, they can complete the missing values with the information from databases such as the mean values of other observed values of the variables. However, the distribution of the data may be changed. Advanced approaches including maximum likelihood estimation (Schafer and Graham, 2002), Bayesian multiple imputation (Rubin, 1987), machine learning (Lakshminarayan, et al., 1996), Bayesian networks (Zio, et al., 2004; Hruschka and Ebecken, 2002), k-nearest neighbor, regression (Kim, et al., 2004; Heckerman, 1995), and singular value decomposition (Liu, et al., 2003) have been applied to complete the missing values in databases and microarray gene expression data sets.

One advantage of Bayesian networks is that they support probabilistic reasoning from data with uncertainty. However, for learning Bayesian networks from incomplete databases, the parameter values and the scores of networks cannot be computed directly on the records having missing values. Moreover, the scoring metric cannot be decomposed directly. Thus, a local change in the network structure will lead to the re-evaluation of the score of the whole network.

For parameter learning, existing methods either use different inference algorithms to get the expected values of statistics or complete the missing values. Two commonly adopted methods are Gibbs sampling and EM (Heckerman, 1995). Gibbs sampling tries to complete the database by inferring from the available information and then learns from the completed database (Geman and Geman, 1984). On the other hand, EM calculates the expected values of the statistics via inference and then updates the parameter values using the previously calculated expected values (Dempster, et al., 1977; Lauritzen, 1995). It will converge to a local maximum of the parameter values under certain conditions. Furthermore, EM usually converges faster than Gibbs sampling. Both Gibbs sampling and EM assume that the missing values appear randomly or follow a certain distribution. In order to encode prior knowledge of the pattern of missing data, Ramoni and Sebastinani proposed a new deterministic BC method that does not need to guess the pattern of missing data (Ramoni and Sebastinani, 1997a, 1997b; Petrison, et al., 1997). It firstly bounds the possible estimates consistent with the probability interval by computing the maximum and minimum estimates that would have been inferred from all possible completions of the database. Then the interval is collapsed to a unique value via a convex combination of the extreme estimates using information on the assumed pattern of missing data.

For structure learning from incomplete databases, the score-and-search approach can still be employed. The main issues are how to define a suitable scoring metric and how to search for Bayesian networks efficiently and effectively. Many variants of SEM were proposed for this kind of learning in the past few years (Friedman, 1997, 1998).

4.1   BASIC SEM ALGORITHM

The basic SEM algorithm can learn Bayesian networks in the presence of missing values and hidden variables (Friedman, 1997). It alternates between two steps: an optimization for the Bayesian network parameters conducted by the EM algorithm, and a search for a better Bayesian network structure using a hill-climbing strategy. The two steps iterate until the whole algorithm is stopped. The score of a Bayesian network is approximated by the expected value of statistics. Friedman extended his SEM to directly optimize the true Bayesian score of a network in Friedman, 1998. The framework of the basic SEM algorithm can be described as follows:

1. Let M_1 be the initial Bayesian network structure.
2. For t=1,2,..
3. Execute EM to approximate the maximum-likelihood parameters Θ_t for M_t.
4. Perform a greedy hill-climbing search over Bayesian network structures, evaluating each structure using approximated score $Score(M)$.
5. Let M_{t+1} be the Bayesian network structure with the best score.
6. If $Score(M_t) = Score(M_{t+1})$ then return M_t and Θ_t.

4.2   HYBRID EVOLUTIONARY ALGORITHM (HEA)

The Hybrid Evolutionary Algorithm (HEA) is proposed by Wong and Leung for learning Bayesian networks from complete databases (Wong and Leung, 2004). It employs the results of lower-order CI tests to refine the search space and adopts a HEA to search for good network structures. Each individual in the population represents a candidate network which is encoded by a connection matrix. In addition, each individual has a cutoff value α which is also subject to be evolved. At the beginning, for every pair of nodes (X,Y), the highest p-value returned by the lower-order CI tests is stored in a matrix P_v. If the p-value is greater than or equal to α, the CI assertion $I(X,Z,Y)$ is assumed to be valid, which implies that the nodes X and Y cannot have a direct edge between them. By changing the α values dynamically, the search space of each individual can be modified and each individual conducts its search in a different search space. Four mutation operators are used in HEA. They add, delete, move, or reverse edges in the network structures either through a stochastic method or based on some knowledge. A novel merge operator is suggested to reuse previous search results. The MDL scoring metric is used for evaluating candidate networks. The cycle prevention method is adopted to prevent cycle formation in the network structures.

The experimental results demonstrate that HEA has better performance on some benchmark data sets and real-world data sets than other state-of-the-art algorithms (Wong and Leung, 2004).

5   Direct Marketing Modeling

Direct marketing concerns communication with prospects, so as to elicit response from them. In contrast to the mass marketing approach, direct marketing is targeted at a group of individuals that are potential buyers and are likely to respond. In retrospect, direct marketing emerged because of the prevalence of mail ordering in the nineteenth century (Petrison, et al., 1997). As technology advances, marketing is no longer restricted to mailing but includes a variety of media. Nevertheless, the most important issue in the business remains to be the maximization of the profitability, or return on investment (ROI), of a marketing campaign.

In a typical scenario, we often have a huge list of customers. The list could be records of existing customers or data bought from *list brokers*. But among the huge list, there are usually few real buyers which amount to only a few percent (Cabena, et al., 1997). Since the budget of a campaign is limited, it is important to focus the effort on the most promising prospects so that the response rate can be improved.

Before computers became widely used, direct marketers often used simple heuristics to enhance the response rate. One straightforward approach is to use common sense to make the decision. In particular, we could match prospects by examining the demographics of the customers in the list. For example, in the life insurance industry, it is natural to target the advertising at those who are rich and aging. Another common approach to enhance the response rate is to conduct list testing by evaluating the response of samplings from the list. If a certain group of customers gives a high response rate, the actual campaign may be targeted to the customers similar to this group. A more systematic approach, which was developed in 1920s but is still being used today, is to differentiate potential buyers from non-buyers using the recency-frequency-monetary model (RFM) (Petrison, et al., 1997). In essence, the profitability of a customer is estimated by three factors including the recency of buying, the frequency of buying, and the amount of money spent. Hence, only individuals that are profitable will be the targets of the campaign.

With the advancement of computing and database technology, people seek computational approaches to assist in decision making. From the data set that contains demographic details of customers, the objective is to develop a *response model* and use the model to predict promising prospects. In a certain sense, response models are similar to classifiers in the classification problem. However, unlike the classifier which makes a dichotomous decision (that is, active or inactive respondents), the response model needs to score each customer in the data set with the likelihood of purchase. The customers are then ranked according to the score. A ranked list is desirable because it allows decision makers to select the portion of customer list to roll out (Zahavi and Levin, 1997). For instance, out of the 200,000 customers on the list, we might wish to send out catalogs or brochures to the most promising 30 percent of customers so that the advertising campaign is cost-effective (the 30 percent of the best customers to be mailed is referred to as the *depth-of-file*) (Bhattacharyya, 1998). Hence, one way to evaluate the response model is to look at its performance at different depth-of-file. In the literature, there are various approaches proposed for building the response model. Here, we give a brief review in the following paragraphs.

Earlier attempts often adopted a statistical analysis approach. Back in 1967, a company already used multiple regression analysis to build the response model. In 1968, the Automatic Interaction Detection (AID) system was developed which essentially uses tree analysis to divide consumers into different segments (Petrison, et al., 1997). Later, the system was modified and became the Chi-Squared Automatic Interaction Detector (CHAID). One statistical analysis technique, which is still widely used today, is logistic regression. Essentially, the logistic regression model assumes that the *logit* (that is, the logarithm of the *odd ratios*) of the dependent variable (active or inactive respondents) is a linear function of the independent variables (that is, the attributes). Because the approach is popular, newly proposed models are often compared with the logistic regression model as the baseline comparison (Bhattacharyya, 1998, 2000; Zahavi and Levin, 1997).

Zahavi and Levin (1997) examined the possibility of learning a back-propagation neural network as the response model. However, due to a number of practical issues and that the empirical result did not improve over a logistic regression model, it seems that the neural network approach does not bring much benefit.

Because there are striking similarities between classification and the direct marketing problem, it is straightforward to apply classification algorithms to tackle the problem. As an example, Ling and Li (1998) used a combination of two well-known classifiers, the naïve Bayesian classifier and C4.5, to construct the response model. Because scoring is necessary, they modified the C4.5 classifier so that a prediction (that is, active and inactive respondents) comes with a *certainty factor*. To combine the two classifiers, they applied ada-boosting (Freund and Schapire, 1996) to both classifiers in learning. When they evaluated their response model across three different real-life data sets, the result showed that their approach are effective for solving the problem.

Bhattacharyya formulated the direct marketing problem as a multi-objective optimization problem (1998, 2000). He noted that the use of a single evaluation criterion, which is to measure the model's accuracy, is often inadequate (2000). For practical concern, he suggested that the evaluation criterion needs to include the performance of the model at a given depth-of-file. In an early attempt, he proposed to use GAs to learn the weights of a linear response model while the evaluation function is a weighted average of the two evaluation criteria. When comparing the learnt model with the logit model on a real-life data set, the new approach indicates a superior performance (Bhattacharyya, 1998). Recently, he attempted to use genetic programming (GP) to learn a tree-structured symbolic rule form as the response model (Bhattacharyya, 2000). Instead of using a weighted average criterion function, his new approach searches for *Pareto-optimal* solutions. From the analysis, he found that the GP approach outperforms the GA approach and is effective at obtaining solutions with different levels of tradeoffs (Bhattacharyya, 2000).

6   The Evolutionary Bayesian Network (EBN) Algorithm

Although HEA outperforms some existing approaches, it cannot deal with incomplete databases. Thus, we propose a novel evolutionary algorithm, called the Evolutionary Bayesian Network (EBN) learning method), that utilizes the efficient and effective global search ability of HEA and applies EM to handle missing values. Some strategies are also introduced to speed up EBN and to improve its performance. EBN is described in Figure 3.5 on the opposite page.

In EBN, there are two special kinds of generations. *SEM generation* refers to one generation in the SEM framework (step 9 of Figure. 3.5) while *HEA generation* refers to the iteration in HEA search process (step 9(g) of Figure 3.5).

Firstly, the database is separated and stored into two parts in the data preprocess phase. The set of records having missing values is marked as H and the set of records without missing values is marked as O. Order-0 and order-1 CI tests are then conducted on O and the results are stored in the matrix P_v for refining the search space of each individual in the following procedures.

At the beginning of the SEM phase, for each individual, we check a randomly generated α value with the stored values in the matrix P_v to refine its search space. It should be noted that the search space will not be refined if O is not available. A DAG structure is then randomly constructed from the refined search space for this individual. Thus, the initial population is generated (step 7 of Figure 3.5). Through some specific strategies, an initial network structure is generated for the current best network which is denoted as G_{best}. EBN will then be executed for a number of SEM generations until the stopping criteria are satisfied, that is, the maximum number of SEM generations is reached or the log-likelihood of G_{best} does not change for a specified number of SEM generations (step 9 of Figure 3.5).

Within each SEM generation, EM will be conducted first to find the best values for the parameters of G_{best} (step 9(a) of Figure 3.5). The missing values in H will be filled according to G_{best} and its parameters (step 9(c) of Figure 3.5). Combining the newly completed result of H with O, we get a new complete data set O'. Then, the HEA search process will be executed on O' for a certain number of HEA generations to find a better network to replace G_{best}. The MDL scoring metric is again employed in the search process to evaluate the fitness of the candidate networks. The whole process will iterate until it stops.

7   Application in Direct Marketing Modeling

In this section, we apply EBN in a real-world direct marketing modeling problem. We compare the performance of the Bayesian networks evolved by EBN (EBN models) with those obtained by LibB [3] and Bayesware Discoverer [4] from incomplete real-world data

---

3   LibB is available at http://compbio.cs.huji.ac.il/LibB/

4   A trial version of Bayesware Discoverer is available at http://www.bayesware.com/

DATA PREPROCESSING

1. Store incomplete records together, mark the whole set as H.
2. Store other records together, mark the whole set as O.

CI TEST PHASE

3. If O is available
   a. Perform order-0 and order-1 CI tests on O.
   b. Store the highest p-value in the matrix P_v.

   else store negative values in the matrix P_v.

SEM PHASE

4. Set t, the generation count, to 0.
5. Set t_{SEM}, the SEM generation count, to 0.
6. Set t_{uc}, the count of generations with unchanged log-likelihood, to 0.
7. For each individual G_i in the population $Pop(t)$
   - Initialize the α value randomly, where $0 \le \alpha \le 1$.
   - Refine the search space by checking the α value against the stored P_v value.
   - Inside the reduced search space, create a DAG randomly.
8. Generate the initial network structure for G_{best}.
9. While t_{SEM} is less than the maximum number of SEM generations or t_{uc} is less than MAX_{uc},
   a. Find G_{best} by using **EM**.
   b. If the log-likelihood of G_{best} does not change, increment t_{uc} by 1; else set t_{uc} to 0.
   c. Complete missing data in H using G_{best} and its parameters, and get updated complete data O'.
   d. Execute order-0 and order-1 CI-tests on O', and store the highest P-value in P_v.
   e. For each individual G_i in the population $Pop(t)$
      * Refine the search space by checking the α value against the P_v value.
      * Evaluate G_i using the MDL metric on O'.
   f. Set t_{HEA}, the HEA generation count in each SEM generation, to 0.
   g. While t_{HEA} is less than the maximum number of HEA generations in each SEM generation,
      * execute **HEA search phase**.
      * increment t_{HEA} and t by 1, respectively.
   h. Pick up the individual that has the lowest MDL score on O' to replace G_{best}.
   i. increment t_{SEM} and t by 1, respectively.
10. Return the individual that has the lowest MDL score in any HEA generation of the last SEM generation as the output of the algorithm.

Figure 3.5   EBN algorithm

sets, as well as the performance of Bayesian neural network (BNN) (Neal, 1996), logistic regression (LR), naïve Bayesian classifier (NB) (Friedman, et al., 1997), and TAN (Friedman, et al., 1997).

We also present the performance of the Bayesian networks evolved by HEA using two missing values handling methods. They transform an incomplete data set into a completed one and employ HEA as search method for learning Bayesian networks from the new data set.

In the first method, denoted as HEA1, we simply replace missing values for each variable with the mode of the observed data of the variable (the state that has the largest number of observations). In the second method, denoted as HEA2, we consider the missing values as a new additional state for each variable, thus a new completed data set is generated.

7.1   METHODOLOGY

The response models are evaluated on a real-life direct marketing data set. It contains records of customers of a specialty catalog company, which mails catalogs to good customers on a regular basis. In this data set, there are 5,740 active respondents and 14,260 non-respondents. The response rate is 28.7 percent. Each customer is described by 361 attributes. We applied the forward selection criteria of logistic regression (Agresti, 2002) to select nine relevant attributes out of the 361 attributes.

Missing values are then introduced randomly into the data set. The percentages of the missing values in our experiments are 1 percent, 5 percent, and 10 percent, respectively. In our experiments, EBN, LibB, and Bayesware Discoverer are executed directly on the data sets with missing values. For BNN, LR, NB, TAN, and HEA1, we replace the missing values with the mean value or the mode for each variable. For HEA2, the missing values are treated as an additional new state for each variable.

For EBN, the maximum number of iterations in EM is 10, the maximum number of HEA generations in each SEM generation is 100, the maximum number of SEM generations is 50, the population size is 50, tournament size is 7, and MAX_{uc} is set to 10. For both HEA1 and HEA2, the maximum number of generations is set to 5000, the population size is 50, and the tournament size is 7.

To compare the performance of different response models, we use decile analysis which estimates the enhancement of the response rate for ranking at different depth-of-file. Essentially, the descending sorted ranking list is equally divided into ten deciles. Customers in the first decile are the top-ranked customers that are most likely to give response. Correspondingly, customers in the last decile are least likely to buy the specified products. A *gains table* will be constructed to describe the performance of the response model. In a gains table, we tabulate various statistics at each decile, including (Rud, 2001):

- *Predicted Probability of Active*: the average of the predicted probabilities of active respondents in the decile by the response model.
- *Percentage of Active*: the percentage of active respondents in the decile.
- *Cumulative Percentage of Active*: the cumulative percentage of active respondents from decile 0 to this decile.
- *Actives*: the number of active respondents in this decile.
- *Percentage of Total Actives*: the ratio of the number of active respondents in this decile to the number of all active respondents in the data set.
- *Cumulative Actives*: the number of active respondents from decile 0 to this decile.

- *Cumulative Percentage of Total Actives*: the ratio of the number of cumulative active respondents (from decile 0 to this decile) to the total number of active respondents in the data set.
- *Lift*: calculated by dividing the percentage of active respondents by the response rate of the file. Intuitively, it estimates the enhancement by the response model in discriminating active respondents over a random approach for the current decile.
- *Cumulative Lift*: calculated by dividing the cumulative percentage of active respondents by the response rate. This measure evaluates how good the response model is for a given depth-of-file over a random approach. It provides an important estimate of the performance of the model.

7.2   CROSS-VALIDATION RESULTS

In order to compare the robustness of the response models, we adopt a tenfold cross-validation approach for performance estimation. A data set is randomly partitioned into ten mutually exclusive and exhaustive folds. Each time, a different fold is chosen as the test set and other nine folds are combined together as the training set. Response models are learned from the training set and evaluated on the corresponding test set.

In Table 3.1, the average of the statistics of the EBN models for the ten test sets of the data set with 1 percent missing values at each decile are tabulated. Numbers in the parentheses are the standard deviations. The EBN models have the cumulative lifts of 320.62 and 232.24 in the first two deciles respectively, suggesting that by mailing to the top two deciles alone, the Bayesian networks generate over twice as many respondents as a random mailing without a model. For this data set, the average learning time of EBN is 49.1 seconds on a notebook computer with an Intel$^{(R)}$ Core$^{(TM)}$ 2 Duo 1.8GHz processor and 3 GB of main memory running Windows XP operating system.

For the sake of comparison, the average of the cumulative lifts of the models learned by different methods from data sets with different percentages of missing values are summarized in Tables 3.2, 3.3, and 3.4, respectively. Numbers in the parentheses are the standard deviations. For each data set, the highest cumulative lift in each decile is highlighted in bold. The superscript [+] represents that the cumulative lift of the EBN models from the corresponding data set is significantly higher at the 0.05 level than that of the models obtained by the corresponding methods. The superscript [−] represents that the cumulative lift of the EBN models is significantly lower at the 0.05 level than that of the corresponding models.

In Table 3.2, the average and the standard deviations of the cumulative lifts of the models learned by different methods for the data set with 1 percent missing values are shown. In the first two deciles, the networks learned by LibB have cumulative lifts of 211.19 and 185.59, respectively; and 213.04 and 189.43 respectively for Bayeseware Discoverer models. It can be observed that EBN models get the highest cumulative lifts in the first three deciles, and the cumulative lifts of the EBN models in the first two deciles are significantly higher at the 0.05 level than those of the other eight models.

In Table 3.3, the average and the standard deviations of the cumulative lifts for different models learned from the data set with 5 percent missing values are shown. In the first two deciles, the EBN models have the highest cumulative lifts of 320.27 and 224.07 respectively, and they are significantly higher than those of the other eight methods at 0.05 level. The average learning time of EBN is 200.5 seconds for this data set.

Table 3.1 Gains table of the EBN models for the ten test sets of the data set with 1 percent missing values

Decile	Prob. of Active	% of Active	Cumulative % of Active	Actives	% of Total Actives	Cumulative Actives	Cumulative % of Total Actives	Lift	Cumulative Lift
0	44.61% (1.66%)	91.96% (6.41%)	91.96% (6.41%)	183.00 (12.75)	31.90% (2.35%)	183.00 (12.75)	31.90% (2.35%)	320.62 (23.64)	320.62 (23.64)
1	43.23% (0.82%)	41.37% (8.45%)	66.67% (5.55%)	82.33 (16.81)	14.31% (2.76%)	265.33 (22.10)	46.22% (3.54%)	143.86 (27.78)	232.24 (17.78)
2	42.92% (1.95%)	2.09% (7.63%)	45.14% (2.65%)	4.17 (15.19)	0.72% (2.62%)	269.50 (15.83)	46.94% (2.24%)	7.26 (26.30)	157.25 (7.50)
3	31.20% (1.72%)	30.30% (3.20%)	41.43% (1.91%)	60.30 (6.37)	10.51% (1.10%)	329.80 (15.22)	57.45% (1.94%)	105.60 (11.03)	144.33 (4.88)
4	24.61% (0.33%)	27.92% (3.55%)	38.73% (1.44%)	55.57 (7.07)	9.69% (1.30%)	385.37 (14.33)	67.14% (1.85%)	97.40 (13.03)	134.95 (3.71)
5	23.17% (0.37%)	58.26% (12.40%)	41.98% (1.99%)	115.93 (24.67)	20.20% (4.22%)	501.30 (23.70)	87.33% (3.47%)	202.99 (42.43)	146.29 (5.81)
6	22.69% (0.24%)	1.99% (6.05%)	36.27% (1.25%)	3.97 (12.05)	0.69% (2.08%)	505.27 (17.47)	88.02% (1.92%)	6.90 (20.90)	126.38 (2.76)
7	22.45% (0.55%)	4.30% (8.76%)	32.28% (1.19%)	8.57 (17.43)	1.48% (3.00%)	513.83 (18.98)	89.50% (1.89%)	14.91 (30.14)	112.44 (2.37)
8	17.12% (0.61%)	24.29% (4.65%)	31.39% (0.83%)	48.33 (9.25)	8.43% (1.66%)	562.17 (14.90)	97.94% (0.63%)	84.74 (16.65)	109.36 (0.70)
9	14.96% (0.87%)	5.66% (1.71%)	28.70% (0.71%)	11.83 (3.58)	2.06% (0.63%)	574.00 (14.17)	100.00% (0.00%)	19.75 (6.01)	100.00 (0.00)

Note: The statistics are obtained from the 10 test sets.

Table 3.2 Cumulative lifts of the networks learned by different methods for the real-world data sets with 1 percent missing values

Decile	EBN	LibB	Bayesware Discoverer	BNN	LR	NB	TAN	HEA1	HEA2
0	**320.62** (23.64)	211.19[+] (28.00)	213.04[+] (41.61)	200.11[+] (11.00)	188.30[+] (12.23)	198.50[+] (9.99)	195.80[+] (6.41)	195.60[+] (9.03)	195.10[+] (11.17)
1	**232.24** (17.78)	185.59[+] (17.44)	189.43[+] (14.53)	171.01[+] (9.76)	168.80[+] (9.73)	169.70[+] (7.15)	168.30[+] (7.35)	169.80[+] (8.65)	170.10[+] (6.79)
2	**157.25** (7.50)	156.79 (7.08)	155.99 (7.46)	156.56 (5.74)	152.30[+] (6.72)	154.30 (4.45)	150.90[+] (4.89)	154.00 (5.54)	155.00 (5.83)
3	144.33 (4.88)	**146.54** (5.56)	146.07 (7.90)	144.26 (4.67)	141.40[+] (3.13)	139.40[+] (2.55)	139.70[+] (2.75)	142.60 (5.23)	144.30 (3.80)
4	134.95 (3.71)	136.43 (6.92)	**140.78** (12.08)	135.60 (1.98)	132.80[+] (1.23)	131.20[+] (1.75)	132.50 (4.17)	132.70[+] (3.09)	134.30 (3.02)
5	**146.29** (5.81)	134.65[+] (10.05)	136.09[+] (4.35)	127.33[+] (2.15)	125.80[+] (2.86)	124.70[+] (2.79)	124.10[+] (2.69)	126.40[+] (2.88)	128.30[+] (2.45)
6	**126.38** (2.76)	119.16[+] (4.11)	119.63[+] (1.82)	120.20[+] (2.02)	118.30[+] (2.26)	116.70[+] (1.64)	118.70[+] (1.70)	120.80[+] (3.01)	118.80[+] (1.48)
7	112.44 (2.37)	113.69 (3.87)	112.53 (1.84)	**113.80[-]** (1.61)	112.50 (1.35)	111.90 (1.45)	113.40[-] (1.17)	113.10[-] (1.52)	112.90[-] (0.57)
8	**109.36** (0.70)	108.58 (2.03)	107.64[+] (1.86)	107.71[+] (0.98)	106.60[+] (1.07)	106.20[+] (0.92)	106.20[+] (1.03)	106.20[+] (1.14)	106.10[+] (0.88)
9	100.00 (0.00)	100.00 (0.00)	100.00 (0.00)	100.00 (0.00)	100.00 (0.00)	100.00 (0.00)	100.00 (0.00)	100.00 (0.00)	100.00 (0.00)

Note: The statistics are obtained from the 10 test sets.

Table 3.3 Cumulative lifts of the networks learned by different methods for the real-world data sets with 5 percent missing values

Decile	EBN	LibB	Bayesware Discoverer	BNN	LR	NB	TAN	HEA1	HEA2
0	**320.27** (22.43)	217.63+ (47.64)	246.59+ (31.34)	199.37+ (10.33)	188.50+ (11.45)	195.40+ (10.27)	197.80+ (9.84)	193.30+ (5.79)	192.40+ (12.97)
1	**224.07** (16.29)	186.30+ (21.35)	165.69+ (19.94)	171.09+ (9.50)	167.80+ (9.20)	170.30+ (6.33)	169.60+ (7.38)	167.90+ (6.82)	169.90+ (7.58)
2	153.53 (6.98)	155.28 (6.96)	152.60 (7.80)	**155.97** (5.60)	151.40 (4.77)	152.60 (4.14)	151.50 (5.23)	153.30 (4.47)	153.80 (5.85)
3	143.41 (5.83)	**145.15** (8.33)	143.24 (6.71)	143.21 (3.67)	140.40+ (2.67)	139.50+ (2.72)	139.90+ (2.85)	143.60 (3.89)	142.90 (4.51)
4	135.63 (3.67)	136.75 (6.21)	**144.16-** (5.18)	134.18 (2.61)	132.40+ (1.58)	130.50+ (1.27)	131.30+ (3.27)	133.00+ (2.54)	133.10+ (3.38)
5	**145.72** (5.51)	133.47+ (10.49)	124.27+ (3.38)	126.88+ (2.49)	125.60+ (2.67)	125.00+ (2.62)	123.60+ (1.65)	126.30+ (2.95)	128.10+ (3.21)
6	**126.11** (2.86)	118.90+ (4.94)	118.10+ (1.85)	120.07+ (2.29)	118.40+ (2.41)	117.00+ (1.70)	118.10+ (1.66)	119.30+ (2.06)	118.90+ (1.79)
7	111.74 (2.05)	113.57- (3.69)	113.09- (2.18)	**113.73-** (1.48)	112.40 (1.17)	111.50 (1.35)	112.50 (1.27)	112.70 (1.42)	113.20- (0.79)
8	**109.20** (1.11)	108.08+ (1.89)	106.80+ (1.56)	107.64+ (0.87)	106.60+ (0.97)	106.00+ (1.15)	106.10+ (1.10)	106.20+ (1.23)	105.90+ (0.88)
9	100.00 (0.00)	100.00 (0.00)	100.00 (0.00)	100.00 (0.00)	100.00 (0.00)	100.00 (0.00)	100.00 (0.00)	100.00 (0.00)	100.00 (0.00)

Note: The statistics are obtained from the 10 test sets.

Table 3.4 Cumulative lifts of the networks learned by different methods for the real-world data sets with 10 percent missing values

Decile	EBN	LibB	Bayesware Discoverer	BNN	LR	NB	TAN	HEA1	HEA2
0	**320.18** (24.36)	239.06+ (64.44)	196.86+ (18.50)	195.71+ (13.60)	185.10+ (12.56)	190.40+ (13.55)	194.90+ (11.43)	194.10+ (9.87)	195.80+ (9.27)
1	**212.88** (15.96)	188.42+ (21.09)	171.22+ (9.13)	169.89+ (9.75)	164.90+ (10.46)	167.70+ (6.29)	167.20+ (8.83)	167.00+ (6.36)	168.50+ (7.63)
2	152.76 (5.65)	153.36 (6.38)	152.20 (6.40)	**154.32** (6.76)	149.30 (8.11)	151.30 (3.95)	151.30 (5.38)	152.40 (6.06)	153.00 (5.50)
3	141.78 (4.40)	**142.46** (9.31)	139.63 (4.50)	142.28 (4.66)	138.90+ (3.57)	138.40+ (2.91)	139.40 (3.63)	139.90 (3.96)	141.00 (4.29)
4	**136.15** (5.39)	134.86 (5.83)	131.55+ (4.84)	133.14+ (3.55)	130.70+ (2.31)	128.60+ (1.78)	129.80+ (4.16)	132.30+ (2.67)	132.40+ (3.86)
5	**143.02** (6.50)	134.62+ (10.86)	124.17+ (5.17)	125.38+ (1.82)	123.60+ (2.01)	123.50+ (1.72)	123.20+ (1.99)	124.50+ (2.37)	125.50+ (2.46)
6	**125.51** (3.20)	119.65+ (5.40)	117.23+ (2.73)	119.27+ (2.25)	117.70+ (2.67)	116.10+ (2.33)	117.30+ (1.42)	118.30+ (2.26)	118.40+ (1.84)
7	111.58 (2.08)	**112.61** (4.21)	112.36 (1.85)	113.25- (1.28)	111.90 (1.85)	111.20 (1.81)	112.50- (1.27)	112.30 (1.25)	113.10- (0.88)
8	**109.35** (0.91)	108.97 (1.81)	105.51+ (1.22)	107.09+ (0.67)	106.40+ (0.84)	105.60+ (0.97)	106.30+ (0.82)	106.20+ (0.92)	106.30+ (0.82)
9	100.00 (0.00)	100.00 (0.00)	100.00 (0.00)	100.00 (0.00)	100.00 (0.00)	100.00 (0.00)	100.00 (0.00)	100.00 (0.00)	100.00 (0.00)

Note: The statistics are obtained from the 10 test sets.

In Table 3.4, the average and the standard deviations of the cumulative lifts for different models discovered from the data set with 10 percent missing values are shown. Again, it demonstrates that the discovered EBN models have the highest cumulative lifts in the first two deciles, which are 320.18 and 212.88 respectively. The cumulative lifts of EBN models in the first two deciles are significantly higher at 0.05 level than those of the other eight methods. For this data set, the average learning time of EBN is 559.2 seconds.

To summarize, the networks generated by EBN always have the highest cumulative lifts in the first two deciles. Moreover, the cumulative lifts of the EBN models are significantly higher at 0.05 level than those of the other models in the first two deciles. Thus, we can conclude that EBN is very effective in learning Bayesian networks from data sets with different missing value percentages.

Since an advertising campaign often involves huge investment, a Bayesian network which can categorize more prospects into the target list is valuable as it will enhance the response rate. From the experimental results, it seems that EBN are more effective than the other methods.

8   Conclusion

In this chapter, we have introduced the basic concepts of Bayesian networks, their inference methods, different Bayesian network classifiers, and some existing Bayesian network learning approaches. We have described a new evolutionary algorithm called EBN that can learn Bayesian networks from incomplete databases. We have applied EBN to a real-world data set of direct marketing and compared the performance of the networks obtained by EBN with the models generated by other methods. The experimental results demonstrate that EBN outperforms other methods in the presence of missing values.

The main advantage of EBN lies in the integration of EM and a hybrid evolutionary algorithm. While using EM and Bayesian inference to complete the missing values of a variable, the relationships of these variables with other variables are also considered instead of examining only the observed values of the variable. Thus better missing value imputations can be obtained. At the same time, the HEA facilitates the discovery of much better Bayesian network structures effectively and efficiently.

Acknowledgments

This work is supported by Hong Kong GRF LU310111.

References

Agresti, A. (2002). *Categorical Data Analysis*. New York, NY: Wiley.

Andreassen, S., Woldbye, M., Falck, B. and Andersen, S. (1987) MUNIN: A causal probabilistic network for interpretation of electromyographic findings. *Proceedings of the 10th International Joint Conference on Artificial Intelligence*, 366–72.

Beaumont, G.P. and Knowles, J.D. (1996). *Statistical Tests: An Introduction with MINITAB Commentary*. London; New York, NY: Prentice-Hall.

Bhattacharyya, S. (1998). Direct marketing response models using genetic algorithms. *Proceedings of the 4th International Conference on Knowledge Discovery and Data Mining*, 144–8.

Bhattacharyya, S. (2000). Evolutionary algorithms in data mining: Multi-objective performance modeling for direct marketing. *Proceedings of the 6th International Conference on Knowledge Discovery and Data Mining*, 465–73.

Bouckaert, R.R. (1995). *Bayesian Belief Networks: From Inference to Construction*. PhD thesis, Utrecht University.

Cabena, P., Hadjinian, P., Stadler, R., Verhees, J. and Zansi, A. (1997). *Discovering Data Mining: From Concept to Implementation*. Upper Saddle River, NJ: Prentice-Hall Inc.

Cai, Z., Heydari, M. and Lin, G. (2006). Microarray missing value imputation by iterated local least squares. *Proceedings of the 4th Asia-Pacific Bioinformatics Conference*, 159–68.

Cheeseman, P., Kelly, J., Self, M., Stutz, J., Taylor, W. and Freeman, D. (1988). Autoclass: A Bayesian classification system. *Proceedings of the 5th International Workshop on Machine Learning*, 54–64.

Cheng, J., Bell, D.A. and Liu, W. (1997). Learning Bayesian Networks from data: An efficient approach based on information theory. *Proceedings of the 6th ACM International Conference on Information and Knowledge Management*, 325–31, Las Vegas, Nevada.

Cheng, J. and Greiner, R. (1999). Comparing Bayesian Network classifiers. In K.B. Laskey and H. Prade (Eds), *Proceedings of the 15th Conference on Uncertainty in Artificial Intelligence*. Stockholm: Morgan Kaufmann, 101–8.

Cheng, J., Greiner, R., Kelly, J., Bell, D. and Liu, W. (2002). Learning Bayesian Networks from data: An information-theory based approach. *Artificial Intelligence, 137*(1–2), 43–90.

Chickering, D.M., Geiger, D. and Heckerman, D.E. (1994). *Learning Bayesian Network is NP-Hard*. Technical report, Microsoft Research.

Chow, C.K. and Liu, C.N. (1968). Approximating discrete probability distributions with dependency trees. *IEEE Transactions on Information Theory, 14*(3), 462–7.

Cooper, G.F. and Herskovits, E.H. (1992). A Bayesian Method for the induction of probabilistic networks from data. *Machine Learning, 9*(4), 309–47.

Dash, D. and Druzdzel, M.J. (1999). A hybrid anytime algorithm for the construction of causal models from sparse data. In K.B. Laskey and H. Prade (Eds), *Proceedings of the 15th Conference on Uncertainty in Artificial Intelligence*. Stockholm: Morgan Kaufmann, 142–9.

de Campos, L.M. and Huete, J.F. (1999). *Approximating Causal Orderings for Bayesian Networks Using Genetic Algorithms and Simulated Annealing*. Technical report, Department of Computer Science and Artificial Intelligence, University of Granada, Spain.

Dempster, A.P., Laird, N.M. and Rubin, D.B. (1997). Maximum likelihood from incomplete data via the EM algorithm. *Journal of the Royal Statistical Society(B), 39*(1), 1–38.

Domingos, P. and Pazzani, M. (1997). On the optimality of the simple Bayesian classifier under zero-one loss. *Machine Learning, 29*, 103–30.

Duda, R.O. and Hart, P.E. (1973) *Pattern Classification and Scene Analysis*. New York, NY: John Wiley & Sons Inc.

Ezawa, K.J. and Norton, S.W. (1996). Constructing Bayesian Networks to predict uncollectible telecommunications accounts. *IEEE Expert-Intelligent Systems and Their Applications, 11*(5), 45–51.

Freund, Y. and Schapire, R.E. (1996). Experiments with a new boosting algorithm. *Proceedings of the 13th International Conference on Machine Learning*, 148–56.

Friedman, N. (1997). Learning belief networks in the presence of missing values and hidden variables. Proceedings of the 14th International Conference on Machine Learning, 125–33.

Friedman, N. (1998). The Bayesian Structural EM Algorithm. *Proceedings of the 14th Conference on Uncertainty in Artificial Intelligence*.

Friedman, N., Geiger, D. and Goldszmidt, M. (1997). Bayesian Network classifiers. *Machine Learning*, *29*, 131–63.

Fung, R.M. and Crawford, S.L. (1990). Constructor: A system for the induction of Probabilistic models. *Proceedings of the 7th National Conference on Artificial Intelligence*, 762–9.

Geman, S. and Geman, D. (1984). Stochastic relaxation, Gibbs distributions and the Bayesian restoration of images. *IEEE Transactions on Pattern Analysis and Machine Intelligence*, *6*(6), 721–42.

Haddawy, P. (1999) An overview of some recent developments in bayesian problem solving techniques. Introduction to *AI Magazine Special Issue on Uncertainty in Artificial Intelligence*, Summer, 1999.

Heckerman, D. (1995). *A Tutorial on Learning Bayesian Networks*. Technical report, MSR-TR-95-06, Microsoft Research Adv. Technol. Div., Redmond, WA.

Heckerman, D. and Wellman, M.P. (1995). Bayesian Networks. *Communications of the ACM*, *38*(3), 27–30.

Hruschka, E.R. Jr. and Ebecken, N.F.F. (2002). Missing values prediction with K2. *Intelligent Data Analysis*, *6*(6), 557–66.

Kim, H., Golub, G.H. and Park, H. (2004). Imputation of missing values in DNA microarray gene expression data. *Proceedings of IEEE Computational Systems Bioinformatics Conference*, 572–3.

Jensen, F. V. (1996). *An Introduction to Bayesian Network*. London: University of College London Press.

Keogh, E.J. and Pazzani, M.J. (1999). Learning augmented Bayesian classifiers: A comparison of distribution-based and classification-based approaches. In D. Heckerman and J. Whittaker (Eds), *Proceedings of the 7th International Workshop on AI and Statistics*. Fort Lauderdale, FL: Morgan Kaufmann, 225–30.

Koller, D. and Murphy, K. (2012). Course Notes. Available at: https://www.coursera.org/course/pgm. CS228 [accessed September 28, 2012]. "Probabilistic Graphical Models", at Stanford University.

Kononenko, I. (1991). Semi-naïve Bayesian classifier. In *Proceedings of the 6th European Working Session on Learning*. Porto: Springer-Verlag, 206–19.

Lakshminarayan, K., Harp, S.A., Goldman, R. and Samad, T. (1996). Imputation of missing data using machine learning techniques. *Proceeding of the 2nd International Conference on Knowledge Discovery and Data Mining*, 140–46.

Lam, W. and Bacchus, F. (1994). Learning Bayesian belief networks – an approach based on the MDL principle. *Computer Intelligence*, *10*(4), 269–93.

Langley, P. and Sage, S. (1994). Induction of selective Bayesian classifier. In R. Lopez de Mantaras and D. Poole (Eds), *Proceedings of the 10th Conference on Uncertainty in Artificial Intelligence*. Seattle, WA: Morgan Kaufmann, 366–406.

Larrañaga, P., Kuijpers, C., Mura, R. and Yurramendi, Y. (1996a). Learning Bayesian network structures by searching for the best ordering with genetic algorithms. *IEEE Transactions on System, Man and Cybernetics*, *26*(4), 487–93.

Larrañaga, P., Poza, M., Yurramendi, Y., Murga, R. and Kuijpers, C. (1996b). Structural learning of Bayesian network by genetic algorithms: A performance analysis of control parameters. *IEEE Transactions on Pattern Analysis and Machine Intelligence*, *18*(9), 912–26.

Lauritzen, S.L. (1995). The EM algorithm for graphical association models with missing data. *Computational Statistics and Data Analysis*, *19*(2), 191–201.

Ling, C.L. and Li, C. (1998). Data mining for direct marketing: Problems and solutions. *Proceedings of the 4th International Conference on Knowledge Discovery and Data Mining*, 73–9.

Liu, L., Hawkins, D.M., Ghosh, S. and Young, S. (2003). Robust singular value decomposition analysis of microarray data. *Proceedings of the National Academy of Sciences of the United States of America*, *100*(23), 13167–72.

Meilà-Predoviciu, M. (1999). *Learning with Mixtures of Trees*. PhD thesis, Massachusetts Institute of Technology.

Monti, S. and Cooper, G.F. (1999). A Bayesian network classifier that combines a finite mixture model and a naïve-Bayes model. In K.B. Laskey and H. Prade (Eds), *Proceedings of the 15th Conference on Uncertainty in Artificial Intelligence*. Stockholm: Morgan Kaufmann, 447–56.

Myers, J.W., Laskey, K.B. and DeJong, K.A. (1999). Learning Bayesian Networks from incomplete data using evolutionary algorithms. *Proceedings of the 1st Annual Conference on Genetic and Evolutionary Computation Conference 1999*. Orlando, FL: Morgan Kauffman, 458–65.

Neal, R.M. (1996). *Bayesian Learning for Neural Networks*. New York, NY: Springer-Verlag.

Pea, J.M., Lozano, J.A. and Larrañaga, P. (2000). An improved Bayesian Structural EM algorithm for learning Bayesian networks for clustering. *Pattern Recognition Letters*, 21(8), 779–86.

Pea, J.M., Lozano, J.A. and Larrañaga, P. (2002). Learning recursive bayesian multinets for data clustering by means of constructive induction. *Machine Learning*, 47(1), 63–89.

Pearl, J. (1988). *Probabilistic Reasoning in Intelligent Systems: Networks of Plausible Inference*. San Mateo, CA: Morgan Kaufmann.

Petrison, L.A., Blattberg, R.C., and Wang, P. (1997). Database marketing: Past, present, and future. *Journal of Direct Marketing*, 11(4), 109–25.

Ramoni, M. and Sebastiani, P. (1997a). *Efficient Parameter Learning in Bayesian Networks from Incomplete Databases*. Technical report, KMI-TR-41.

Ramoni, M. and Sebastiani, P. (1997b). *The Use of Exogenous Knowledge to Learn Bayesian Networks from Incomplete Databases*. Technical report, KMI-TR-44.

Ramoni, M. and Sebastiani, P. (2001). Robust learning with missing data. *Machine Learning*, 45(2), 147–70.

Rissanen, J. (1978). Modelling by shortest data description. *Automatica*, 14(5), 465–71.

Rubin, D.B. (1987). *Multiple Imputation for Nonresponse in Surveys*. New York, NY: John Wiley & Sons Inc.

Rud, O.P. (2001). *Data Mining Cookbook: Modeling Data for Marketing, Risk and Customer Relationship Management*. New York, NY: John Wiley & Sons Inc.

Schafer, J.L. and Graham, J.W. (2002). Missing data: Our view of the state of art. *Psychological Methods*, 7(2), 147–77.

Singh, M. (1998). *Learning Bayesian Networks for Solving Real-world Problems*. PhD thesis, University of Pennsylvania.

Spatz, C. and Johnston, J.O. (1981). *Basic Statistics: Tales of Distribution* (2nd ed.). Monterey, CA: Brooks/Cole Publishing Company.

Spirtes, P., Glymour, C. and Scheines, R. (2000). *Causation, Prediction, and Search* (2nd ed.). Cambridge, MA: MIT Press.

Suzuki, J. (1999). Learning Bayesian belief networks based on the minimum description length principle: Basic properties. *IEICE Transactions Fundamentals*, E82-A 10, 2237–45.

Tian, J. (2000). A branch-and-bound algorithm for MDL learning Bayesian networks. In C. Boutilier and M. Goldszmidt (Eds), *Proceedings of the 16th Conference on Uncertainty in Artificial Intelligence*. San Francisco, CA: Morgan Kaufmann, 580–88.

Weiss, S.M. and Kulikowski, C.A. (1991). *Computer Systems that Learn: Classification and Prediction Methods from Statistics, Neural Nets, Machine Learning and Expert Systems*. San Francisco, CA: Morgan Kaufmann.

Wong, M.L., Lam, W. and Leung, K.S. (1999). Using evolutionary programming and minimum description length principle for data mining of Bayesian networks. *IEEE Transactions on Pattern Analysis and Machine Intelligence*, 21(2), 174–8.

Wong, M.L. and Leung, K.S. (2004). An efficient data mining method for learning Bayesian networks using an evolutionary algorithm-based hybrid approach. *IEEE Transactions on Evolutionary Computation*, *8*(4), 378–404.

Zahavi, J. and Levin, N. (1997a). Applying neural computing to target marketing. *Journal of Direct Marketing*, *11*(4), 76–93.

Zahavi, J. and Levin, N. (1997b). Issues and problems in applying neural computing to target marketing. *Journal of Direct Marketing*, *11*(4), 63–75.

Zio, M.D., Scanu, M., Coppola, L., Luzi, O. and Ponti, A. (2004). Bayesian networks for imputation. *Journal of the Royal Statistical Society (A)*, 167(2), 309–22.

4 Quantile Regression for Database Marketing: Methods and Applications

DRIES F. BENOIT AND DIRK VAN DEN POEL

1 Introduction

Statistics is a tool that helps researchers or analysts to summarize their data in a smaller amount of comprehensive numbers. For example, when a business analyst has information on the monetary value of last year's purchases of all customers of the company, a straightforward way to deal with this information is to summarize the possibly thousands of data points with the mean value. Indeed, the mean value gives us some idea about last year's sales, but it gives a rather incomplete picture of what really is going on. For example, is the mean value a good approximation for the typical customer, or is this value overrated because of a few outstanding customers? Do customers deviate strongly from this mean value or not? These questions can only be answered by calculating other summary statistics than the mean on our sample.

In many situations, researchers are interested in how some factors influence an outcome variable. Going back to the sales example, management might ask their analysts to investigate the influence of issuing coupons on sales. A very simple approach could be to compare the mean sales of the customers that received the coupon versus the ones that did not. The workhorse model in this context is the ordinary least squares (OLS) regression model. Alternatively, a more complex model that focuses on the conditional mean could be used. However, just like the fact that the mean sales gives only limited information on the overall last year's sales of the customer base, conditional mean models give only partial information on the effect of coupons on sales. Nonetheless, until recently, only very few analysts go beyond this conditional mean model.

The classical theory of linear models focuses on the conditional mean function, that is, the function that describes how the mean of y changes with the vector of covariates x. Quantile regression (Bassett and Koenker, 1978) extends the well-known mean regression model to conditional quantiles of the response variable, such as the median. This approach provides a more robust, but also nuanced view of the relationship of the dependent variable and the covariates, since it allows the user to examine the relationship between a set of covariates and the different parts of the distribution of the response variable. An additional advantage is that quantile regression parameter estimates are not biased by outliers or heteroskedasticity.

Recently, interest in quantile regression methods has increased tremendously. Since the now seminal overview book of Koenker (2005), the number of research papers on quantile regression increased rapidly. Quantile regression has shown to be a valuable technique in many research areas, ranging from ecology over genetics to economics. The method is also relevant in the domain of database marketing which will be shown in the applications in this chapter.

This chapter aims to give an overview of the state-of-the-art in quantile regression for cross-sectional data, using both Bayesian and frequentist approaches. In addition, quantile regression for binary dependent variables will be treated. Next to these methodological sections, the applicability of the methods for business analysts will be shown in some comprehensive examples. The goal of this chapter is to familiarize database marketers with a statistical tool that goes beyond the incomplete picture that OLS-like models provide.

2 Methodological Background

This methodology section starts with the frequentist or classical approach to quantile regression. It consists of the original method as proposed by Bassett and Koenker (1978). The central components of the approach are to set up a specific objective function that, when minimized, gives the parameters that describe the linear relation between the dependent and independent variables for a given quantile of the response distribution. Sampling theory then is used to make inference about the model parameters. This is in contrast with the Bayesian approach that is discussed in Section 2.2 (and beyond). In the Bayesian approach a likelihood function is built and then combined with prior distributions on the model parameters. The resulting posterior distribution then represents the uncertainty there is about the quantile regression coefficients. As will be shown, the latter approach has some attractive computational advantages over the former method in the context of quantile regression. A good textbook about the importance of Bayesian methods in general for the field of marketing is given by Rossi et al. (1996).

2.1 QUANTILE REGRESSION: THE FREQUENTIST APPROACH

Regression analysis helps us understand how the typical value of a variable of interest changes when any one of the independent variables is varied, while the other independent variables are held fixed. At least three reasons can explain why the least squares approach has been so dominant in regression problems. First, calculating the linear estimators is relatively straightforward. Knowing that the first interest in regression models appeared in the late eighteenth century when calculations were still to be made using pen and paper, this advantage obviously was extremely important. Second, this type of estimator has been shown to be optimal if the observed deviation from the regression line is normally distributed. Today however, the most compelling motivation of least squares is the observation that these methods provide a general approach to estimating conditional mean functions.

As Mosteller and Tukey (1977) point out, just as the mean often gives a rather incomplete picture of a single distribution, similarly the regression curve gives an incomplete picture for a set of distributions. Quantile regression makes it possible to get a more complete view of the statistical landscape and the relationships among stochastic variables. This approach provides a more nuanced view of the relationship of the dependent variable and the covariates, since it allows the analyst to examine the relationship between a set of covariates and the different parts of the distribution of the response variable.

Next to the motivation in terms of "richer view," quantile regression can also be motivated from the robustness point of view. Since Gauss, it has been recognized that the mean enjoys a strong optimality if the density of the errors happens to be proportional to e^{-x^2}. On the other hand, if there are occasional, very large errors the performance of the median can be superior, a point stressed by Laplace and many subsequent authors (Koenker, 2005). As such, median estimators, and more general quantile estimators, are less influenced by outlying observations in the data. This property on its own can be a motivation to utilize quantile regression methods. Linked to this issue is the finding that quantile regression is not influenced by heteroskedasticity, that is, the variance of the regression error varies over the different values of the covariates. It is well known that in OLS this causes the estimate of the variance parameter to be biased and thus leading to biased standard errors of the OLS estimates. This is avoided when using quantile regression.

The classical way to derive quantile regression is to start from the well-known regression model. Consider the standard linear model where y and x are both continuous variables:

$$y_i = x_i'\beta + \epsilon_i \tag{1}$$

If we assume that $E(\varepsilon|x) = 0$, then $\mu(x_i)$ is a conditional mean function, while if $Med(\varepsilon|x) = 0$, then $\mu(x_i)$ is a conditional median function. Since the equation above implies that the relation between y and x is linear, we obtain a linear conditional expectation model:

$$E(y_i \mid x_i) = x_i'\beta \tag{2}$$

or a linear conditional median model:

$$Med(y_i \mid x_i) = x_i'\beta \tag{3}$$

depending on what restriction we have put on the error term.

In the conditional expectation model, we can find the regression coefficients by solving:

$$\underset{\beta \in \mathbb{R}}{argmin} \sum_{i=1}^{n} (y_i - x_i'\beta)^2 \tag{4}$$

One could say that we try to find a value for β that minimizes the sum of squared errors. In median regression, we proceed in exactly the same way, but here, we try to find an estimate of β that minimizes the sum of the absolute deviations:

$$\underset{\beta \in \mathbb{R}}{argmin} \sum_{i=1}^{n} |y_i - x_i'\beta| \tag{5}$$

Quantile regression proceeds by extending the median case to all other quantiles of interest. Recall that the general τ^{th} sample quantile $\xi(\tau)$, $0 < \tau < 1$, can be formulated as the minimizer:

$$\xi(\tau) = \underset{\xi \in \mathbb{R}}{argmin} \sum_{i=1}^{n} \rho_\tau (y_i - \xi) \tag{6}$$

where $\rho_\tau(z) = z(\tau - I(z < 0))$ and where $I(\cdot)$ denotes the indicator function. The loss function assigns a weight of τ to positive residuals and a weight of $(1 - \tau)$ to negative residuals. Using this loss function, the linear conditional quantile function extends the τth sample quantile $\xi(\tau)$ to the regression setting in the same way as the linear conditional mean or median function.

$$\hat{\beta}(\tau) = \underset{\beta \in \mathbb{R}}{argmin} \sum_{i=1}^{n} \rho_\tau (y_i - x_i ' \beta) \tag{7}$$

for any quantile $\tau \in (0,1)$. The quantile $\hat{\beta}(\tau)$ is called the τth regression quantile. Note that the case where τ equals 0.5, which minimizes the sum of absolute residuals, corresponds to the median regression. The classical approach then usually continues by constructing confidence intervals based on the bootstrap.

2.2. QUANTILE REGRESSION: A BAYESIAN APPROACH

Koenker and Machado (1999) were the first to show that likelihood-based inference using independently distributed asymmetric Laplace densities (ALD) is directly related to the minimization problem in Equation (7). Nonetheless, the real take-off of Bayesian quantile regression started with the paper of Yu and Moyeed (2001) who elaborated further on the Laplace distribution approach. It should be noted however, that some other Bayesian approaches have emerged mostly for median, rather than full quantile regression. Tsionas (2003) proposed an approach based on a scale mixture of normals, which itself leads to an ALD. Other methods are based on Dirichlet Process Priors (Kottas and Gelfand, 2001) or substitution likelihoods (Dunson, Watson, and Taylor, 2003). However, the above semiparametric methods for quantile regression require complex choices of prior distributions and prior (hyper-) parameters. This is avoided in the methodology proposed here. We concur with Hewson and Yu (2008) and (Yu and Stander, 2007) that this is one of the distinct advantages of Bayesian quantile regression based on the ALD.

In contrast to other parameterizations of the ALD (see Kotz, et al., 2001), Yu and Zhang (2005) propose a three-parameter ALD with a skewness parameter that can be used directly to model the quantile of interest:

$$f_p(y \mid \mu, \sigma, \tau) = \frac{\tau(1-\tau)}{\sigma} \exp\{-\rho_\tau (\frac{y - \mu}{\sigma})\} \tag{8}$$

Where:

$$\rho_\tau(y) = y(\tau - I(y < 0)) \tag{9}$$

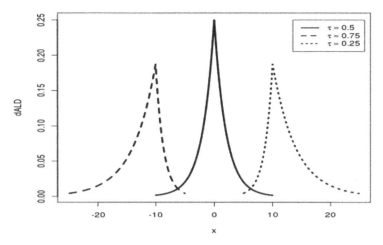

Figure 4.1   The asymmetric Laplace distribution

Minimizing Equation (7) is equivalent to maximizing a regression likelihood (8) using ALD errors with $\mu = x_i'\beta$. Bayesian implementation of quantile regression begins by forming a likelihood comprised of independent ALD with $\mu = x_i'\beta$, specifying the quantile of interest, τ, and placing priors on the model parameters β and σ. Inference about model parameters then follows conventional Bayesian procedures which lead to exact inference about $\beta_{hat}(\tau)$ as opposed to the frequentist asymptotic inference which has shown to be unreliable in this context (Bilias, et al., 2000).

Figure 4.1 shows how the skewness of the ALD changes with altering values for τ. For example where $\tau = 0.25$ the majority of the mass of the ALD is situated in the left tail. In the case where $\tau = 0.5$ both tails of the ALD have equal mass and the distribution then equals the more common double exponential distribution. In contrast to the normal distribution with a quadratic term in the exponent, the ALD is linear in the exponent. This results in a more peaked mode for the ALD together with thicker tails. On the other hand, the normal distribution has heavier shoulders compared to the ALD.

2.3   QUANTILE REGRESSION FOR BINARY DEPENDENT VARIABLES

Consider the standard binary regression model:

$$y_i = I(y_i^* \geq 0) = x_i'\beta + \epsilon_i \tag{10}$$

Where y_i is the indicator of the ith individual's response determined by the underlying latent variable y^*, xi is a 1 x k vector of explanatory variables, β is a k x 1 vector of parameters, ϵ_i is a random error term and i = 1, ..., n.

The first step toward a binary quantile regression model in econometrics was set by Manski's Maximum Score Estimator (Manski, 1975, 1985). He mainly focused on the median case, but he later acknowledged extending the estimation to the more general quantiles. This leads to the following form of the Maximum Score estimator:

$$\hat{\beta}(\tau) = \underset{\beta \in \mathbb{R}}{argmax} \, n^{-1} \sum_{i=1}^{n} \rho_\tau (2y_i - 1)(2y_i - 1) sgn(x_i' \beta) \qquad (11)$$

for any quantile $\tau \in (0,1)$. With, sgn($\cdot$), is the signum function and again $\rho_\tau(\cdot)$ is the loss function. Scale normalization is necessary because the parameter β can only be identified up to a scale.

Benoit and Van den Poel (2010) discuss a number of issues that make Manski's Maximum Score estimator difficult to use in practice. The first problem that arises is directly related to the nature of the objective function in Equation (11). Because of the signum function sgn($\cdot$) and the loss function $\rho\tau(\cdot)$, the objective function results in a multidimensional step-function. This is problematic because this specific type of function is very difficult to optimize, mainly because the lack of first-order conditions that could be exploited. Secondly, the Maximum Score estimator has a very complicated asymptotic distribution, which limits making inference about the model parameters (Kim and Pollard, 1990). Bootstrapping of subsampling has been proposed to solve the issue, but these solutions rely on a large sample size and may become computationally infeasible.

These issues make clear that in the frequentist approach to binary quantile regression, both calculating a consistent estimator and making inferences about this estimator is problematic. Benoit and Van den Poel (2010) propose a Bayesian approach to binary quantile regression that avoids the problems of optimization and inference. Their method makes use of data augmentation (Tanner and Wong, 1987) combined with the Laplace distribution approach described by Yu and Moyeed (2001).

Introduce n Asymmetric Laplace distributed random variables, $y_1^*, .., y_n^*$, into the problem. The scale parameter of these latent variables is set to unity for identification reasons similar as for the Maximum Score estimator discussed earlier. The parameter τ should be specified at the quantile of interest. For example, set $\tau = 0.5$ in the case of binary median regression. Further, define $y_i = 1$ if $y^* > 0$ and $y_i = 0$ otherwise. Then:

$$P(y_i = 1 | x_i, \beta) = 1 - F_{y^*}(-x_i' \beta) \qquad (12)$$

where $F_y(\cdot)$ is the cumulative distribution function of the asymmetric Laplace variable y^*. The joint posterior density of the unobservables β and y^* given the data y and the quantile of interest, τ, is then given by:

$$\pi\left(\beta, y^*, \tau\right) \propto \pi\left(\beta\right) \prod_{i=1}^{n} \left\{ I\left(y_i^* > 0\right) I\left(y_i = 1\right) + I\left(y_i^* \leq 0\right) I\left(y_i = 0\right) \right\} ALD(y_i^*; x_i' \beta, \sigma = 1, \tau) \quad (13)$$

where $\varpi(\beta)$ is the prior on the regression coefficients and I($\cdot$) is the indicator function. This joint posterior distribution is not in a known class of distributions. Therefore, it is not possible to sample from this posterior directly. However, with the development of Markov Chain Monte Carlo (MCMC) algorithms, computing this kind of posterior becomes fairly straightforward. Splitting up the complicated posterior in the posterior distribution of β conditional on y^* and in the posterior distribution of y^* conditional on β, often facilitates sampling from the joint posterior. In the current case, one of the two fully conditional distributions is of a known form. This suggests that a Metropolis-Hastings within Gibbs algorithm is an appropriate sampling scheme for the current setting.

The conditional distribution of y^* is given by:

$$\pi(y^* \mid \beta, y, \tau) \sim ALD\ (x_i{}'\beta, \sigma = 1, \tau) \tag{14}$$

truncated at the left by 0, if $y_i = 1$ or truncated at the right by 0, if $y_i = 0$. This is a distribution of a known form and thus can be sampled from directly. Algorithms for sampling from the three parameter Asymmetric Laplace distribution can be found, for example, in Yu and Zhang (2005).

Next, note that the posterior density of β given y*, τ and data is given by:

$$\pi(\beta \mid y^*, y, \tau) \propto \pi(\beta) \prod_{i=1}^{n} F_{y^*}(y_i^*; \beta, \sigma = 1, \tau) \tag{15}$$

This fully conditional posterior density is in fact the posterior density for the regression parameters in Bayesian quantile regression as discussed in above. In contrast to the fully conditional posterior density for the latent data, this posterior is of an unknown form. A standard conjugate prior distribution is not available for the quantile regression formulation, so MCMC methods, for example, Metropolis-Hastings, may be used for extracting this posterior distribution. This allows the use of virtually any prior distribution on the regression parameters and, as proven in Yu and Moyeed (2001), even an improper uniform prior, $\varpi(\beta)$, will result in a proper posterior distribution.

The Metropolis-Hastings within Gibbs sampler is now easy to implement. Given the data, the prior and the quantile of interest, the joint posterior distribution in Equation (13) can then be sampled from by sequentially drawing values from the distributions given in Equation (14) and (15). In every step, one should condition on the most recently drawn value of the conditioning arguments. Any value can be taken as starting value, but good choices of starting values can strongly reduce the burn-in period of the proposed algorithm. For example, in the case where $\tau = 0.5$, a good starting value could be the maximum likelihood estimates of the model under a probit or logit link function. When a sufficiently large set of values are drawn from the joint posterior distribution, it becomes straightforward to compute credible intervals or whatever other quantity of interest on the model parameters.

3 Case Studies

This section of the chapter intends to show the practical relevance of quantile regression and binary quantile regression in the context of database marketing. The first case study deals with the problem of customer lifetime value (CLV) prediction and is based on the application in the paper of Benoit and Van den Poel (2009). The second case study deals with another important topic in Customer Relationship Management (CRM), that is, cross-sell modeling and also contains an example from financial services.

3.1 QUANTILE REGRESSION: CUSTOMER LIFETIME VALUE (CLV) MODELING

3.1.1 Introduction

Customer Lifetime Value (CLV) has been studied under the name of LTV, Customer Value, Customer Equity, and Customer Profitability. The concept is defined as the sum of the revenues gained from a company's customers over the lifetime of transactions after deduction of the total cost of attracting, selling, and servicing customers, taking into account the time value of money. The basic formula for calculating CLV for customer i at time t for a finite time horizon T (Berger and Nasr, 1998) is:

$$CLV_{i,t} = \sum_{T=0}^{T} \frac{Profit_{i,t+T}}{(1+d)^T} \tag{16}$$

where d is a pre-determined discount rate. In multi-services industries, $Profit_{i,t}$ is defined as:

$$Profit_{i,t} = \sum_{j=1}^{J} Serv_{i,j,t} * Usage_{i,j,t} * Margin_{i,j,t} \tag{17}$$

Here J is the number of different services sold, $Serv_{ij,t}$ is a dummy indicating whether customer i purchases service j at time t, $Usage_{ij,t}$ is the amount of that service purchased and $Margin_{ij,t}$ is the average profit margin for service j.

Theoretically, CLV models should estimate the value of a customer over the entire customer's lifetime. However, in practice most researchers use a finite time horizon of three or four years (for example, Donkers, et al., 2007; Zeithaml, et al., 2001). Three to four years is a good estimate for the horizon over which the current business environment would not substantially change and even then, there is significant uncertainty in predicting customer behavior (Venkatesan, et al., 2007). Moreover, some research considers an even shorter time horizon (Hwang, et al., 2004).

CLV has been analyzed in a substantial number of different domains, varying from econometric models to machine learning. However, the key questions are usually very similar: "What are the drivers of CLV?," "Which customers are the most valuable ones in the future?," "How to address the top customers?," and so on. Several authors give an overview of the variety of modeling procedures that were used in search for answers to these key questions (Berger and Nasr, 1998; Donkers et al., 2007; Gupta et al., 2006; Venkatesan and Kumar, 2004). In general, one can distinguish two broad classes of models that apply to a contractual setting. First, a large group of models focuses on the choices customers face when buying an additional service or product. A customer's lifetime value is then seen as the sum of the distinct contributions per service or product. This approach is appealing because of the natural way in which the CLV prediction is built up. In a first stage, an estimation is made on the probability of a customer buying a given product or service. The second stage is then to combine these probabilities with the margins associated with the product or service into an aggregate prediction of a customer's lifetime value. This approach also has the advantage of providing more insight into the factors that drive customer value. The main drawbacks are the amount of modeling required and the often poorer predictions. Examples of this approach are found in Venkatesan and Kumar (2004) and Hwang et al. (2004). The second large group of models does not follow the two-stage method, but focuses directly on relationship length and total profits. Since the individual-level choice modeling is left aside, the process of producing CLV estimates is much more straightforward and prediction accuracy is higher (Verhoef and Donkers, 2001). As such, this approach turns the disadvantages of the first approach into benefits. However, due to aggregation, insight into the factors that drive consumer profitability is limited compared to the choice-based approach. Examples of CLV research following this direct approach are found in Malthouse and Blattberg (2005) and in Hansotia and Rukstales (2002).

One of the key issues when decision makers use the CLV metric is whether the firm can provide an adequate prediction of the CLV of each customer in the database. Furthermore, these predictions are often used as guidelines for investments in segments of customers (Zeithaml et al., 2001). However, the regression techniques used in the past are often not ideally suited for the purpose of modeling CLV. When evaluating customer profitability, marketers are often reminded of the 80/20 rule (80 percent of the profits are produced by the top 20 percent of profitable customers and 80 percent of the costs are produced by the top 20 percent of unprofitable customers). This finding has important implications for both the two-stage approach as well as for the approach that models CLV directly. For researchers using the two-step CLV approach, the problem arises when modeling the choice problem. Since the largest group of customers buys no or only a very limited amount of products or services and only a small group of customers buys many products or services, the researcher should be aware of the fact that he or she is modeling rare events. In this rare-event situation, it is known that parametric choice models easily break down (Gupta et al., 2006). The other approach, where the researcher focuses directly on the relationship length and total profits, leaves aside the individual-level choice modeling step. However, the problem of rare events cannot be totally avoided. This is because the underlying process (the 80/20 rule) results in a lifetime value variable that tends to have a strong non-normal distribution and the usual assumption of homoskedasticity is hard to maintain (Fader, et al., 2005; Malthouse and Blattberg, 2005). In contrast, the proposed quantile regression technique does not suffer from these particularities of the CLV variable (Buchinsky, 1998). Quantile regression can be seen as part of the second approach since it models CLV directly. This direct approach often leads to high predictive performance, but quantile regression also provides the manager with insights in the covariates that are totally missed with other methods from the direct approach (for example, linear regression). Thus, quantile regression combines somewhat the best of the two approaches.

3.1.2   Data

The data are provided by a large European financial services company. The database contains both transactional and socio-demographic information about the customers. For the current analysis, we work at the household level. Households are studied, instead of individuals, because in this market the household is the principal decision-making unit. A household is defined as all customers living on the same address. A total of 22,665 families are retained that had at least one active product on December 31, 2003. The CLV is then computed, using Equations (16) and (17), for the four subsequent years. In line with the business practice of the company, we use margins that are not consumer specific and the usage levels are set to their expected values. Also note that the margin is calculated taking into account the defection rates of the customers buying service j. The entire dataset is divided into training set and validation set at the ratio 60/40, respectively. Performance measures are reported only on the validation set. For the independent variables, we include past behavioral data as well as socio-demographic data. Table 4.1 gives an overview of the different variables that are used in the analysis. Most of these

Table 4.1   Overview of the variables in the analysis

Code	Description
CLV	The dependent variable: lifetime value based on Equations 1 and 2.
nbr_FamInd	Number of individuals that are part of the household.
Social_Class_Score	A score (between 0 and 1000) indicating the social class of the neighborhood. A high score means a higher social class.
FTHB_gez	A dummy variable indicating whether the household is in a given segment or not. This is: household members are under 35 and the household is a stable economic entity with a first real estate project.
freq	Total number of purchases ever made by all household members.
lor	Number of days since the date of the first purchase of all household members.
recency	Number of days since the date of the last purchase of all household members.

variables have proven to be good predictors of lifetime value in previous studies (Fader et al., 2005; Kim, et al., 2006; Rossi, McCulloch, and Allenby, 1996). Other variables are chosen because they are of special interest for the company. Note that all continuous variables are standardized around their mean value. This is done for numerical stability, but also because of the confidential nature of the data.

As pointed out in the introduction, the dependent variable is often strongly right-skewed in lifetime value modeling. Malthouse and Blattberg (2005) suggest a variance stabilizing transformation of the CLV variable when using linear regression. According to their practice, the logarithmic transformation is used and a constant is added to every value to avoid taking the logarithm of a negative value or zero. By doing so, a more fair comparison is made between the different modeling techniques. Note that in the current application this transformed variable is not only used for linear regression, but also for quantile regression.

3.1.3   Results

Although much research on CLV has employed conventional least squares regression methods, it has been recognized that the resulting estimates of various effects on the conditional mean of CLV were not necessarily indicative of the size and nature of these effects on the lower or upper tail of the CLV distribution (Gupta et al., 2006). A more complete picture of covariate effects can be provided by estimating a family of conditional quantile functions.

Figure 4.2 presents a graphical summary of the quantile regression results for a selection of the predictors. Full results can be found in Benoit and Van den Poel (2009). Each subplot depicts one variable in the quantile regression model, $\{\hat{\beta}(\tau)_j(\tau) : j = 1,...,11\}$. Note that the plots in Figure 4.2 are obtained using Bayesian estimation with vague priors on the unknown model parameters. The plotted point estimates and the credible intervals are the expectation, Q.025 percentile and Q.975 percentile obtained from the marginal posterior distribution of the different parameters. The solid line with filled dots represents the point estimates of the regression coefficients for the different quantiles,

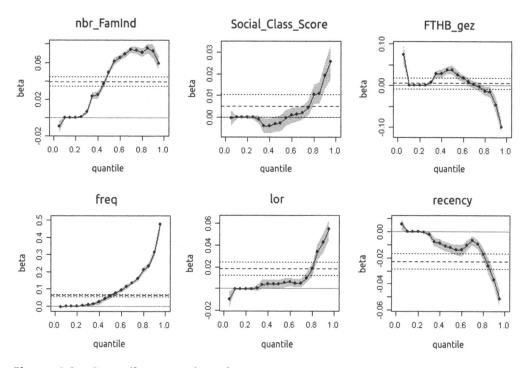

Figure 4.2 Quantile regression plots

$\{\tau_q : q = 0.5,\ldots,0.95, \text{ by } 0.5\}$. The shaded area depicting a 95 percent point wise credible band is obtained from the marginal posterior distribution of the different parameters. Superimposed on the plot is a dashed line representing the ordinary least squares estimate of the mean effect, with two dotted lines representing a 95 percent confidence interval.

At first glance one can see that for this application it might be worthwhile to split up the effects of the covariates in three distinct parts when the results are discussed, τ in [0.05,0.3], τ in [0.3,0.7], τ in [0.7,0.95]. For most variables, the effect on the lower conditional quantiles is very small and often not significant. When considering the effects on the more central conditional quantiles, one can see that the effect of the variables is often quite constant over the interval (for example, Social_Class_Score, FTHB_gez, lor and recency). However, this is not the case for all variables (for example, nbr_FamInd and freq). For the upper quantiles of the conditional CLV distribution, the effect of most variables shows to increase or decrease a lot, compared to the lower quantiles. For all variables displayed here the effect of the covariate is most pronounced in the upper quantiles of the conditional CLV distribution.

Not surprisingly, the number of household members has a positive impact on the expected lifetime value. The estimated conditional quantile function reveals that the effect of the covariate is getting more extreme for the higher quantiles. For this variable, the effect on the conditional mean is quite similar to the effect on the conditional median of CLV distribution.

The least squares estimate for the social class score suggests that the effect is positive. However, the confidence bands around the OLS estimate show that this effect is not different from zero (p>0.05). Here, quantile regression gives a more detailed insight in the effect of the covariate. The plot reveals that the covariate has no significant effect on the conditional CLV distribution for the lower and middle quantiles. However, for the higher quantiles this effect is clearly different from zero. Ample research supports the finding that higher social class families are more profitable than lower social class families (Reinartz and Kumar, 2003). While on average the effect is insignificant, quantile regression provides the additional insight that for the higher quantiles of the conditional CLV distribution social class has a significantly positive effect on CVL. Moreover, it becomes more pronounced for higher quantiles of the CLV distribution.

The segmenting variable (FTHB_gez) is a striking example of how misleading the OLS estimates can be. Again, the OLS estimate suggests that the effect of the variable is not different from zero. But when considering the quantile regression results, a different picture becomes clear. The conditional quantile function of CLV reveals a positive effect for the middle quantiles. However, in the upper quantiles of the CLV distribution, the covariate has a negative effect. Recall that this variable is a dummy indicating whether the household is a young family with a first real-estate project. It could be argued that families being in that specific stage of their family lifecycle acquire a rather modest amount of financial products. On the other hand, those families are often financially immature and therefore they are often buying products from product categories that are less profitable for the financial services company (Javalgi and Dion, 1999), which is indicated by the negative relationship in the upper quantiles of the CLV distribution. This is in line with the findings of (Zeithaml et al., 2001) that young professionals who purchase homes at the upper end should be tagged as potential top customers.

From literature one could expect a positive relationship for the frequency variable (Reinartz and Kumar, 2003). Note that the OLS estimate is very similar to the median conditional quantile estimate. However, for the higher quantiles, the OLS estimate is strongly underestimating the effect of the variable.

The length of relationship exerts a rather outspoken effect on the conditional CLV distribution. For the lower quantiles the effect is not significant, for the middle quantiles the effect remains rather constant, but for the higher quantiles the effect of the variable increases fast. The variable recency seems to exert a similar effect, but here in the opposite direction. For these three variables, the OLS estimate is a bit more extreme than the effect in the middle quantiles. For the extreme quantiles, the OLS estimate is again a substantial under- or overestimation of the real effect.

The added value of quantile regression is not limited to the richer insights into the effects of the covariates. In this part we focus on the out-of-sample predictive performance of the quantile regression models. In a first step, we will focus first on predicting the level of individual CLV. Secondly, our interest is on predicting the ordering of the customers based on CLV.

Correct predictions for the level of CLV are relevant when a company wants to target customers with a CLV above a given level. This is the case in situations where the expected CLV has to be above a certain level in order to have a profitable customer. Often used measures as (root) mean squared error (MSE) or the mean absolute deviation (MAD) criteria are not appropriate to make the current comparison, since the regression techniques optimize for one of the two criteria. Linear regression will have the best predictive performance when the root MSE criterion is used, while quantile regression (with $\tau=0.5$) excels when the MAD criterion is considered. To analyze how well each model predicts the level of CLV for each individual, we therefore use the hit-rate criterion proposed by (Donkers et al., 2007). For this hit rate, we categorize all customers based on their true CLV into four equal-sized groups with increasing levels of CLV. The hit rate is then computed as the percentage of customers of whom the predicted CLV falls into the same category as their actual CLV.

More often the management will be interested in targeting their most profitable customers without being interested in the precise level of CLV. In the latter case, it is more appropriate to use an ordering-based measure of predictive performance. Since CLV is more often used as a segmentation device than as a tool to manage profitability of marketing activities at the individual level (Zeithaml et al., 2001), the ordering-based measure will be more relevant. The predictive performance with respect to the ordering of the customers is also evaluated with a hit-rate criterion. Several studies (Donkers et al., 2007; Malthouse and Blattberg, 2005) use it as a measure of predictive performance with respect to the ordering of the customers. In contrast to the hit rate for levels, this hit rate does not consider the level of CLV, but only the ordering of the customers with respect to CLV. The ordering-based hit rate measures what percentage of customers with an actual CLV in the top-x percent have a predicted CLV that is also in the top-x percent based on predicted CLV.

We start by investigating the performance of the different models for predicting the absolute level of CLV. Therefore, we set τ=0.5 and the quantile regression reduces to median regression. Three different models are compared, that is, the normal linear regression model, the quantile regression model and a naïve model. The naïve model is a model without explanatory variables and always predicts the mean. The results for the hit-rate criterion explained in above are as follows. The linear regression model has a hit-rate of 36 percent, the quantile regression model has a hit-rate of 38 percent and the naïve model has a hit-rate of 27 percent. Several Chi-square tests indicated significant ($p<0.01$) differences between all models. This means the quantile regression model performs better than the models without explanatory variables and better than the mean regression model in terms of absolute predictions. Thus, when management wants to target a group of customers with an expected CLV above a specific threshold level, the quantile regression approach is more appropriate. In the case of lifetime value, however, the managers' focus is often not on the absolute CLV levels, but rather on the ordering of the customer base. As explained earlier the main reason for this is the popularity of CLV as a basis for customer segmentation. Therefore, it might be more relevant to evaluate the predictive performance of the ordering of the customers.

Figure 4.3, on the following page, gives the results for the different models regarding the predictive performance of the ordering of the customers. The criterion used is explained and justified above. Note that a naïve model would randomly assign the customers to the top group. When, for example, one tries to predict the top 30 percent customers, the naïve model randomly assigns 30 percent of the customers to that condition. The horizontal axis represents the top x percent one tries to predict. The vertical axis is then the performance of the models based on the ordered hit-rate criterion. The quantile regression model used τ=0.98. A Chi-square test is performed to check the significance of the difference in performance; when significant ($p<0.05$) the area between the two curves is shaded.

Where the ordering of the customers is of primary interest, quantile regression takes advantage of its properties of handling asymmetrical errors. As shown in the figure, the advantage of using quantile regression is most pronounced when the interest is in the

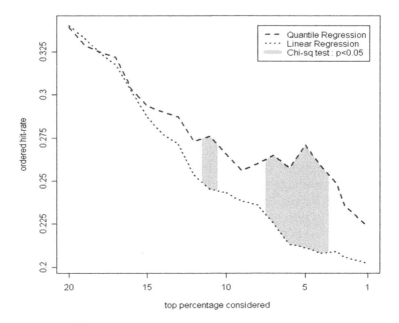

Figure 4.3   Ordered predictive performance

high-end customers and wears off when larger top groups are considered. Also note that the performance of the mean regression deteriorates at a higher rate than the quantile regression performance when the focus is on decreasing top segments. Knowing that those top groups are often of central interest for the decision makers, the use of quantile regression in this context makes a real difference.

3.2   QUANTILE REGRESSION: CHURN PREDICTION

3.2.1   Introduction

Personal retail banking is characterized by customers who typically spread their assets over only one or two companies and stay with a company for long periods of time. From the point of view of the financial services company, this produces a stable environment for CRM. It is argued that these companies need to operate on a long-term "cradle-to-grave" customer management strategy (Li, et al., 2005). This means that they recognize that young customers are often unprofitable in their earlier years, but become profitable at a later stage. The longer customers stay with the bank, the more they become tied to such an extent that the perceived cost of defection outweighs the benefits of shifting their banking business to another provider.

Although the process of attracting new customers is important, most financial services companies make customer retention a top priority for several reasons: in general, the longer a customer stays with a bank, the more that customer is worth (Benoit and Van den Poel, 2009). Long-term customers buy more, take less of a company's time, are less sensitive to price differences, and bring in new customers (Ganesh, et al., 2000; Reichheld, 1996). Long-term customers become less costly to serve because of the bank's greater knowledge of the existing customer base and reduced servicing costs (Ganesh, et al., 2000). In addition, the cost of winning a new customer is about five times greater than the cost of keeping an existing one (Colgate and Danaher, 2000). A study by Reichheld and Sasser (1990) showed that reducing defections by just 5 percent can generate 85 percent more profits for a bank. The latter findings corroborate the results of a study of Dirk Van den Poel and Larivière (2004), which illustrated how increasing retention by just 1 percent resulted in substantial profit gains.

As such, the goal is to identify the customers with a high churn probability in order to target them with appropriate actions and consequently try to keep them within the company. These actions may include targeting these customers with appropriate actions, for example, proposing an incentive to renew the contract with the company, and so on.

3.2.2   Data

A European financial services company provided the data for this example. A stratified random sample of all active customers at the end of June 2006 were selected, a group of 24,364 clients in total. Information about the customers was extracted from the company data warehouse from the moment they joined the company until June 29th 2006. This information was then captured into explanatory variables. The dependent variable in this setting is whether a given customer churns or not. Here a churned customer is defined as someone who closed all his/her bank accounts with this company. The dependent variable is based on the churn behavior in the period from June 30, 2006 until December 31, 2006.

Table 4.2 gives an overview of all variables used in this study. Traditional churn models usually take socio-demographic variables (age, gender, and so on) as predictors in addition to past behavior that is summarized in terms of recency, frequency, and monetary value (RFM). For reasons of clarity, this data example does not contain any other variables than the basic CRM variables discussed above.

To avoid overfitting of the model, the dataset is divided into a training set and a validation set. The model is trained on the training set and tested on the validation set. The training set is composed by randomly assigning 70 percent of the customers, while the other 30 percent are assigned to the validation set. In order to get an equal churn rate in both of the sets, stratification is performed on the churn variable. Note that only a very small percentage, that is, 2 percent, of the dataset churns in the six-month follow-up period.

Table 4.2   Description of variables

Code	Description
gender	Gender of the respondent
social class	Social class of the respondent
lor	Number of days since first purchase
freq	Total number of purchases ever made
recency	Number of days since last purchase

3.2.3 Results

The Bayesian approach to binary quantile regression, as proposed earlier in this chapter, is applied to this dataset using two different quantiles, that is, τ=0.5 and τ=0.98. The τ=0.5 model will give an estimate of the median of the response distribution of the latent utility associated with the churn behavior. As such, this model can be seen as a robust alternative to the popular logit or probit models. On the other hand, the τ=0.98 model will estimate the model parameters penalizing false negatives more than false positives. That is, if τ=0.50 the training error number will be minimized. When τ<0.5 more weight will be put on false positives. For a formal proof see Zheng (2012). As will be shown, this is a very interesting feature of binary quantile regression when applied to the context of churn prediction. Finally, the results are compared with those obtained by the familiar logistic regression model.

The evaluation criterion used in this example is lift. This evaluation criterion focuses exclusively on the top x percent of most critical customers. The top x percent riskiest customers (that is, the group of customers with the highest predicted churn probabilities) represents an ideal segment for targeting in a retention-marketing campaign (Lemmens and Croux, 2006). This performance measure is very attractive because it incorporates somewhat the fact that marketing budgets are limited. As a result, actions to reduce churn (for example, direct mail campaigns) are limited to a segment of customers that is at high risk. In practice, the metric is calculated by ordering the customers on decreasing predicted churn probability. Next, the proportion of real churners in the top x percent is compared with the proportion of churners in the total dataset. The higher the lift, the better is the model. For example, a top 10 percent lift of 2 means that the model under investigation identifies twice as many churners in the top 10 percent than a random assignment would do.

Table 4.3 gives a summary of the parameter estimates of the models applied on the churn dataset. It is important to note that the parameter estimates of the frequentist approach (that is, logistic regression) are very different in nature compared to the Bayesian parameter estimates. That is, the frequentist logit model gives us the maximum likelihood estimates of the parameters together with the standard error of these point estimates. On the other hand, the Bayesian methods give the expected value of the posterior distribution of the model parameters, together with the posterior standard deviation. It is clear that both the traditional logit model and the median binary quantile regression model have quite similar results. However, when estimating more extreme quantiles, another set of predictor variables seem to be important.

Table 4.3   Parameter estimates of the different methods

	logit		QRb τ = 0.50		QRb τ = 0.98	
intercept	-0.89	(0.10)	-1.16	(0.16)	-0.15	(0.12)
gender	0.10	(0.14)	0.11	(0.19)	0.04	(0.15)
soc_class	-0.03	(0.07)	-0.05	(0.09)	-0.04	(0.07)
lor	-0.46	(0.09)	-0.65	(0.15)	-0.50	(0.11)
freq	-0.91	(0.75)	-1.82	(1.58)	-1.31	(0.99)
recency	0.39	(0.07)	0.50	(0.11)	0.55	(0.10)

Table 4.4   Confusion matrices

		logit		QRb τ = 0.50		QRb τ = 0.98	
Predicted		0	1	0	1	0	1
True	0	7100	119	7062	157	3300	3919
	1	135	5	135	5	37	103

Table 4.4 gives an overview of the predictive performance of the different models in terms of their confusion matrices (calculated on the test data). Again, the results are very similar for the traditional logistic regression model and the Bayesian binary median regression model. It is clear that the extreme low incidence of the response variable makes it hard to correctly predict the churners. However, as explained above, by increasing the quantile of the Bayesian binary quantile regression, it becomes possible to increase the true positive rate. However, this comes at the expense of an increase false positive rate. Figure 4.4 shows how these different models compare in terms of lift.

Figure 4.4 plots the lift curves for the different models considered here. Note that a naïve model that predicts the churn incidence (here 0.02) for every customer, would result in a horizontal lift curve at y=1. As such, it is clear that all models perform better that the naïve model. However, it has been stated earlier that interest is often in the performance of the models in terms of predicting the order of the customers. That is, how well does a model perform when the goal is to predict the top x percent of customers that are likely to churn. This can be seen in the graph above for the low values of "decile." Again, both the frequentist logit model and the Bayesian binary quantile regression model perform very

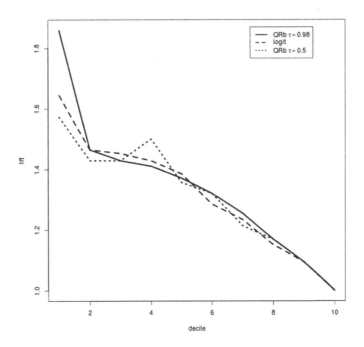

Figure 4.4   Lift curves

similar. However, the model focusing on the extreme quantile clearly outperforms the other models in terms of predicting the top group of customers that are at high risk of churning. Identifying this group of customers is of great importance to the company and this Bayesian approach to binary quantile regression shows to be a valuable tool in achieving this goal.

4 Summary

Although the ideas behind quantile regression date back to the first attempts to calculate a least squares regression, it's only quite recent that quantile regression regained interest. Much has to do with the more difficult computation compared to least squares. As was shown, this is definitely the case for binary dependent variables. Problematic optimization of the objective function as well as difficulties with making inference about the point prediction limited the applicability of the methods. The Bayesian approach to quantile regression, as discussed in this chapter, does not suffer from these difficulties. This comes, however, at the expense of computer-intensive MCMC estimation. But, with modern computing power this is not a real issue any more.

As has been shown in the methodology section of this chapter, the advantages of median regression or full quantile regression are clear: the resulting parameter estimates are robust to outliers in the data, the hard-to-hold assumption of normality is not required and possible heteroskedasticity will not influence the results. In addition to these more technical advantages, quantile regression also gives a much more detailed insight of the effects of the covariates on the response variables. Taken together, these characteristics of quantile regression make the technique an ideal tool for understanding as well as predicting both qualitative and continuous variables.

Until now, applications of quantile regression are mainly found in ecology, medicine, economics, etc. In this chapter, we tried to show the value of the methodology for database marketing. The first and most elaborate example discussed how quantile regression can be used in the context of CLV estimation. The results showed that both in predictive accuracy as well as insight in the effects of the covariates, quantile regression is a valuable approach. The second example dealt with the qualitative problem of customer churn estimation. For this example the focus was on the predictive accuracy of the model. It was shown how estimating different quantiles influences the false positive and false negative rate and how this can be used to optimize the selection of customers at risk. Again, it was shown that binary quantile regression could improve on existing methods.

The quantile regression models discussed in this chapter are available as a library ("package") for the free statistical software R (Benoit, et al., 2011). The software can easily be installed on any operating system. Downloading and installing the bayesQR package is straightforward (see R manual for a step-by-step guide). The help files that come with the bayesQR package contain simple examples that are illustrative of how to use the package with your own data.

References

Bassett, G. and Koenker, R. (1978). Asymptotic theory of least absolute error regression. *Journal of the American Statistical Association, 73*(363), 618–22.

Benoit, D.F., Al-Hamzawi, R., Yu, K. and Van den Poel, D. (2011). R-package: bayesQR – Bayesian quantile regression. Published on CRAN.

Benoit, D.F. and Van den Poel, D. (2009). Benefits of quantile regression for the analysis of customer lifetime value in a contractual setting: An application in financial services. *Expert Systems with Applications, 36*(7), 10475–84.

Benoit, D.F. and Van den Poel, D. (2012). Binary quantile regression: A Bayesian approach based on the asymmetric Laplace distribution. *Journal of Applied Econometrics, 27*(7), 1174–88.

Berger, P.D. and Nasr, N.I. (1998). Customer lifetime value: Marketing models and applications. *Journal of interactive marketing, 12*(1), 17–30.

Bilias, Y., Chen, S. and Ying, Z. (2000). Simple resampling methods for censored regression quantiles. *Journal of Econometrics, 99*(2), 373–86.

Buchinsky, M. (1998). Recent advances in quantile regression models: A practical guideline for empirical research. *The Journal of Human Resources, 33*(1), 88.

Colgate, M.R. and Danaher, P.J. (2000). Implementing a customer relationship strategy: The asymmetric impact of poor versus excellent execution. *Journal of the Academy of Marketing Science, 28*(3), 375–87.

Donkers, B., Verhoef, P.C. and Jong, M.G. (2007). Modeling CLV: A test of competing models in the insurance industry. *Quantitative Marketing and Economics, 5*(2), 163–90.

Dunson, D.B., Watson, M. and Taylor, J.a. (2003). Bayesian latent variable models for median regression on multiple outcomes. *Biometrics, 59*(2), 296–304.

Fader, P.S., Hardie, B.G.S. and Lee, K.L. (2005). RFM and CLV: Using Iso-Value curves for customer base analysis. *Journal of Marketing Research, 42*(4), 415–30.

Ganesh, J., Arnold, M.J. and Reynolds, K.E. (2000). Understanding the customer base of service providers: An examination of the differences between switchers and stayers. *Journal of Marketing, 64*(3), 65–87.

Gupta, S., Hanssens, D., Hardie, B., Kahn, W., Kumar, V., Lin, N., Ravishanker, N. and Sriram, S. (2006). Modeling customer lifetime value. *Journal of Service Research, 9*(2), 139–55.

Hansotia, B. and Rukstales, B. (2002). Incremental value modeling. *Journal of Interactive Marketing, 16*(3), 35–46.

Hewson, P. and Yu, K. (2008). Quantile regression for binary performance indicators. *Applied Stochastic Models in Business and Industry, 24*(5), 401–18.

Hwang, H., Jung, T. and Suh, E. (2004). An LTV model and customer segmentation based on customer value: A case study on the wireless telecommunication industry. *Expert Systems with Applications, 26*(2), 181–8.

Javalgi, R.G. and Dion, P. (1999). A life cycle segmentation approach to marketing financial products and services. *The Services Industries Journal, 19*(3), 74–96.

Kim, J. and Pollard, D. (1990). Cube root asymptotics. *The Annals of Statistics, 18*(1), 191–219.

Kim, S., Jung, T., Suh, E. and Hwang, H. (2006). Customer segmentation and strategy development based on customer lifetime value: A case study. *Expert Systems with Applications, 31*(1), 101–7.

Koenker, R. (2005). *Quantile Regression*. Cambridge: Cambridge University Press, 366.

Koenker, R. and Machado, J.A.F. (1999). Goodness of fit and related inference processes for quantile regression. *Journal of the American Statistical Association, 94*(448), 1296–310.

Kottas, A. and Gelfand, A.E. (2001). Bayesian semiparametric median regression modeling. *Journal of the American Statistical Association, 96*(456), 1458–68.

Kotz, S., Kozubowski, T.J. and Podgorski, K. (2001). *The Laplace Distribution and Generalizations*. Boston, MA: Birkhäuser.

Lemmens, A. and Croux, C. (2006). Bagging and boosting classification trees to predict churn. *Journal of Marketing Research*, *43*(2), 276–86.

Li, S., Sun, B. and Wilcox, R.T. (2005). Cross-selling sequentially ordered products: An application to consumer banking services. *Journal of Marketing Research*, *42*(2), 233–9.

Malthouse, E.C. and Blattberg, R.C. (2005). Can we predict customer lifetime value? *Journal of Interactive Marketing*, *19*(1), 2–16.

Manski, C.F. (1975). Maximum score estimation of the stochastic utility model of choice. *Journal of Econometrics*, *3*(3), 205–28.

Manski, C.F. (1985). Semiparametric analysis of discrete response: Asymptotic properties of the maximum score estimator. *Journal of Econometrics*, *27*(3), 313–33.

Mosteller, F. and Tukey, J.W. (1977). *Data Analysis and Regression: A Second Course in Statistics*. Boston, MA: Addison Wesley, 588.

Reichheld, F.F. (1996). Learning from customer defections. *Harvard Business Review*, *74*(2), 56–69.

Reichheld, F.F. and Sasser, W. E. (1990). Zero defections – quality comes to services. *Harvard Business Review*, *68*(5), 105–11.

Reinartz, W.J. and Kumar, V. (2003). The impact of customer relationship characteristics on profitable lifetime duration. *Journal of Marketing*, *67*(January), 77–99.

Rossi, P.E., Allenby, G.M. and McCulloch, R.E. (2006). *Bayesian Statistics and Marketing*. New York, NY: Wiley.

Rossi, P.E., McCulloch, R.E. and Allenby, G.M. (1996). The value of purchase history data in target marketing. *Marketing Science*, *15*(4), 321–40.

Tanner, M. and Wong, W.H. (1987). The calculation of posterior distributions by data augmentation. *Journal of the American Statistical Association*, *82*(398), 528–40.

Tsionas, E. (2003). Bayesian quantile inference. *Journal of Statistical Computation and Simulation*, *73*(9), 659–74.

Van den Poel, D. and Larivière, B. (2004). Customer attrition analysis for financial services using proportional hazard models. *European Journal of Operational Research*, *157*(1), 196–217.

Venkatesan, R. and Kumar, V. (2004). A customer lifetime value framework for customer selection and resource allocation strategy. *Journal of Marketing*, *68*(4), 106–25.

Venkatesan, R., Kumar, V. and Bohling, T. (2007). Optimal customer relationship management using Bayesian decision theory: An application for customer selection. *Journal of Marketing Research*, *44*(4), 579–94.

Verhoef, P. and Donkers, B. (2001). Predicting customer potential value an application in the insurance industry. *Decision Support Systems*, *32*(2), 189–99.

Yu, K. and Moyeed, R. (2001). Bayesian quantile regression. *Statistics & Probability Letters*, *54*(4), 437–47.

Yu, K. and Stander, J. (2007). Bayesian analysis of a Tobit quantile regression model. *Journal of Econometrics*, *137*(1), 260–76.

Yu, K. and Zhang, J. (2005). A three-parameter asymmetric Laplace distribution and its extension. *Communications in Statistics: Theory and Methods*, *34*(9–10), 1867–79.

Zeithaml, V.A., Rust, R.T. and Lemon, K.N. (2001). The customer pyramid: Creating and serving profitable customers. *California Management Review*, *43*(4), 118–42.

Zheng, S. (2012). QBoost: predicting quantiles with boosting for regression and binary classification. *Expert Systems with Applications*, *39*(2), 1687–1697.

5 *Ensemble Learning in Database Marketing*

KOEN W. DE BOCK AND KRISTOF COUSSEMENT

1 Introduction

As illustrated by its prevalence throughout this work, predictive modeling is a cornerstone method in database marketing. The reason is straightforward: companies can strongly benefit from deploying stored consumer information to infer future behavior or characteristics of their consumers and, by using these predictions, making marketing campaigns more effective. Strong model performance is vital, as a direct link exists between the accuracy of the predictions and the profitability of marketing campaigns. As Neslin et al. (2006) concluded from their analysis of the results of the Teradata Center for CRM and Duke University churn modeling tournament organized in 2002: *methods do matter*. Consequently, a vast number of studies on predictive modeling in database marketing have been devoted to introducing and benchmarking (novel) algorithms. Techniques that have been suggested in literature throughout the years include statistical techniques (for example, logistic regression (Smith, et al. 2000), generalized additive models (GAMs) (Coussement, et al. 2010), discriminant analysis (Ganesh, et al. 2000)) and classifiers originating from the data mining literature (for example, neural networks (Mozer et al. 2000), support vector machines (Coussement and Van den Poel, 2008) and decision trees (Smith, et al. 2000)).

This chapter introduces ensemble learners, a category of methods for statistical learning that have been praised for their competitive nature in comparison to other methods (Bauer and Kohavi 1999; Dietterich 2000b). The rationale of ensemble learning depicts that, in order to improve performance, models for supervised (for example, classification and regression) or unsupervised learning (such as clustering) could benefit from combining several methods instead of focusing on just one. Until now, most methods have focused on classification. Ensemble classifiers or multiple classifier systems (MCS) are defined as a combination of many constituent member classification models, whereby aggregate ensemble predictions are taken as combinations of the ensemble member outputs. Given the prevalence of binary classification problems in algorithms and applications in database marketing, the remainder of the chapter focuses on two-class classification.

An illustration of the power of ensemble learning is provided in Figure 5.1. It demonstrates how classification performance (measured in AUC[1] and top-decile lift) for

---

1   Area Under the Receiver Operating Characteristic Curve.

the publicly available[2] *churn* dataset in the UCI repository (Asuncion and Newman, 2007) evolves when an ensemble of CART decision trees is created rather than a single tree. The plots clearly indicate that when more trees are added to the ensembles (that is, when one moves from left to right on the X-axis), the performance quickly surpasses that of a single decision tree, even when it has been *pruned* (that is, reduced in complexity to improve its generalizability to unseen data). Note that the plot compares four strategies to create ensemble learners: Bagging, the Random Subspace Method (RSM), the combined approach of Bagging and RSM and Rotation Forest. See Section 3 for a detailed discussion of these ensemble strategies.

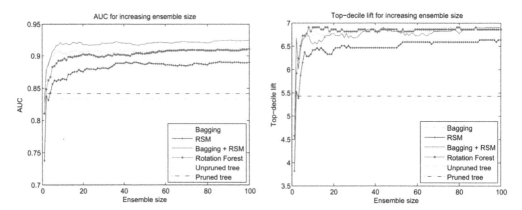

Figure 5.1   Increasing classification performance as a result of creating an ensemble of CART classifiers

Note: The figure shows AUC (a) and top-decile lift (b) for a CART decision tree (pruned and unpruned) versus four ensembles combining CART decision trees: Bagging, RSM, Bagging + RSM, and Rotation Forest as a function of ensemble size.

The practice of combining models into ensemble learners has also proven to be a very successful strategy to increase the accuracy of predictive models in real-life business applications. To illustrate this, consider Table 5.1, providing an overview of the most important data mining contests that have been organized in the past decennium and top-ranked by ensemble learning algorithms. It also shows the nature of the challenge offered to contestants, and the exact algorithm used by the winning entries in these tournaments.

Table 5.1 demonstrates the supremacy of ensemble learning algorithms in many different contests and contexts during the past decennium. Three of these contests issued challenges related to database marketing. While it is hard to assess adoption of these techniques by companies for predictive modeling in database marketing, these results at least demonstrate the potential strength on large-scale data sets in real-life business cases.

The remainder of this chapter is organized as follows. In Section 2, a generic framework of ensemble learning is provided that offers the shared components of the numerous methods that have been proposed and common configuration options for

---

2   Freely downloadable via http://www.sgi.com/tech/mlc/db/

Table 5.1   Data mining contests won using ensemble learning algorithms

Contest	Challenge	Winning algorithm
Duke/Teradata Center for CRM Competition 2002	*Churn prediction*	Stochastic gradient Boosting
KDD Cup 2005	Search query categorization	Hybrid ensemble with weighted sum of ranks
KDD Cup 2006	Computer aided embolism detection	Real AdaBoost (Task 1), Hybrid ensemble with voting (Task 2)
KDD Cup 2007	Netflix rating frequency prediction	Classifier selection
Netflix Prize 2008	Movie rating prediction	Stacked generalization and Stochastic Gradient Boosting
Fico / UC San Diego Data Mining Contest 2009	Detecting anomalous e-commerce transactions	Random Forests
KDD Cup 2009	*Churn prediction, cross-sell analysis and up-sell analysis*	Hybrid ensemble selection (Fast Track), Boosting with classification trees and shrinkage, using Bernoulli loss (Slow Track)
Fico / UC San Diego Data Mining Contest 2010	*Customer acquisition*	Hybrid ensemble selection (Fast Track)
KDD Cup 2010	Student performance prediction	Hybrid ensemble with multiple feature sets and classifier, and combination using regularized linear regression
KDD Cup 2011	Personalized music recommendation	Hybrid ensemble with multi-step member model combination

Note: Challenges situated in database marketing are highlighted in italic and bold font type.

the dimensions of ensemble learners are provided. Moreover, Dietterich's (2000a) three intuitive arguments on the origins of the competitive performance are described. Section 3 focuses on a selection of well-known algorithms. Subsequently, Section 4 discusses results of applications in database marketing literature. Section 5 is devoted to a number of advanced issues in ensemble learning usage, while a final Section concludes this chapter.

2   Basics of Ensemble Learning

2.1   A GENERIC FRAMEWORK

Ensemble learners are combinations of individual models. These constituent models are generally denominated ensemble *members,* and the aggregated model is in the remainder of this chapter called an *ensemble learner.* Sometimes different terminology is used: ensemble methods are sometimes called *multiple classifier systems, model committees,* or *expert fusion methods,* and the constituent models *base learners* or *weak learners.* It is generally assumed that an ensemble improves classification performance over an individual classifier if an ensemble algorithm succeeds in reconciling two ingredients: strong performance and diversity amongst its ensemble members. In other words, the constituent models need to have a level of expertise, while a certain level of

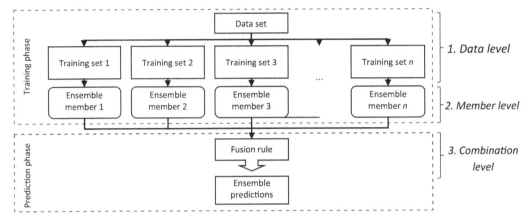

Figure 5.2   Generic ensemble classifier structure

disagreement has to emerge among the ensemble members. Methods to quantify and visualize diversity are discussed in Section 5. Amongst the many different ensemble algorithms, most have been proposed bearing in mind a strategy to increase diversity while maintaining or enhancing member accuracy.

Ensemble classifiers broadly differ along three structural dimensions of ensemble design, that is:

1. the treatment of the input training data (the *data level*);
2. the choice of the base classifier (the *member level*); and
3. the aggregation strategy for the base classifiers (the *combination level*).

Most algorithms can be explained as configurations of the generic structure in Figure 5.2. The remainder of this section discusses configuration choices for these three dimensions of ensemble algorithm design.

2.1.1   Data level: Training data treatment

First, many algorithms inject diversity amongst ensemble members by training every member on an altered version of the original data set. Hence, the training data set, fed to the algorithm, is modified in some way to create member training sets. As such, it is hoped that the subsequently trained ensemble members will be more diverse. Several strategies to manipulate training data have been proposed. Brown et al. (2005) make a distinction between *resampling* and *distortion* methods. In resampling methods, subsets of variables and/or observations are derived which may or may not be overlapping, while distortion methods transform the data. Possibilities of such transformations include data sampling schemes (for example, Bagging), random variable selection (for example, Random Forest, RSM), feature extraction (Rotation Forest, RotBoost), instance reweighting (for example, AdaBoost) and random variable weights (Maudes, et al., 2012).

2.1.2   Member level: Ensemble member algorithm choice

Second, broadly two strategies exist for choosing the members of an ensemble. In *hybrid* ensembles, different types of algorithms are combined, whilst in *non-hybrid* ensembles, one classifier algorithm is chosen and replicated multiple times in order to constitute an ensemble. An example of the first category is the combination of a neural network, a decision tree, a naïve Bayes model and a boosted naïve Bayes model into a single ensemble classifier to tackle churn prediction presented in (Hu, 2005). Examples of non-hybrid ensemble algorithms are Bagging, Random Forest, and GAMens, described in Section 3. In hybrid ensembles, diversity is expected naturally due to inherent differences between algorithms, such as the implicitly minimized loss function, the difference between parametric and nonparametric models (for example, linear regression versus GAMs), implicit feature selection (for example, node splits in decision trees) and so on. However, it is advisable to stimulate diversity further by implementing a training data transformation scheme. An investigation by Duin and Tax (2000) indicated that it is more effective to replicate a single classification algorithm on several randomly taken feature sets than to use different algorithms on the same set.

In non-hybrid ensembles, diversity is pursued using either multiple model specifications or parameter settings, or by using data level transformation in combination with techniques that are not robust to perturbations in training data. In the latter case, often the term *weak* or *unstable* base learner is used, indicating a model with low bias and high variance, and usually, low generalization power. This explains the popularity of (unpruned) decision trees (CART, CHAID, C4.5, or decision stumps) in ensemble algorithms extracting diversity from training data transformations. Similarly, other popular candidate algorithms are often also non-parametric in nature: K-nearest neighbors (Maudes, et al., 2009), artificial neural networks (Schwenk and Bengio, 2000), and GAMs (De Bock, et al., 2010). Overall, the most popular classifier ensemble schemes are non-hybrid and thus apply a base classification algorithm to differently permutated training sets. The two most well-known algorithms in this category are Bagging and Boosting (see Section 4). The popularity of non-hybrid ensembles could be attributed to their ease of implementation, reduced complexity over hybrid algorithms, and widespread availability in software packages.

Note that depending on the algorithm, training of the ensemble members could be organized sequentially or simultaneously. Sequential member training is necessary when the results of the training step of one member is impacted by results obtained from previous iterations. For example, in Boosting, erroneously classified observations obtain more weight in the training data fed to subsequently trained members, whereas the members of Bagging and Random Forest models could in theory be trained in parallel. This distinction becomes relevant when data is physically dispersed, or when training time is an issue and the potential of distributed or multi-core computing power can be exploited.

2.1.3   Combination level: Fusion rules

A third important element of any ensemble classifier algorithm is the fusion rule, used to aggregate ensemble member's outputs to ensemble predictions. Fusion rules can be categorized along the following dimensions:

1. whether they accommodate class or continuous member predictions (posterior probability estimates or other degrees of confidence);
2. whether the rule requires training or not; and
3. whether all members contribute to ensemble predictions or only one member is selected to deliver the prediction.

A first distinction is made between fusion rules for label outputs, that is, appropriate when ensemble members generate class predictions, and fusion rules for continuous outputs, suitable when the ensemble members output a value that represents a degree of confidence (Kuncheva, 2004). A well-studied and simple combiner that belongs to the first category is *majority voting*. This rule attributes the most frequently predicted class amongst the ensemble members as the final class prediction, as expressed in Equation 1:

$$C(x) = \frac{argmax}{c \in \Phi} \sum_{j=1}^{m} I(h_j(x) = c)$$ (1)

where m is the number of ensemble members, Φ represents the set of possible class labels, $h_j(x)$ is the class prediction of ensemble member j for an instance x, $I(.)$ is an index function that solves to a value of 1 if its argument is true and 0 otherwise, and finally, $C(x)$ is the ensemble prediction. Some algorithms (for example, the RSM, GAMens, or Rotation Forest) by default implement a fusion rule for continuous member outputs such as estimates of posterior probabilities. Rules of this type are often preferred in database marketing applications where a ranking of customers is often desirable and therefore, continuous predictions are required. The most straightforward form is *average aggregation* (also sometimes referred to as *mean combination*), which simply takes the average of the ensemble members' outputs. Weights can be assigned to ensemble members which score higher on a performance metric of choice to obtain weighted majority voting or weighted average aggregation (Kuncheva, 2004). The latter is provided in Equation 2:

$$C(x) = \frac{1}{m} \sum_{j=1}^{m} w_j h_j(x)$$ (2)

where w_j is the weight associated with ensemble member j, $\sum_{j=1}^{m} w_j = 1$; and $h_j(x)$ is the prediction of ensemble member j for an instance x. Training error rates are often used as weights, but other metrics such as AUC, lift, or misclassification cost can be used as well and are often more appropriate in marketing. An experiment on the use of lift in alternative weighting schemes for fusion rules in the context of churn prediction is conducted by De Bock and Van den Poel (2010). In their experiments, overall top-decile lift performance of Bagging and AdaBoost improved by weighting members according to their individual lift performance.

A second categorization differentiates between *trainable* and *non-trainable* fusion rules. Some fusion rules, such as average aggregation, do not require additional training once the ensemble has been populated with members. Other algorithms require the additional step of configuration of the fusion rule. Accuracy-weighted majority voting would fall in this category, but more advanced rules are possible as well. A common strategy is to merge all ensemble member predictions into a new training set on which an additional model is then trained, such as a simple linear regression, a neural network or a regularized (lasso) regression (Friedman and Popescu, 2008). Another strategy involves the creation of *decision templates*. These are prototype ensemble member prediction profiles that are created for every class by taking the average prediction of every ensemble member for all observations belonging to that class. To classify a new observation, the ensemble members' predictions are collected, and a distance measure (Euclidian, Mahalanobis, and so on) is calculated between the predictions and the average values in the decision template. This is repeated for every class and the closest matching decision template indicates the final class prediction.

A third categorization distinguishes between *ensemble fusion* and *classifier selection*. The difference lies in the decision on which members contribute to predictions. In ensemble fusion, all members' outputs are used, such as through majority voting. In classifier selection, it is assumed that ensemble members vary in their expertise to make predictions for observations belonging to different regions in the feature space and as such, the member or members in the ensemble that will contribute to the predictions vary depending on the nature of the observation. In most cases, an *oracle*, that is, a meta model, is used to indicate the competency of each member in the ensemble and the best candidate is chosen to deliver the prediction. In terms of fusion rules, this implies that depending on the characteristics of an observation to be scored, one member will be chosen to make the prediction. This corresponds to a dynamically weighted fusion rule with a weight of 1 for the most competent member while the other members in the ensemble receive a weight of 0.

2.2   DIETTERICH'S ARGUMENTS OF ENSEMBLE LEARNING PERFORMANCE

Ensembles are often observed to boast stronger performance on test set data and hence, they are assumed to have better generalization ability compared to individual models. Dieterrich (2000a) determined three fundamental reasons that explain why an ensemble classifier might improve upon the performance of a single classifier. The three arguments are represented visually in Figure 5.3.

The first argument is one of a statistical nature. This argument emphasizes the risk-reducing and generalizing nature of ensemble learners. Suppose that an analyst in search for the optimal model for the problem at hand, h^*, has the choice between several

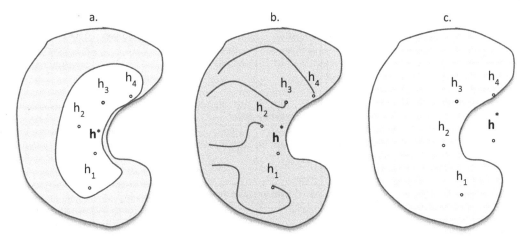

Figure 5.3   Graphical representation of Dietterich's three reasons for ensemble learning performance

alternative models h_1 to h_m, each with acceptable performance. In Figure 5.3(a), this set is represented by the light central region. A viable strategy would involve selecting the model with maximum performance on the training set, a set of *unseen* data. However, one can never be sure whether this selected model will also obtain the best performance on a new data sample. To avoid choosing wrongly, and reduce the risk introduced by such a choice, it is desirable to use all models and average them. As such, creating an ensemble of models is comparable to other risk-reducing strategies such as cross-validation or model averaging.

The second reason is of a computational nature (shown in Figure 5.3(b)). Several algorithms optimize until an arbitrarily chosen convergence threshold is met, or operate using a type of random search. In other cases, the final model depends upon the choice of a random seed value. In such cases, during the training process, the model evolves toward the optimal model h^* but might result in a suboptimal solution. Aggregation of models might in that case lead to a model that is closer to the globally optimal model.

Finally, the third reason is representational in nature. It might be possible that the optimal model is not a part of the space of possible models. In other words, the chosen technique is not suitable to model the problem at hand. For example, linear discriminant analysis is probably not a good choice if there are clear non-linear relationships between predictors and the dependent variable. In combining these classifiers, the probability that the true hypothesis becomes part of the space of hypotheses is increased.

3 Algorithms

A multitude of algorithms have been proposed throughout the past 15-odd years. This section provides an overview of the most notable ones. A first subsection discusses basic

Table 5.2 Configurations of basic ensemble learner algorithms: Bagging, the Random Subspace Method, Random Forest and AdaBoost

Ensemble taxonomy	Bagging	RSM	Random Forest	AdaBoost
1. Data level				
Data set → Training set member 1 … Training set member *n* → Ensemble member 1 … Ensemble member *n* → Fusion rule → Ensemble predictions	Bootstrap samples	Random feature subsets	Bootstrap samples	Sequential resampling/ reweighting
2. Member level				
	CART (or other decision tree)	C4.5 (or other)	Randomized CART	Decision stumps
3. Combination level				
	Majority voting	Average aggregation	Majority voting	Weighted majority voting (weights based on error rate)

algorithms: Bagging, Boosting, the RSM, and Random Forests. An overview of these methods is provided in Table 5.2. A second subsection focuses on a selection of more advanced algorithms: GAMens, rotation-based ensemble algorithms, and Stochastic Gradient Boosting. These techniques are summarized in Table 5.3.

3.1   BASIC ALGORITHMS

3.1.1   Bagging

Bagging is an early ensemble algorithm developed by Leo Breiman (1996) and is an abbreviation for bootstrap aggregation. This algorithm seeks diversity by influencing the data level within the ensemble, by feeding a different training data set to every member. In particular, to construct a bagged ensemble consisting of m members (the only parameter to be specified), every constituent classifier $h_j(x)$ is trained upon a bootstrap sample, that is, a random sample drawn with replacement from and maintaining the same size as the training data. To generate predictions, the ensemble members are aggregated in one final classifier by a majority vote. Bagging is an example of an ensemble technique where classifiers can be trained in parallel.

The ability of Bagging to deliver improved predictive performance has been investigated in experiments by Bauer and Kohavi (1999), who found that Bagging is especially able to decrease the variance of unstable base learners. Because Bagging relies upon variations in training data and deploys no other strategies to increase diversity amongst its members, it is very important that the algorithm used at the member level should be unstable (cfr. Section 2.1.2). Breiman introduced Bagging as an ensemble strategy for CART decision trees. Other candidate algorithms include neural networks and k-nearest neighbors.

Several variations of Bagging have been proposed and proven to further improve performance. The RSM and Random Forest are presented in subsections 3.1.2 and 3.1.3. Further, it was shown that a bagged ensemble can benefit from trimming, that is, having its worst performing members excluded from the ensemble (Croux, et al., 2007). In their algorithm called *Trimmed Bagging*, a parameter α is introduced that indicates the percentage of weakest performing members to be removed based on training set accuracy. Second, in *Wagging* (Bauer and Kohavi, 1999), sampling is replaced by random instance weighting based on Gaussian noise, and the base learner is assumed to accept weights for its training instances. Other variations are *suBagging*, replacing bootstrap samples by sampling without replacement and *Bragging*, replacing majority voting by median predictions (Bühlmann, 2002).

3.1.2   Random Subspace Method (attribute Bagging)

A related method to Bagging is the RSM, (Ho, 1998)), also sometimes referred to as *attribute Bagging* (Bryll, et al., 2003) based on its resemblance to Bagging. Similarly, in the RSM, diversity is introduced by constructing an ensemble of decision trees that are trained on variations of the training data. For every member, a training set is constructed by taking a random selection of features from the feature space without replacement. Consider a training sample that is described by p features. From these p features, r will randomly be selected (with $r < p$). In this way, a first random subspace of the original feature space is obtained. This subspace is r-dimensional and thus smaller than the p-dimensional feature space. This procedure is repeated a certain number of times and a decision tree is trained on each subspace. The final classifier is obtained through majority voting.

The RSM is preferred in case of a relatively small amount of training objects in comparison to the number of data features (that is, so-called *large p, small n* problems). If no measures are taken, this high level of data dimensionality could cause over-training. The RSM technique avoids overfitting of the training sample while preserving the maximum accuracy (Lai, et al., 2006). As random subspaces contain less features than the original feature space and the number of training objects stays the same, the relative training sample size increases. Sometimes, the feature space contains many redundant features, which can result in poor classifiers. Selecting only a number of features increases the chance to exclude the redundant features and improve the performance of the classifier (Skurichina and Duin, 2002).

Recent research shows that the performance of RSM can be significantly improved by altering the base learner algorithm. In Kuncheva et al. (2010), RSM applied to support vector machines resulted in optimal performance. In De Bock et al. (2010), RSM was found to benefit from adopting GAMs as member classifiers.

3.1.3 Random Forests

A technique that is related to both Bagging and the RSM is Random Forests (Breiman, 2001). A Random Forest implements Bagging to create training sets for each of its member classifiers and implements *randomized* CART decision trees that perform random feature selection *at the node level*. This means that at each node of every member model j, a random number of features r (with $r < p$) is selected and evaluated based on Gini index to choose the best split from these features. All resulting individual classifiers are aggregated using majority voting.

The algorithm smartly exploits a side-effect of the Bagging component. In the training of every individual ensemble member, on average $\frac{1}{e} \approx 36.8$ % of instances are not selected. These *out-of-bag* observations are involved in several ways, of which two seem especially relevant. First, they are used to internally estimate the generalization error without the need for a secondary test or validation data set. This principle could be easily extended to other performance metrics. These internal estimates can for example be used to optimize the random feature subset size parameter. Second, they can be used to estimate the relative importance of variables in the model (see Section 5.2). Note that these estimates can be obtained for every method that applies random subsampling at the ensemble member level.

Random Forests are attributed several advantages. First, the strong performance of Random Forests has been acclaimed in many different domains, such as cancer classification, credit scoring (Brown and Mues, 2012), customer churn prediction (Larivière and Van den Poel, 2005) and business failure prediction. In several experiments, Random Forests outperformed other ensemble methods such as Bagging, RSM, and AdaBoost. Second, the number of parameters to specify remains limited to the ensemble size and the size of random feature subsets. In addition, a cost matrix can be specified to force the algorithm on minimizing misclassification cost rather than accuracy. Third, the algorithm has been found to handle data problems rather well, such as class imbalance (Brown and Mues, 2012), outliers, and noise (Breiman 2001), a large feature-to-instance ratio, and situations where there are many features with a weak ability to distinguish between classes (Breiman, 2001).

3.1.4 AdaBoost

Boosting, like Bagging, has been an inspiration for a large number of algorithm variations (for example, Merler, et al., 2007; Zhang and Zhang, 2008). However, the most important technique within this category of algorithms is *AdaBoost*, an acronym for adaptive Boosting (Freund and Schapire, 1997). To illustrate its importance, AdaBoost has been identified as one of the ten most important data mining algorithms by Wu and Kumar (2009). In AdaBoost, each base classifier $h_j(x)$ is trained either on reweighted versions of the training data set D, obtained by applying different weights (*Boosting-by-reweighting*) or on a resampled version of the training data according to a sampling probability distribution (*Boosting-by-resampling*) to each of the training observations. The idea is that in every iteration the ensemble is forced to concentrate on those observations with which it experiences most difficulties, by attributing higher weights to observations that were wrongly classified in earlier iterations.

At the start of the training process, the instance weights $D_1(i)$ are initialized so that every observation $i = 1,\ldots, n$ in the training data set receives an equal weight of $\frac{1}{n}$ where n is the number of observations. In each iteration of the training process, three tasks are performed:

1. an ensemble member is trained;
2. a corresponding member weight is determined for that particular learner; and
3. the instance weight distribution is updated.

In particular, in any iteration j, first a learner $h_j(x)$ is trained on D using weights $D_j(i)$. Further, the weight α_j of the respective ensemble member is obtained via:

$$\alpha_j = \frac{1}{2}\ln(\frac{1-\varepsilon_j}{\varepsilon_j}) \tag{3}$$

based upon the error of $C_j(x)$, calculated as:

$$\varepsilon_j = \frac{1}{\sum_{i=1}^{n}D_j(i)}\sum_{i=1}^{n}D_j(i)I(h_j(x_i) \neq y_i) \tag{4}$$

Finally, the instance weights are updated as follows:

$$D_{j+1}(i) = \frac{D_j(i)}{N_j} \times \begin{cases} \exp(-\alpha_j) \text{ if } h_j(x_i) \neq y_i \\ \exp(\alpha_j) \text{ if } h(x_i) \neq y_i \end{cases} \tag{5}$$

Where N_j is simply a normalization factor so that D_{j+1} is a probability distribution function: $N_j = \sum_{i=1}^{n}D_j(i)\exp(-\alpha_j y_i h_j(x_i))$. In case ε_j is larger than 0.5 then the training is halted, or the weights are reinitialized to $\frac{1}{n}$. Once trained, the ensemble is deployed to generate predictions using a weighted majority vote:

$$C\left(x\right) = \underset{c \in \Phi}{argmax} \sum_{j=1}^{m} a_j I(h_j\left(x\right) = c)) \tag{6}$$

AdaBoost inherently minimizes an exponential loss function which can be shown to minimize the probability of a misclassification (that is, the Bayesian error). Several authors have investigated the origin of its strong performance. Experiments by Bauer and Kohavi (1999) have found that the strong performance of AdaBoost is linked to its ability to reduce both the variance and bias in comparison to its (unstable) base learner. Friedman et al. (2000) approach Boosting from a statistical point of view and explain AdaBoost as a method to fit an additive logistic regression in a stagewise forward manner, using a criterion that is similar to Binomial log-likelihood. Hence, AdaBoost substantially extends the range of functional relationships that can be modeled using an arbitrarily simple base learner, which explains its potential for increased performance.

Variations of AdaBoost include *AdaBoost.M1*, an extension to multi-class classification, *LogitBoost*, which adopts a logistic loss function (Friedman, et al., 2000) and *MultiBoost*, a combination of Wagging and AdaBoost (Webb, 2000).

3.2 ADVANCED ALGORITHMS

Over the years, many interesting algorithms have been proposed in a continuous search for superior performance, often as improvements upon the basic algorithms discussed in the previous section. In this section, a selection of promising, more recent algorithms is discussed. The configurations of these algorithms are summarized in Table 5.3.

Table 5.3 Configurations of advanced ensemble learner algorithms: Stochastic Gradient Boosting, Rotation Forest, and RotBoost

Ensemble taxonomy		Stochastic Gradient Boosting	Rotation Forest	GAMens
		1. Data level		
		Sequential resampling/ reweighting	Rotated data (through e.g. PCA)	Bootstrap samples with random feature subsets
		2. Member level		
		Decision stumps	CART	Semi-parametric additive logistic regression
		3. Combination level		
		Weighted majority voting	Average aggregation	Average aggregation

3.2.1 Stochastic Gradient Boosting

Stochastic Gradient Boosting is a powerful ensemble method proposed by Jerome Friedman (Friedman, 2001, 2002). The goal of gradient Boosting is to find the model $C^*(X)$ that minimizes the expected value over all points (x_i, y_i) of an arbitrarily chosen and differentiable loss function $L(Y, C(X))$:

$$C^*(X) = \frac{argmin}{C(X)} E_{y,x} L(Y, C(X)) \qquad (7)$$

The model $C^*(X)$ is approximated by an ensemble $C(x)$ that is a weighted sum of base learners $h_j(x, a_j)$ where a_i represents the set of parameters that describe the configuration of the base learner j and its fit to the data:

$$C(x) = \sum_{j=1}^{m} w_j h_j(x, a_j) \qquad (8)$$

The ensemble is built in an iterative manner that is similar to AdaBoost. Instead of training members upon reweighted versions of the training data, in every iteration j, a base learner is fit to so-called *pseudo-residuals* in a least squares fashion. First, the ensemble is initialized with the following initial constant function and extended by iteratively adding members:

$$C_0(x) = \frac{argmin}{w} \sum_{i=1}^{n} L(y_i, w) \qquad (9)$$

$$C_j(x) = C_{j-1}(x) + \frac{argmin}{h \in} \sum_{i=1}^{n} L(y_i, C_{j-1}(x_i) + h(x_i)) \qquad (10)$$

To solve these minimization problems, the strategy of gradient descent is applied. This translates to the following minimization problem:

$$C_j(x) = C_{j-1}(x) - w_j \sum_{i=1}^{n} \nabla_f L(y_i, F_{j-1}(x_i) + h(x_i)) \qquad (11)$$

$$w_j = \frac{argmin}{w} \sum_{i=1}^{n} L(y_i, C_{j-1}(x_i)) - w \frac{\partial L(y_i, C_{j-1}(x_i))}{\partial h(x_i)} \qquad (12)$$

Note that this expression minimizes the loss function for the predictions made for observations in the training set However, the aim is to find a model that generalizes to other data sets and hence, a model that approximates the gradient of L as close as possible. This goal is achieved by fitting a model $h_j(x, a_j)$ to so-called pseudo-residuals:

$$\tilde{y}_{ij} = -\left[\frac{\partial L(y_i, C_{j-1}(x_i))}{\partial C(x_i)} \right]_{C(x) = C_{j-1}(x)} \quad \text{with } i = 1, \dots, n \qquad (13)$$

The weight of the respective ensemble member j is then simply found by solving:

$$w_j = \underset{w}{argmin} \sum_{i=1}^{n} L(y_i, C_{j-1}(x_i) - wh_j(x_i)) \tag{14}$$

Friedman suggested two improvements to his initial formulation of gradient Boosting. The first was an adaptation to better handle CART decision trees as base learners. In the *TreeBoost* algorithm, a weight w_j is chosen per tree leaf instead of per member tree. The second adaptation introduces a heuristic for randomization in the model to enhance its capability to generalize and avoid overfitting. At each iteration, a base learner is fit upon a subsample of the training data set, randomly drawn without replacement. Hence the term *Stochastic Gradient Boosting*. This modification was found to significantly improve performance and allows the introduction of out-of-bag estimates as discussed in Section 3.1.4. Stochastic Gradient Boosting has proven to be a very powerful technique, as illustrated in the overview of data mining contests (Table 5.1) and in the database marketing literature in Section 4.

3.2.2 Rotation-based ensemble classifiers

Rotation-based ensembles aim at an additional injection of diversity into an ensemble of decision trees by rotating the feature space with principal component analysis (PCA), or, in extension, by applying any feature extraction technique. Two algorithms have been proposed in this family of methods: *Rotation Forest* (Rodríguez, et al., 2006) and the derived *RotBoost* (Zhang and Zhang, 2008). A Rotation Forest is constructed as an ensemble classifier C of m decision trees taking as training data for each base classifier a rotated version using a (linear) feature extraction algorithm φ. In particular, to train each base classifier C_j a rotation matrix R_j^a is first obtained by randomly taking s subsets from the feature space $X; X = \{X_1, X_2, ..., X_p\}$ (or dividing X into feature subsets of size r), for each subset performing feature extraction algorithm φ on a bootstrap sample containing 75 percent of the training data, and finally rearranging the coefficients. The training data for C_j is then obtained by rotating the input vector using R_j^a and combining the result with the outcome variable. At the combination level, ensemble predictions are obtained by taking an average. *Rotboost* is defined as the combination of Rotation Forest and AdaBoost: every base classifier C_j in Rotation Forests is replaced by an AdaBoost classifier (see Section 3.1.2).

Rotation Forests was found superior over Bagging, AdaBoost, and Random Forests on a broad range of UCI data sets in Rodríguez et al. (2006). The strong performance is attributed to a simultaneous improvement of (1) diversity within the ensemble, obtained by the use of feature extraction on training data and the use of decision trees, known to be sensitive to variations in the training data, as base classifiers; and (4) accuracy of the base classifiers, by keeping all extracted features in the training data. Zhang and Zhang (2008) indicated superior performance of RotBoost over Bagging, AdaBoost and MultiBoost, and a slight improvement over Rotation Forests in terms of accuracy.

Feature extraction plays an important role in rotation-based ensemble classifiers. In the original Rotation Forest algorithm, feature extraction through PCA is applied (Rodríguez, et al., 2006). In Kuncheva and Rodríguez (2007), the value of using alternative feature extraction algorithms is investigated. Experiments replace PCA by non-parametric discriminant analysis (NDA), random projections (RP), and sparse random projections

(SRP). More elaborate experiments on the adoption of alternative feature extraction algorithms have been conducted in the context of customer churn prediction in (De Bock and Van den Poel, 2011) (see Section 4).

3.2.3   GAMens

In (De Bock, et al., 2010), GAMs are introduced as base learners for ensemble classification. *GAMens* is an algorithm that combines Bagging and the RSM, and adopts GAMs as member classifiers. Intended for binary classification, GAMens adopts the semi-parametric additive logistic regression model as base learner:

$$C_i(X) = logit\left(P(Y = 1|X)\right) \equiv log\left\{\frac{P(Y = 1|X)}{1 - P(Y = 1|X)}\right\} = \sum_{k=1}^{p_c} s_k(X_k) + \sum_{l=1}^{p_b} \beta_l X_l \tag{15}$$

where features $X_k; k = 1, \dots, p_c$ are continuous variables, $X_l; l = 1, \dots, p_b$ are dummy variables that result from a transformation from categorical variables (see Chapter 1) and the functions $s_1(X_1), s_2(X_2), \dots, s_{p_c}(X_{p_c})$ are smoothing splines that estimate the nonparametric relationships between the continuous variables $X_1, X_2, \dots, X_{p_c}$ and the logit. Ensemble predictions are obtained via average aggregation which takes the simple average of the predicted class membership probabilities by the individual ensemble members. Parameters that need to be specified are ensemble size (m), the desired number of variables to be selected as random feature subspaces is required (r parameter), and the number of degrees of freedom to be used in the smoothing spline estimation is required (df parameter). Experiments on 12 UCI datasets demonstrated superior performance of GAMens over Bagging and RSM adopting CART base learners, and a slight improvement (albeit not significant) over Random Forest and Rotation Forest (De Bock, et al., 2010).

4   Applications in Database Marketing

As noted earlier, the classification technique used to create a model to predict customer churn has a direct impact upon the prediction quality, and hence, of the profitability of all subsequent marketing efforts to sustain customer retention (Neslin, et al., 2006). Motivated by the suggested increase in classification performance, ensemble learning has received significant attention in churn prediction literature during the past decade (De Bock and Van den Poel, 2011). Table 5.4 presents an overview of studies that apply ensemble learning to database marketing. It indicates the application that is focused upon, the types of algorithms used, and the number and origin of data sets used in the experiments.

It is clear from the table that the majority of these papers focus on churn prediction. The first applications of ensemble learning to the prediction of customer churn emerged in data mining and operational research-oriented journals at the beginning of this century. Mozer et al. (2000) conducted experiments on US mobile carrier data. Their results show that Boosting is a viable strategy to improve the predictive performance of C5.0 decision trees and neural networks. Further evidence of the potential of ensemble learning was found by Hu (2005). Experiments on data from a financial services company

Table 5.4   Ensemble learning applications in database marketing

Study	Application	Ensemble learner	Nr. of datasets	Industry
(Mozer, et al., 2000)	Churn	AdaBoost, ANN Boosting	1	Telecom
(Hu, 2005)	Churn	Boosted Naive Bayesian Networks, Hybrid ensemble	1	Bank
(Buckinx and Van den Poel, 2005)	Churn	Random Forests	1	FMCG retail
(Ha, et al., 2005)	Response modeling	ANN Bagging	1	Gift mail-order
(Larivière and Van den Poel, 2005)	Churn, Customer profitability	Random Forests, Regression Forests	1	Bank
(Kim, 2006)	Churn	Logit and ANN ensembles	1	Telecom
(Lemmens and Croux, 2006)	Churn	Bagging, Stochastic Gradient Boosting	1	Telecom
(Burez and Van den Poel, 2007)	Churn	Random Forests	1	Pay TV
(van Wezel and Potharst, 2007)	Customer brand choice modeling	Bagging, LogitBoost, MultiBoost	2	US household data
(Burez and Van den Poel, 2008)	Churn	Random Forests	1	Pay TV
(Coussement and Van den Poel, 2008)	Churn	Random Forests	1	Newspaper subscriptions
(Bose and Chen, 2009)	Churn	C5.0 Boosting	1	Telecom
(Burez and Van den Poel, 2009)	Churn	Random Forests, Weighted Random Forests, Stochastic Gradient Boosting	6	Bank, Telecom, Pay TV, Supermarket, Newspaper subscriptions
(Prinzie and Van den Poel, 2008)	Cross-sell	Random Multinomial Logit; Random Forests	1	Home appliances retail
(Coussement and Van den Poel, 2009)	Churn	Random Forests	1	Newspaper subscriptions
(Glady, et al., 2009)	Churn	AdaCost	1	Bank
(Xie, et al., 2009)	Churn	Improved Balanced Random Forests (IBRF)	1	Bank
(De Bock and Van den Poel, 2010)	Churn	Bagging, RSM and AdaBoost with lift-based fusion rules and probability estimation trees	5	Bank (3), Supermarket, DIY
(Risselada, et al., 2010)	Churn	Bagging of CART and logit	2	ISP, Insurance provider

Table 5.4   Continued

(De Bock and Van den Poel, 2011)	Churn	Rotation-based ensembles: Rotation Forests, RotBoost and variations	4	DIY, Bank, Telecom, Mail-order apparel
(De Bock and Van den Poel, 2012)	Churn	GAMensPlus	6	DIY, Bank, Supermarket, Telecom, Mail-order apparel
(Coussement and De Bock, 2012)	Churn	GAMens, Random Forests	1	Online gambling

compared a decision tree, a selective Bayesian network and a neural network to two ensemble learning strategies, that is, a boosted naïve Bayesian network and a hybrid ensemble learner consisting of all benchmarked algorithms. Their evaluation indicated a performance improvement by the ensemble learning strategy.

In their reference work, Lemmens and Croux (2006), introduced the usage of ensemble learning for customer churn prediction into the marketing literature stream. They compared logistic regression to two prominent strategies to create non-hybrid ensembles of decision trees, that is, Bagging and (Stochastic Gradient) Boosting, for an anonymous US wireless telecom operator. Their results demonstrate that both ensemble learning algorithms significantly outperform logistic regression. Other applications of ensemble learning include Kim (2006) who constructed non-hybrid ensemble learners of neural networks and logistic regression models using an adapted version of Bagging whereby ensemble member are trained on random samples taken without replacement and with a size equal to half the number of instances in the calibration data set. Glady et al. (2009) created cost-sensitive churn prediction models based on the customer's expected customer lifetime value (CLV) using the AdaCost algorithm, a variant of AdaBoost. Finally, De Bock and Van den Poel (2011) conducted experiments on the use of rotation-based ensemble learners, transforming the input data of the ensemble members using feature extraction. They demonstrated favorable performance of this new approach over existing ensemble learners and single classifiers. The best performance, measured in terms of top-decile lift, was observed for Rotation Forests implementing independent component analysis (ICA).

A popular non-hybrid ensemble classification algorithm that received a lot of attention in customer churn prediction is Random Forests. Larivière and Van den Poel (2005) introduced this ensemble learner to the churn prediction domain. Using data from a European financial services company, Random Forests demonstrated superior prediction performance compared to logistic regression. Ample churn prediction research has been shown how Random Forests outperformed single classifiers in a pay TV setting (Burez and Van den Poel 2007, 2008) and in the newspaper publishing industry (Coussement and Van den Poel 2008, 2009). However, the superiority of Random Forests in comparison to logistic regression and automatic relevance detection (ARD) neural networks was not confirmed by Buckinx and Van den Poel (2005) in an FMCG retail setting. Additionally, Random Forests have been indicated to be particularly suitable to deal with class imbalance, a frequently encountered issue in customer churn prediction. Burez and Van den Poel (2009) demonstrated that weighted Random Forests are superior in the presence of class imbalance. Xie et al. (2009) modified the Random Forest algorithm to be more robust to this problem. Their *Improved Balanced Random Forests* (IBRF) algorithm introduces cost-sensitive learning by iteratively altering the class distribution and by increasing the importance of misclassified observations belonging to the minority class. Their experiments on data from a Chinese bank demonstrated performance improvements over conventional Random Forests and a selection of single classifiers.

Finally, recent research has highlighted the added value of using GAMs as base learners in churn prediction ensembles. In De Bock and Van den Poel (2012), GAMensPlus is proposed as an update of GAMens (see Section 3.2.3), including two instruments to make the resulting models interpretable. Experiments show that over six different data sets, GAMensPlus outperforms single GAMS and other ensemble methods significantly in terms of several performance metrics. In Coussement and De Bock (2012), the competitive performance of GAMens in churn prediction was confirmed in an application to online gambling.

5 Advanced Topics

5.1 DIVERSITY

Diversity is a very important concept in ensemble learning. As explained earlier, an ensemble of learners can only improve the performance of a single learner if the members differ to some extent in the predictions they assign to instances in a data set. When assuming the use of member learners that generate class predictions, an ensemble will work best if the member classifiers are as accurate as possible while they disagree as much as possible. This implies a tradeoff between diversity amongst members and their accuracy: (1) if all member classifiers generate perfect predictions, they do not disagree and the ensemble obtains maximum performance as well; (2) if all members are characterized by an accuracy of just above 50 percent and the errors they make are totally uncorrelated, the ensemble accuracy will converge toward 100 percent as the ensemble grows larger.

Virtually all ensemble algorithms impose diversity in some way. In Bagging and the RSM, every member is trained upon a modified version of the training set. Rotation Forests take it a step further by rotating the feature space using a feature extraction method such as PCA on feature subsets and maintaining all identified factors. Some algorithms explicitly increase diversity in the ensemble. An example is the collective-agreement-based ensemble pruning method proposed by Rokach (2009).

Several measures can be used to measure diversity in classifier ensembles (Kuncheva and Whitaker, 2003). A distinction is made between pairwise and non-pairwise measures. In the first class, pairs of member classifiers are compared in order to obtain an overall measure of diversity, an average has to be taken across member pairs. The non-pairwise measures calculate a single measure for an ensemble as a whole. For an overview of diversity metrics, we kindly refer the reader to Kuncheva and Whitaker (2003) and Kuncheva (2004).

An intuitive means for visualizing the accuracy-diversity tradeoff is the kappa-error diagram (Margineantu and Dietterich, 1997). This diagram is a scatterplot where every point corresponds to a pair of ensemble members and plots their average error rate on the Y-axis, and their kappa-value, a measure of agreement, on the X-axis. In the case of binary classification, the kappa of a pair of members i and j is calculated as:

$$\kappa_{i,j} = \frac{2(c_{1,1}c_{2,2} - c_{1,2}c_{2,1})}{\left(c_{1,1} + c_{1,2}\right)\left(c_{1,1} + c_{2,1}\right) + \left(c_{1,2} + c_{2,2}\right)\left(c_{2,1} + c_{2,2}\right)} \qquad (16)$$

where $c_{v,w}$ is the number of instances where ensemble member $h_i(X)$ predicts class v and member $h_j(X)$ predicts class w. When there is maximum agreement (that is, both members consistently predict the same classes), the kappa attains a value of 1. Total disagreement would lead to a value of 0. The right pane (a) of Figure 5.4 shows the kappa-error diagram for four algorithms (AdaBoost, RSM, Rotation Forest, and Bagging) applied to the UCI churn data set. The diagram demonstrates the diversity-seeking nature of AdaBoost by iteratively changing the weight distribution of the training data. Bagging and Rotation Forest seem to be similarly situated. Both generate accurate but little diverse members. In Rodríguez et al. (2006), it is argued that Rotation Forest on average (evaluated over many data sets) benefits from a minimal improvement on both the accuracy and diversity dimensions, which could not be confirmed for this particular data set. Rotation Forest generates some member pairs that are more accurate but less diverse.

In database marketing, predictive modeling is seldom evaluated in terms of accuracy (or, equivalently, error rate). Instead, oftentimes analysts are interested in the ability of an algorithm to rank customers according to their probability to behave in a certain way (as for example measured using AUC (Huang and Ling, 2005)), or the ability to identify the customers most likely to engage in the behavior of interest well (as measure by top-decile lift and gain ratio). Therefore, it could be desirable to evaluate the pairwise performance and diversity of members in an ensemble classifier using different metrics than the well-established kappa-error diagrams. For example, one way to accommodate probability predictions instead of crisp class predictions is to use correlation to measure agreement between member pairs, and average AUC values to quantify their average performance. This approach is applied in pane b of Figure 5.4. Here, both RSM and AdaBoost seem to be able to generate very diverse member pairs, while the composition of Bagging and Rotation Forests is again comparable.

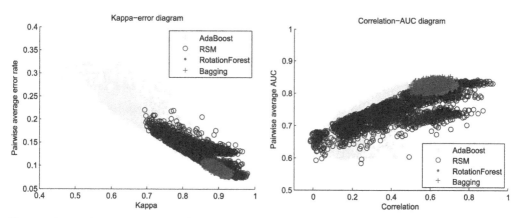

Figure 5.4 **Kappa-error and correlation-AUC diagram for the UCI churn data set comparing AdaBoost, the Random Subspace Method, Rotation Forest, and Bagging**

5.2 INTERPRETABILITY

In various domains, ensemble learning has been often found to outperform uncombined methods. However, in fields such as medical diagnostics (Tan, et al., 2003) and credit scoring (Martens, et al., 2007; Setiono, et al., 2009), comprehensibility or ability to derive insight into a model's functioning is equally important, or even primordial to high-quality predictions. Depending on the managerial objectives and priorities, this applies to database marketing as well. For example, several authors have emphasized model comprehensibility as a requirement for successful churn prediction models (Qi, et al., 2009; Shaw, et al., 2001). Interpretable, intuitive models enable marketing decision makers to gain insight into customer behavior and identify factors with an impact upon customer loyalty, churning behavior (Masand, et al., 1999) or other relevant customer choices.

Some of the most popular techniques in predictive database marketing offer interpretability in a very natural manner. Possible algorithms that have been found to reconcile acceptable performance with ease of interpretation are logistic regression (Buckinx and Van den Poel, 2005; Kim and Yoon, 2004), GAMs (Coussement, et al., 2010), and decision trees (Kim and Yoon, 2004). Unfortunately, as Neslin et al. (2006) suggest, full explanatory power and superior predictions are rarely reconciled. Powerful techniques such as neural networks or ensemble learners are so-called black-box models that exhibit an increased level of complexity that often allows a better fit of the data at the cost of model comprehensibility. For such techniques, other strategies have to be applied to derive insights from these models. One option is to apply rule extraction methods where the black-box model is replaced or complemented by an interpretable one (see Chapter 6). In this section, two alternative strategies are discussed that can be used to derive insight from ensemble classification methods without the need to train an additional model.

5.2.1 Variable importance measures

Variable importance measures allow insight into the relative importance of features used for training. They were initially introduced by Breiman (2001) as a by-product of Random Forests. While several types have been proposed, permutation accuracy importance scores are the more advanced and reliable variant, as reported in Strobl et al. (2007). Permutation accuracy importance scores are calculated using data that was not used for training. This can be a validation sample, or, when random sampling was applied to obtain ensemble member training sets, the out-of-bag observations (see Section 3.1.4). Permutation accuracy importance scores for feature X_j are then obtained by calculating, for every member, the average difference in accuracy before and after permuting the values of variable x_j in the out-of bag data, and averaging the result over all ensemble members $h_j(X); j = 1, \ldots, m$. These permutation-based accuracy scores can be tested for significance (Strobl, et al., 2008).

Figure 5.5 shows variable importance scores based on accuracy for a Random Forest model that was estimated for the UCI churn data set. The plot shows that 13 variables are influential predictors in the model, while others do not exhibit explanatory power.

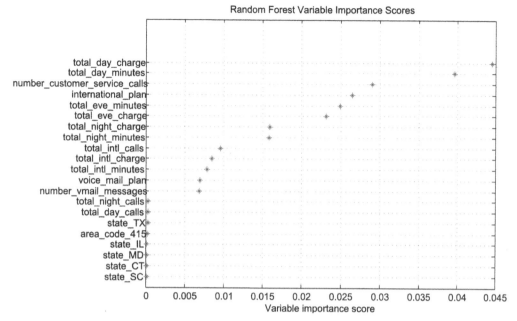

Figure 5.5 Original permutation accuracy-based Random Forest variable importance scores for the UCI churn data set

The score of 0.045 for the variable *total_day_charge* indicates that on average, accuracy of member trees drop by 4.5 percent when this variable is cancelled out.

In database marketing, several performance metrics are used for evaluation and comparison or models. In the case of binary classification, one could choose for example accuracy, AUC, or lift. Based on this observation, in De Bock and Van den Poel (2012), generalized feature importance scores are introduced that measure the relative impact of features on an arbitrarily chosen performance metric. The authors also point out that, when applied to GAMens, variable importance scores avoid bias that is present in decision tree ensembles based upon (1) biased variable selection at node splits in CART decision trees; and (2) the artificial promotion of categorical variables introduce through bootstrap sampling (Strobl, et al., 2007).

5.2.2 Partial Dependence Plots

While variable importance scores allow an analyst to identify the relative importance of variables in the model, partial dependence plots provide insight into the nature of the relationship between a variable and the outcome variable. For models containing more than two independent variables, a graphical representation of the model $C(X)$ becomes difficult. However, it can be also useful to investigate the partial dependence of every variable in the model upon the outcome variable, which shows the relationship conditional upon the variables. For any black-box model, these partial dependence functions of a subset of variables X_{S_1} ; $X = \left(X_{S_1}, X_{S_2} \right)$ can be estimated using:

$$F_{S_1}\left(X_{S_2}\right)=\frac{1}{n}\sum_{i=1}^{n}C(X_{S_1},x_{iS_2})\tag{17}$$

where $\left\{x_{1S_2},x_{2S_2},\ldots,x_{nS_2}\right\}$ are the values of subset X_{S_2} in the training data set. While this approach can be quite computationally expensive, for ensembles consisting of decision trees these partial dependence functions can be easily derived from the tree members without any additional pass through the data (Hastie, et al., 2001).

Figure 5.6 shows partial depence plots for a selection of variables in a Random Forest model estimated in the UCI churn data set. The selected variables all emerged as relevant drivers of customer churn through the variable importance measures and illustrate different types of non-linear functional relationships with the logit transformation of the probability to churn. Indicative histograms for churners (red) and non-churning customers (blue) are included to illustrate the relative distribution of classes over the variables' value ranges.

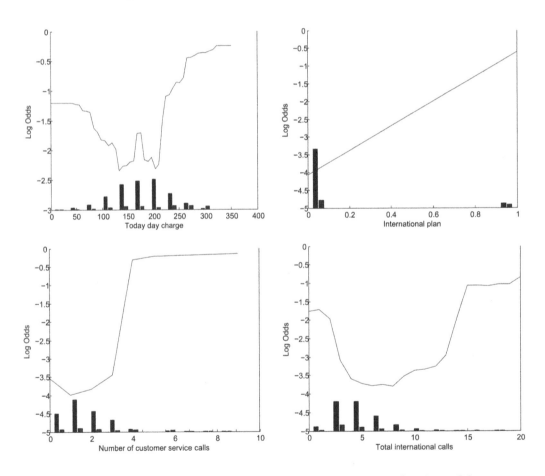

Figure 5.6   Random Forest partial dependence plots for a selection of four variables in the UCI churn data set

6   Software

Numerous commercial and open-source software packages for statistical analysis and data mining now implement ensemble learning algorithms. In the first category, SAS Enterprise Miner[3] offers nodes for Bagging, Boosting, and hybrid model combination. IBM's SPSS Modeler[4] features Bagging and Boosting. Finally, Salford Systems' Predictive Modeler (SPM)[5] offers Random Forest and Stochastic Gradient Boosting (TreeNet) implementations, as well as several functions for model interpretation and post-processing. More variety in algorithms is offered in open source packages. Firstly, via the CRAN software repository[6] many freely available add-on packages for R can be accessed. A non-exhaustive selection of package names includes *adabag* (Bagging and AdaBoost.M1), *ada* (AdaBoost, GentleBoost and LogitBoost), *randomForest*, *GAMens*, and *party* (Bagging and Random Forests based on conditional inference trees). Secondly, wide variety of methods (Bagging, AdaBoost, LogitBoost, Stacking, RSM,...) is available in the WEKA data mining package.[7] Finally, RapidMiner[8] offers an interface to the WEKA algorithms as well as several proprietary algorithm implementations.

7   Summary

In this chapter, an introduction to ensemble learning was provided in the context of database marketing. A prominent tool in a database marketer's arsenal is predictive modeling, a practice that is typically applied to forecast future customer behavior or characteristics, an asset that can in turn be deployed to make marketing campaigns more targeted and efficient. In ensemble learning, it is recognized that it is hard to find a single model that is assumed to perform well in several situations. Rather, by combining several techniques and models, one can create a model that demonstrates performance that is more robust, and in general, superior in comparison to its uncombined model constituents. This strong performance of ensemble learners, and most prominently, ensemble classifiers, has been demonstrated empirically in a growing body of literature on database marketing. Moreover, ensemble learners have consistently emerged as winning entries in data mining contests in a variety of domains.

Several algorithms have been developed that each implement a unique strategy to create ensembles that consist of well-performing, but simultaneously, diverse member models. Only when models vary in their expertise, synergy will emerge, and the combined model can be expected to outperform the uncombined model. In an overview of models, it is argued that the best known algorithms combine several replications of the same unstable base algorithm, and pursue diversity through varying the training data. Possible strategies involve sampling, feature selection, sequential weighting, or rotation of feature

---

3   More details can be found via http://www.sas.com

4   See http://www.ibm.com/software/analytics/spss/products/modeler/

5   See http://www.salford-systems.com

6   Available at http://cran.r-project.org

7   See http://www.cs.waikato.ac.nz/ml/weka

8   See http://rapid-i.com/

spaces. Other configuration choices of interest are the base learner algorithms, and the rule applied to combine ensemble members' outputs.

Two special topics that were addressed are diversity and interpretability. First, diversity is a necessary condition to the aspiration of performance improvement over uncombined models. Intuitively, a tradeoff exists between member performance and diversity within the ensemble, while both have to be present for the ensemble to perform well. While this tradeoff is hard to quantify or prove, a hint can be given in so-called accuracy-diversity diagrams. Second, combining multiple interpretable models usually renders them increasingly complex to the extent where it becomes impossible to evaluate the relative importance of features in the model, and the nature of their relationship with the outcome. While rule extraction can provide a solution, other strategies that do not require the estimation of a meta-model are variables importance scores and partial dependence plots.

Ensemble learning is a promising field of research with great potential for database marketing. While its usage in business may still be scarce today, evolutions in terms of computational power, increasing software support, and the development of techniques to make these models more interpretable will contribute to their adoption. However, research on ensemble learning in database marketing has merely scratched the surface of its full potential. While this chapter focused on classification tasks, the philosophy of ensemble learning equally applies to regression and unsupervised learning. Moreover, ensemble learning has been successfully deployed to tackle class imbalance and cost-sensitive learning, both relevant in database marketing. Hence, future research is needed to address these promising opportunities. Finally, ensemble learning applications have been disproportionally focused on churn prediction. Future research should the potential of these methods in other disciplines.

References

Asuncion, A. and Newman, D. J. (2007). *UCI Machine Learning Repository*. Irvine, CA: University of California, School of Information and Computer Science.

Bauer, E. and Kohavi, R. (1999). An empirical comparison of voting classification algorithms: Bagging, boosting, and variants. *Machine Learning, 36*(1–2), 105–39.

Bose, I. and Chen, X. (2009). Quantitative models for direct marketing: A review from systems perspective. *European Journal of Operational Research, 195*(1), 1–16.

Breiman, L. (1996). Bagging predictors. *Machine Learning, 24*(2), 123–40.

Breiman, L. (2001). Random forests. *Machine Learning, 45*(1), 5–32.

Brown, G., Wyatt, J., Harris, R. and Yao, X. (2005). Diversity creation methods: A survey and categorisation. *Information Fusion, 6*(1), 5–20.

Brown, I. and Mues, C. (2012). An experimental comparison of classificaiton algorithms for imbalanced credit scoring data sets. *Expert Systems with Applications, 39*, 3446–53.

Bryll, R., Gutierrez-Osuna, R. and Quek, F. (2003). Attribute bagging: Improving accuracy of classifier ensembles by using random feature subsets. *Pattern Recognition, 36*(6), 1291–302.

Buckinx, W. and Van den Poel, D. (2005). Customer base analysis: Partial defection of behaviourally loyal clients in a non-contractual FMCG retail setting. *European Journal of Operational Research, 164*(1), 252–68.

Bühlmann, P. (2002). Bagging, subagging and bragging for improving some prediction algorithms. In *Recent Advances and Trends in NonParametric Statistics*, M.G. Akritas and D.N. Politis (Eds). Amsterdam: Elsevier.

Burez, J. and Van den Poel, D. (2007). CRM at a pay-TV company: Using analytical models to reduce customer attrition by targeted marketing for subscription services. *Expert Systems with Applications, 32*(2), 277–88.

Burez, J. and Van den Poel, D. (2008). Separating financial from commercial customer churn: A modeling step toward resolving the conflict between the sales and credit department. *Expert Systems with Applications, 35*(1–2), 497–514.

Burez, J. and Van den Poel, D. (2009). Handling class imbalance in customer churn prediction. *Expert Systems with Applications, 36*(3), 4626–36.

Coussement, K., Benoit, D.F. and Van den Poel, D. (2010). Improved marketing decision making in a customer churn prediction context using generalized additive models. *Expert Systems with Applications, 37*(3), 2132–43.

Coussement, K. and De Bock, K.W. (Forthcoming). Customer churn prediction in the online gambling industry: The beneficial effect of ensemble learning. *Journal of Business Research.*

Coussement, K. and Van den Poel, D. (2008). Churn prediction in subscription services: An application of support vector machines while comparing two parameter-selection techniques. *Expert Systems with Applications, 34*(1), 313–27.

Coussement, K. and Van den Poel, D. (2009). Improving customer attrition prediction by integrating emotions from client/company interaction emails and evaluating multiple classifiers. *Expert Systems with Applications, 36*(3), 6127–34.

Croux, C., Joossens, K. and Lemmens, A. (2007). Trimmed bagging. *Computational Statistics & Data Analysis, 52*(1), 362–8.

De Bock, K.W., Coussement, K. and Van den Poel, D. (2010). Ensemble classification based on generalized additive models. *Computational Statistics & Data Analysis, 54*(6), 1535–46.

De Bock, K.W. and Van den Poel, D. (2010). Ensembles of probability estimation trees for customer churn prediction. In N. García-Pedrajas, F. Herrera, C. Fyfe, J.M. Benítez and M. Ali (Eds), *23rd International Conference on Industrial Engineering and Other Applications of Applied Intelligent Systems (IEA/AIE 2010)* (Vol. 6097). Cordoba: Springer-Verlag.

De Bock, K.W. and Van den Poel, D. (2011). An empirical evaluation of rotation-based ensemble classifiers for customer churn prediction. *Expert Systems with Applications, 38*(10), 12293–301.

De Bock, K.W. and Van den Poel, D. (2012). Reconciling performance and interpretability in customer churn prediction modeling using ensemble learning based on generalized additive models. *Expert Systems with Applications, 39*(8), 6816–26.

Dietterich, T.G. (2000a). Ensemble methods in machine learning. In J. Kittler and F. Roli (Eds), *1st International Workshop on Multiple Classifier Systems (MCS 2001)* (Vol. 1857). Cagliari: Springer-Verlag.

Dietterich, T.G. (2000b). An experimental comparison of three methods for constructing ensembles of decision trees: Bagging, boosting, and randomization. *Machine Learning, 40*(2), 139–57.

Duin, R. and Tax, D. (2000). *Experiments with Classifier Combining Rules, in Workshop on Multiple Classifier Systems (MCS 2000)* (Vol. 1857). Berlin/Heidelberg: Springer.

Freund, Y. and Schapire, R.E. (1997) A decision-theoretic generalization of on-line learning and an application to boosting. *Journal of Computer and System Sciences, 55*(1), 119–39.

Friedman, J.H. (2001). Greedy function approximation: A gradient boosting machine. *Annals of Statistics, 29*(5), 1189–232.

Friedman, J.H. (2002). Stochastic gradient boosting. *Computational Statistics and Data Analysis, 38*(4), 367–78.

Friedman, J., Hastie, T. and Tibshirani, R. (2000). Additive logistic regression: A statistical view of boosting. *Annals of Statistics, 28*(2), 337–74.

Frieman, J.H. and Popescu, B.E. (2008). Predictive learning via rule ensembles. *Annals of Applied Statistics, 2*(3), 916–54.

Ganesh, J., Arnold, M.J. and Reynolds, K.E. (2000). Understanding the customer base of service providers: An examination of the differences between switchers and stayers. *Journal of Marketing, 64*(3), 65–87.

Glady, N., Baesens, B. and Croux, C. (2009). Modeling churn using customer lifetime value. *European Journal of Operational Research, 197*(1), 402–11.

Ha, K., Cho, S. and MacLachlan, D. (2005). Response models based on bagging neural networks. *Journal of Interactive Marketing, 19*(1), 17–30.

Hastie, T., Tibshirani, R. and Friedman, J. (2001). *The Elements of Statistical Learning: Data Mining, Inference and Prediction*. New York, NY: Springer-Verlag.

Ho, T.K. (1998). The random subspace method for constructing decision forests. *IEEE Transactions on Pattern Analysis and Machine Intelligence, 20*(8), 832–44.

Hu, X.H. (2005). A data mining approach for retailing bank customer attrition analysis. *Applied Intelligence, 22*(1), 47–60.

Huang, J. and Ling, C.X. (2005). Using AUC and accuracy in evaluating learning algorithms. *Ieee Transactions on Knowledge and Data Engineering, 17*(3), 299–310.

Kim, H.S. and Yoon, C.H. (2004). Determinants of subscriber churn and customer loyalty in the Korean mobile telephony market. *Telecommunications Policy, 28*(9–10), 751–65.

Kim, Y.S. (2006). Toward a successful CRM: Variable selection, sampling, and ensemble. *Decision Support Systems, 41*(2), 542–53.

Kuncheva, L.I. (2004). *Combining Pattern Classifiers: Methods and Algorithms*. Hoboken, NJ: John Wiley & Sons.

Kuncheva, L.I. and Rodríguez, J.J. (2007). An experimental study on rotation forest ensembles. In M. Haindl, J. Kittler and F. Roli (Eds), *7th International Workshop on Multiple Classifier Systems (MCS 2007)* (Vol. 4472). Prague: Springer-Verlag.

Kuncheva, L.I., Rodriguez, J. J., Plumpton, C.O., Linden, D.E.J. and Johnston, S.J. (2010). Random subspace ensembles for fMRI classification. *IEEE Transactions on Medical Imaging, 29*(2), 531–42.

Kuncheva, L.I. and Whitaker, C.J. (2003). Measures of diversity in classifier ensembles and their relationship with the ensemble accuracy. *Machine Learning, 51*(2), 181–207.

Lai, C., Reinders, M. and Wessels, L. (2006). Random subspace method for multivariate feature selection. *Pattern Recognition Letters 27*, 1067–76.

Larivière, B. and Van den Poel, D. (2005). Predicting customer retention and profitability by using random forests and regression forests techniques. *Expert Systems with Applications, 29*(2), 472–84.

Lemmens, A. and Croux, C. (2006). Bagging and boosting classification trees to predict churn. *Journal of Marketing Research, 43*(2), 276–86.

Margineantu, D.D. and Dietterich, T.G. (1997). Pruning adaptive boosting. In *Proceedings of the Fourteenth International Conference on Machine Learning*. Florida, FL: Morgan Kaufmann Publishers Inc.

Martens, D., Baesens, B., Van Gestel, T. and Vanthienen, J. (2007). Comprehensible credit scoring models using rule extraction from support vector machines. *European Journal of Operational Research, 183*(3), 1466–76.

Masand, B., Datta, P., Mani, D.R. and Li, B. (1999). CHAMP: A prototype for automated cellular churn prediction. *Data Mining and Knowledge Discovery, 3*(2), 219–25.

Maudes, J., Rodriguez, J.J. and Garcia-Osorio, C. (2009). Disturbing neighbors ensembles for linear SVM. In J.A. Benediktsson, J. Kittler and F. Roli (Eds), *Multiple Classifier Systems, Proceedings* (Vol. 5519).

Maudes, J., Rodríguez, J.J., García-Osorio, C. and García-Pedrajas, N. (2012). Random feature weights for decision tree ensemble construction. *Information Fusion, 13*(1), 20–30.

Merler, S., Caprile, B. and Furlanello, C. (2007). Parallelizing AdaBoost by weights dynamics. *Computational Statistics & Data Analysis, 51*(5), 2487–98.

Mozer, M.C., Wolniewicz, R., Grimes, D.B., Johnson, E. and Kaushansky, H. (2000). Predicting subscriber dissatisfaction and improving retention in the wireless telecommunications industry. *IEEE Transactions on Neural Networks, 11*(3), 690–96.

Neslin, S.A., Gupta, S., Kamakura, W., Lu, J.X. and Mason, C.H. (2006). Defection detection: Measuring and understanding the predictive accuracy of customer churn models. *Journal of Marketing Research, 43*(2), 204–11.

Prinzie, A. and Van den Poel, D. (2008). Random forests for multiclass classification: Random MultiNomial Logit. *Expert Systems with Applications, 34*(3), 1721–32.

Qi, J.Y., Zhang, L., Liu, Y.P., Li, L., Zhou, Y.P., Shen, Y., Liang, L. and Li, H.Z. (2009). ADTreesLogit model for customer churn prediction. *Annals of Operations Research, 168*(1), 247–65.

Risselada, H., Verhoef, P.C. and Bijmolt, T.H.A. (2010). Staying power of churn prediction models. *Journal of Interactive Marketing, 24*(3), 198–208.

Rodríguez, J.J., Kuncheva, L.I. and Alonso, C.J. (2006). Rotation forest: A new classifier ensemble method. *IEEE Transactions on Pattern Analysis and Machine Intelligence, 28*(10), 1619–30.

Rokach, L. (2009). Collective-agreement-based pruning of ensembles. *Computational Statistics & Data Analysis, 53*(4), 1015–26.

Schwenk, H. and Bengio, Y. (2000). Boosting neural networks. *Neural Computation, 12*(8), 1869–87.

Setiono, R., Baesens, B. and Mues, C. (2009). A note on knowledge discovery using neural networks and its application to credit card screening. *European Journal of Operational Research, 192*(1), 326–32.

Shaw, M.J., Subramaniam, C., Tan, G.W. and Welge, M.E. (2001). Knowledge management and data mining for marketing. *Decision Support Systems, 31*(1), 127–37.

Skurichina, M. and Duin, R.P.W. (2002). Bagging, boosting and the random subspace method for linear classifiers. *Pattern Analysis & Applications 5*, 121–35.

Smith, K.A., Willis, R.J. and Brooks, M. (2000). An analysis of customer retention and insurance claim patterns using data mining: A case study. *Journal of the Operational Research Society, 51*(5), 532–41.

Strobl, C., Boulesteix, A., Kneib, T., Augustin, T. and Zeileis, A. (2008). Conditional variable importance for random forests. *BMC Bioinformatics, 9*(1), 307.

Strobl, C., Boulesteix, A.L., Zeileis, A. and Hothorn, T. (2007). Bias in random forest variable importance measures: Illustrations, sources and a solution. *Bmc Bioinformatics, 8*(25).

Tan, K.C., Yu, Q., Heng, C.M. and Lee, T.H. (2003). Evolutionary computing for knowledge discovery in medical diagnosis. *Artificial Intelligence in Medicine, 27*(2), 129–54.

van Wezel, M. and Potharst, R. (2007). Improved customer choice predictions using ensemble methods. *European Journal of Operational Research, 181*(1), 436–52.

Webb, G.I. (2000). MultiBoosting: A technique for combining boosting and wagging. *Machine Learning, 40*(2), 159–96.

Wu, X. and Kumar, V. (2009). *The Top Ten Algorithms in Data Mining.* Boca Raton, FL: Chapman & Hall/CRC.

Xie, Y.Y., Li, X., Ngai, E.W.T. and Ying, W.Y. (2009). Customer churn prediction using improved balanced random forests. *Expert Systems with Applications, 36*(3), 5445–9.

Zhang, C.X. and Zhang, J.S. (2008), RotBoost: A technique for combining Rotation Forest and AdaBoost. *Pattern Recognition Letters, 29*(10), 1524–36.

6 *Advanced Rule-based Learning: Active Learning, Rule Extraction, and Incorporating Domain Knowledge*

THOMAS VERBRAKEN, VÉRONIQUE VAN VLASSELAER,
WOUTER VERBEKE, DAVID MARTENS, AND BART BAESENS

1 Introduction

Different data mining tasks, such as regression, classification, association rule mining, and clustering, are widely discussed in the literature. The task of interest in this chapter is classification. We will focus on the state-of-the-art in rule-based learning. From a user perspective, a classification model should be comprehensible and justifiable (that is, intuitively correct and in accordance with domain knowledge), and provide correct predictions (Martens et al., 2011). The last requirement is that the model generalizes well, in the sense that it provides correct predictions on new, unseen data instances. This generalization behavior is typically measured by the percentage of correctly classified test instances (PCC). Other commonly used measures include sensitivity and specificity, the receiver operating curve (ROC), and the area under the ROC curve (AUC).

Comprehensibility is often a key requirement, demanding that the user is able to understand the logic behind a prediction of the model. In some domains a lack of comprehensibility is a major issue, and causes a reluctance to use the classifier or even a complete rejection of the model. Moreover, legal incentives with regards to discrimination or privacy issues may exist that require models to be comprehensible. Furthermore, comprehensibility is required to check whether a model is in line with current domain knowledge, that is, whether it is justifiable. For instance, a prediction model which estimates a customer who has made several complaints with the customer service to have a lower churn probability than an identical customer who did not complain, is counter-intuitive and thus unacceptable for implementation. Note that when justifiability is required, comprehensibility will be needed as well. Only when a classification model satisfies all three performance requirements, – accuracy or predictive power, comprehensibility, and justifiability – it is acceptable for implementation. Thus, there is clearly a need for comprehensible white box models, as opposed to black-box models which are often used. On the other hand, also predictive performance, which tends to be higher for black-box models, is crucial, and as such typically a tradeoff exists.

In this chapter, rule extraction is discussed, a technique which supplements the superior predictive performance of black-box models with a set of comprehensible rules. These methods effectively open up the black-box and provide insight in the working of a black-box model. The remainder of this chapter is structured as follows: in the next section we will discuss the basic concepts related to rule extraction. Sections 3 and 4 give an overview of rule extraction algorithms for neural networks and support vector machines respectively. In section 5, the so-called pedagogical rule extraction algorithms, which can be combined with any type of black-box model, are outlined. Finally, Section 6 provides a convenient way to visualize rule sets whereas in Section 7 the concept of rule extraction is demonstrated on a real-life case study.

2   Rule Extraction

Comprehensibility can be added to black-box models by extracting symbolic rules from the trained model. Rule extraction techniques attempt to open up the black-box and generate symbolic, comprehensible descriptions with approximately the same predictive power as the model itself. An advantage of using an incomprehensible black-box model as a starting point for rule extraction, such as a support vector machine (SVM) or a neural network, is that they are capable of modeling more complex relations.

Andrews et al. (1995) proposed a classification scheme for neural network rule extraction techniques that can easily be extended to SVMs (Martens et al., 2007), and which is based on the following criteria:

1. translucency of the extraction algorithm with respect to the underlying black-box model;
2. expressive power of the extracted rules or trees;
3. specialized training regime of the neural network;
4. quality of the extracted rules;
5. algorithmic complexity of the extraction algorithm.

In this chapter, we will focus mainly on two dimensions when discussing the rule extraction algorithms: the translucency of the rule extraction algorithm and the expressive power of the extracted rules. The translucency criterion considers the technique's perception of the black-box model. A *decompositional* approach is closely intertwined with the internal workings of a black-box model. On the other hand, a *pedagogical* algorithm considers the trained model as a black-box. Instead of looking at the internal structure, these algorithms directly extract rules which relate the inputs and outputs of the model. These techniques typically use the trained model as an oracle to label or classify (artificially generated) training examples which are then used by a symbolic learning algorithm. The idea behind these techniques is the assumption that the trained model can better represent the data than the original dataset. That is, the data is cleaner and free of apparent conflicts. Since the model is viewed as a black-box, most pedagogical algorithms lend themselves very easily to rule extraction from other machine learning algorithms. The difference between

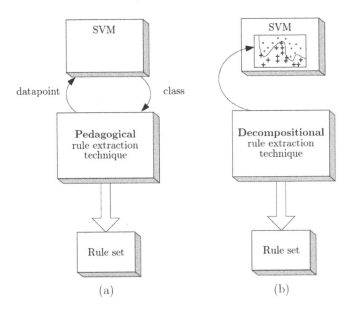

Figure 6.1   Pedagogical (a) and decompositional (b) rule extraction techniques

decompositional and pedagogical rule extraction techniques is schematically illustrated in Figure 6.1.

The expressive power of the extracted rules depends on the language used to express the rules. Many types of rules have been suggested in the literature, of which propositional rules, M-of-N rules, and fuzzy rules are the most relevant. *Propositional if-then* rules are simple implications of the form: If $X = a$ and $Y = b$, then class = 1. *M-of-N rules* (If at least M-of-N conditions (C1,C2,...,CN) Then ...) can be used to represent complex classification concepts. Although they come at a decreased comprehensibility, the antecedent will always be either true or false, which is not the case with fuzzy rules. An example of a *fuzzy classification rule* is: If X is low and Y is medium, then class = 1, whereby low and medium are fuzzy sets with corresponding membership functions. They allow for more flexibility and are usually expressed in terms of linguistic concepts which are easier to interpret for humans. Nevertheless, human interpretation depends from person to person and is hard to objectify.

In general, five criteria are used to evaluate the rule extraction algorithms: comprehensibility, fidelity, accuracy, scalability, and generality. *Comprehensibility* is the extent to which the extracted rules are humanly comprehensible. The *fidelity* criterion indicates the extent to which the extracted rules model the black-box from which they were extracted, and is measured by the percentage of test points where the classifier and the extracted rules agree on the class label. The ability to make accurate predictions on previously unseen cases is called the *accuracy*. The *scalability* specifies the ability of the model to handle large input spaces and large number of data. Finally, the *generality* is the extent to which the method requires special training regimes or restrictions on the model architecture.

3   Decompositional Rule Extraction from Artificial Neural Networks

This section will discuss how rules can be extracted from a commonly used black-box model with strong predictive power, artificial neural networks. Firstly, we will discuss how neural networks work which reveals their complexity and incomprehensibility, after which two decompositional techniques for rule extraction from neural networks will be explained: Neurorule and Nefclass.

3.1   NEURAL NETWORKS

Neural networks are mathematical representations inspired by the functioning of the human brain. Many types of neural networks have been suggested in the literature for both supervised and unsupervised learning (Bishop, 1995). Because our focus is on classification, the Multilayer Perceptron (MLP) neural network will be discussed in more detail. An MLP is typically composed of an input layer, one or more hidden layers, and an output layer, each consisting of several neurons. Each neuron processes its inputs and generates one output value which is transmitted to the neurons in the subsequent layer. One of the key characteristics of MLPs is that all neurons and layers are arranged in a feedforward manner and no feedback connections are allowed. Figure 6.2 provides an example of an MLP with one hidden layer and two output neurons for a binary classification problem. The output of hidden neuron i is computed by processing the weighted inputs and its bias term $b_j^{(1)}$ as follows:

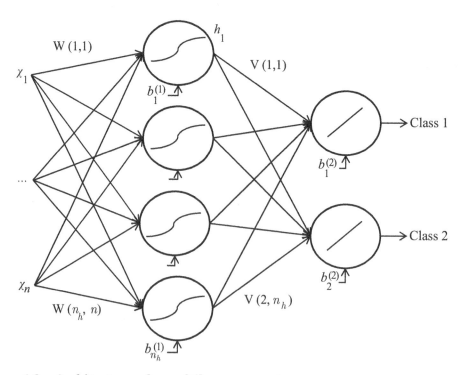

Figure 6.2   Architecture of a multilayer perceptron

$$h_i = f^{(1)}\left[b_j^{(1)} + \sum_{j=1}^{n} W(i,j)x_j\right] \tag{1}$$

W is a weight matrix, whereby $W(i,j)$ denotes the weight connecting input j to hidden unit i. In an analogous way, the output of the output neurons is computed:

$$z_i = f^{(2)}\left(b_j^{(1)} + \sum_{j=1}^{n_h} V(i,j)h_j\right) \tag{2}$$

with n_h the number of hidden neurons and V a weight matrix, whereby $V(i,j)$ denotes the weight connecting hidden unit j to output unit i. The bias inputs play a role analogous to that of the intercept term in a classical linear regression model. The class is then assigned according to the output neuron with the highest activation value (winner take all learning). The transfer functions $f^{(1)}$ and $f^{(2)}$ allow the network to model non-linear relationships in the data. Examples of transfer functions that are commonly used are the sigmoid:

$$f(x) = \frac{1}{1+\exp(-x)} \tag{3}$$

the hyperbolic tangent:

$$f(x) = \frac{\exp(x) - \exp(-x)}{\exp(x) + \exp(-x)} \tag{4}$$

and the linear transfer function $f(x)=x$.

The weights $\mathbf{W}$ and $\mathbf{V}$ are the crucial parameters of a neural network and need to be estimated during a training process which is usually based on gradient-descent learning to minimize some kind of error function over a set of training observations (Bishop, 1995). Note that multiple hidden layers may be used, but theoretical works have shown that one hidden layer is sufficient to approximate any continuous function to any desired degree of accuracy (universal approximation property) (Bishop, 1995).

As universal approximators, neural networks can achieve significantly better predictive accuracy compared to models that are linear in the input variables. However, their complex mathematical internal workings prevent them from being used as effective management tools in real-life situations where, besides having accurate predictions, explanation of the predictions being made is essential. In the literature, the problem of explaining the neural network predictions has been tackled by techniques that extract symbolic rules from the trained networks. These neural network rule extraction techniques attempt to open up the neural network black-box and generate symbolic rules with (approximately) the same predictive power as the neural network itself. An advantage of using neural network rule extraction methods is that the neural network considers the contribution of the inputs toward classification as a group, while decision-tree algorithms like C4.5 measure the individual contribution of the inputs one at a time as the tree is grown.

In the following subsections we will discuss Neurorule and Nefclass, which both are decompositional algorithms for rule extraction from neural networks.

3.2 NEURORULE

Neurorule is a decompositional algorithm which extracts propositional rules from trained three-layered feedforward neural networks (Setiono and Liu, Symbolic representation of neural networks, 1996). It consists of the following steps:

1. Train a neural network to meet the pre-specified accuracy requirement.
2. Remove the redundant connections in the network by pruning while maintaining its accuracy.
3. Discretize the hidden unit activation values of the pruned network by clustering.
4. Extract rules that describe the network outputs in terms of the discretized hidden unit activation values.
5. Generate rules that describe the discretized hidden unit activation values in terms of the network inputs.
6. Merge the two sets of rules generated in Steps 4 and 5 to obtain a set of rules that relates the inputs and outputs of the network.

Neurorule assumes the data are discretized and represented as binary inputs using the thermometer encoding for ordinal variables and dummy-encoding for nominal variables (Setiono and Liu, Symbolic representation of neural networks, 1996). Table 6.1 illustrates thermometer encoding for a continuous variable, for example the average monthly bill (AMB) of a telecom customer.

The continuous variable AMB is first discretized into four bins, which can be done by a discretization algorithm (for example the algorithm of Fayyad and Irani (Multi-interval discretization of continuous-valued attributes for classification learning, 1993)) or according to the recommendation from a domain expert. The four values are then represented by three thermometer inputs I_1, I_2, and I_3. If I_3 is equal to 1, this corresponds to categorical monthly bill being larger than 2, or the original monthly bill being larger than 10 euro. This encoding scheme facilitates the generation and interpretation of the propositional if-then rules. Furthermore, Neurorule assumes the nominal variables are represented by dummies. For example, when a nominal variable has three values, it is encoded with two binary dummy variables.

Neurorule typically starts from a one-hidden-layer neural network with hyperbolic tangent hidden neurons and linear output neurons. For a classification problem with C classes, C output neurons are used and the class is assigned to the output neuron with the highest activation value (*winner-take-all learning*). The network is then trained to minimize

Table 6.1   The thermometer encoding procedure for ordinal variables

	Categorical Input	Thermometer Input		
		I_1	I_2	I_3
AMB ≤ 10 euro	1	0	0	0
AMB > 10 euro and AMB ≤ 39 euro	2	0	0	1
AMB > 39 euro and AMB ≤ 122 euro	3	0	1	1
AMB > 122 euro	4	1	1	1

a regularized cross-entropy error function using the Broyden-Fletcher-Goldfarb-Shanno (BFGS) method, which is a modified quasi-Newton algorithm (Setiono, A neural network construction algorithm which maximizes the likelihood function, 1995).

Determining the optimal number of hidden neurons is not a trivial task. Neurorule starts from an oversized network and then gradually removes the irrelevant connections. This pruning step is achieved by applying an iterative algorithm in which weights of irrelevant inputs converge gradually to zero (Setiono, A penalty function approach for pruning feedforward neural networks, 1997). When all connections to a hidden neuron have been pruned, this neuron can be removed from the network. A connection with sufficiently small weight can be pruned from the network without affecting the network's classification accuracy. Once a trained and pruned network has been obtained, the activation values of all hidden neurons are clustered to simplify the rule extraction process. In the case of hyperbolic tangent hidden neurons, the activation values lie in the interval [–1,1]. A simple greedy clustering algorithm then starts by sorting all the hidden activation values in increasing order (Setiono, Thong, and Yap, Symbolic rule extraction from neural networks: An application to identifying organizations adopting IT, 1998). Adjacent values are merged into a unique discretized value as long as the class labels of the corresponding observations do not conflict. The merging process hereby first considers the pair of hidden activation values with the shortest distance in between. Another discretization algorithm that can be used is the Chi2 algorithm, which is an improved and automated version of the ChiMerge algorithm and makes use of the ς^2 test statistic to merge the hidden activation values (Setiono and Liu, Symbolic representation of neural networks, 1996).

In Step 4 of Neurorule, a new data set is composed consisting of the discretized hidden unit activation values and the class labels of the corresponding observations. Duplicate observations are removed and rules are inferred relating the class labels to the clustered hidden unit activation values. This can be done using an automated rule-induction algorithm such as X2R (Liu and Tan, 1995) or manually when the pruned network has only a few unique discretized hidden unit activation values. Note that Steps 3 and 4 can be performed simultaneously by C4.5 (rules), because C4.5 (rules) can work with both discretized and continuous data (Quinlan, 1993). In the last two steps of Neurorule, the rules of Step 4 are translated in terms of the original inputs. First, the rules are generated describing the discretized hidden unit activation values in terms of the original inputs. To this end, one might again use an automated rule-induction algorithm (for example, X2R, C4.5). This rule set is then merged with that of Step 4 by replacing the conditions of the latter with those of the former.

3.3 NEFCLASS

The category of neural network fuzzy-rule extraction techniques is often referred to as neurofuzzy systems. Basically, these systems encompass methods that use learning algorithms from neural networks to tune the parameters of a fuzzy system. In this section, we will further elaborate on Nefclass, which is a well-known neurofuzzy system (Nauck, 2000).

Nefclass has the architecture of a three-layer fuzzy perceptron, whereby the first layer consists of input neurons, the second layer of hidden neurons, and the third layer of output neurons. The difference with a classical multilayer perceptron is that the weights

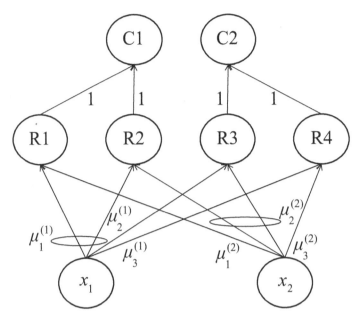

Figure 6.3   Example of Nefclass network

now represent fuzzy sets and that the activation functions are now fuzzy set operators. The hidden-layer neurons represent the fuzzy rules and the output-layer neurons the different classes of the classification problem with 1 output neuron per class. Figure 6.3 depicts an example of a Nefclass network. The fuzzy rule corresponding to rule unit R_1 is expressed as follows:

$$\text{If } x_1 \text{ is } \mu_1^{(1)} \text{ and } x_2 \text{ is } \mu_1^{(2)} \text{ then } Class = C_1,$$

whereby $\mu_1^{(1)}$ and $\mu_1^{(2)}$ represent the fuzzy sets defined for x_1 and x_2. Nefclass enforces all connections representing the same linguistic label (for example, x_1 is small) to have the same fuzzy set associated with them. For example, in Figure 6.3 the fuzzy set $\mu_1^{(1)}$ is shared by the rule units R_1 and R_2, and thus has the same definition in both fuzzy rules.

Nefclass allows the user to model a priori domain knowledge before starting to learn the various parameters, or the classifier can also be created from scratch. In both cases, the user must start by specifying the fuzzy sets and membership function types for all inputs, which can be trapezoidal, triangular, Gaussian, or List.

Nefclass starts by determining the appropriate number of rule units in the hidden layer. Suppose we have a data set D of N data points $\{(x_i, y_i)\}_{i=1}^{N}$, with input data $\mathbf{x}_i \in \mathbb{R}^n$ and target vectors $y_i \in \{0,1\}^m$ for an m-class classification problem. For each input x_i, q_i fuzzy sets $\mu_1^{(i)}, \ldots, \mu_{q_i}^{(i)}$ are defined. The rule-learning algorithm then proceeds as follows.

1. Select the next pattern (x_j, y_j) from D.
2. For each input unit x_i, $i = 1, \ldots, n$, find the membership function $\mu_{l_i}^{(i)}$ such that

$$\mu_{l_i}^{(i)}(x_i) = \max_{l \in \{1,\ldots,q_i\}} \left\{ \mu_l^{(i)}(x_i) \right\} \tag{5}$$

3. If there is no rule node R with

$$W\left(x_1, R\right) = \mu_{l_1}^{(1)}, \ldots, W\left(x_n, R\right) = \mu_{l_n}^{(n)} \tag{6}$$

with $W(x_p, R)$ the fuzzy weight between input x_i and rule node R, then create such a node and connect it to output class node p if $y_j(p) = 1$.
4. Go to Step 1 until all patterns in D have been processed.

Obviously, the above procedure will result in a large number of hidden neurons and fuzzy rules. This can be remedied by specifying a maximum number of hidden neurons and keeping only the first k rule units (simple rule learning). Alternatively, one could also keep the best k rules (*best rule learning*) or the best k/m rules for each class (*best per class rule learning*).

Once the number of hidden units has been determined, the fuzzy sets between the input and hidden layer are tuned to improve the classification accuracy of the network. Hereto, Nefclass employs a fuzzy variant of the well-known backpropagation algorithm to tune the characteristic parameters of the membership functions (Nauck, 2000). Nefclass also offers the possibility of pruning the rule base by removing rules and variables based on a simple greedy algorithm. The goal of this pruning is to improve the comprehensibility of the created classifier (see (Nauck, 2000) for more details).

4 Decompositional Rule Extraction from Support Vector Machines

Due to their ability to model non-linearities, support vector machines (SVM) (Vapnik, 1995) are a widely used classification technique. Generally speaking, SVMs exhibit very good predictive performance. However, their strength is also their main weakness, as the generated non-linear models are typically regarded as incomprehensible black-box models. This opaqueness can be remedied through the use of rule extraction techniques, which induce rules that mimic the black-box SVM model as closely as possible. Through rule extraction, some insight is provided into the logics of the SVM model (Martens et al., 2007). This explanation capability is of crucial importance in any domain where the model needs to be validated before being implemented. This section first discusses the theory of SVMs, and then two decompositional algorithms for rule extraction are outlined.

4.1 SUPPORT VECTOR MACHINES

Given a training set of N data points $\{(x_i, y_i)\}_{i=1}^{N}$, with input data $x_i \in \mathbb{R}^n$ and corresponding binary class labels $y_i \in \{-1, +1\}$, the SVM classifier, according to Vapnik's original formulation satisfies the following conditions (Cristianini and Shawe-Taylor, 2000; Vapnik, 1995):

$$\begin{cases} w^T \varphi\left(x_i\right) + b \geq +1, \text{ if } y_i = +1 \\ w^T \varphi\left(x_i\right) + b \leq -1, \text{ if } y_i = -1 \end{cases} \tag{7}$$

which is equivalent to:

$$y_i[\boldsymbol{w}^T \boldsymbol{\varphi}(\boldsymbol{x}_i) + b] \ge 1, \qquad i = 1, \ldots, N.$$

The non-linear function $\boldsymbol{\varphi}(.)$ maps the input space to a high (possibly infinite) dimensional feature space. In this feature space, the above inequalities basically construct a hyperplane $\boldsymbol{w}^T \boldsymbol{\varphi}(\boldsymbol{x}) + b = 0$ discriminating between both classes.

In primal weight space the classifier then takes the form:

$$y(\boldsymbol{x}) = \text{sign}[\boldsymbol{w}^T \boldsymbol{\varphi}(\boldsymbol{x}) + b] \tag{8}$$

but, on the other hand, is never evaluated in this form. One defines the convex optimization problem:

$$\min_{w,b,\xi} J(\boldsymbol{w}, b, \xi) = \frac{1}{2} w^T w + C \sum_{i=1}^{N} \xi_i \tag{9}$$

subject to:

$$\begin{cases} y_i[\boldsymbol{w}^T \boldsymbol{\varphi}(\boldsymbol{x}_i) + b] \ge 1 - \xi_i & i = 1, \ldots, N \\ \xi_i \ge 0, & i = 1, \ldots, N \end{cases} \tag{10}$$

The variables ξ_i are slack variables which are needed in order to allow misclassifications in the set of inequalities (for example due to overlapping distributions). The first part of the objective function tries to maximize the margin between both classes in the feature space, whereas the second part minimizes the misclassification error. The positive real constant C should be considered as a tuning parameter in the algorithm.

The Lagrangian to the constrained optimization problem is given by:

$$L(w, b, \xi; \alpha, v) = J(\boldsymbol{w}, b, \xi) - \sum_{i=1}^{N} \alpha_i \{y_i[\boldsymbol{w}^T \boldsymbol{\varphi}(\boldsymbol{x}_i) + b] - 1 + \xi_i\} - \sum_{i=1}^{N} v_i \xi_i \tag{11}$$

The solution to the optimization problem is given by the saddle point of the Lagrangian, that is, by minimizing $L(w,b,\xi; \alpha,v)$ with respect to w,b,ξ and maximizing it with respect to α and v. This leads to the following classifier:

$$y(\boldsymbol{x}) = \text{sign}[\sum_{i=1}^{N} \alpha_i y_i K(\boldsymbol{x}_i, \boldsymbol{x}) + b] \tag{12}$$

whereby $K(\boldsymbol{x}_i, \boldsymbol{x}) = \boldsymbol{\varphi}(\boldsymbol{x}_i)^T \boldsymbol{\varphi}(\boldsymbol{x})$ is taken with a positive definite kernel satisfying the Mercer theorem. The Lagrange multipliers α_i are then determined by means of the following optimization problem (dual problem):

$$\max_{\alpha_i} -\frac{1}{2} \sum_{i,j=1}^{N} y_i y_j K(\boldsymbol{x}_i, \boldsymbol{x}_j) \alpha_i \alpha_j + \sum_{i=1}^{N} \alpha_i \tag{13}$$

Subject to:

$$\sum_{i=1}^{N} a_i y_i = 0$$

$$0 \le a_i \le C \qquad i = 1, \ldots, N. \tag{14}$$

The entire classifier construction problem now simplifies to a convex quadratic programming (QP) problem in α_i. Note that one does not have to calculate w nor $\varphi(x_i)$ in order to determine the decision surface. Thus, no explicit construction of the non-linear mapping $\varphi(x_i)$ is needed. Instead, the kernel function K will be used. For the kernel function $K(.,.)$ one typically has the following choices:

$$K(x_i,x) = x_i^T x \qquad \text{(linear kernel)}$$

$$K(x_i,x) = \left(1 + \frac{x_i^T x}{c}\right)^d \qquad \text{(polynomial kernel of degree } d)$$

$$(15)$$

$$K(x_i,x) = \exp\{-\frac{x - x_{i2}^2}{\sigma^2}\} \qquad \text{(RBF kernel)}$$

$$K(x_i,x) = \tanh(\kappa x_i^T x + \theta) \qquad \text{(MLP kernel)}$$

where d, c, σ, κ, and θ are constants.

Typically, many of the α_i will be equal to zero (sparseness property). The training observations corresponding to non-zero α_i are called support vectors and are located close to the decision boundary. The previous equations illustrate that the SVM classifier is a complex, non-linear function. Trying to comprehend the logics behind the classifications that are made is quite difficult, if not impossible. In what follows, two decompositional algorithms for rule extraction from SVMs will be discussed.

4.2 SVM+ PROTOTYPE

A first decompositional method for extracting rules from SVMs has been introduced by Núñez et al. (2002) and creates rule-defining regions based on prototype and support vectors. Prototype vectors are generated using clustering and are the representatives of the obtained clusters. Núñez et al. use vector quantization for the clustering task. Two types of rules can be generated: equation rules and interval rules, respectively corresponding to an ellipsoid and interval region, which can be built in the following manner. Using the prototype vector as center, an ellipsoid is built where the axes are determined by the support vector within the partition that lies the furthest from the center. The straight line connecting these two vectors defines the long axes of the ellipsoid. Simple geometrics allow for the other axes to be determined. The interval regions are defined from ellipsoids parallel to the coordinate axes.

An incremental approach is followed where first a single prototype and associated ellipsoid is generated. A following partition test determines whether the region is transformed into a rule (negative test) or whether new regions will be created (positive partition test). This process is continued until there are no regions with positive partition test or when a predefined number of iterations has passed. The partitioning test tries to keep the number of overlapping regions with different classes as low as possible. The partitioning test will succeed when either the generated prototype belongs to another class, when one of the vertices belongs to another class, or when a support vector with different class exists within the region. This approach may be intuitive and have good accuracy on small datasets, but it does not scale well: with a high number of patterns come just as many rules resulting in low comprehensibility. Also, the clustering will be negatively impacted by overlapping dependent variables.

4.3   FUNG ET AL.

Fung et al. extract non-overlapping rules by constructing hypercubes with axis-parallel surfaces (2005). This approach is similar to the one discussed previously, but requires no computationally expensive clustering. Instead, the algorithm transforms the problem to a simpler, equivalent variant and constructs the hypercubes by solving linear programs in $2n$ variables with n being the feature space dimension, reducing the required run time to a time order of less than a second. Each extracted rule represents a hypercube in the n-dimensional space with edges parallel to the axis. Each hypercube corresponding to an extracted rule has one vertex that lies on the hyperplane, which simplifies the problem and allows generating disjoint rules. Given a region I of equal class label, Fung et al. show the optimal rule can be defined in different ways. The first one is by maximizing the volume of the axis-parallel hypercube, and the second one is by maximizing the point coverage. Using the Volume Maximization Criteria rules are generated corresponding to hypercubes with maximal volume. For the Point Coverage Criteria, the cardinality of the generated hypercube is maximized.

5   Pedagogical Rule Extraction Algorithms

This section discusses pedagogical rule extraction algorithms which can be applied to any black-box model. The reason is that a pedagogical algorithm considers the black-box model as an oracle which it uses to label training instances. In what follows, three pedagogical rule extraction algorithms will be discussed: C4.5, Trepan, and G-REX.

5.1   C4.5

A first pedagogical rule extraction technique is based on the popular C4.5 algorithm (Quinlan, 1993). C4.5 induces decision trees based on information-theoretic concepts. Let p_1 (p_0) be the proportion of examples of class 1(0) in sample S. The entropy of S is then calculated as follows:

$$\text{Entropy}(S) = -p_1 \log_2(p_1) - p_0 \log_2(p_0) \tag{16}$$

whereby $p_0 = 1 - p_1$. Entropy is used to measure how informative an attribute is in splitting the data. Basically, the entropy measures the order (or disorder) in the data with respect to the classes. It equals 1 when $p_1 = p_0 = 0.5$ (maximal disorder, minimal order) and 0 (maximal order, minimal disorder) when p_1 or $p_0 = 0$. In the latter case, all observations belong to the same class. $\text{Gain}(S, x_j)$ is defined as the expected reduction in entropy due to sorting (splitting) on attribute x_j:

$$\text{Gain}(S, x_j) = \text{Entropy}(S) - \sum_{v \in \text{values}(x_j)} \frac{|S_v|}{|S|} \text{Entropy}(S_v) \tag{17}$$

where values (x_j) represents the set of all possible values of attribute x_j, S_v the subset of S where attribute x_j has value v, and $|S_v|$ the number of observations in S_v. The Gain criterion was used in ID3, the forerunner of C4.5, to decide upon which attribute to split at a given node (Quinlan, 1986). However, when this criterion is used to decide upon the node splits, the algorithm favors splits on attributes with many distinct values. In order to rectify this, C4.5 applies a normalization and uses the gain ratio criterion which is defined as follows:

$$\text{Gainratio}\left(S, x_j\right) = \frac{\text{Gain}\left(S, x_j\right)}{\text{SplitInformation}\left(S, x_j\right)} \tag{18}$$

with

$$\text{SplitInformation}\left(S, x_j\right) = - \sum_{k \in \text{values}(x_j)} \frac{|S_k|}{|S|} \log_2 \frac{|S_k|}{|S|} \tag{19}$$

The tree induction algorithm is applied to the data where the output has been changed to the SVM predicted value, so that the tree approximates the SVM. This approach has been used in (Barakat and Diederich, 2004) to extract rules from SVMs. A problem that arises however is that the deeper a tree is expanded, the less data points are available to use to decide upon the splits. The next technique we will discuss tries to overcome this issue.

5.2 TREPAN

Trepan was introduced in Craven and Shavlik (Extracting tree-structured representations of trained networks, 1996). It is a pedagogical algorithm which extracts decision trees from trained neural networks with arbitrary architecture by using a symbolic learning algorithm as explained before. Like in most decision-tree algorithms (Quinlan, 1993), Trepan grows a tree by recursive partitioning. At each step, a queue of leaves is further expanded into subtrees until a stopping criterion is met. A crucial difference with decision-tree-induction algorithms is that the latter have only a limited set of training observations available. Hence, these algorithms typically suffer from having fewer and fewer training observations available for deciding upon the splits or leaf node class labels at lower levels of the tree. On the other hand, the primary goal of neural network rule extraction is to mimic the behavior of the trained neural network. Hence, instead of using the original training observations, Trepan first re-labels them according to the classifications made by the network. The re-labeled training data set is then used to initiate the tree-growing process. Furthermore, Trepan can also enrich the training data with additional training instances which are then also labeled (classified) by the neural network itself. The network is thus used as an oracle to answer class membership queries about artificially generated data points. This way, it can be assured that each node split or leaf node class decision is based upon at least S_{min} data points where S_{min} is a user-defined parameter. In other words, if a node has only m training data points available and $m < S_{min}$, then $S_{min} - m$ data points are additionally generated and labeled by the network.

Generating these additional data points is by no means a trivial task. First of all, care should be taken that the generated data instances satisfy all constraints (conditions) that lie from the root of the tree to the node under consideration. Given these constraints, one approach might be to sample the data instances uniformly. However, a better alternative would be to take into account the distribution of the data. This is the approach followed by Trepan. More specifically, at each node of the tree, Trepan estimates the marginal distribution of each input. For a discrete valued input, Trepan simply uses the empirical frequencies of the various values, whereas for a continuous input a kernel density estimation method is used.

Trepan allows splits with *at least* M-of-N type of tests. Note that the test *at least* 2 of $\{C_1, C_2, C_3\}$ is logically equivalent to: (*C*1 *and C*2) *or* (*C*1 *and C*3) *or* (*C*2 *and C*3). These M-of-N splits are constructed by using a heuristic search procedure. First, the best binary split is selected according to the information-gain criterion (Quinlan, 1993). The best binary test then serves as a seed for the M-of-N search process, which uses the following operators:

- M-of-N+1: Add a new condition to the set; for example, 2 of $\{C1, C2\}$ becomes 2 of $\{C1, C2, C3\}$.
- M+1-of-N+1: Add a new condition to the set and augment the threshold; for example, 2 of $\{C1, C2, C3\}$ becomes 3 of $\{C1, C2, C3, C4\}$.

The heuristic search procedure uses a beam-search method with a beam width of two, meaning that at each point the best two splits are retained for further examination. Again, the information-gain criterion is used to evaluate the splits. Finally, once an M-of-N test has been constructed, Trepan tries to simplify it and investigates if conditions can be dropped and/or M can be reduced without significantly degrading the information gain.

Trepan uses one local and one global criterion to decide when to stop growing the tree. For the local stopping criterion, Trepan constructs a confidence interval around p_c, which is the proportion of instances belonging to the most common class at the node under consideration. The node becomes a leaf when $Pr\left(p_c < 1 - \epsilon\right) < \alpha$, whereby α is the significance level and ϵ specifies how tight the confidence interval around p_c must be. Both values are set to 0.01 by default. The global criterion specifies a maximum on the number of internal nodes of the tree and can be specified in advance by the user. Trees with a small number of internal nodes are more comprehensible than large trees.

5.3 G-REX

Another technique which has been suggested, named G-REX (Genetic Rule EXtraction) (Johansson et al., 2004), is a pedagogical method to extract rules from black-box models with the use of genetic programming, which is based on Darwin's principle of "survival of the fittest." Each individual in the population represents a rule, which can be a Boolean rule, a decision tree, or even a fuzzy rule. All requirements on comprehensibility, fidelity and accuracy are declared in the fitness function. The selection operator chooses an individual that is allowed to reproduce with a probability that is proportional to its fitness; this operator is known as roulette wheel selection. The reproduction phase encompasses crossover and mutation. After a number of generations the fittest program, according to the defined fitness function, is chosen as the extracted rule. As for C4.5 and Trepan, the trained black-box model is mimicked by relabeling training data according to its predictions.

6 Visualizing the Extracted Rule Sets Using Decision Tables

Decision tables (DTs) provide an alternative way of representing data mining knowledge extracted by, for example, neural network rule extraction in a user-friendly way. DTs are a tabular representation used to describe and analyze decision situations (for example, customer churn prediction), where the state of a number of conditions jointly determines the execution of a set of actions (Vanthienen and Wets 1994). In our black-box model rule extraction context, the conditions correspond to the antecedents of the rules (for example monthly bill is larger than 100 Euro), whereas the actions correspond to the outcome classes (for example customer churns or does not churn). A DT consists of four quadrants, separated by double lines, both horizontally and vertically (see Figure 6.4). The horizontal line divides the table into a condition part (above) and an action part (below). The vertical line separates subjects (left) from entries (right).

Condition subjects	Condition entries
Action subjects	Action entries

Figure 6.4   Decision table quadrants

The condition subjects are the criteria that are relevant to the decision-making process. They represent the attributes of the rule antecedents about which information is needed to classify a given applicant as good or bad. The action subjects describe the possible outcomes of the decision-making process (that is, the classes of the classification problem). Each condition entry describes a relevant subset of values (called a state) for a given condition subject (attribute), or contains a dash symbol ("-") if its value is irrelevant within the context of that column. Subsequently, every action entry holds a value assigned to the corresponding action subject (class). True, false, and unknown action values are typically abbreviated by "x", "-", and ".", respectively. Every column in the entry part of the DT thus comprises a classification rule, indicating what action(s) apply to a certain combination of condition states. If each column only contains simple states (no contracted or irrelevant entries), the table is called an expanded DT, whereas otherwise the table is called a contracted DT. Table contraction can be achieved by combining columns that lead to the same action configuration. The number of columns in the contracted table can then be further minimized by changing the order of the conditions. It is obvious that a DT with a minimal number of columns is to be preferred because it provides a more parsimonious and comprehensible representation of the extracted knowledge than an expanded DT.

Several kinds of DTs have been proposed, but it is desired that the condition entry part of a DT satisfies the following two criteria:

- Completeness: all possible combinations of condition values are included.
- Exclusivity: no combination is covered by more than one column.

The results of these restrictions are single-hit tables, wherein columns have to be mutually exclusive, and which have advantages with respect to verification and validation (Vanthienen et al., 1998). It is this type of DT that can be easily checked for potential anomalies, such as inconsistencies (a particular case being assigned to more than one class) or incompleteness (no class assigned). The DT formalism thus allows for easy verification of the knowledge extracted by, for example, a neural network rule extraction algorithm. Additionally, for ease of legibility, the columns are arranged in lexicographical order, in which entries at lower rows alternate first. As a result, a tree structure emerges in the condition entry part of the DT, which lends itself very well to a top-down evaluation procedure: Starting at the first row, and then working one's way down the table by choosing from the relevant condition states, one safely arrives at the prescribed action (class) for a given case. This condition-oriented inspection approach often proves more intuitive, faster, and less prone to human error than evaluating a set of rules one by one. Once the DT has been approved by the expert, it can, in a final stage, be incorporated into a deployable expert system (Vanthienen and Wets, 1994).

7 Case Study: Rule Extraction for Customer Churn Prediction

In this section, a small case study will be carried out to illustrate the concepts introduced in this chapter. The central business problem in this case study is customer churn prediction, which has become increasingly important. During the last decade, the number of mobile phone users has increased drastically, with expectations of 5.6 billion mobile phone subscribers in 2011, which is around 80 per cent of the world population. Hence, telecommunication markets are getting saturated, particularly in developed countries, and in this context, customer churn prediction models play a crucial role. Building a prediction model may serve two distinct purposes. Firstly, prediction models can be used to identify those customers which are most likely to terminate their contract in the near future, allowing the telecom operator to take action such as approaching them with a retention offer. Furthermore, a classification model may also be used to gain insight in the drivers behind customer churn, which gives the opportunity to develop new marketing strategies. In order to optimally fulfill both needs, a classification model needs to be acceptable for implementation, as outlined previously, implying that the model needs to be accurate, comprehensible, and justifiable. This case study will show how the concepts discussed throughout this chapter can be applied to the customer churn prediction problem.

In this case study, an artificial data set will be used, which has been studied previously by Lima et al. (2009) and Verbeke et al. (2011) and which can be obtained freely from the Internet.[1] The data set consists of 5,000 instances and 20 attributes, shown in Table 6.2, and the base churn rate is 14.14 per cent. The data set is split into two stratified random samples. The two samples serve a as a training and test set, and consist of 70 per cent and 30 per cent of the instances respectively. Furthermore, a coarse classification is carried out, to cluster the *state* attribute.

Neural networks are commonly applied because this classification technique generally yields high accuracy. The drawback however is that neural networks are black-box models, which are not easily interpretable. To overcome this problem, rule extraction techniques may be applied to open up the black-box. In what follows, first a neural network is trained after which the rule extraction technique Trepan is employed. Table 6.3 shows the obtained performance.

The performance is measured in terms of PCC (Percentage Correctly Classified). There exist more advanced performance measures, but for the purpose of this case study this is sufficient. The first line shows that the black-box model is able to correctly classify 92.59

---

[1] See www.sgi.com/tech/mlc/db

Table 6.2   Variables of the churn data set

Variable Name	Type	Variable Name	Type
state	discrete	total evening minutes	continuous
account length	continuous	total evening calls	continuous
area code	continuous	total evening charge	continuous
phone number	discrete	total night minutes	continuous
international plan	discrete	total night calls	continuous
voice mail plan	discrete	total night charge	continuous
number voice mail messages	continuous	total international minutes	continuous
total day minutes	continuous	total international calls	continuous
total day calls	continuous	total international charge	continuous
total day charge	continuous	number customer service calls	continuous

Table 6.3   Performance of the classification algorithms

Performance Measure	PCC
Accuracy Neural Network	92.59
Accuracy Decision Table	88.47
Fidelity (Neural Network vs. Decision Tree)	93.88

Total day charge	≤ 42	> 42		
Voice mail plan		Yes		No
Total evening minutes		≤ 208	> 208	–
Non-churner	x	x	–	–
Churner	–	–	x	x

Figure 6.5   Decision table for customer churn prediction

per cent of the instances. For the extracted decision tree, this performance drops to 88.47 per cent. This drop in performance is to be expected, since the rule extraction translates a complex model to a number of comprehensible rules. However, these rules will generally not achieve exactly the same performance as the original model. The fidelity, which measures to which extent the decision tree is consistent with the neural network, is equal to 93.88 per cent in this case. Although the DT has a lower accuracy than the neural network, it provides insight in the classification mechanism. The decision tree which was extracted from the neural network by the use of Trepan is visualized as a DT in Figure 6.5.

Whereas the neural network acts as an oracle without offering any insight, the DT provides an understanding of drivers behind customers churn. In this specific example, it seems that people with a low daily charge are less likely to churn. Furthermore, if the daily charge is high, they are more likely to churn when they call more during the evening, which indicates that the subscription is private instead of business related. Thus, the company might want to develop a new plan for private customers with relatively high bills in order to retain them. It is obvious that the drivers behind churn depend on many factors, such as the type of client base, the available promotions and plans, competitor's promotions, and so on. Therefore, a timely reassessment of the model is necessary in order to capture any structural changes.

8   Conclusion

Nowadays, data mining plays an important role in marketing, such as predicting customer churn and modeling responses to direct marketing. A data mining model is considered acceptable for implementation if it fulfills three requirements, which are comprehensibility, justifiability, and an adequate predictive power. There exist many techniques which achieve superior predictive performance, such as support vector machines and neural networks. However, these two techniques are considered black-box models, since they do not allow for an easy interpretation of what drives classification. This chapter discusses rule extraction techniques, in which a comprehensible rule set is extracted from a black-box model. The rule set can be visualized as a DT, which is an intuitive and compact format allowing for an easy interpretation of the classification behavior. The main advantage these techniques offer is that they enable practitioners to check whether the model is in line with current domain knowledge. Furthermore, it enables the specialist to acquire additional domain knowledge, which can be translated into actionable information, for instance in preventing customer churn.

References

Andrews, R., Diederich, J. and Tickle, A.B. (1995). A survey and critique of techniques for extracting rules from trained neural networks. *Knowledge Based Systems, 8*(6), 373–89.

Barakat, N. and Diederich, D. (2004). Learning-based rule-extraction from support vector machines. In *14th International Conference on Computer Theory and Applications ICCTA 2004 Proceedings*, Alexandria, Egypt.

Bishop, C. (1995). *Neural Networks for Pattern Recognition*. Oxford: Oxford University Press.

Craven, M.W. and Shavlik, J.W. (1996). Extracting tree-structured representations of trained networks. In D. Touretzky, M. Mozer and M. Hasselmo (Eds) *Advances in Neural Information Processing Systems (NIPS)*. Cambridge, MA: MIT Press, 24–30.

Cristianini, N. and Shawe-Taylor, J. (2000). *An Introduction to Support Vector Machines and Other Kernel-Based Learning Methods*. New York, NY: Cambridge University Press.

Fayyad, U.M. and Irani, K.B. (1993). Multi-interval discretization of continuous-valued attributes for classification learning. In *Proceedings of Thirteenth International Joint Conference Artificial Intelligence (IJCAI)*. Chambéry: Morgan Kaufmann, 1022–9.

Fung, G., Sandilya, S. and Bharat Rao, R. (2005). Rule extraction from linear support vector machines. In *KDD '05: Proceeding of the 11th ACM SIGKDD International Conference on Knowledge Discovery in Data Mining*. New York, NY: ACM Press, 32–40.

Johansson, U., König, R. and Niklasson, L. (2004). The truth is in there – rule extraction from opaque models using genetic programming. In *17th International Florida AI Research Symposium Conference FLAIRS Proceedings*.

Lima, E., Mues, C. and Baesens, B. (2009). Domain knowledge integration in data mining using decision tables: Case studies in churn prediction. *Journal of the Operational Research Society, 60*(8), 1096–106.

Liu, H. and Tan, S.T. (1995). A fast rule generator. In *Proceedings of IEEE International Conference on Systems, Man Cybernetics*. Piscataway, NJ: IEE Press, 631–5.

Martens, D., Baesens, B., Van Gestel, T. and Vanthienen, J. (2007). Comprehensible credit scoring models using rule extraction from support vector machines. *European Journal of Operational Research, 183*(3), 1466–76.

Martens D., Vanthienen J., Verbeke W. and Baesens B. (2011). Performance of classification models from a user perspective. *Decision Support Systems, 51*(4), 782–93.

Nauck, D. (2000). *Data Analysis with Neuro-fuzzy Methods*. Magdeburg: University of Magdeburg.

Núñez, H., Angulo, C. and Catala, A. (2002). Rule extraction from support vector machines. In *European Symposium on Artificial Neural Networks Proceedings*, 107–12.

Quinlan, J.R. (1986). Induction of decision trees. *Machine Learning, 1*(1), 81–106.

Quinlan, J.R. (1993). *C4.5 Programs for Machine Learning*. Chambéry: Morgan Kaufmann.

Setiono, R. (1995). A neural network construction algorithm which maximizes the likelihood function. *Connection Science, 7*(2), 147–66.

Setiono, R. (1997). A penalty function approach for pruning feedforward neural networks. *Neural Computing, 9*(1), 185–204.

Setiono, R. and Liu, H. (1996). Symbolic representation of neural networks. *IEEE Computer, 29*(3), 71–77.

Setiono, R., Thong, J.Y. and Yap, C. (1998). Symbolic rule extraction from neural networks: An application to identifying organizations adopting IT. *Information & Management, 34*(2), 91–101.

Vanthienen, J., Mues, C. and Aerts, A. (1998). An illustration of verification and validation in the modelling phase of KBS development. *Data & Knowledge Engineering*, 27(3), 337–52.

Vanthienen, J. and Wets, G. (1994). From decision tables to expert-system shells. *Data & Knowledge Engineering, 13*(3), 265–82.

Vapnik, V.N. (1995). *The Nature of Statistical Learning Theory*. New York, NY: Springer-Verlag New York, Inc.

Verbeke, W., Martens, D., Mues, C. and Baesens, B. (2011). Building comprehensible customer churn prediction models with advanced rule induction techniques. *Expert Systems with Applications, 38*(3), 2354–64

Applications

7 *Hybrid Models for Recommender Systems*

ASIM ANSARI

1 Introduction

Recommender systems are software tools used by firms to recommend items to users. The list of recommended items is personalized for each user taking into account the user's preferences. Recommender systems have become increasingly popular over the past decade given their potential to benefit both firms and users and are widely used in a number of industries. Entertainment firms use them for recommending movies (for example, Netflix), music, and videos (for example, YouTube) to consumers. Content websites use such systems to create personalized newspapers, to suggest webpages and documents, and to customize emails containing links to content of various types. Ecommerce firms (such as Amazon.com) and service firms use recommendation systems to suggest products, house rentals, matches, and travel-related services. Over the past 15 years, many researchers in marketing, human computer interaction, machine learning, and information retrieval have studied different facets of recommender systems. Adomavicius and Tuzhilin (2005b) provide a comprehensive survey of the early literature on recommender systems. Since this publication, there has been an explosion of research spurred by the Netflix competition. Su and Koshgoftaar (2009) survey many different methods, with a special emphasis on collaborative filtering techniques. The recent monograph by Ekstrand et al. (2010) also focusses on collaborative filtering. The recommender systems handbook, edited by Ricci et al. (2011), contains detailed discussions of different aspects of recommender systems, such as techniques and algorithms, applications, evaluation of recommender systems, and user interactions with recommender systems. Most of the above reviews predominantly concentrate on research done in computer science and allied fields. Given these comprehensive expositions, this chapter will emphasize the contributions from marketing scholars and primarily focus on describing model-based recommender systems. Instead of a detailed review, we will develop a general latent variable framework for user modeling and show how such a framework can subsume a number of approaches that have been explored in the literature. Recommendation systems enable firms to target customers or users on a one-on-one basis. They therefore help ecommerce sites improve product sales and enable content providers to improve the usage of products and services. Firms are primarily interested in increasing the number of items they sell. In addition, firms may be motivated to leverage the heterogeneity of preferences within the customer base to increase the diversity of items that are sold or accessed by users. The hope from the firm's side is that personalized recommendations will improve customer satisfaction and thereby enhance usage. Users benefit from recommender systems in identifying relevant and preferred items while engaging in less effortful decision making and with reduced information overload. Users may be unaware of the existence of specific alternatives, or may need assistance in sifting through alternatives, particularly in situations that involve too many items. When information changes rapidly and new items are introduced on a regular basis, recommender systems help users by providing relevant information in a timely manner. In some situations, users seek the best sequence of items (such as a television series), or a set or bundle of products that fit well together. In contrast, some users may not be interested in the recommendations per se, but may instead interact with recommendation systems to help others, or to express one's views.

1.1 RECOMMENDER SYSTEM COMPONENTS

The main components of a typical recommender system can be schematically represented as in Figure 7.1. Such systems use statistical or data mining/machine learning algorithms on data stored in a database to build a "user model" that captures a user's preferences. The output of such an empirical model is then leveraged within an optimization or item selection component to identify items that fulfill different objectives. User responses to recommended items are then fed back into the database and can inform subsequent calibration of the user model.

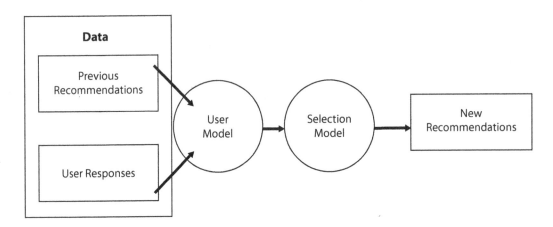

Figure 7.1   Components of a recommender system

1.1.1   Data

Recommender systems use data on users, items, and interactions in making predictions. User data typically consists of demographic information, such as age, gender, or location. In social recommender systems, information about the friendship network of an individual can be used in making predictions for a given user. Item data consists of information about the attributes of the item. For movies, this can be the genre, the director and actors, or the year of release. Interaction data describe aspects of the

Table 7.1   Ratings matrix for four users and nine movies

User	M1	M2	M3	M4	M5	M6	M7	M8	M9
1	4	2	3	.	4	.	5	5	.
2	1	.	.	.	4	.	5	.	.
3	.	2	2	3	1	.	.	.	1
4	4	3	2	5	4	3	5	5	.

interaction of the user with the items and typically take the form of explicit or implicit ratings (that is, measures of preference). Explicit measures or stated preference measures include ratings provided by users, which can be interval scaled, ordinal, or binary in nature. Implicit measures of preference are revealed preference measures and can include purchasing data or data on the time spent browsing or listening to an item. Purchase data can be considered as unary data. Such interactions data can be represented in a "ratings" matrix. Table 7.1 shows an example ratings matrix in which the cells containing "." indicate missing data. Interactions data may also include information about the structure of the object or aspects of the context in which recommendations are made. For example, when making recommendations via email, attributes that specify the layout of the email, or represent the clutter within the email can be used in predicting whether a user will click on a link.

1.2   USER MODEL

The user model captures what is unique about each user's preferences. A number of different algorithmic approaches and specifications have been proposed in the literature to construct such a user model. These models and approaches differ with respect to the types of data they use, and how such data are combined to yield a prediction for an individual user. In the context of Table 7.1, the user model predicts the missing ratings in the data table. Abstracting from the specifics of each approach, a user model can be broadly considered as an empirical model that computes a utility function for each user. The literature distinguishes among the following basic types of user models.

1.2.1   Content-based

Content-based models establish a mapping between the content of an item (for example, the attributes that describe the item) and the item's appeal to a user. Such a mapping establishes the degree of importance that a user places on each attribute of the item. For instance, if a user has positively rated news items pertaining to dieting, then the system will infer that the user prefers such content. Content-based systems overcome the cold-start problem for new items as these can be recommended even if no ratings are available for them, as long as item information is available. Content-based systems are highly useful in situations where item properties can be automatically extracted, as in text documents. In other situations, however, attribute information needs to be entered in the database, and this can be an effortful, time consuming, and error-prone process. Furthermore, it can be difficult to incorporate abstract attributes that deal with product aesthetics and image. Content-based models also use data on user demographics. This is helpful when a new user is added to the system, as the demographic information can be used to infer preferences before the user rates an item. Lops et al. (2011) review the state-of-the-art in content-based recommender systems and identify emerging trends.

1.2.2 Collaborative filtering

Collaborative filtering methods are among the most popular and have been extensively studied over the past 15 years. These methods use only the interactions data and therefore make predictions based on the ratings or preferences of other users or other items. They are therefore useful in situations where content and demographic data are not available readily. Collaborative filtering systems are typically classified into two subgroups: memory-based and model-based methods. Memory-based methods work directly from the ratings matrix and make recommendations for a focal user or item by using the data from other similar users and items. Thus, they are neighborhood-based methods that leverage the correlation in preferences across users or across items. In contrast, model-based methods construct a parameterized statistical model of the ratings matrix and recommend items using the fitted model. Neighborhood-based methods come in two flavors: user-based and item-based. User-based neighborhood methods (Breese, et al., 1998; Herlocker et al. 1999) use the preferences of like-minded users to recommend items to a given user. As an example, if user A and user B have provided similar ratings for a number of movies, and if user A has recently rated highly a movie that B has not yet seen, then this movie would be recommended to user B. Such user-based methods are effective predictors of preference, but suffer from scalability problems in situations involving a large number of users. Item-based collaborative filtering methods have better scalability and are one of the most widely used collaborative filtering methods in the industry. These methods use the correlation in item appeals across users (Sarwar, et al., 2001). In making a prediction on an item for a given user, item-based collaborative filtering first identifies the items that are similar to the focal item and then uses the known ratings made by the user on these similar items to estimate the rating for the user on the focal item. Item-based methods have been shown to have better scalability and improved accuracy (Sarwar, et al., 2001). Improvements in scalability come from the ability to pre-compute the similarity matrix across items. Item-based methods are also preferable in situations where the user needs to understand the reasons behind the recommendations. Users are familiar with items that they had previously preferred, whereas, they may not know the identity of other like-minded users. Desrosiers and Karypis (2011) provide a comprehensive survey of different types of neighborhood-based methods and note that these methods have the advantage of simplicity, justifiability (as they can provide intuitive justifications for the predictions), efficiency of computation (as model estimation is not needed), and stability in the face of a dynamic set of items and users. Model-based methods use a fitted model to make predictions and include, among others, Bayesian classifiers (Miyahara and Pazzani, 2000) and cluster-based methods (Xue, et al., 2005). Recent advances in collaborative filtering have favored latent factor models or low-rank matrix factorization methods (Koren, et al., 2009) that are based on the Singular Value Decomposition (SVD) of the ratings matrix. These methods have become very popular because of their impressive performance on the Netflix competition.[1] Matrix factorization methods represent items and users as vectors (that is, latent factors) in a joint space. Such latent factor representations enable these methods to infer hidden item attributes and characteristics of users. The user-item interactions are represented as inner products in the joint space. Koren and Bell (2011) describe in detail these recent advances in collaborative filtering and document different ways in which basic methods can be extended to improve predictive performance. A number of different matrix factorization approaches have been proposed. These include non-negative matrix factorization (Lee and Seung, 2001), probabilistic matrix factorization (Salakhutdinov and Mnih, 2008), non-parametric matrix factorization (Yu, et al., 2009) and maximum margin matrix factorization (Rennie and Srebro, 2005). Lee et al. (2012) compare the predictive accuracy of many different collaborative filtering methods while varying the number of users, items, sparsity levels, performance criteria, and computational complexity. They report that in general matrix factorization methods perform the best. However, they also report that other methods can exhibit superior performance in specific conditions.

1.2.3 Hybrid recommender systems

As collaborative filtering methods rely solely on the ratings in the database, they suffer from the cold-start problem, that is, they are unable to predict preferences for new items or new users. In such instances, hybrid recommender systems can be used for predictions. These methods utilize a combination of collaborative filtering and content-based approaches and are designed to overcome the problems of each technique. As they integrate the content information about items and the demographic information about users with the ratings, they are capable of predicting preferences for new items and new users. A number of different hybrid approaches have been used in the literature. These include content boosted collaborative filtering which uses a content-based model to fill in the missing entries in the data matrix D and then uses a collaborative filtering algorithm on the pseudo-data matrix. This helps overcome the cold-start and scalability problems (Melville, et al., 2002; Basu, et al., 1998). Burke (2002) analyzes in detail many classes of hybrid recommender systems. These include weighted methods which combine the predictions from different recommendation methods using a variety of weighting schemes (Su, et al., 2007) and switching methods that switch among different algorithms, instead of combining them. Hybrid recommenders have been shown to outperform simpler alternatives. In terms of the bias-variance tradeoff, the performance improvements from combining algorithms come from the reduction in variance. It should be noted that the winning entry in the Netflix competition was a hybrid of more than 100 different algorithms. In particular, feature-weighted linear stacking (Sill et al., 2009) which uses functions of item features in weighting the different prediction algorithms was found to perform very well. A detailed exposition of stacking is given in LeBlanc and Tibshirani (1996).

---

1   The competition ran between October 2006 and July 2009 and the goal of the competition was to improve the predictive accuracy of the Netflix movie recommendation system by 10 percent on a dataset of 480,046 users, 17,770 items, and 95,947,878 ratings.

1.3 OVERVIEW

In this chapter, we focus predominantly on hybrid model-based recommender systems. The next section develops a comprehensive hybrid latent factor model and shows how it can subsume other approaches as special cases. Section 3 discusses model extensions that involve different types of preference data, user models that treat the missing ratings as informative, models that accommodate implicit preference data such as purchase or unary data, contextual recommendations, and preference evolution. Section 4 contains a brief discussion of popular estimation methods and highlights the pros and cons of each method in light of scalability challenges and accuracy of predictions. Section 5 discusses different aspects regarding the item selection component of recommender systems. The chapter ends with a brief discussion about the opportunities for further research.

2 Hybrid Latent Factor Models

We focus on hybrid recommendation system models that combine observed variables with unobserved factors. These models can be considered as generalized versions of the basic model developed in Ansari et al. (2000). They combine the best features of content and collaborative filtering approaches as they integrate user and item-specific covariates with latent factors that capture different sources of unobserved heterogeneity. It is well known that accounting for sources of unobserved heterogeneity is crucial for improving predictive performance. We illustrate hybrid recommendation models on ratings data. Suppose ratings r_{ui} are available for $u = 1$ to U users and $i = 1$ to I items. These ratings can be conceptually arranged in a data matrix D whose rows represent the U users and whose columns correspond to the I items. As a given user typically rates only a few items, data are available for only a small subset $D_0 \subset D$ of all the user-item dyads (u,i) within D. The task of a recommender system is to predict the missing ratings. Ansari et al. (2000) modeled the observed ratings using a hierarchical regression approach. We begin with a simple instantiation of the Ansari et al. framework to develop an intuitive understanding of how the different components of a hybrid model contribute toward its performance.

2.1 SIMPLE EXAMPLE

Consider a recommendation system for movies. The movie ratings in such a system can be explained in terms of observable dyad-specific, item-specific (for example, movie genre) and user-specific variables (for example, demographics). For simplicity, assume that data includes a single dyad-specific binary variable, $FavTheme_{ui}$, that indicates whether the movie i has the user u's favorite theme, a single item-specific binary variable, $Action_i$, that indicates whether movie i is an action movie and a single user variable, $Male_u$, that specifies whether user u is a male. We now show how such data can be used in a hierarchical regression model that accounts for unobserved sources of user heterogeneity.

2.1.1 Model with user heterogeneity

We focus here on modeling the rows of D. Suppose user u rates n_u items belonging to the set I_u. These ratings can be modeled via a user-level regression that includes observed dyad-specific and item-specific variables as predictors. The model for user u can be written as:

$$r_{ui} = \beta_{u1} + \beta_{u2}\, FavTheme_{ui} + \beta_{u3}\, Action_i + \varepsilon_{ui}, \quad \varepsilon_{ui} \sim N(0, \sigma^2), \tag{1}$$

for items $i \in I_u$. The regression errors ε_{ui} capture the impact of unobserved dyad-specific variables and are assumed to be normally distributed with a zero mean and a scalar variance σ^2. Notice that the regression coefficients in Equation 1 are user-specific (hence the subscript u). In principle, if enough data are available for all users, the above model can be estimated using a separate regression for each user. However, this is generally infeasible as many users typically rate very few items. A separate regression model for such users would require estimating more coefficients than the number of observations available for the user. Thus, a hierarchical approach (also called a random coefficient, or a multilevel approach) is necessary to pool information (that is, collaborate) appropriately across users. This is done by specifying a population distribution that captures the variation in the regression coefficients across users.

Let β_u be the vector of all regression coefficients for user u. A population model can explain the variation in these regression coefficients. A portion of this variation is explained using observable demographic variables (for example, $Male_u$). The remaining portion is accounted for by random effects, λ_u, that capture unobserved sources of user heterogeneity. In our simple example, this population model can be written as a system of Seemingly Unrelated Regression (SUR) equations (Zellner, 1962) as follows:

$$
\begin{aligned}
\beta_{u1} &= \mu_1 + \mu_2\, Male_u + \lambda_{u1}, \\
\beta_{u2} &= \mu_3 + \mu_4\, Male_u + \lambda_{u2}, \\
\beta_{u3} &= \mu_5 + \mu_6\, Male_u + \lambda_{u3}.
\end{aligned}
\tag{2}
$$

The SUR coefficients (collected in the vector μ) capture the impact of the observed sources of heterogeneity. The random effects, $\lambda_u = \{\lambda_{u1}, \lambda_{u2}, \lambda_{u3}\}$, represent latent demographic variables and thus accommodate unobserved sources of individual differences. We assume that λ_u follows a multivariate normal distribution $N(0, \Lambda)$, with a zero mean, 0, and a covariance matrix Λ. The diagonal terms in Λ reflect the extent of variation in β_u's due to unobserved factors, and the off-diagonal elements capture the covariance between the unobserved factors impacting the different user-specific coefficients. A mixed model representation of the user heterogeneity model can be obtained by substituting Equation 2 into Equation 1. We then have

$$
\begin{aligned}
r_{ui} &= \mu_1 + \mu_2\, Male_u + \mu_3\, FavTheme_{ui} + \mu_4\, FavTheme_{ui}\, Male_u + \mu_5\, Action_i + \mu_6\, Action_i\, Male_u \\
&\quad + \lambda_{u1} + \lambda_{u2}\, FavTheme_{ui} + \lambda_{u3}\, Action_i + \varepsilon_{ui},
\end{aligned}
\tag{3}
$$

which clarifies how the observed ratings are influenced by different groups of covariates. In particular, the model captures the interactions between the observed demographics and the dyad and item-specific covariates. The user-specific random effects in λ_u and their interaction with the dyad and item-specific variables, however, are crucial for predictive performance. The random effects for a given user allow the model to capture the unique aspects of the user's preference structure. For example, the random effect λ_{u1} captures how user u differs from the population in his average rating for the items and λ_{u3} shows how the user differs from the population in his preference for action movies. The user heterogeneity specification captures the uniqueness of users (that is, the rows of the ratings matrix D). The inclusion of observed covariates and random effects allows the model to overcome the cold-start problem pertaining to new items (that is, movies). As long as a movie can be described in terms of its genre variables, the model can be used to predict how much a specific user will like that movie. However, it is unlikely to predict well the preferences of new users, as random effects for such users are not available before they contribute ratings to the database. In such situations, a model that focuses on modeling the uniqueness of specific items can be beneficial.

2.1.2 Model with item heterogeneity

We now shift focus to the columns in D. Let the data contain n_i ratings for item i. These ratings can be modeled via an item-level regression that includes observed dyad-specific and user-specific predictors. In our simple example, we can write the regression equation for item i as follows:

$$r_{iu} = \beta_{i1} + \beta_{i2} FavTheme_{ui} + \beta_{i3} Male_u + \varepsilon_{iu}, \quad \varepsilon_{iu} \sim N(0, \sigma^2), \tag{4}$$

where the observations in this regression are the observed ratings within column i. These are the ratings provided by users u in the set U_i. Notice that now the regression coefficients are item-specific (hence we use r_{iu} instead of r_{ui} and the subscript i for the coefficients), and that item-specific variables such as the genre of the movie cannot be included in such a regression. As before, one can use a hierarchical approach and specify a population distribution that captures the variability in the regression coefficients across items. Continuing with the simple example, the population SUR equations will now be:

$$\begin{aligned} \beta_{i1} &= \mu_1 + \mu_2 \, Action_i + \gamma_{i1}, \\ \beta_{i2} &= \mu_3 + \mu_4 \, Action_i + \gamma_{i2}, \\ \beta_{i3} &= \mu_5 + \mu_6 \, Action_i + \gamma_{i3}. \end{aligned} \tag{5}$$

The mixed model representation for this model can be obtained by substituting Equation 5 into Equation 4. We then have:

$$\begin{aligned} r_{ui} &= \mu_1 + \mu_2 Action_i + \mu_3 FavTheme_{ui} + \mu_4 FavTheme_{ui} Action_i + \mu_5 Male_u + \mu_6 Male_u Action_i \\ &+ \gamma_{i1} + \gamma_{i2} FavTheme_{ui} + \gamma_{i3} Male_u + \varepsilon_{ui} \end{aligned} \tag{6}$$

where the random effects, $\gamma_i = \{\gamma_{i1}, \gamma_{i2}, \gamma_{i3}\}$, represent unobserved item-specific variables that are assumed to follow a multivariate normal distribution $N(0, \Gamma)$, with a zero mean and a covariance matrix Γ. They capture what is unique about the item's appeal to users. For instance, γ_{i1} represents how item i differs from the population in terms of its average rating. Similarly, γ_{i3} represents how the item is differentially attractive to males. As can be seen in Equation 6, this model includes the interactions between the genre variables (observed or unobserved) and the dyad and user-specific covariates. The model helps overcome the cold-start problem pertaining to new users. As long as a new user can be described in terms of demographics, the model can be used to predict how much a specific item will appeal to the new user. However, it is unlikely to predict very well the ratings for new items, as random effects for such items are not available before users contribute ratings for these items in the database. However, as we discussed before, in such situations, the user-heterogeneity model is particularly useful. Ansari et al. (2000) showed how the two sources of unobserved heterogeneity can be gainfully combined into a single comprehensive model. In terms of our ratings matrix D, such a model can be considered as focusing on the cells, that is, the dyads (u, i).

2.1.3 Model of user and item heterogeneity

Such a joint model can be written directly using its mixed effects representation. Continuing with our simple example, we can represent the ratings as:

$$
\begin{aligned}
r_{ui} = & \mu_1 + \mu_2 Male_u + \mu_3 Action_i + \mu_4 FavTheme_{ui} \\
& + \mu_5 FavTheme_{ui} Male_u + \mu_6 FavTheme_{ui} Action_i + \mu_6 Male_u Action_i \\
& + \lambda_{u1} + \lambda_{u2} FavTheme_{ui} + \lambda_{u3} Action_i \\
& + \gamma_{i1} + \gamma_{i2} FavTheme_{ui} + \gamma_{i3} Male_u + \varepsilon_{ui}.
\end{aligned}
\tag{7}
$$

As before, the user-specific random effects λ_u represent unobserved demographics and interact with the dyad-specific and item-specific observed variables, whereas, the item-specific random effects γ_i represent unobserved item descriptors and interact with the dyad-specific and user-specific observed variables. The above model allows for a full accounting of all the interaction effects, and given its comprehensive characterization of heterogeneity, predicts well in a variety of situations.

2.2 GENERAL MODEL

We now abstract from the simple illustrative example above to the more general framework as developed in Ansari et al (2000). Let x_{ui} be a vector containing dyad-specific covariates, x_i be a vector of item-specific variables and x_u be a vector of user-specific variables. The mixed model can be written in terms of these groups of predictors as:

$$
r_{ui} = w_{\mu}' \mu + w_{\lambda}' \lambda_u + w_{\gamma}' \gamma_i + \varepsilon_{ui}, \quad \varepsilon_{ui} \sim N(0, \sigma^2), \quad \lambda_u \sim N(0, \Lambda), ; \gamma_i \sim N(0, \Gamma), \tag{8}
$$

for $(u, i) \in D_0$. The vector W_{μ} contains the different groups of observed covariates and their interactions, that is, $W_{\mu} = \{x_{ui}, x_u, x_i, x_{ui} \% x_i, x_i \% x_u\}$, where we use the notation $a \% b$ to denote interactions formed from the vectors a and b. The vector w_{λ} contains the dyad and item-specific covariates and their interactions, that is, $W_{\lambda} = \{x_{ui}, x_i, x_{ui} \% x_i\}$

and the vector W_λ contains the dyad and user-specific variables and their interactions, that is, $W_\gamma = \{x_{ui}, x_u, x_{ui}\% x_u\}$. The parameters in μ contain the fixed effects, and the vectors λ_u and γ_i are the random effects. It is clear that the model in Equation 8 combines both *content* and *collaborative filtering* approaches. It includes "content" (that is, observed variables) and it also collaborates across users and items via the population distributions that govern item and user heterogeneity. The estimated random effects for a given user are based on a weighted combination of the data provided by the user and the data from other users, and hence are collaborative in nature. Similarly, the random effects for a given item collaboratively leverage data on that item as well as the data on other items. The model in Equation 8 is expected to do a good job in predicting user preferences in situations where a large number of content variables are available. However, in many recommendation contexts, such content descriptors or user-specific covariates are unavailable or very difficult to collect. When content variables are not available, the above model reduces to a bare bones version:

$$r_{ui} = \mu + \lambda_u + \gamma_i + \varepsilon_{ui}, \tag{9}$$

where μ is a population-level intercept, λ_u is a user-specific random effect (the user's offset from the population intercept), and γ_i, a single item-specific random-effect that captures the item's popularity relative to the mean population rating. Such a simple model, however, will be unable to predict well, as it does not incorporate meaningful differences either across users or across items. The collaborative filtering literature deals with such data paucity via matrix factorization methods which incorporate multiplicative latent terms.

2.2.1 Matrix factorization via a bilinear component

Matrix factorization methods (Koren, et al., 2009; Koren and Bell, 2011) have become very popular in the recent collaborative filtering literature because of their impressive performance in the Netflix challenge. These methods add a bilinear term $\eta'_u \eta_i$ to Equation 9:

$$r_{ui} = \mu + \lambda_u + \gamma_i + \eta'_u \eta_i + \varepsilon_{ui}, \tag{10}$$

to compensate for the lack of observed content variables. The latent variables η_i represent unobserved item characteristics, whereas, the latent variables η_u represent how user u values these unobserved item characteristics. Both these variables are inferred from the similarity and differences in the observed ratings across items. In this setup, users and items are represented as vectors in a joint space as in the vector multidimensional scaling model (Tucker, 1960; Slater 1960, Carroll, 1980; DeSarbo, et al., 2008). Such matrix factorization methods can be considered as adaptations of the SVD of the ratings data, and thus have close links to correspondence analysis (Greenacre, 1984; Hoffman and Franke, 1986). The dimensionality of these latent variables is determined based on the predictive performance of the resulting model. To reduce the chance of overfitting, which can result in poor predictions, the collaborative filtering literature uses regularization when estimating parameters. The same bilinear term can be included in Equation 8 to yield a general model:

$$
\begin{aligned}
r_{ui} &= w'_{\mu}\,\mu + w'_{\lambda}\,\lambda_{u} + w'_{\gamma}\,\gamma_{i} + \eta'_{u}\,\eta_{i} + \varepsilon_{ui}, \\
\lambda_{u} &\sim N(0, \Lambda), \quad \gamma_{i} : N(0, \Gamma), \\
\eta_{u} &\sim N(0, \Sigma_{u}), \quad \eta_{i} : N(0, \Sigma_{i}), \\
\varepsilon_{ui} &\sim N(0, \sigma^{2}).
\end{aligned}
\tag{11}
$$

The, independent multivariate normal priors for η_{u} and η_{i} are useful for automatic regularization within this framework. The covariance matrices Σ_{u} and Σ_{i} for these priors are used to capture the variability in these latent space vectors. The above yields a fairly general model that can perform well across a range of recommendation contexts. Such a model has been recently proposed by Agarwal and Chen (2009) in the context of recommendation systems, although, it has close parallels to models in social network analysis (Hoff, 2005; Ansari et al. 2011). Agarwal and Chen (2009) show that the model is capable of impressive performance on multiple datasets. Appropriate parameter restrictions are needed to identify the model parameters. The model can also be used in tandem with variable selection frameworks to reduce the possibility of overfitting.

3   Model Extensions

In the previous section, we focused on a framework for modeling the observed continuous ratings data in D. A number of researchers have extended this framework in several directions. These extensions handle situations involving binary preference data (Ansari and Mela, 2003) or ordinal data and when the missing ratings are informative about preference (Ying, et al., 2006). Other researchers have focused on modeling implicit preference data, such as purchase or unary data (Bodapati, 2008). Some researchers have explored the role of context in recommending products, or have accommodated the temporal evolution of preferences or item appeals to improve the predictive power in non-stationary environments. We discuss below a few of these extensions.

3.1   BINARY/ORDINAL PREFERENCES AND MISSING DATA

Often times, explicit preference data is binary in nature (for example, thumbs up or down data). Such data collection places fewer demands on the user, particularly when data are collected from devices or interfaces that may not be easy to navigate or manipulate. In other situations, when data are collected using Likert scales, it may be beneficial to treat these ratings as ordinal instead of assuming them to be continuous. Such binary or ordinal data can be handled via a straightforward extension of the hybrid modeling approach outlined above. Instead of modeling such ratings directly, an additional set of latent variables, that is, random utilities are assumed to underly the observed ratings. This is consistent with the elaborate literature on random utility discrete choice models within marketing and economics (Train, 2009; Ben-Akiva and Lerman, 1985; McFadden, 1973). The framework described in Section 2 focusses on modeling only the observed ratings in D. This ignores the information that may be contained in the missing entries within the database. Preference data could be missing in a given cell of D because of a variety of reasons. It could be that the user is not aware of the item. Alternatively, it is possible that the user is aware of the item, but did not rate it because he or she does not have a strong preference for the item. Alternatively, it is possible that the recommendation system did not seek input from the user on such items, and this selection mechanism could itself be correlated with the user preferences. Given the above reasons, it is quite likely that the missing cells in D are not missing at random, and could therefore be informative about user preferences. Ying et al. (2006) developed an ordinal data model that leverages the information in the missing ratings. They use a hierarchical Bayesian selectivity approach (Heckman, 1979) to simultaneously model the observed ordinal ratings r_{ui} and the missing data mechanism m_{ui}. Here, m_{ui} is a binary variable that indicates whether the rating in cell (u,i) of D is missing. The observed ratings r_{ui} is modeled using an underlying latent utility r^*_{ui} and a set of user-specific thresholds contained in a vector θ_I. The missing data indicator is modeled using another latent utility variable m_{ui}. The selectivity model developed by Ying et al. (2006) involves a SUR system of two regression equations for the two random utilities as follows:

$$
\begin{aligned}
r^*_{ui} &= w'_{r,\mu}\,\mu_r + w'_{r,\lambda}\,\lambda^r_u + w'_{r,\gamma}\,\gamma^r_i + \varepsilon^r_{ui}, \\
m^*_{ui} &= w'_{m,\mu}\,\mu^m + w'_{m,\lambda}\,\lambda^m_u + w'_{m,\gamma}\,\gamma^m_i + \varepsilon^m_{ui},
\end{aligned}
\tag{12}
$$

where the first equation above is a special case of our general hybrid model, but now involves the latent utilities r_{ui} instead of the observed ratings. The second equation models the missing data mechanism, that is, it handles the selectivity problem. The two regression errors ε^r_{ui} and ε^m_{ui} are assumed to be distributed bivariate normal $N(0,\Upsilon)$. Selectivity is present when the correlation parameter in the bivariate correlation matrix Υ is of significant magnitude, as this implies that the two equations share common unobservable variables. Ying et al. (2006) estimate the above model on a subset of movies from the EachMovie data and show that accounting for selectivity results in significant improvements in predictive power. They also find a positive correlation between the errors in the two equations, which also confirms that the missing data on movie ratings can be informative about preferences.

3.2 IMPLICIT PREFERENCES AND UNARY DATA

In many situations, explicit preference data are not available. However, it is common to observe implicit preference information in the form of purchase data. Such data, however, are inherently ambiguous. While observed purchases can be clearly interpreted as indicating preference for the product, non-purchases are ambiguous indicators of preference. A customer may not purchase a product because he or she is a) not aware of the product or b) is aware of the product but does not like it. Because of this asymmetry between purchase and non-purchases, such data are named unary data (Herlocker, et al., 2004). Bodapati (2008) developed a sophisticated modeling framework to handle such unary data. His framework can be best understood in the context of Table 7.2. He combines purchase data of two types in order to break the asymmetry inherent in purchase data. The first type of purchasing data can be called firm-initiated purchases. These are the starred entries in Table 7.2. These are purchases (1^*'s) or non-purchases (0^*'s) that a user makes as a response to recommendations made by the firm. Non-purchases resulting from such recommendations represent the situation where the customer is aware of the product (due to forced exposure), but does not buy because he/she is not satisfied with the item that is recommended. The second type of data involves self-initiated purchases or non-purchases. These are represented by the unstarred entries in the table. For this type of data, the researcher knows that the purchases (1's) imply a preference for the product. However, the researcher does not know whether non-purchases imply that the user is unaware (!'s) or is aware but does not like the product (⊕'s). Thus, the researcher is unable to separate the two types of non-purchases, (that is, !'s from the ⊕'s), on the self-initiated data. However, when both sources of data are available, they can be combined in a unified modeling framework. Bodapati shows that one can disentangle the underlying causes of non-purchasing when the different model components that deal with these two sources of data share common model parameters. We now succinctly cover the essence of his framework below.

Table 7.2   Ratings matrix with unary data

User	M1	M2	M3	M4	M5	M6	M7	M8	M9
1	1*	0*	1	!	1	!	1*	1	!
2	1	!	!	!	0*	⊕	1	⊕	!
3	⊕	0*	0*	1	1*	!	!	!	1*
4	0*	1	0*	1	1	0*	0*	1	!

Bodapati assumes that a user u buys an item i because of two sequential steps. First, the user becomes aware of the product, represented by the probabilistic event A_{ui}, and then buys the product if the utility from the product exceeds a threshold, captured by the probabilistic event S_{ui}. The probability of buying the product can be written as the product of the unconditional probability of becoming aware and the conditional probability of being satisfied given awareness. Bodapati models these probabilities using a hierarchical logistic regression approach on the self-initiated and firm-initiated data. The probabilities are specified as functions of user-specific coefficients and unobserved item specific variables, η_i. For the self-initiated data, the resulting specification can be written as:

$$Prob(r_{ui} = 1) \quad = Prob(A_{ui} = 1) \times Prob(S_{ui} = 1 \mid A_{ui} = 1)$$
$$= logistic(\ \alpha'_u\ \eta_i) logistic(\ \beta'_u\ \eta_i). \tag{13}$$

The probability of no-purchase is just the complement of the above probability. For the firm-initiated data, the user is aware of the product because of the recommendation. Therefore, the probability of purchase can be written as:

$$Prob(r_{ui} = 1^*) \quad = Prob(S_{ui} = 1 \mid A_{ui} = 1)$$
$$= logistic(\ \beta'_u\ \eta_i). \tag{14}$$

Notice that the models for both types of data share the vector β_u of user-specific parameters, and therefore, when both datasets are combined and the model is estimated simultaneously on the entire data, it is possible to identify all model parameters. In addition to the above, Bodapati (2008) also discusses how to select the items to recommend to users. We will discuss this aspect later in this chapter.

3.3 CONTEXTUAL RECOMMENDATIONS

Users interact with and consume items within a particular context. The psychology literature offers strong support for the notion that preferences are context dependent. A given user may like horror movies when viewing movies with his male friends, whereas the same user may prefer romantic movies in the company of his spouse or girlfriend. Context is a multifaceted concept that has been explored from a variety of perspectives across a range of disciplines. Within marketing, the interaction between a user and the environment, and how this influences behavior, has been studied by a number of researchers (Belk, 1974, 1975; Payne, et al., 1992). Belk (1975) identifies five groups of situational characteristics that impact preferences. These include:

1. physical surroundings, which has implications for location aware systems and mobile recommendations;
2. social surroundings, which has implications for recommending products and services in the context of joint consumption, or gift-giving behavior;
3. temporal context, which implies taking into account the time of the day when recommending content or products, or time constraints that impact the suitability of particular recommendations;
4. task definition, which may include consumer intent behind the purchase; and
5. antecedent states, which capture transient impacts on preferences, such as moods, in contrast with more stable preferences.

The use of context implies modeling three-way data. This means that the resulting data structure is a cube, instead of a two-way array such as D. The third dimension of such a data cube involves different contexts that may influence user preferences or product appeal. Incorporating context requires context dependent preference elicitation, as is done in the literature on three-way analysis preferences (Green and Rao, 1972; DeSarbo, et al., 2008). A number of researchers have studied context-aware recommender systems (Adomavicius, et al, 2005; Mokbel and Levandoski, 2009; Palmisano, et al., 2008). Adomavicius and Tuzhilin (2011) review the role and importance of incorporating context in recommendation systems and describe three different paradigms for incorporating contextual information in making recommendations. The first such approach is called *contextual pre-filtering*, which involves first filtering the ratings data in the database to match those observations that were elicited in a particular context and then making recommendations using a standard two-way recommendation model on these pre-filtered observations. This approach is useful if the context definitions are sufficiently broad such that enough data are available within each context. The second approach, named *contextual post-filtering*, involves making predictions without considering the context and then filtering these to remove recommendations that are not relevant for the context under consideration. The third approach, named *contextual modeling*, is the most appealing from a modeling perspective. In this approach, the three-way nature of the data is fully exploited and directly integrated within the recommendation model. The area of contextual modeling is ripe for further exploration and development. Opportunities exist to contribute via the construction of hierarchical multilinear models (Hoff, 2011) that leverage multiple layers of hierarchical specifications to accommodate contextual preferences. One such approach is that of Adomavicius and Tuzhilin (2005a) who show how the Ansari et al. (2000) model can be extended to a third dimension (time) that incorporates unobserved temporal factors and their interaction with user and item variables. While time can be considered as a contextual variable, it plays a more general role in recommender systems. We now explore how temporal evolution of preferences can be modeled.

3.4 PREFERENCE EVOLUTION

Recommendation systems use data that are collected over an extended time period. Customer preferences can evolve over such time frames. For instance, a customer who likes only action movies at one time may experience a gradual shift in preference towards drama or mystery. Such changes in preferences can occur because of consumer learning, as the user samples items of different types, or due to a variety of other life experiences that can impact the preference structure. Apart from a shift in the underlying preference structure, the scale usage behavior of a user may also exhibit temporal dynamics. For example, a user who uses the middle of the rating scale to rate just acceptable movies may become more extreme in response styles because of accumulated experience and an enhanced ability to discriminate. The overall appeal of an item may also wax and wane over time. For example, a movie may experience transient periods of renewed popularity because of random shocks such as the winning of an award. A movie's appeal could also exhibit a more stable and gradual decline due to aging. News items may lose their appeal because they may no longer be current or news worthy. The evolution of user preferences and the changes in the appeal of an item can be captured in recommendation models via time varying parameters. Koren and Bell (2011) discuss in detail the different sources of temporal dynamics. They show that a matrix factorization model that accommodates such time varying parameters can be written as:

$$r_{ui} = \mu + \lambda_{ut} + \lambda_{it} + \eta'_{ut}\,\eta_i + \varepsilon_{ui}, \tag{15}$$

where λ_{ut}, λ_{it} and η_{ut} are assumed to vary over calendar time. They note that the estimation of user-specific time varying parameters can be particularly challenging as users often do not provide ratings in every time period of interest. Koren and Bell (2011) report that incorporating such time varying latent factors resulted in substantial gains in predictions on the Netflix challenge data. Alternatively, dynamics can also be handled by giving greater weight to recent data in estimating the random effects (Agarwal and Chen, 2009). Greater research is needed to fully explore the potential of dynamic models in recommendation systems. It would be interesting to study how state-space methods based on Kalman filtering or particle filtering (Chung et al., 2009), which allow online learning, can be adapted to handle such dynamics. In this regard, little is known about the utility of updating different model parameters at different time scales. For instance, it appears reasonable to update the population distribution infrequently while allowing for more frequent adaptation of random effects.

4 Estimation Methodologies and Issues

A variety of estimation methods have been used in the recommendation system literature. The choice of the estimation algorithm depends upon a number of factors such as, the type of recommendation model, the need for uncertainty estimates in making recommendations, the need for justification, data size, and scalability concerns. Bayesian methods of estimation are popular in the literature, particularly within marketing. Bayesian inference involves summarizing the joint posterior distribution of the model parameters. Recommendations are then based on the posterior predictive distribution. The posterior distribution is typically unavailable in closed form. This is also the case for the hybrid model in Equation 8. Researchers have, therefore, used Markov Chain Monte Carlo (MCMC) methods to perform simulation-based inference. This involves iteratively simulating parameter draws from the full conditional distributions of the joint posterior density. If these full conditional distributions are completely known, then Gibbs sampling (Geman and Geman, 1984) can be used (Ansari, et al., 2000). In more complex situations involving binary and ordinal preferences or when missing data mechanisms are leveraged in predictions (Ying et al., 2006; Bodapati, 2008), a Metropolis-Hastings scheme (Metropolis, et al., 1953; Hastings, 1970) is used, given the non-conjugacy of the priors. The machine learning community has explored a greater variety of methods of estimation. This diversity has been mostly driven by the need to have scalable algorithms that can be estimated on datasets involving millions of observations. The matrix factorization literature has typically used either alternating least squares or stochastic gradient descent methods (Bottou, 2010). These methods have become popular given their computational ease and their good predictive performance. These are online learning methods, that is, they operate on one observation at a time, and therefore do not require the entire dataset to be available in memory, thus making parameter updating scalable. Other researchers have used either Maximum A Posteriori (MAP) estimation or have relied on variational approximations of the posterior distribution when estimating probabilistic matrix factorization models. Variational approximations aim to mimic the posterior using a simpler factorized distribution under which the user-specific latent variables are independent of the item-specific random effects. This results in greater computational efficiency. MAP estimation circumvents the need to draw from the posterior as it focuses on finding the posterior mode. In contrast, MCMC methods involve simulating from the posterior, and are thus computationally intensive relative to MAP and variational methods. In MCMC methods, a large number of iterations are needed to fully explore the joint posterior distribution and each iteration requires a complete pass through the entire dataset. However, Salakhutdinov and Mnih (2008) show that MCMC methods can be successfully applied to the rather large Netflix dataset which contains more than 100 million movie ratings. They highlight that the conditional independence (CI) structure of the hierarchical models can be used to sample from the full conditionals of the user-specific parameters in parallel within each iteration of the MCMC scheme. This is possible because the user-specific random effects, as well as the item-specific random effects are conditionally independent given the other model parameters and can therefore be drawn in parallel within each MCMC iteration. Salakhutdinov and Mnih (2008) demonstrate that MCMC methods predict significantly better than MAP-trained models on the Netflix dataset and report that the performance gain from using MCMC methods over MAP is larger than the corresponding gain that variational approaches yield. Other researchers have used Monte Carlo Expectation Maximization (MCEM) methods for estimating within the classical framework of statistics. Agarwal and Chen (2009) show that the MCEM algorithm is scalable on large datasets such as the MovieLens and the Yahoo Front Page data and can be parallelized easily. They also report that the MCEM algorithm performs better than the Iterated Conditional Mode (ICM) algorithm in predictive performance and in its ability to control overfitting. Recent advances in computing are enabling researchers to estimate increasingly sophisticated recommendation models on large datasets. Many of these gains are possible because of the improvements in hardware and software that are enabling easier parallelization. It is to be noted that almost all computers that are available in the market nowadays come with multiple CPU cores. Moreover, researchers are beginning to utilize the potential of Graphics Processing Units (GPUs) for computational purposes. The availability of parallel computing platforms and programming models such as CUDA from NVIDIA (Sanders and Kandrot, 2011) and the OpenCL standard for parallel programming is facilitating both GPU computing and hybrid computing in which the computing capabilities of multiple CPUs and GPUs can be simultaneously used. Of particular importance is GraphLab, which is a new parallel framework for machine learning. Its collaborative filtering library (accessible from graphlab.org/pmf.html) contains software for all the major matrix factorization techniques. These developments bode well for the ability of companies to unleash the potential inherent in large databases of customer preferences.

5   Item Selection Model

The item selection component of a recommender system focusses on selecting items that balance what the user wants and what the firm desires. Typically, a list of items that are predicted to be of highest utility to the user is recommended. In addition, users may also want novel items, that is, those items that they would like when experienced, but do not expect. This is akin to the notion of recommending items that the user would not purchase on their own. Bodapati (2008) emphasizes the point that an item needs to be selected based on its sensitivity to recommendation. The paper argues that instead of recommending items with the highest predicted utility, the system should take into account the expected incremental number of purchases relative to a situation involving no recommendations. From a decision theoretic view point, the selection of items can depend upon the loss function. For instance, in certain applications, the risk associated with recommending the wrong outcome could be large, as in recommending stocks. In other situations, the cost of a wrong recommendation would be minimal, as in the case of a song recommendation. In constructing a set of items to recommend, diversity is often valued. A diverse set of recommendations can handle heterogeneity in preferences for the same user across different contexts. Often these contexts are latent, and thus diversity can be beneficial. Alternatively, diversity could be valuable in accommodating a variety of tastes, as users may have multiple ideal points. When diversity is a consideration, the set of items does not typically contain only those items that have the highest predicted utility. The system also needs to focus on the interactions among products within the set, as certain products may not gel well with each other. In selecting such sets, utility estimates based on models that evaluate preferences for an assortment or collection of items (Farquhar and Rao, 1976) can be useful. The firm may have specific objectives when recommending items. This could include profitability as well as coverage objectives. Given a long tail of items, firms may be interested in recommending items that are not that popular. Similarly, firms may need to balance what the user wants with what may be profitable to recommend. Other objectives may include optimizing the probability of visiting the website, when recommendations are offered as part of an email (Ansari and Mela, 2003). Finally, the system needs to consider the tradeoff between exploration (learning a customer's preferences) and exploitation (utilizing the customer's preferences). Thus, active learning principles involving the adaptive presentation of recommendations can be used to learn actively the preferences of a user, while recommending items. This is crucial for providing new information to the system, as preferences are dynamic in nature. Here, the literature on adaptive conjoint estimation can be handy. Rubens et al. (2011) describe in detail how active learning is relevant for recommender systems. Chung et al. (2009) illustrate how playlists of songs can be generated using Bayesian sequential experimental design so as to maximize consumer listening, improve future parameter estimates, and facilitate surprising (serendipitious) songs. They show that a sole focus on maximizing expected listening duration results in subsequent difficulties in estimating model parameters for the user model. They, therefore, dynamically optimize listening duration and parameter efficiency. The optimal set of songs is constructed using a modified Fedorov algorithm (Cook and Nachtsheim, 1980), which iteratively converges to the optimal list.

6   Conclusions

There has been considerable progress in recommender systems research over the past 20 years. A variety of different user modeling approaches have been proposed and researchers have studied many different facets of recommender systems. In this chapter, we primarily focussed on describing hybrid model-based systems that integrate data of many types. We developed a general hybrid model for ratings data and showed how it can subsume many different types of recommendation algorithms as special cases. We discussed how this framework can be extended to handle missing data, binary, ordinal preferences, and unary data. We also explored how information about the recommendation context and the dynamic nature of preferences can be handled. Despite the rapid progress in research, a number of challenges remain. Prominent among these are the challenge of scalability in light of the availability of very large datasets and keeping in mind the dynamic nature of such data. A number of efforts are underway to tackle this problem, and more research on parallelization technologies and distributed computing frameworks will be beneficial in this regard. Further research on accommodating the diversity in preferences in recommending sets of items is needed for systems to be able to satisfy customers' variety seeking and context dependent needs. Researchers can also focus on modeling the dynamics of preferences with a view toward determining the right balance between short-term and longer-term preferences in recommending items. In terms of item-selection, more research is needed on the use of active learning to manage the tradeoff between exploration and exploitation.

References

Adomavicius, G., Samkaranarayanan, R., Sen, S. and Tuzhilin, A. (2005). Incorporating contextual information in recommender systems using a multidimensional approach. *ACM Transactions of Information Systems (TOIS)*, *23*(1), 103–45.

Adomavicius, G. and Tuzhilin, A. (2005a). Incorporating context into recommender systems using multidimensional rating estimation methods. In *Proceedings of the 1st International Workshop on Web Personalization, Recommender Systems and Intelligent User Interfaces at the (WPR-SIUI 2005) at the 2nd International Conference on E-Business and Telecommunication Networks*.

Adomavicius, G. and Tuzhilin, A. (2005b). Toward the next generation of recommender systems: A survey of the state-of-the-art and possible extensions. *IEEE Transactions on Knowledge and Data Engineering*, *17*(6), 734–49.

Adomavicius, G. and Tuzhilin, A. (2011). Context-aware recommender systems. In Ricci, F., Rokach, L., Shapira, B. and Kantor, P. (Eds) *Recommender Systems Handbook*. New York: Springer, 217–53.

Agarwal D. and Chen, B.-C. (2009). Regression based latent factor models. In Elder, J.F., Fogelman-Soulié, F., Flach, P.A. and Javeed Zaki, M. (Eds) *Proceedings of the 15th ACM SIGKDD International Conference on Knowledge Discovery and Data Mining (KDD 2009)*. New York: ACM, 19–28.

Ansari, A., Essegaier, S. and Kohli, R. (2000). Internet recommendation systems. *Journal of Marketing Research*, *37*(3), 363–75.

Ansari, A., Koenigsberg, O. and Stahl, F. (2011). Modeling multiple relationships in social networks. *Journal of Marketing Research*, *48*(4), 713–28.

Ansari A. and Mela, C. (2003). E-customization. *Journal of Marketing Research*, *40*(2), 131–45.

Basu, C., Hirsh, H. and Cohen, W. (1998). Recommendation as Classification: Using Social and Content-based Information in Recommendation. In *Proceedings of the 15th National Conference on Artificial Intelligence (AAAI' 98)*. Anaheim, CA, Madison, WI: AAAI Press/MIT Press, 714–20.

Belk, R.W. (1974). An exploratory assessment of situational effects in buyer behavior. *Journal of Marketing Research*, *11*(2), 156–63.

Belk, R.W. (1975). Situational variables and consumer behavior. *Journal of Consumer Research*, *2*(3), 157–64.

Ben-Akiva, M. and Lerman, S. (1985). *Discrete Choice Analysis: Theory and Applicaton to Travel Demand*. Boston, MA: MIT Press.

Bodapati, A. (2008). Recommendation systems with purchase data. *Journal of Marketing Research*, *45*(February), 77–93.

Bottou, L. (2010). Large-scale machine learning with stochastic gradient descent. In Y. Lechavallier and G. Saporta (Eds) *Proceedings of the 19th International Conference on Computational Statistics (COMPSTAT'2010)*. New York/Heidelberg: Springer, 177–87.

Breese, J., Heckerman, D. and Kadie, C. (1998). Empirical analysis of predictive algorithms for collaborative filtering. In *Proceedings of the Fourteenth Conference Annual Conference on Uncertainty in Artificial Intelligence (UAI-98)*. San Francisco, CA: Morgan Kaufmann, 43–52.

Burke, R. (2002). Hybrid recommender systems: Survey and experiments. *User Modeling and User-Adapted Interaction*, *12*(4), 331–70.

Carroll, J.D. (1980), Models and methods for multidimensional analysis of preferential choice (or other dominance data). In E.D. Lantermann and H. Feger (Eds) *Similarity and Choice*. Bern, Stuttgart, Vienna: Hans Huber Publishers, 234–89.

Chung, T.S., Rust, R.T. and Wedel, M. (2009). My mobile music: An adaptive personalization system for digital audio players. *Marketing Science, 28*(1), 52–68.

Cook, R.D. and Nachtsheim, C.J. (1980). A comparison of algorithms for constructing exact D-optimal designs. *Technometrics, 22(3)*, 315–24.

DeSarbo, W., Grewal, R. and Scott, C. (2008). A clusterwise bilinear multidimensional scaling methodology for simultaneous segmentation and positioning analyses. *Journal of Marketing Research*, 45(3), 280–92.

DeSarbo, W., Atalay, A. and Blanchard, S.J. (2009). A three-way clusterwise multidimensional unfolding procedure for the spatial representation of context dependent preference. *Computational Statistics and Data Analysis, 53(8)*, 3217–30.

Desrosiers, C. and Karypis, G. (2011). A comprehensive survey of neighborhood-based recommendation methods. In Ricci, F., Rokach, L., Shapira, B. and Kantor, P. (Eds) *Recommender Systems Handbook*. New York: Springer, 107–44.

Ekstrand, M., Riedl, J. and Konstan, J. (2010). Collaborative filtering recommender systems. *Foundations and Trends in Human-Computer Interaction, 4*(2), 81–173.

Farquhar, P.F. and Rao, V.R. (1976). A balance model for evaluating subsets of multiattributed items. *Management Science, 22*(January), 528–39.

Geman, S. and Geman, D. (1984). Stochastic relaxation, Gibbs distributions, and the Bayesian restoration of images. *IEEE Transactions on Pattern Analysis and Machine Intelligence, 6(6)*, 721–41.

Green, P.E. and Rao, V.R. (1972). *Multidimensional Scaling*. Hinsdale, IL: Dryden Press.

Greenacre, M.J. (1984), *Theory and Applications of Correspondence Analysis*. London: Academic Press.

Hastings, W. (1970). Monte Carlo sampling methods using Markov chains and their applications. *Biometrika, 57*(1), 97–109.

Heckman, J. (1979). Sample selection bias as a specification error. *Econometrica, 47*(1), 153–61.

Herlocker, J.L., Konstan, J.A., Borchers, A. and Riedl, J. (1999). An algorithmic framework for performing collaborative filtering. In *Proceedings of the 22nd Annual International ACM SIGIR Conference on Research and Development in Information Retrieval (SIGIR '99)*. New York, NY: ACM, 230–37.

Herlocker, J., Konstan, J., Terveen, L. and Riedl, J. (2004). Evaluating collaborative filtering recommender systems. *ACM Transactions on Information Systems, 22*(1), 5–53.

Hoff, P. (2005). Bilinear mixed-effects models for dyadic data. *Journal of American Statistical Association, 100*(469), 286–95.

Hoff, P.D. (2011). Hierarchical multilinear models for multiway data. *Computational Statistics and Data Analysis, 55(1)*, 530–43.

Hoffman, D.L. and Franke, G. (1986). Correspondence analysis: The graphical representation of categorical data in marketing research. *Journal of Marketing Research, 23*(August), 213–27.

Koren, Y. and Bell, R. (2011). Advances in collaborative filtering. In Ricci, F., Rokach, L., Shapira, B. and Kantor, P. (Eds) *Recommender Systems Handbook*. New York, NY: Springer, 145–86.

Koren, Y., Bell, R. and Volinsky, C. (2009). Matrix factorization techniques for recommender systems. *Computer*, 42(8), 41–9.

LeBlanc, M. and Tibshirani, R. (1996). Combining estimates in regression and classification. *Journal of the American Statistical Association, 91*(436), 1641–50.

Lee, D. and Seung, H. (2001). Algorithms for non-negative matrix factorization. *Advances in Neural Information Processing Systems (NIPS) 13: Proceedings of the 2000 Conference.* Madison, MI: MIT Press, 556–62.

Lee, J., Sun, M. and Lebanon, G. (2012). A comparative study of collaborative filtering algorithms. *arXiv:1205.3193.*

Lops, P., Gemmis, M. de and Semeraro, G. (2011). Content-based recommender systems: State of the art and trends. In Ricci, F., Rokach, L., Shapira, B. and Kantor, P. (Eds) *Recommender Systems Handbook.* New York, NY: Springer-Verlag, 73–105.

McFadden, D. (1973), Conditional logit analysis of qualitative choice behavior. In P. Zarembka (Ed.) *Frontiers in Economics.* New York, NY: Academic Press, 105–42.

Melville, P., Mooney, R.J. and Nagarajan, R. (2002). Content boosted collaborative filtering for improved recommendations. In Dechter, R. and Sutton, R.S. (Eds) *Proceedings of the 18th National Conference on Artificial Intelligence (AAAI' 02).* Anaheim, CA, Madison, WI: AAAI Press/MIT Press, 187–92.

Metropolis, N., Rosenbluth, A., Rosenbluth, M., Teller, A. and Teller, E. (1953). Equations of state calculations by fast computing machines. *Journal of Chemical Physics, 21*(6), 1087–92.

Miyahara K. and Pazzani, M. (2000). Collaborative filtering with the simple Bayesian classifier. In Mizoguchi, R. and Slaney, J.K. (Eds) *Proceedings of the 6th Pacific Rim International Conference on Artificial Intelligence (PRICAI'00).* Berlin, Heidelberg: Springer-Verlag, 679–89.

Mokbel, M.F. and Levandoski, J.J. (2009). Toward context and preference-aware location-based services. In *Proceedings of the Eighth ACM International Workshop on Data Engineering for Wireless and Mobile Access.* New York, NY: ACM, 25–32.

Payne, J.W., Bettman J.R. and Johnson, E.J. (1992). Behavioral decision research: A constructive processing perspective. *Annual Review of Psychology, 43*(1), 87–131.

Palmisano, C., Tuzhilin, A. and Gorgoglione, M. (2008). Using context to improve predictive modeling of customers in personalization applications. *IEEE Transactions on Knowledge and Data Engineering, 20*(11), 1535–49.

Rennie, J. and Srebro, N. (2005). Fast maximum margin matrix factorization for collaborative prediction. In De Raedt, L. and Wrobel, S. (Eds) *Proceedings of the 22nd International Conference on Machine Learning.* New York, NY: ACM, 719.

Ricci, F., Rokach, L., Shapira, B. and Kantor, P. (Eds) (2011). *Recommender Systems Handbook.* New York, NY: Springer Science+Business Media. LLC, Springer Verlag.

Rubens, N., Kaplan, D. and Sugiyama, M. (2011). Active learning in recommender systems. In Ricci, F., Rokach, L., Shapira, B. and Kantor, P. (Eds) *Recommender Systems Handbook.* New York, NY: Springer, 735–67.

Salakhutdinov, R. and Mnih, A. (2008). Bayesian probabilistic matrix factorization using Markov Chain Monte Carlo, *Proceedings of the 25th International Conference on Machine Learning,* 880–87.

Sanders, J. and Kandrot, E. (2011). *CUDA by Example: An Introduction to General-Purpose GPU Programming.* Upper Saddle River, NJ: Addison-Wesley.

Sarwar, B., Karypis, G., Konstan, J. and Riedl, J. (2001). Item-based collaborative filtering recommendation algorithms. In *Proceedings of the 10th International Conference on the World Wide Web.* New York, NY: ACM, 285–95.

Sill, J., Takacs, G., Mackey, L. and Lin, D. (2009). Feature-weighted linear stacking. *Arxiv:0911.0460.*

Slater, P. (1960). The analysis of personal preferences *The British Journal of Statistical Pscyhology, 13*(2), 119–35.

Su, X., Greiner, R., Khoshgoftaar, T. M. and Zhu, X. (2007). Hybrid collaborative filtering algorithms using a mixture of experts. In *Proceedings of the IEEE/WIC/ACM International Conference on Web Intelligence (WI' 07)*. Washington, DC: IEEE Computer Society, 645–9.

Su, X. and Khoshgoftaar, T.M. (2009). A survey of collaborative filtering techniques. *Advances in Artificial Intelligence*. Available at: http://www.hindawi.com/journals/aai/2009/421425/ [accessed 28 September 2012].

Train, K. (2009). *Discrete Choice Methods with Simulation*. New York: Cambridge University Press.

Tucker, L.R. (1960). Intra-individual and inter-individual multidimensionality. In H. Gullikson and S. Messick (Eds) *Psychological Scaling: Theory and Applications*. New York, NY: Holt, Rinehart and Winston.

Xue, G.-R, Lin, C., Yang, Q., Xi, W., Zeng, H.-J., Yu, Y. and Chen, Z. (2005). Scalable collaborative filtering using cluster-based smoothing. In *Proceedings of the 28th Annual International ACM SIGIR Conference on Research and Development in Information Retrieval (SIGIR '05)*. New York, NY: ACM, 114–21.

Ying, Y., Feinberg, F. and Wedel, M. (2006). Leveraging missing ratings to improve online recommendation systems. *Journal of Marketing Research, 43*(3), 355–65.

Yu, K., Zhu, S., Lafferty, J. and Gong, Y. (2009). Fast nonparametric matrix factorization for large-scale collaborative filtering. In *Proceedings of the 32nd international ACM SIGIR Conference on Research and Development in Information Retrieval (SIGIR '09)*. New York, NY: ACM, 211–18.

Zellner, A. (1962). An efficient method of estimating seemingly unrelated regression equations and tests for aggregation bias. *Journal of the American Statistical Association, 57*(293), 348–68.

8 Marketing in the New Mobile Economy

ANINDYA GHOSE AND SANG-PIL HAN

1 Introduction

Rapid advances in mobile Internet technologies now allow consumers to interact and create and share content based on physical location. In mobile settings, consumers can immediately share their experiences, thoughts, and even their real-time location information. This dramatic growth in mobile activities has led to a corresponding torrent of granular data that capture these behaviors. Whether mobile device users are communicating with others using voice or SMS, consuming digital content, acquiring information, alerting others to their location, engaging in transactions, or posting content to be consumed by others, they are creating an "electronic trail" that lends itself to modeling and analysis which can ultimately lead to a better understanding of customers and more effective marketing.

With a proliferation of mobile channels, managing the marketing mix is also critical for firms today. Firms operate on multiple platforms to track individual-level behavior within and across channels, deriving valuable insights regarding customer behavior and the effectiveness of marketing actions. Among the questions this chapter will raise: What are the implications of mobile channel for managing customer relationships, marketing communications, and branding? How should firms use mobile channels to interact with and enhance relationships with customers and influence their purchase behavior? How do mobile and traditional marketing activities work together to influence consumer perceptions, preferences, and behaviors? How do different consumer groups respond to mobile communications activities and channels for different categories and markets? How do peers affect individual behavior, especially in the adoption and use of new services in mobile settings?

Furthermore, one of the most fundamental changes brought forth by the advent of the mobile phone has been the widespread adoption of mobile applications that perform all kinds of feats, such as accessing social networks, reading eBooks, playing games, music, videos, and so on. Recent media reports document that 91 percent of top brands have a presence in at least one of the major mobile app stores. This is a significant increase compared to 18 months ago when only 51 percent of the brands published or licensed an application. Brands have realized that publishing applications in the various app stores offers a viable channel to promote their brand, reach consumers, and sell products. This

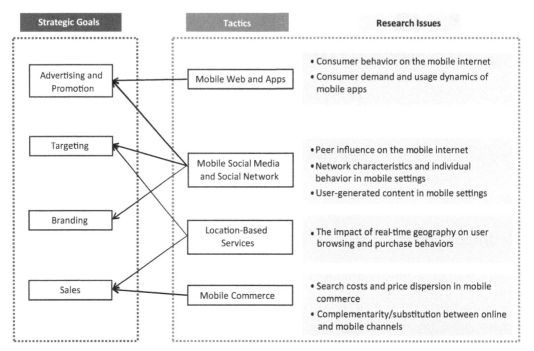

Figure 8.1   Framework for strategic goals, tactics, and research issues on mobile marketing

is especially true of companies in the media, services, and entertainment industries who actively use app stores as a way to market their products.

One of the trends driving the growth in in-app advertising is the growing amount of time mobile users are spending on casual gaming and social media activity using their mobile devices. Recent reports show that time spent in mobile apps has now exceeded mobile web usage, so it makes sense that there is a systematic reallocation of advertising dollars. In addition to the heavy usage mobile apps receive, another reason why marketers would want to invest marketing dollars in apps is that these ads can produce strong results because they can provide more information about a user than browser-based use can, potentially enabling them to better target their efforts. Among the questions this chapter raises are: How can firms manage their brand marketing in mobile application platforms (that is, in-app ads, brand apps)? How should firms convert users' app browsing and usage to actual purchases in their offline/online stores? Should marketers invest in in-app advertising or in mobile display ads?

Figure 8.1 depicts a pictorial framework. The left-hand side lists strategic/managerial goals of firms including advertising, targeting, branding, and sales, and the right-hand side shows related tactics of mobile marketing landscape along with relevant research issues. For example, to achieve a strategic goal of "advertising and promotion" in a mobile environment, we propose to execute new marketing tactics on "mobile web and apps" and "mobile social media and social network." In what follows, we survey the literature on each of these topics in detail. Then we outline some possible directions for future research for each of these topics.

2   Mobile Web and Apps

2.1   CONSUMER BEHAVIOR ON THE MOBILE INTERNET

Mobile content services constitute one of the fastest-growing applications on the web today. Consumers are increasingly engaged in not only content usage but also content generation using their mobile phones. For example, a consumer can upload his photos to social networking sites to share with friends and family, and the consumer can download content from mobile app stores and content that is uploaded by friends. Indeed, advanced mobile technologies allow consumers not only to entertain themselves, to enhance productivity, but also to build and maintain their social relationships through co-creation and joint usage of content.

Content generation and usage may not be independent decision-making processes at all. There are two relevant streams of literature on the dynamic interdependence between user content generation and usage behaviors – economic behavior under resource constraints and reciprocity stemming from social exchange theory. Researchers have long recognized that time acts as a constraint (Becker, 1965; Jacoby, et al., 1976). In online and mobile settings, users need to allocate their resources between content generation and content usage activities since users can take on the dual role of creators as well as consumers (Ghose and Han, 2010, 2011; Trusov, et al., 2010; Albuquerque, et al., 2010). On the mobile Internet, not only do users need to invest time, but also incur explicit transmission charges to generate and use content in certain countries. This suggests that there is a negative temporal interdependence between content generation and content usage activities over time. For example, Ghose and Han (2011) find that there is a negative and statistically significant temporal interdependence between content generation and usage on the mobile Internet. These findings raise a number of interesting directions for future research. For example, the above study does not incorporate information about the specific type of content uploaded or downloaded (for example, photo, audio, text, and so on) and the destination websites (for example, social networking sites, mobile portal sites, and so on) in its analysis. Future work could examine this information. Another area for future research is to study how content generated via mobile phones diffuses through different kinds of social networks, such as text-messaging-based networks, multimedia content-based networks, and offline location-based spatial networks.

In another example, Ghose and Han (2010) develop and estimate a dynamic structural model of how consumers learn about different kinds of content on the mobile Internet. Two common categories of website users access through their cell phones are:

1.   regular social networking and community-oriented (hereafter, SNC) sites; and
2.   mobile portal sites.

This distinction is important because of the fundamental differences in the operation of mobile portal sites from regular websites. Mobile portal sites are owned and hosted by mobile phone companies. Examples include AT&T App Center, Vodafone live, and T-Mobile's Web'n'Walk. In addition to user-generated content, a substantial part of the content on these sites comes from professional content creators who have signed contracts with mobile phone operators. As a result, mobile operators have more control on the kinds of content that is available on these websites. This is as opposed to social networking and community websites such as Facebook, MySpace, Twitter, and so on where the content is generated primarily by users. Hence, an understanding of differences in user behavior (both uploading and downloading) between mobile portal sites and SNC sites can be useful toward examining their potential as advertising platforms.

Ghose and Han (2010) model user behavior with respect to two different categories of content – content from SNC sites and content from mobile portal sites and with respect to two different kinds of activities – content creation (uploading) and consumption (downloading). In their model, users can learn about how well a particular content activity matches their "taste." They also analyze a competing model in which user behavior can be influenced by content quality, rather than taste. User learning in either model (content taste or content quality) occurs through direct signals such as their own content creation and usage behavior as well as through indirect word-of-mouth (WOM) signals such as the content creation and usage behavior of their social network neighbors. They find that learning based on own experience is more accurate than learning from social networks.

These studies raise some potential questions for future research. First, they did not consider the actual amount of content generation and usage activities in our analysis. Instead, they focused only on the frequency of these activities. Second, they do not have information on the actual content of voice calls between social network neighbors. Such information could shed light on exactly what information is shared between members of a mobile phone-based social network. Third, these papers do not study the privacy implications of such granular data and examine if there are any privacy friendly methods that can utilize such data for superior targeting. Future academic work could explore each of these areas and make significant contributions to the literature.

2.2   CONSUMER DEMAND AND USAGE DYNAMICS OF MOBILE APPS

One of the most fundamental changes brought forth by the advent of the mobile phone has been the widespread adoption of mobile applications. Mobile apps have existed for years but clunky user interfaces on devices and hard-to-use apps stores made it difficult for consumers to download apps. And then came Apple in 2008 with its App Store for the iPhone. The iPhone, which was easy to use, coupled with the App Store that allowed users to search and download apps from iTunes, turned mobile apps into an overnight success. Today, the Apple App Store is considered the largest and most successful mobile app store out there. Mobile apps perform all kinds of feats, such as accessing social networks, reading eBooks, playing games, music, videos, and so on, and thus are changing the way consumers entertain and work in the new mobile economy. In 2010 more than 300,000 applications were downloaded 10.9 billion times and global downloads will reach 76.9 billion in 2014 will be worth US$35 billion.

As consumers increasingly use mobile apps, it is important to understand consumer demand for mobile apps and quantify the value created by the availability of these apps. Knowledge of heterogeneous consumer demand toward app characteristics in mobile apps markets can help app developers and managers to design and improve their app features, to determine optimal pricing strategies, to better monetize their apps, and eventually to increase profits. For example, there are so called premium "grossing apps" which are becoming popular. TomTom Navigation app is $99.99 and Golfshot: Golf GPS app is $29.99. Such grossing apps are about four times more expensive than other popular apps (Distimo, 2011). In contrast, there are thousands of popular free apps as well. A free version of Angry Birds gaming app has more than millions of downloads. This example demonstrates that some consumers are willing to pay more for additional features or/and high-quality apps while some consumers are only downloading free versions of apps with limited features.

App developers use consumer demand information to determine whether to offer an app for free, and if not free, how much to charge for it. Moreover, given that app stores often collect one-off or subscription fees for paid apps, it can be critical for them to obtain precise estimates of user demand. Such demand-side information can also be used for app stores to determine whether to develop mobile apps in-house or to outsource high-quality app developers, or both. Ghose and Han (2012) estimate a random coefficient-based structural model of user demand in a mobile app setting and estimate the resultant change in consumer surplus from the availability of mobile apps. In their model, the utility for consumer i from choosing app j in market t can be represented as:

$$u_{ijt} = X_{jt}\beta_i + \alpha_i P_{jt} + \xi_{jt} + \varepsilon_{ijt}, \tag{1}$$

where X_{jt} is a vector of observable characteristics of app j in market t and $_i$ is a vector of the random coefficients (that is, taste parameters) associated with those app characteristics. P_{jt} is the price of app j in market t and α_i is a scalar for a random coefficient that captures consumers' heterogeneous tastes toward app price. ξ_{jt} represents the unobserved (by researchers) characteristics of app j. ε_{ijt} is a mean-zero stochastic term representing an app-level taste shock. The observed app characteristics in the authors' sample include:

- app file size (megabytes);
- app age (days elapsed since app release);
- length of textual app description by the app developer (number of characters);
- number of visual app description by the app developer (number of screenshots);
- app age-restrictions (4+, 9+, 12+, and 17+); and
- app categories.

Using the BLP (Berry, et al., 1995) estimation method, the authors find that besides prices, observed app characteristics such as file size, app tenure, length of the app description, and number of screenshots have a statistically and economically significant effect on app demand.

From a broader perspective, mobile technologies facilitate the delivery of many new products and services across mobile platforms. As these platforms develop and mature, it will be important to quantify their value for customers, firms, and society. As millions of consumers use mobile apps, companies also attempt to grab the attention of their customers and increase value as well as brand recognition. For example, companies can place their brand ads into popular apps. In doing so, it is required to create catchy tag lines and graphics that will remind customers of the existence of the brand as well as to align the mobile app's customer base with the company's target customer groups.

While much of the attention in academic research and in the press has been on examining user behavioral differences in the mobile channel versus traditional channels, we believe that important benefits lie in new products and services made available through these mobile platforms. While prior work has studied the impact of the mobile web on users' multimedia content creation and consumption behavior (for example,

Ghose, et al., forthcoming, 2011), the value of new apps and services made available through mobile platforms has remained unquantified.

Future research in this domain can make an important contribution by estimating user demand for mobile apps, imputing the resultant change in consumer surplus from the availability of mobile apps, and generating managerial insights for app developers, app stores, and advertisers.

2.3 INTERDEPENDENCE BETWEEN WEB AND MOBILE ADS

In the increasingly advertising-filled online environment, it is well-known that consumers are often exposed to more than one message from a marketer before they buy the product. Gartner (2011) projects that brand spending on mobile advertising will grow from 0.5 percent of the total advertising budget in 2010 to over 4 percent in 2015. Mobile advertising comes in a variety of forms, including display, SMS/text message, location-based, and rich media. Of these, mobile banner images displayed on top of the screen in a Wireless Application Protocol (WAP) browser constitute the most common form of such advertising. Recently, this advertising unit has also been embedded in various mobile smartphone applications (apps), which has afforded app developers with another potential source of revenues.

Companies operate on multiple platforms to track individual-level behavior within and across channels, deriving valuable insights regarding customer behavior and the effectiveness of marketing actions. As companies divert more and more funds from traditional media toward digital advertising, they are interested in understanding what effects, if any, the two possible channels of advertising – web advertising and mobile advertising – have on each other. For example, consider the following scenario. A consumer sees a brand advertisement on the PC Internet on one day, an advertisement for the same brand on the mobile channel the next day, and maybe the day after that, the consumer clicks on the mobile ad link. However, any analysis where the mobile channel is the only one getting the credit for the last click-through or where web and mobile advertisings are measured in silos, remains incomplete and potentially flawed. Instead, one needs to look at whether web and mobile advertising work together in a synergistic manner, and if so, then one needs to be able to measure and quantify that effect. While lab experiments would be easier to execute, an ideal test would have to be carried out in the field. Researchers would need to work with advertisers such that they can switch off and on their ads in each of the two channels periodically.

A number of interesting research opportunities exist in this space. A related question is about the interplay between mobile display ads and mobile in-app advertising and how to allocate ad budgets between these two media. Should marketers invest more in one versus the other? Should they invest equally in both? Recent reports show that time spent in mobile apps has now exceeded mobile web usage, so it makes sense that there is a systematic reallocation of advertising dollars. Given the tremendous reach of apps on smartphones, advertisers who are not marketing within apps are probably missing a big opportunity. On the other hand, the growth in tablets, and the iPad in particular, which can significantly improve the mobile web browsing experience, also suggests mobile web-based display ads still have an important role to play. Given the superior experience offered by a larger screen, brands interested in reaching this high-quality audience should invest in both mobile web and in-app ads. In any case, this does raise a series of interesting questions that future researchers can examine and highlight how moderating factors such as industry sector and brand equity influence such choices.

Any future research in this space could build on several streams of research in the traditional online web. First, there is an emerging stream of work that examines the interdependence between different kinds of online advertising channels. For example, Yang and Ghose (2010) analyze the relationship between organic and sponsored search advertising. They analyze the impact of paid ads on organic search listings for several product categories. Their results show that click-throughs on organic listings have a positive interdependence with click-throughs on paid listings, and vice-versa. Ghose et al. (2011) examine the relationship between sponsored search and display advertising to infer whether this interaction between search and display advertising leads to higher or lower conversion rates. In a similar vein, Goldfarb and Tucker (2011a, 2011b) examine the inter-relationship between offline and online advertising for a variety of firms using different media such as search ads, billboard ads, and direct solicitations. In addition, Forman et al. (2009) have also examined substitution and complementarity between offline and online channels.

More broadly, such a study would also be related to an emerging stream of work that examines interdependence in search advertising. Rutz and Bucklin (2011) show that there are spillovers between search advertising on branded and generic keywords; some customers may start with a generic search to gather information, but they later use a branded search to complete their transaction. Ghose and Yang (2009) quantify the impact of keyword attributes on consumer search and purchase behavior as well as on advertiser's cost per click and the search engine's ranking decision for different ads. Ghose and Yang (2011) build a model to map consumers' search–purchase relationship in sponsored search advertising. They provide evidence of horizontal spillover effects from search advertising resulting in purchases across other product categories. Agarwal et al. (2011) provide quantitative insights into the impact of organic search results on the sponsored search especially when there is an overlap in the results. Yao and Mela (2011) build a dynamic structural model to explore how the interaction of consumers, search engines, and advertisers affects consumer welfare and firm profits.

3   Mobile Social Media and Social Network

3.1   PEER INFLUENCE ON THE MOBILE INTERNET

Recently Forrester reported that just 16 percent of the US population is responsible for 80 percent of the impressions and posts about products and services in social media channels. There is a stream of literature on peer influence in social media platforms. Individuals can be influenced by others with whom they communicate. Prior studies commonly define the notion of peer influence as how the behaviors of one's peers change the likelihood that (or extent to which) one engages in a behavior. There is some evidence of this influence in the business world – such as adoption of new services and products (Hill, et al., 2006; Tucker, 2008; Aral, et al., 2009; Nair, et al., 2010; Nam, et al., 2010; Iyengar, et al; 2010; Oestricher-Singer and Sundararajan, 2010), switching from an existing service provider (Dasgupta, et al., 2008), and diffusion of user-generated content in online space (Susarla, et al., 2010). On the mobile Internet, Ghose and Han (2011) find that the social network has a strong positive effect on user behavior in their content generation and usage, respectively.

Peer influence is difficult to identify in observational data (Manski, 1993). Aral (2011) summarizes that there are several sources of bias in data on social interactions and outcomes among peers can confound assessments of peer influence and social contagion, including simultaneity (Godes and Mayzlin, 2004), unobserved heterogeneity (Van den Bulte and Lilien, 2001), homophily (Aral, et al., 2009), time-varying factors (Bemmaor, 1994; Van den Bulte and Lilien, 2001), and other contextual and correlated effects (Manski, 1993).

On the mobile Internet, the ubiquity of mobile devices and their accessibility to mobile Internet allow people to stay connected to each other through various social networking technologies (that is, Facebook, Twitter, Foursquare). Companies are able to distinguish whether a user tweeted on their platform via the mobile web or the PC web (Ghose, et al., 2012a). Consequently, this has generated tons of social interaction data and observed behavioral patterns within social networks. On the one hand, the active use of mobile social media by the population will provide companies and researchers with more detailed information on who interacted with whom at exactly what time and which location, which can be key ingredients to disentangle any peer influence from other confounding factors. On the other hand, sometimes friends are exposed to the same stimuli in terms of time and geography (that is, going to a concert together) and may broadcast their experience real time via social media using their mobile devices. This will generate seemingly very similar behavioral patterns (that is, posting pictures on their Facebook walls). Based on the correlated behavioral observations, one may conclude that there is evidence one influenced the other. However, the observed similarity in behaviors arose due to the same contextual stimuli. Therefore, it will be more challenging to distinguish the peer influence from other alternative explanations in the mobile Internet setting. Future research in this domain can make a valuable contribution by conducting randomized field experiments to identify peer influence and social contagion in the mobile social media, quantifying and comparing the magnitude of peer influence between online and mobile social networks, and formulate effective social contagion management policies in the multichannel social media environment.

3.2   NETWORK CHARACTERISTICS AND INDIVIDUAL BEHAVIOR IN MOBILE SETTINGS

In the last few years, there has been a significant increase in user engagement with various kinds of Internet-based platforms for content creation and consumption. This has led to marketers becoming keen to better understand how various aspects of consumers' social network (for example, their social connections, behavior of contacts) affect their adoption and usage of such platforms. While the medium through which users accessed these platforms in the past was mostly computers, increasingly web-enabled mobile phones have become a more popular device to access content on the Internet.

One stream of research has considered how the structural properties of social networks (for example, the strength of interpersonal connections) impact individual behavior. In general, the impact of network characteristics on behavior is explained through their effect on the level of information that individuals have access to. The classic work of Granovetter (1973, 1982) on the strength of weak ties laid the foundations for such work.

Granovetter noted that weak ties (for example, acquaintances) provide information that strong ties (for example, close friends that a user frequently interacts with) may not have access to. Recent research (for example, Centola and Macy, 2007) offers a more nuanced view of how weak ties may impact consumer behavior. Still other work has emphasized the relationship between other network characteristics and information sharing among individuals (Aral and Van Alstyne 2011; Burt, 2001; Coleman, 1990; Godes and Mayzlin, 2004). For example, Aral and Van Alstyne (2011) find that cohesive networks tend to have greater channel bandwidth, such that an individual can access more detailed information.

On the mobile Internet, Ghose et al. (2012) model the impact of network characteristics – tie strength and network density – and social contagion on the usage of mobile Internet. The tie strength can be operationalized in various ways. They use two metrics, call frequency and call duration based on voice call records (or message frequency based on SMS or MMS records), to capture the strength of the communication between a user and his or her network neighbors. They measured the tie strength at an individual level as the average amount of call (message) frequency or call duration among users. Network density of an individual's network measures the extent to which his direct contacts are connected to each other. To measure the network density for each user, they use local clustering coefficient (Watts and Strogatz, 1998). Ego-centric network density is low for networks of disconnected contacts and high in a network of contacts densely connected to one another. They find that both tie strength and network density significantly impact individual usage of mobile Internet service after controlling for the other. Their results are largely attributable to the information redundancy that occurs within highly connected social networks.

There is an increasing amount of social interaction through mobile devices such as smartphones and tablets. This will change the network structure developed by online social interactions. For example, the extent of tie strength is in general much higher in a mobile setting as compared to in an online setting. Moreover, consumers communicate with different subsets of contacts by access channels. For example, one can communicate primarily with close contacts in mobile as compared to in PC. So the impact of network characteristics on consumer behavior can potentially be very different between two channels. Future research in this domain can make an important contribution by exploring how network structures and characteristics differ between online and mobile communication channels and examine resultant changes in consumer behaviors from the usage of mobile channels.

3.3   USER-GENERATED CONTENT IN MOBILE SETTINGS

There is a stream of literature on user-generated content in social media platforms. Ghose et al. (forthcoming) examine an increasingly popular form of user-generated content in microblogs that can potentially have a strong economic and social impact. A handful of papers have focused on microblogs in particular, including for example, Java et al. (2007) and Boyd et al. (2010). Stephen et al. (2011) use data from Twitter to study transmission activity as a driver of retransmission and diffusion in online social networks.

An emerging stream of literature studies the economic value of user-generated content in online settings as well as the means for monetizing such content, for example, through sponsored search advertising and prediction markets. For example, Archak et al. (2011) examined the pricing power of product features by mining consumer-generated reviews in Amazon.com. These kinds of studies combine established techniques from economics and marketing with text mining algorithms from computer science as well as theories from social psychology to measure the economic value of each text snippet, understand how user-generated content in these systems influence economic exchanges between various agents in electronic markets, and empirically estimate the performance of mechanisms that are being used to monetize such online content.

Consumers can buy products online and leave a short feedback posting, summarizing their interaction with the seller, such as "Lightning fast delivery! Sloppy packaging, though." Increasingly these information exchanges are having some business impact that is being reflected in one or more economic variables (for example, product sales, pricing premiums, profits) that can be measured to examine the effect of a particular information exchange. Consumers now can not only create such content using PCs at home or office but also do so using their mobile devices anywhere and anytime. That popular social media mobile apps (that is, mobile Facebook) constitute the most downloaded apps demonstrates that there has been a dramatic increase in the amount of user-generated content via mobile devices.

One of the distinct features of user-generated content in mobile settings is that it can contain more time-relevant and geographically-specific information about the content. A new study from Forrester Research explains how Yelp.com, which offers customer reviews of local businesses, is leveraging mobile to make it easy for consumers to add information while out and about, thus strengthening its core website. For example, mobile users can upload photos that add details and visual elements to reviews on the website. Mobile users can add a picture from the main menu screen of the Yelp app as well as from a mobile review page. Yelp receives an image from a mobile device every 30 seconds. Moreover, much like Foursquare or Gowalla, mobile Yelp users can check in at a specific location. The Yelp app uses GPS to display to mobile users a list of nearby places or a user can check in directly from a review page. Yelp also shows a ranking of who has checked in at an establishment the most and shows users their friends who have checked in nearby. The feature also allows businesses to offer special deals to customers who have checked in. Future research in this domain can make an important contribution by identifying key determinants of consumers' content generation in the mobile setting, quantifying the economic value of mobile-specific user-generated content, and generating managerial insights for sellers in the mobile commerce, advertisers, and mobile app developers.

4 Location-based Services: The Impact of Real-time Geography on User Browsing and Purchase Behaviors

A long literature documents the role of distance in social and economic behavior. Tobler's (1970) first law of geography is that "all things are related, but near things are more related than far things." The Internet reduces the cost of communication. Therefore, the popular press has frequently emphasized the ability of the Internet ends this relationship and brings about the "Death of Distance" (Cairncross, 1997) or a "Flat World" (Friedman, 2005). In the academic literature, this idea has been explored in depth. Balasubramanian (1998) and Zhang (2009) analytically discuss the role of distance to offline stores in an online and offline substitution setting. Several empirical studies show that the online channel is more valuable when consumers have to travel further to reach an offline store (Forman, et al., 2009; Anderson, et al., 2010). Therefore, the online channel helps reduce the importance of distance in many ways, generally increasing the competition faced by any particular firm. Still, the consequences of lowered communications costs depend on several local factors. Therefore, much online behavior is local. Blum and Goldfarb (2006) show that surfing behavior is disproportionately local and Hampton and Wellman (2002) find that online social interactions are also disproportionately local. Overall, the literature suggests an important role for distance in determining online behavior.

If the benefit of accessing local information is different when people access the Internet on a mobile phone, even though communication costs fall it suggests that online behavior more broadly may change. Hence, if surfing behavior becomes more local then local retailers may disproportionately benefit. For example, people might access the Internet on a mobile phone to sort or filter information by location to make it more relevant to their surroundings (Mountain, et al., 2009). Location-based services are tools that tailor retrieved information based on the location at which a query was made (Brimicombe and Li, 2006; Jiang and Yao, 2006). The location-based services allow for "where's my nearest" services, for example, they include searches for local news, weather or sports reports, navigation, friend-finder services, location-based gaming, and so on (Mountain, et al., 2009). In this sense, distance between a user and a store interacts with whether the user accesses the Internet through a mobile phone or a PC. For example, Ghose et al. (2012a) document a stronger impact of distance on click-through decisions when the Internet is accessed on a mobile phone, and they argue that the distance effects are higher on the mobile Internet.

Recent studies also examined the impact of the extent of the geographical mobility on individual behavior. There are two possible scenarios. The first is that the more a user travels, the more travel-related discretionary time the user is likely to have. Shim et al. (2008) analyze mobile usage patterns where people view TV programs on their phone screens. They find that the highest usage occurs between 6 AM and 9 AM in the morning and between 6 PM and 8 PM in the evening, which is consistent with the notion that most users view content using mobile phones while commuting from home to work and back. O'Hara et al. (2007) find that people use mobile video content to pass time, manage solitude, and disengage from others. In contrast, it is possible that mobile Internet usage can occur at geographically fixed places as well. To address this issue, Ghose and Han (2011) examine the interplay between user Internet usages and geographical mobility. They use a unique dataset on individual-level mobile content generation and usage behavior in conjunction with traveling pattern data of the same user. They find that users more frequently engage in content usage compared to content generation when they are traveling. Future research in this domain can make an important contribution by testing consumers' preference for local products, quantifying the economic value of convenience and instant gratification when transacting products using mobile devices, and generate key managerial insights for content providers, advertisers, and mobile platforms.

5 Mobile Commerce

5.1 SEARCH COSTS AND PRICE DISPERSION IN MOBILE COMMERCE

There is a long stream of literature on search costs in the online environment. As the ranking effect is often interpreted as a type of search cost in an online setting (for example,

Yao and Mela, 2011), Brynjolfsson et al. (2010) have quantified such search costs as being quite substantial in online settings when users are exposed to multiple offers on a computer screen, as in a shopbot setting. The reduction in search costs associated with the Internet affected prices, price dispersion, product quality, online demand, market structure, unemployment, and many other areas of economic life (see, Lynch and Ariely, 2000; Autor, 2001; Ellison and Ellison, 2009; Kim, et al. 2010, and so on). Further, a long literature suggests that there are primacy effects on choice, or benefits to being first or early in a sequence (Becker, 1954; Miller and Krosnick, 1998; Carney and Banaji, 2008, and so on). Most people start browsing from the top of lists, so higher-ranked items are likely to receive more attention. These effects have been documented in a variety of contexts such as food and beverages (Coney, 1977; Dean, 1980), election (Miller and Krosnick, 1998), and elsewhere. In online contexts, a number of papers have shown that primacy effects have important market consequences. For example, better-ranked links are more likely to be clicked in desktop environments (Ansari and Mela, 2003; Drèze and Zufryden, 2004; Baye, et al., 2009; Ghose and Yang, 2009; Yang and Ghose, 2010; Agarwal, et al., 2011).

The wider literature on search also emphasized that lower search costs reduce price dispersion. These effects have been documented in a variety of industries including books and CDs (Brynjolfsson and Smith, 2000), life insurance (Brown and Goolsbee, 2002), and automobiles (Scott Morton, et al., 2001). Overall, however, the evidence suggests that lower search costs online lead to lower prices and lower price dispersion. If search costs via the ranking effect on the mobile Internet differ from those on the PC-based Internet, price dispersion online may change.

Ghose et al. (forthcoming) examine whether a ranking effect is different on the mobile Internet as compared to on the PC-based Internet. That type of search cost is the cognitive effort consumers engage in while scrolling down a list of links displayed on small screens. They cognitively process incoming posting feeds before choosing to click one to learn more about it. Screen sizes have important consequences. A small screen view can cause information chunking and users to lose a global view of the task, incurring cognitive load (Nunamaker, et al., 1987, 1988). Numerous studies have documented that the small screens of mobile phones create a serious obstacle to users' navigation activities and perceptions (Chae and Kim, 2004), the effectiveness of the learning experience (Maniar, et al., 2008), and in mobile marketing (Shankar, et al., 2010). Since only a small amount of information can be shown on the screen, users need to scroll up/down and left/right continuously within a webpage, making it difficult to find target information (Jones, et al., 1999). These search processes place a heavy cognitive load on users (Albers and Kim, 2000). Due to the small screen, users need to remember the content and context of a webpage that they have already viewed, which further increases the cognitive load and the potential for errors (Davison and Wickens, 1999). Hence, adapting the presentation of webpages to the unique mobile context is critical to enabling effective mobile web browsing and information searching (Adipat, et al., 2011).

Future research in this domain can make an important contribution by modeling consumer search behavior using data on both online and mobile browsing and purchase data. Product prices are in general the same between online and mobile channels. So the difference in extent of dispersion of transaction prices between two channels mainly result from consumers' browsing patterns across two channels. The theoretical literature typically model consumer search behavior in two ways: fixed search behavior based on Stigler's original model (1961) and sequential search behavior based on McCall (1970) and Mortensen (1970). Hence future research on consumer search in mobile platforms could shed light on exactly what type of search process consumers typically follow in the mobile environment.

5.2 COMPLEMENTARITY/SUBSTITUTION BETWEEN ONLINE AND MOBILE CHANNELS

An emerging stream of relevant literature has discussed the role of mobile technologies in marketing. Shankar and Balasubramanian (2009) provide an extensive review of mobile marketing. Shankar et al. (2010) develop a conceptual framework on mobile marketing in the retailing environment and provide discussions on retailers' mobile marketing practices. For example, retailers can communicate with consumers near their stores via mobile phones by transmitting relevant information such as the store's location, product availability, quality, price, and coupon in its response to the customer's mobile phone-initiated requests. Moreover, specific consumer segments such as the Gen Y youth market increasingly use mobile phones as single-source communication devices (Sultan, et al., 2009) to gain greater access to social circles, location-based information, and content. Sinisalo (2011) examines the role of the mobile medium among other channels within multichannel CRM communication.

A long stream of literature has examined the interdependence between channels/ platforms. The outcome of such research has important managerial implications on whether a firm invests in both channels/platforms (if there exists synergistic effect) or just either of the two (if there is no synergistic effect). For example, research on multichannel retailing demonstrates consumer substitution between online and offline channels utilizing various theoretical models of spatially differentiated commodity markets derived from Salop's (1979) circular city model (Balasubramanian, 1998; Cheng and Nault, 2007) and from Hotelling's (1929) linear city model (Pan, et al., 2002). Common assumptions in all of these models are the presence of transportation costs when consumers use the offline channel and of disutility costs when buying online. In some cases the size of the transportation costs plays a key role in determining the equilibrium that prevails in these models.

The mobile channel is distinct from online channel. The web not only looks and feels different on a mobile device, but people engage with it differently, at different moments of the day, on the go, and often with different objectives/intent. More importantly, consumers can enjoy instant gratification by using the purchased item immediately. For example, consumers could purchase restaurant deals from Groupon using mobile app, and then redeem them offline shortly afterwards. While consumers will not incur any transportation costs in the mobile channel similar as in the online channel, they can even make purchase decisions real-time anywhere they are. The ubiquity of mobile devices and their accessibility to mobile Internet will allow consumers to seamlessly browse or/and shop products from one device (that is, PC) to another device (that is, smartphones). According to a recent Yahoo Research report, 59 percent of users who visit a website on mobile devices follow up visiting that website on the PC. Similarly, 34 percent of users who visit a website on a PC follow up visiting that website on mobile devices.

These studies raise some potential questions for future research. Consumers can go back and forth between online and mobile websites before they make purchase decisions. With the proliferation of mobile channels, companies operate on multiple platforms to track individual-level behavior within and across channels, deriving valuable insights regarding customer behavior and the effectiveness of marketing actions. No research has empirically examined whether there exists substituting effects or complementary effects between online and mobile channels. Put simply, in order to assess any synergistic effect from the addition of a mobile channel, future research should consider its direct impact (that is, visit a mobile website/app and purchase immediately) as well as its indirect impact (that is, visit a mobile website/app and not make immediate purchases, but later revisit the website on a PC and make purchase). Hence, future research in this domain can make an important contribution by developing rigorous attribution model for the mobile channel.

6 Conclusion

Mobile technology has become the cornerstone of our personal and professional lives. Consumers have the power to socialize, shop, game, and perform several other tasks using handheld devices. The massive growth and adoption of mobile technologies has had many managers and practitioners working on how to effectively position their firms to benefit from the trend. In the face of a rapidly evolving marketing landscape triggered by advances in mobile devices, firms need a structured process for assessing opportunities, testing tactics, and measuring results in these newly emerging channels. Hence, the drive for mobility has become a key part of the technology agenda for most companies today. The integration of mobile devices such as laptops, tablets, PDAs, and smartphones, along with their various applications, make it easier than ever for businesses to communicate with internal employees and external entities such as customers and vendors. Mobile technology allows people to use company data and resources without being tied to a single location. Users can download applications on their mobile devices that allow them to connect with others through social media. Firms are using web-based applications to communicate directly with customers in a variety of ways. Mobile technology has introduced a new dimension into advertising and marketing for businesses worldwide. Consumers now see advertisements on mobile phones through a wide variety of mobile marketing technologies including SMS, mobile websites, mobile applications, banner ads, QR codes, and so on. These advertisements can be customized to reach a more specific, targeted audience thanks to software that parses the information individuals are seeking on their mobile device and then displaying advertisements related to that information. Mobile commerce is taking off in a big way too as mobile technologies are being used to distribute vouchers, coupons, and location-specific deals. In a nutshell, mobile-based devices are changing the way a firm does business because these new technologies are enabling the creation of new products and services for customers. In this chapter, we have summarized the state-of-the-art academic knowledge in this space. We have also pointed out several interesting research opportunities in this domain. We hope our article paves the way for future research that has deep managerial implications and insights, and advances the academic work in this important domain.

References

Adipat, B., Zhang, D. and Zhou, L. (2011). The effects of tree-view based presentation adaptation on mobile web browsing. *Management Information Systems Quarterly, 35*(1), 99–121.

Agarwal, A., Hosanagar, K. and Smith, M.D. (2011). Location, location, location: An analysis of profitability of position in online advertising markets. *Journal of Marketing Research, 48*(6), 1057–73.

Albers, M. and Kim, L. (2000). User web browsing characteristics using Palm handhelds for information retrieval. In Jones, S.B., Moeller, B.W., Priestley, M. and Long, B. (Eds) *Proceedings of IEEE Professional Communication Society International Professional Communication Conference.* Washington, DC: IEEE Computer Society, 125–35.

Albuquerque, P., Pavlidis, P., Chatow, U., Chen, K., Jamal, Z. and Koh, K. (2010). Evaluating promotional activities in an online two-sided market for user-generated content, Working paper, SSRN.

Anderson, E., Fong, N., Simester, D. and Tucker, C. (2010). How sales taxes affect customer and firm behavior: The role of search on the Internet. *Journal of Marketing Research, 47*(2), 229–39.

Ansari, A. and Mela, C. (2003). E-customization. *Journal of Marketing Research, 40*(2), 131–45.

Aral, S. (2011). Identifying social influence: A comment on opinion leadership and social contagion in new product diffusion. *Marketing Science, 30*(2), 217–23.

Aral, S., Muchnik, L., and Sundararajan, A. (2009). Distinguishing influence-based contagion from homophily-driven diffusion in dynamic networks. *Proceedings of the National Academy of Sciences, 106*(51).

Aral, S. and Van Alstyne, M. (2011). The diversity-bandwidth tradeoff. *American Journal of Sociology, 117*(1), 90–171.

Archak, N., Ghose, A. and Ipeirotis, P. (2011). Deriving the pricing power of product features by mining consumer reviews. Management Science, *57*(8), 1485–509.

Autor, D. (2001). Wiring the labor market. *Journal of Economic Perspectives, 15*(1), 25–40.

Balasubramanian, S. (1998). Mail versus mall: A strategic analysis of competition between direct marketers and conventional retailers. *Marketing Science, 17*(3), 181–95.

Baye, M., Gatii, R., Kattuman, P. and Morgan, J. (2009). Clicks, discontinuities, and firm demand online. *Journal of Economics and Management Strategy, 18*(4), 935–75.

Becker, S. (1954). Why an order effect? *Public Opinion Quarterly, 18*(3), 271–78.

Becker, G.S. (1965). A theory of the allocation of time. *Economic Journal, 75*(299), 493–517.

Bemmaor, A.C. (1994). Modeling the diffusion of new durable goods: Word-of-mouth effect versus consumer heterogeneity. In G. Laurent, G.L. Lilien and B. Pras (Eds) *Research Traditions in Marketing.* Boston, MA: Kluwer Academic Publishers, 201–23.

Berry, S., Levinsohn, J. and Pakes, A. (1995). Automobile prices in market equilibrium. *Econometrica, 63*(4), 841–90.

Blum, B. and Goldfarb, A. (2006). Does the Internet defy the law of gravity? *Journal of International Economics, 70*(2), 384–405.

Boyd, D., Golder, S. and Lotan, G. (2010). Tweet, Tweet, Retweet: Conversational Aspects of Retweeting on Twitter. *Proceedings of the 43th Hawaii International Conference on System Sciences* (HICSS), 1–10.

Brimicombe, A. and Li, Y. (2006). Mobile space-time envelopes for location-based services. *Transactions in Geographical Information* Systems, *10*(1), 5–23.

Brown, J. and Goolsbee, A. (2002). Does the Internet make markets more competitive? Evidence from the life insurance industry. *Journal of Political Economy, 110*(3 June), 481–507.

Brynjolfsson, E. and Smith, M. (2000). Frictionless commerce? A comparison of Internet and conventional retailers. *Management Science, 46*(4), 563–85.

Brynjolfsson, E., Dick, A. and Smith, M. (2010). A nearly perfect market? Differentiation versus price in consumer choice. *Quantitative Marketing and Economics, 8*(1), 1–33.

Burt, R.S. (2001). Structural holes versus network closure as social capital. In N. Lin, K.S. Cook and R.S. Burt (Eds) *Social Capital: Theory and Research.* New York, NY: Aldine De Gruyter, 31–56.

Cairncross, F. 1997. *The Death of Distance.* Cambridge, MA: Harvard University Press.

Carney, D.R. and Banaji, M.R. (2008). First is Best. Working Paper, Columbia University.

Centola, D. and Macy, M. (2007). Complex contagions and the weakness of long ties. *American Journal of Sociology, 113*(3), 702–34.

Chae, M. and Kim, J. (2004). Do size and structure matter to mobile users? An empirical study of the effects of screen size, information structure, and task complexity on user activities with standard web phones. *Behaviour & Information Technology, 23*(3), 165–81.

Cheng, Z. and Nault, B.R. (2007). Internet channel entry: Retail coverage and entry cost advantage. *Information Technology and Management, 8*(2), 111–32.

Coleman, J.S. (1990). *Foundations of Social Theory.* Cambridge, MA: Harvard Business School Press.

Coney, K. (1977). Order bias: The special case of letter preference. *Public Opinion Quarterly, 41*(3), 385–88.

Dasgupta, K.R., Singh, B., Viswanathan, D., Chakraborty, S., Mukherjea, A. and Nanavati, A.J. (2008). Social ties and their relevance to churn in mobile telecom networks. *Proceedings of the 11th International Conference on Extending Database Technology Conference,* Nantes, France.

Davison, H. and Wickens, C. (1999). Rotocraft hazard cueing: The effects on attention and trust. Technical Report ARL-99-5/NASA-99-1, University of Illinois, Aviation Research Lab, Savoy, IL.

Dean, M. (1980). Presentation order effects in product taste tests. *Journal of Psychology, 105*(1), 107–10.

Distimo. (2011). In-depth view on download volumes in the Google Android Market. Available at: http://www.distimo.com/blog/2011_05_in-depth-view-on-download-volumes-in-the-google-android-market/

Drèze, X. and Zufryden, F. (2004). The measurement of online visibility and its impact on Internet traffic. *Journal of Interactive Marketing, 18*(1), 20–37.

Ellison, G. and Ellison, S.F. (2009). Search, obfuscation, and price elasticities on the Internet. *Econometrica, 77*(2), 427–52.

Forman, C., Ghose, A. and Goldfarb, A. (2009). Competition between local and electronic markets: How the benefit of buying online depends on where you live. *Management Science, 55*(1), 47–57.

Friedman, T. (2005). *The World is Flat: A Brief History of the Twenty-first Century.* New York, NY: Farrar, Straus, and Giroux.

Gartner. (2011). Gartner Says Worldwide Mobile Application Store Revenue Forecast to Surpass $15 Billion in 2011. Available at: http://www.gartner.com/it/page.jsp?id=1529214 [accessed October 16, 2012).

Ghose, A., Goldfarb, A. and Han, S. (forthcoming). How is the mobile internet different? Search costs and local activities, *Information Systems Research.*

Ghose, A., Goldfarb, A. and Han, S. (2011). An Empirical Analysis of the Relationship between Display and Sponsored Search Advertising, Working Paper, NYU.

Ghose, A. and Han, S. (2010). A Dynamic Structural Model of User Learning in Mobile Media Content, Working Paper, SSRN.

Ghose, A. and Han, S. (2011). An empirical analysis of user content generation and usage behavior on the mobile Internet. *Management Science, 57*(9), 1671–91.

Ghose, A., and Han, S. (2012). Estimating Demand for Applications in the New Mobile Economy, Working Paper, NYU.

Ghose, A., Han, S. and Iyengar, R. (2012). Estimating Demand for Mobile Apps in the New Economy. Working Paper, SSRN.

Ghose, A. and Yang, S. (2009). An empirical analysis of search engine advertising: sponsored search in electronic markets. *Management Science, 55*(10), 1605–22.

Ghose, A. and Yang, S. (2011). Modeling Cross-category Purchases in Sponsored Search Advertising, Working Paper, NYU.

Godes, D. and Mayzlin, D. (2004). Using online vonversations to study word-of-mouth communication. *Marketing Science, 23*(4), 545–60.

Goldfarb, A. and Tucker, C. (2011a). Search engine advertising: Channel substitution when pricing ads to context. *Management Science, 57*(3), 458–70.

Goldfarb, A. and Tucker, C (2011b). Advertising bans and the substitutability of online and offline advertising. *Journal of Marketing Research, 57*(3), 458–70.

Granovetter, M.S. (1973). The strength of weak ties. *American Journal of Sociology, 78*(6) 1360–1380.

Granovetter, M.S. (1982). The strength of weak ties: A network theory revisited. In P.V. Marsden and N. Lin (Eds) *Social Structure and Network Analyses*. New York, NY: John Wiley and Sons, 105–30.

Hampton, K. and Wellman, B. (2002). Neighboring in Netville: How the Internet supports community and social capital in a wired suburb. *City and Community, 2*(3), 277–311.

Hill, S., Provost, F. and Volinsky, C. (2006). Network-based marketing: Identifying likely adopters via consumer networks. *Statistical Science, 21*(2), 256–76.

Hotelling, H. (1929). Stability in competition. *Econometric Journal, 39*, 41–57.

Iyengar, R., Van den Bulte, C. and Valente, T. (2011). Opinion leadership and social contagion in new product diffusion. *Marketing Science, 30*(2), 195–212.

Jacoby, J., Szybillo,. G.J. and Berning, C.K. (1976). Time and consumer behavior: An interdisciplinary overview. *Journal of Consumer Research, 2*(4), 320–39.

Java, A., Song, X., Finin, T. and Tseng, B. (2007). Why we twitter: Understanding microblogging usage and communities. *Proceedings of the Joint 9th WEBKDD and 1st SNA-KDD Workshop*, San Jose, CA.

Jiang, B. and Yao, X. (2006). Location-based services and GIS in perspective. *Computers, Environment and Urban Systems, 30*(6), 712–25.

Jones, M., Marsden, G., Mohd-Nasir, N. and Boone, K. (1999). Improving web interaction on small displays. *Computer Networks, 31*(11–16), 1129–37.

Kim, J., Albuquerque, P. and Bronnenberg, B. (2010). Online demand under limited consumer search. *Marketing Science, 29*(6), 1001–23.

Lynch, J.G. and Ariely, D. (2000). Wine online: Search costs affect competition on price, quality, and distribution. *Marketing Science, 19*(1), 83–103.

Maniar, N., Bennett, E., Hand, S. and Allan, G. (2008). The effect of mobile phone screen size on video based learning. *Journal of Software, 3*(4), 51–61.

Manski, C.F. (1993). Identification of endogenous social effects: The reflection problem. *Review of Economic Studies, 60*(3), 531–42.

McCall, J. (1970). Economics of information and job search. *Quarterly Journal of Economics, 84*(1), 113–26.

Miller, J. and Krosnick, J. (1998). The impact of candidate name order on election outcomes. *Public Opinion Quarterly, 62*(3), 291–330.

Mortensen, D. (1970). A theory of wage and employment dynamics. In E. Phelps (Ed.) *Microeconomic Foundations of Employment and Inflation Theory*. New York, NY: W. Norton.

Mountain, D., Myrhaug, H. and Goker, A. (2009). Mobile search. In A. Göker and J. Davis (Eds) *Information Retrieval: Searching in the 21st Century*. Chichester: John Wiley and Sons, 103–30.

Nair, H., Manchanda, P. and Bhatia, T. (2010). Asymmetric social interactions in physician prescription behavior: The role of opinion leaders. *Journal of Marketing Research, 47*(5), 883–95.

Nam, S., Manchanda, P. and Chintagunta, P.K. (2010). The effect of signal quality and contiguous word of mouth on customer acquisition for a video-on-demand service. *Marketing Science, 29*(4), 690–700.

Nunamaker, J.F., Applegate, L.M. and Konsynski, B.R. (1987). Facilitating group creativity: Experience with a group decision support system. *Journal of Management Information Systems, 3*(4), 5–19.

Nunamaker, J.F., Applegate, L.M. and Konsynski, B.R. (1988). Computer-aided deliberation: Model management and group decision support. *Journal of Operations Research, 36*(6), 826–848.

Oestreicher-Singer, G., and Sundararajan, A. (2010). The Visible Hand of Social Networks in Electronic Markets. Working Paper, SSRN.

O'Hara, K., Mitchell, A. and Vorbau, A. (2007). Consuming video on mobile devices. *Proceedings of the SIGCHI Conference on Human Factors in Computing Systems*, San Jose, CA.

Pan, X., Ratchford, B., and Shankar, V. (2002). Price Competition between Pure Play versus Bricks-and-Clicks e-retailers: Analytical Model and Empirical Analysis. In M. Baye (Ed.) *The Economics of the Internet and E-Commerce* (Advances in Applied Microeconomics, Vol. 11). Amsterdam: Elsevier, 29–62.

Rutz, O.J. and Bucklin, R.E. (2011). From generic to branded: A model of spillover dynamics in paid search advertising. *Journal of Marketing Research, 48*(1), 87–102.

Salop, S.C. (1979). Monopolistic competition with outside goods. *Bell Journal of Economics, 10*(1), 141–56.

Scott Morton, F., Zettlemeyer, F. and Silva-Risso, J. (2001). Internet car retailing. *Journal of Industrial Economics, 49*(4 Dec), 501–20.

Shankar, V. and Balasubramanian, S. (2009). Mobile marketing: A synthesis and prognosis. *Journal of Interactive Marketing, 23*(2), 118–29.

Shankar, V., Venkatesh, A., Hofacker, C. and Naik, P. (2010). Mobile marketing in the retailing environment: Current insights and future research avenues. *Journal of Interactive Marketing, 24*(2), 111–20.

Shim, J.P., Park, S. and Shim, J.M. (2008). Mobile TV phone: Current usage, issues, and strategic implications. *Industrial Management and Data Systems, 108*(9), 1269–82.

Sinisalo, J. (2011). The role of the mobile medium in multichannel CRM communication. *International Journal of Electronic Customer Relationship Management, 5*(1), 23–45.

Stephen, A., Dover, Y. and Goldenberg, J. (2011). Social Sharing by Social Pumps: The Effect of Transmitter Activity on Information Diffusion over Online Social Networks, Working Paper, University of Pittsbrugh.

Stigler, G. (1961). The economics of information. *Journal of Political Economy, 69*, 213–25.

Sultan, F., Rohm, A. and Gao, T. (2009). Factors influencing consumer acceptance of mobile marketing: A two country Study of Youth Markets. *Journal of Interactive Marketing, 23*(4), 308–20.

Susarla, A., Oh, J. and Tan, Y. (2012). Social networks and the diffusion of user-generated content: Evidence from YouTube. *Information Systems Research, 23*(1), 23–41.

Tobler, W. (1970). A computer movie simulating urban growth in the Detroit region. *Economic Geography, 46*(2), 234–40.

Trusov, M., Bodapati, A.V. and Bucklin, R.E. (2010). Determining influential users in internet social networks. *Journal of Marketing Research, 47*(4), 643–58.

Tucker, C. (2008). Identifying formal and informal influence in technology adoption with network externalities. *Management Science, 54*(12), 2024–38.

Van den Bulte, C. and Lilien, G. (2001). Medical innovation revisited: Social contagion versus marketing effort. *American Journal of Sociology, 106*(5), 1409–35.

Watts, D. and Strogatz, S. (1998). Collective dynamics of small-world networks. *Nature, 393*, 440–42.

Yang, S. and Ghose, A. (2010). Analyzing the relationship between organic and sponsored search advertising: Positive, negative, or zero interdependence? *Marketing Science, 29*(4), 602–23.

Yao, S. and Mela, C. (2011). A dynamic model of sponsored search advertising. *Marketing Science, 30*(3), 447–68.

Zhang, X. (2009). Retailers' multichannel and price advertising strategies. *Marketing Science, 28*(6), 1080–94.

9 Targeting Display Advertising

WENDY W. MOE

1 Introduction

Before sponsored search advertising, pop-up ads and email campaigns, there was display advertising. From the very beginning, display ads have been an important source of revenues for online content providers and as such have played a critical role in supporting the free content provided on the Internet. Figure 9.1 illustrates the growth in online advertising expenditures over the past eight years. Even with the development of a wide array of new online advertising vehicles, expenditures on displays ads continue to grow and accounted for 24 percent of the $26.04 billion online advertising industry in 2010. The term display ad refers to a family of online advertisements that include text, images, and/or animation presented on content sites. Large display ads appearing across the top of a content page are typically referred to as banner ads whereas ads presented along the side of a content page are referred to as skyscraper ads. Regardless of the location of the

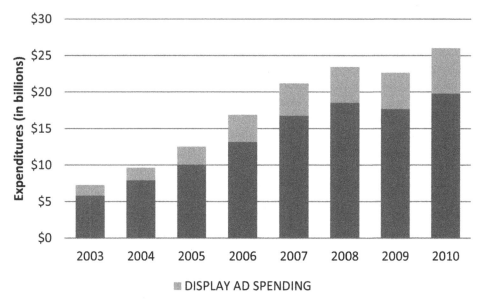

Figure 9.1　Online advertising expenditures
Source: Interactive Advertising Bureau (2003–2010).

ad, display ads expose the website visitor to the brand featured in the ad and provide interested individuals the ability to click on the ad for more information.

Over the years, as online marketers gather more data and establish better metrics and analytics, advertisers have developed and refined their ability to target display ads to the most promising prospects. This chapter will provide an overview of some of the metrics and analytics used to evaluate display ads and then describe how they are leveraged for targeting policies.

2 Measuring the Effectiveness of Online Display Advertising

While online marketers have more data available, it can still be a challenge to accurately measure advertising effectiveness. The ideal metric would provide some measure of return on investment (ROI) reflecting the added profitability generated by advertising expenditures.

$$ROI = \frac{Incremental\,profits\,generated\,by\,advertising}{Advertising\,expenditure} \tag{1}$$

While the denominator for any ROI calculation can be relatively straightforward to obtain, the numerator presents a greater challenge. This is true for both online and offline marketers. The advantage that online marketers have is the abundance of performance metrics available for online ads. Offline advertisers must rely on response models that link aggregate sales to advertising activities (which can be difficult) or surveys that gauge consumer awareness of and attitudes toward advertisements. In contrast, online advertisers are able to track a variety of consumer behaviors that can be directly related to a specific online ad.

Table 9.1 describes common metrics used to evaluate online advertising. Ad impression measures are comparable to offline metrics of audience exposure and reach and represent the number of website visitors exposed to the ad. This metric is determined by the level of visitor traffic at the website on which the ad space is purchased. Unique to the online environment is the ability to measure behavioral responses to the ad exposure. Two common metrics are click-through rates (CTR) and purchase conversion. CTR are computed as the percent of exposures associated with a click on the ad and are a measure of the consumer's immediate behavioral response to the ad. Online advertisers can also link a consumer's click-through to subsequent purchasing behavior at the advertiser's website, an endeavor that has been a challenge for offline advertisers. However, online web retailers can easily compute purchase conversion rates (number of visitors who purchase/total number of visitors) associated with visitors who enter the site through an ad click-through and compare it to their regular visitors. The aforementioned metrics provide marketers with the ability to directly measure an ad's effect on sales and thus allows for more accurate calculations of advertising ROI (if the selection effects resulting from ad targeting are adequately controlled for).

Websites selling ad space also try to capitalize on the availability of these metrics by linking their price to many of the performance metrics mentioned above. Web pages that benefit from high visitor traffic often price based on the number of impressions they deliver. Their proposition is that simply exposing individuals to an ad can be beneficial to the advertiser's brand and long-term sales. This is referred to as CPM (or cost per

Table 9.1   Online advertising performance metrics

	Description	Pricing Model	
Impressions	Number of exposures to ad	CPM (cost per thousand impressions)	Hybrid model
Click-Through Rates (CTR)	% of exposures associated with a click on the ad	CPC (cost per click)	
Purchase Conversion	% of web retailer visitors who purchased	Difficult for ad seller to measure	
Return on Investment (ROI)	Incremental profits from ad expenditure		

thousand impressions) pricing. Other sites (especially those with very targeted audiences) price according to the number of click-throughs they deliver with the presumption that the visitors to their site are more valuable consumers than the untargeted audience delivered by high traffic web pages. This pricing model is referred to as cost-per-click (or CPC) pricing. Some efforts have also been made to price ads according to the subsequent purchases that may result. However, this can be difficult since it requires that the web retailer track and share data pertaining to purchasing activity at their site, which can raise potential privacy problems thus limiting this practice.

CPM models capitalize on exposure effects while CPC models capitalize on measureable behavioral responses. However, advertising is likely to provide both long-term brand-building effects from exposure (Drèze and Hussherr, 2003) as well as immediate behavioral effects as measured by click-throughs (Chatterjee, et al., 2003). Thus, increasingly websites are instituting hybrid models where the cost of advertising on their site is function of both the impressions and the clicks delivered.

2.1 PERFORMANCE METRICS BASED ON IMMEDIATE AD EFFECTS

The online advertising industry has focused heavily on CTR metrics. While offline ads have been priced almost exclusively according to the level of exposure they provide, pricing for online ads has been based largely on CTR. In a 2010 report by the Interactive Advertising Bureau (IAB), 62 percent of all online ads were priced using performance metrics only (for example, CTR) while the remaining considered exposure measures (33 percent were priced exclusively based on exposure while 5 percent considered a hybrid pricing model).

Because of this focus on CTR, several researchers have directed their attention to the factors that impact click-through performance of display ads. A study by Chatterjee et al. (2003) examined intrasession versus intersession effects on CTR. They found that, within a browsing session, individuals tend to click on the first exposure of any given ad and are far less likely to click on repeat exposures. Across sessions, individuals become more responsive to an ad as time since the last exposure increases. In other words, the researchers argue that ad performance depends on the location of the ad in the individual's navigational clickstream. The study also found high variation in "click proneness" across people, highlighting the potential opportunity to individually target online display advertisements.

Rutz and Bucklin (2011) considered a different performance metric. Rather than examining CTR, they investigated how display ads affect browsing paths. Across industries, CTR are quite low. In 2009, a study by the National Advertising Initiative showed that the average click-through rate for an untargeted display ad was 2.8 percent (Beales, 2010). However, display ads can affect behaviors other than ad click-through. Rutz and Bucklin (2011) show how consumers exposed to a display ad (even if they don't click on it) will change their online shopping behavior to include searches for the brand featured in the ad.

2.2   LONG-TERM PERFORMANCE OF ONLINE DISPLAY ADVERTISING

Long-term effects of advertising can be very difficult to measure, whether online or offline. The theory is that advertising builds awareness and preference for a brand and that this ultimately translates to increased sales. While performance metrics such as CTR measure the immediate effect of display advertising, they fail to capture long-term benefits for the brand.

To highlight the drawbacks of relying exclusively on CTR, Drèze and Hussherr (2003) use eye-tracking technology in a controlled experiment to examine how individuals interact with online display ads. Their findings suggest that low CTR are driven in large part by the fact that many individuals avoid looking at display ads altogether (rather than looking but not clicking), a finding supported by Cho and Cheon (2004) who found that consumers avoid looking at display ads because they are perceived as goal impediments. However, Drèze and Hussherr (2003) further find that although website visitors avoid looking at display ads, the presence of the ad is still able to influence traditional brand equity measures such as awareness, recall, and recognition. The implication is that CTR underestimates the returns on display ads as these ads can benefit a brand even when consumers are not actively engaged with the ad itself.

The long-term impact of display ads on the brand is further demonstrated by Manchanda et al. (2006). In their study, display ads were shown to influence future repurchasing behavior for a frequently purchased consumer product. Rather than examining CTR, Manchanda et al. (2006) modeled an individual's inter-purchase time as a hazard process where exposure to display ads can speed up purchase frequency. In other words, they show that display ads can increase customer lifetime value. This benefit of display advertising is ignored by simple performance metrics such as CTR, and thus any ROI calculations based on CTR would undervalue display advertising activities.

2.3   ADVERTISING RESPONSE MODELS

The alternative to using CTR is to construct an advertising response model that allows for both immediate and short-term effects. Decades of offline research has resulted in a family of models that employ a construct that has often been referred to as advertising goodwill (Nerlove and Arrow, 1962). The theory is that advertising effects accumulate as consumers are repeatedly exposed to advertising. At the same time, consumers also forget, and the effects of previously seen advertisements decay as time passes. Marketing researchers have operationalized this accumulation and decay of advertising effects by defining advertising goodwill as follows:

$$\text{Goodwill}_t = \alpha \, \text{Goodwill}_{t-1} + A_t \tag{2}$$

where Goodwill_t represents the inventory of advertising goodwill at time t, α is the decay rate of goodwill from period to period, and A_t is the effect of the advertisement presented at time t. This model is sometimes also referred to as a "leaky bucket" model as the mechanism driving the goodwill measure can be likened to attempts to fill a leaky bucket with water.

The above model has also been extended to allow for advertising wear-out and restoration effects. In a study of TV advertising effects on product sales, Naik et al. (1998) propose a model that allows ads in a campaign to decrease in effectiveness with repetition (wear-out) but regain effectiveness as time passes (restoration). As a result, the effectiveness of any given ad campaign would depend on the ad schedule and the timing of each ad exposure (for example, *when* should an ad air?), a key component of the media buying decision.

However, advertisers buying online display ads cannot pre-determine the schedule of ad exposures. With offline media, the audience passively absorbs the schedule of ads that is pushed out to them. In contrast, the online consumer interacts with the media and controls what they see as well as the sequence in which they see it. As a result, the schedule of ad exposures is dependent on an individual's sequence of page views and therefore unique across individuals. While it is possible for an advertiser to design an online campaign to generally increase or decrease exposures, notable difference will still exist across individuals due to differences in their browsing behaviors.

Braun and Moe (2010) extend the response models developed for offline advertising to explicitly measure the effects of individually varying ad schedules. Their model attributes the effects of an online display ad campaign to:

1. the various advertising copy utilized in the campaign;
2. the schedule of ad impressions (for example, wear-out and restoration effects); and
3. individual differences across consumers.

Since the nature of online data provide detailed behavioral data at the individual-level, Braun and Moe (2010) examine how individual visits to the advertiser's website and subsequent conversion at the website are affected by that individual's unique schedule of ad impressions.

Specifically, they employ a zero-inflated Poisson model for the number of visits (v_{it}) an individual makes to the advertiser's website in time *t*, and a zero-inflated Binomial model for that individual's conversion rate at the site (where s_{it} represents the number of successful conversions resulting from the v_{it} visits). In both models, r_v and r_s captures the inflated observations at zero.

$$f\left(v_{it}\right) = (1 - r_v)\mathbf{I}\left[\sum_t v_{it} = 0\right] + r_v \frac{e^{-\alpha_{it}} \alpha_{it}^{v_{it}}}{v_{it}!} \tag{3}$$

$$f\left(s_{it}\right)=(1-r_{s})\mathbf{I}\left(\sum_{t}s_{it}=0\right)+r_{s}\binom{v_{it}}{s_{it}}p_{it}^{s_{it}}\left(1-p_{it}\right)^{v_{it}-s_{it}} \tag{4}$$

Both model components include covariate effects that capture the variation in impression schedules across individuals. Methodologically, they employ an advertising goodwill construct with creative-specific, wear-out and restoration effects as a covariate for the individual's Poisson visit rate (l_i) and Binomial conversion rate (p_i). Bayesian methods are used to allow for heterogeneity across individual baseline visit and conversion rates. The resulting model measures the effects of a display ad campaign on visits to and successful conversions at the advertiser's website as ad exposures vary across individuals, both in terms of the creative content as well as the schedule of ad impressions presented to the target consumer.

$$log\, \alpha_{it}=log\, \alpha_{0i}+\beta_{\alpha i}GOODWILL_{it}+\gamma SEASONALITY_{t} \tag{5}$$

$$logit\, p_{it}=logit\, p_{0i}+\beta_{pi}GOODWILL_{it} \tag{6}$$

where advertising goodwill (GOODWILL) decays over time at rate α and increases with each new ad impression. The magnitude of the increase depends on the creative-specific effect associated with the impression, repetition wear-out effects after u repeat exposures of creative j, and restoration effects after a period of τ has elapsed since the last exposure of creative j.

$$GOODWILL_{it}=\alpha GOODWILL_{i,t-1}+\sum_{j=1}^{J}\overset{Effect\,of}{Creative\,j}\sum_{u=1}^{\overset{Cumulative}{Ad\,Exposures}_{ijt}}\left(\frac{repetition}{wearout}\right)^{u-1}\left(\frac{restoration}{effect}\right)^{\tau_{ij}} \tag{7}$$

Braun and Moe (2011) also control for potential correlations between how frequently an individual is exposed to an ad and their underlying visitation and purchasing behavior. They do so by explicitly modeling each individual's impression schedule as a separate zero-inflated Poisson process (with impression rate λ) and correlate each individual's rate of impressions with the rate of visits and purchases. This allows for variation across individuals as well as any correlation between ad exposure and visitation and purchasing behavior that may be a result of simply increasing online browsing activity.

$$log\, \lambda_{i},log\, \mu_{0i},logit\, p_{0i},\beta_{\mu i},\beta_{pi}\sim MVN\left(\phi,\Sigma\right) \tag{8}$$

Their empirical results show substantial ad accumulation, wear-out, and restoration effects and have implications for how advertisers should schedule ad impressions for a given individual. For example, in some cases, it may be beneficial to serve an ad with less effective creative content if ads with more effective content are sufficiently "worn-out." A more in-depth discussion of how this study impacts behavioral targeting policies appears later in this chapter.

2.4 CROSS-CHANNEL EFFECTS

Increasingly, consumers are multi-channel shoppers (Inman, et al., 2004; Neslin and Shankar, 2009). Many consumers research a purchase in one channel while transacting the purchase itself in a different channel. However, when evaluating the effectiveness of online ads, researchers tend to consider only the online channel and assume channel/ marketing congruency. That is, they assume that shoppers respond to online ads with online purchases (Blattberg, et al., 2008).

However, Dinner et al. (2011) found evidence of multi-channel advertising effects. They decompose sales revenue into online and offline revenues and then distinguish between customer count and customer spend as two separate sources of revenue, allowing them to examine how various forms of advertising affects each.

$$REVENUES_{mt} = OfflineCustomerCount_{mt} \times OfflineCustomerSpend_{mt}$$
$$OnlineCustomerCount_{mt} * OnlineCustomerSpend_{mt} \qquad (9)$$

While previous research found that advertising and promotional efforts tend to affect customer count but have limited effects on customer spend (Ansari, et al., 2008), Dinner et al. found empirical evidence that advertising affects both customer count and customer spend. But perhaps their most interesting finding is that online advertising can affect offline sales (more so than how much offline advertising affects online sales). This cross-channel effect can be substantial with online advertising affecting offline sales as much as it affects online sales. These results imply that measures of online advertising effectiveness focused exclusively on online sales will underestimate the overall impact of the advertising expenditures for those companies with both an online and offline presence.

2.5 SUMMARY OF MEASUREMENT METHODS FOR ONLINE DISPLAY ADVERTISING

What the abovementioned studies have shown us is that online display advertising can have both immediate effects, which can be captured by CTR, as well as longer-term effects, which tend to be overlooked by such performance metrics. As a result, a number of studies have set forth to document and measure the long-term effects of display advertising on the brand, navigational path, repeat purchasing rate, and future visitation and conversion behavior. Table 9.2 provides a summary of these studies and the effects they found.

Table 9.2   Summary of online display ad effects

	Effects of Display Ads	Research Study
Immediately observable effects	Click-through rate	Chatterjee et al. (2003) Beales (2010)
	Navigational/search behavior	Rutz and Bucklin (2009)
Long-term effects	Repurchase frequency	Manchanda et al. (2006)
	Brand equity metrics (awareness, recall, recognition)	Drèze and Hussherr (2003)
	Advertising goodwill Visits to advertiser's website Conversion at advertiser's website	Braun and Moe (2011)
Multi-channel effects	Customer counts (online vs. offline)	Dinner, van Heerde and Neslin (2011)
	Customer spend (online vs. offline)	

In the process, these studies have also documented notable differences across individual consumers in terms of how they respond to online display advertising. This compels us to think about how we can target online display advertising to improve our returns on online advertising investments.

3 Targeting Strategies

The goal with target advertising is to selectively expose your advertisements to those individuals who are most likely to respond positively. The challenge is identifying these individuals. A number of different approaches have been used to target display ads (see Table 9.3).

Table 9.3 Overview of targeting approaches

Targeting Strategy	Description
Targeting based on user characteristics	Identify individuals for ad targeting based on demographic and/or interest profiles which they have self-reported
Geotargeting	Present display ads to individuals in certain geographic locations based on IP address of computer
Contextual targeting	Identify webpages for ad placement based on content
Behavioral targeting	Identify individuals for ad targeting based on online browsing behaviour

3.1 TARGETING BASED ON USER CHARACTERISTICS

Traditional approaches such as demographic and/or interest-based targeting have been transported to the online environment. Many online communities (for example, Facebook) allow advertisers to serve ads to community members who self-report certain demographic characteristic and/or interests in their member profiles. For example, an advertiser interested in reaching college students in the mid-Atlantic region may design a Facebook ad campaign that serves their ads to University of Maryland students when they log in.

Additionally, researchers have also developed methods that use website visitors' clickstream behavior to infer demographic characteristics for the purposes of online ad targeting. In a study by De Bock and Van den Poel (2010), Random Forest classifiers were used to predict the demographic attributes of anonymous website visitors using their Internet clickstream behavior. Their methodology was applied to clickstream data that tracked user behavior across 260 associated websites. This data was coupled with data from an online survey that solicited demographic information from a random sample of website visitors, allowing the researchers to both train and validate their method. Their approach provides additional demographic information that can be useful for online targeting, both in terms of the individualized targeting of ads as well as the profiling of websites for ad placement decisions.

Advertisers can also geotarget their ads by delivering their ad content to only individuals in certain geographic regions based on their computer's IP address (while the precise location of the computer is difficult to ascertain since most home computers are assigned rotating IP addresses by their broadband provider, the geographic region to which the IP belongs can still be informative for targeting purposes). Geotargeting can be effective in limiting advertising efforts to the advertiser's geographic reach, making the advertising spending more efficient. However, it is less effective in matching the ad content to individual interests.

3.2 CONTEXTUAL TARGETING

Contextual targeting, which relies on matching the content of the ad to the context in which the ad is seen, provides another targeting approach. For example, a brand like Nike may choose to purchase ad space in the sports section of the WashingtonPost.com website while a brand like Nordstrom may purchase ad space in the fashion section. The theory is that an individual viewing the webpage on which the ad appears has an interest in the topic featured on that page and therefore potentially has an interest in the advertiser if the content of the ad is matched to the content of the page.

A number of studies have investigated the impact of contextually targeted ads on behavior. In an early study conducted by Shamdasani et al. (2001), controlled experiments showed that relevance between website content and the product category featured in the display ad can induce:

1.   more favorable attitude toward the ad;
2.   more favorable attitude toward the product;
3.   higher intention to click on the ad; and
4.   higher purchase intentions.

In other words, advertisers that match the content of their ad to the content of the webpage on which the ad appears will benefit from more successful ad campaigns. This study by Shamdsani et al. (2001) provided early evidence that contextual targeting improves ad performance.

Other studies found similar effects. Moore et al. (2005) also found that context congruity between the ad and the website resulted in more favorable attitudes toward the advertised brand. However, they also found that context congruity decreased recall and recognition of the ad since congruent information is easily overlooked (in contrast, incongruent information is more likely to attract the consumer's attention). Thus, an advertiser must trade off the benefits achieved in terms of improved consumer attitudes resulting from contextual targeting with the loss in recall and recognition associated with the practice.

Finally, two other studies examined how context congruity affects the intrusiveness of online ads (Edwards, et al., 2002; Goldfarb and Tucker, 2010). In a controlled experiment, Edwards et al. (2002) demonstrated how context congruity decreases ad intrusiveness, which can improve advertising performance as consumers tend to avoid more intrusive ads. Edwards et al. (2002) argue that context congruent ads are *more* effective since they are *more* likely to attract the attention of the consumer, contradicting the conclusions of Moore et al. (2005) and suggesting that context congruent ads are *less* effective as they are *less* likely to attract the attention of the consumer. Thus, further research to explore this relationship is needed. A formal scale to measure ad intrusiveness was developed in a separate study by Li et al. (2002). Like the abovementioned researchers, Goldfarb and Tucker (2010) also examined the effects of context congruity and ad intrusiveness. In a large-scale field experiment, they found that both context congruity and ad intrusiveness can increase purchasing intent. Specifically, when ads are both contextually targeted and perceived to be intrusive, ad performance decreases as the practice raises privacy concerns that the consumer may already have. This effect is strongest among people in their study who choose not to share sensitive information (for example, income, age, and so on).

The practice of matching an advertisement to website content is analogous to the offline practice of matching ads with the appropriate newspaper section, TV show, or radio station. What is unique about contextually targeting online is the opportunity to identify very specific individual interests. For example, Google serves contextually targeted ads in user's Gmail accounts by scanning the content of emails and serving ads that are contextually congruent. If an individual is viewing an email from a friend in which they are talking about planning a ski vacation, an ad for a local ski resort may appear on the page.

The abovementioned studies and practices employ contextual targeting simply to match the ad content with the website content. In a study by Sherman and Deighton (2001), contextual targeting strategies were extended to help identify websites for ad placement based not just on the content of the websites but based on whether targeted customers were likely to visit these websites. In their analysis, the websites visited by an advertiser's customers were cluster analyzed. The resulting clusters effectively identified website genres that were popular amongst their target customers, providing target websites for ad placement. When banner ads were offered on these targeted websites, conversion rates (purchases per impression) were ten times higher than when the ads were offered on non-targeted websites.

The study by Sherman and Deighton (2001) began to leverage customer behaviors for the purpose of ad targeting. In the next section, we further discuss behavioral targeting as a strategy for online display advertising.

3.3 BEHAVIORAL TARGETING

An increasingly popular targeting strategy online is behavioral targeting. Behavioral targeting leverages observed behavioral histories to infer an individual's interest in and likelihood of purchasing from a particular product category. Ads are then targeted at individuals whose interests are aligned with the product being advertised. For example, if an individual visits a number of automobile-related website, it would be fair to assume that this individual has an interest in cars and may be in the market for a new car, making this individual a prime target for car ads.

A study conducted by the National Advertising Initiative (2010, see www.net workadvertising.org/) estimated that spending on behaviorally targeted display ads account for 17.9 percent of all spending for online display advertising, and it is expected to grow. The popularity and growth of behavioral targeting can be easily explained by the dramatic improvements in performance metrics associated with behaviorally targeted ads when compared to untargeted, or run-of-network, advertisements. In the same study by the NAI, behaviorally targeted ads achieved a CTR of 6.8 percent compared to just 2.8 percent for untargeted ads. As a result of this drastic difference in CTR, advertising networks are able to sell behaviorally targeted ad space at a price of 2.68 times more than what they charge for untargeted ad space.

Clearly, there are tremendous opportunities to improve advertising ROI by turning to behavioral targeting. Therefore, we will review how the technology driving behavioral targeting works and discuss some of the methodological approaches available for identifying target individuals and customizing advertising for them. We discuss both behavioral targeting within a website and across a network of websites below.

3.3.1 Behavioral targeting within a website

Within-site behavioral targeting relies on individual clickstream and purchase history data, both of which are easily obtainable from website server logs. These behavioral histories can reveal consumer interests without the need to ask individuals to self-report their interests. For example, an individual who has viewed or purchased a product from a particular category can be assumed to have an interest in that category.

A common practice is for multi-category web retailers to target category-specific promotional offers to those customers who have previously purchased or shopped for products in that category. For example, Amazon may target a frequent book buyer with a display ad on their site that offers 20 percent off of her next book purchase. In theory, these targeted customers are more likely to respond positively to promotional messages that are matched to their interests (as indicated by their behavioral histories).

To this end, researchers have developed advanced methodologies that utilize pageview and purchase history data to decipher visitor preferences. For example, Moe (2006) developed a two-staged choice model where both product pageviews and purchase choices at an online retailer were modeled to identify shoppers' search criteria and attribute preferences. In stage one of the model, a product is included in a shopper's search set if its attributes meet or exceed the individual's decision criteria for that attribute. A multinomial logit choice model (with a no-choice option) is employed where the utility of viewing one product out of all the products available in the category is determined by product j's K attributes, x_{jk}, and how that attribute would contribute to the variety of attributes in the search set (D). The latter component of the utility function accommodates behaviors where consumer i actively seeks out variety along a specific attribute for comparison shopping purposes.

$$U_i(j) = \sum_{k=1}^{K} \beta_k \cdot x_{jk} + \gamma_k \cdot D_{ijk} \tag{10}$$

To operationalize the use of simplified decision criteria in the search stage, not all attributes contribute to the utility function specified in (10). Instead, the inclusion of an attribute is dependent on a latent indicator variable which is estimated. For example, if price is used as a screening criterion in the search stage while color is not, the indicator for price is 1 and the indicator for color is 0. This variable is estimated with heterogeneity across individuals.

The above conceptualization of screening criteria follows established research on how different decision rules are used in various stages of the decision process (Gensch, 1987; Bettman, et al., 2000; Fader and McAlister, 1990; Gilbride and Allenby, 2004). The resulting model provided estimates that describe both the search criteria in stage one as well as the underlying preference structure driving both search and purchasing decisions.

In stage two, the shopper is assumed to choose a product from the resulting search set using a more effortful compensatory decision rule. Again, a multinomial logit choice model (with a no-choice option) is estimated. However, unlike the formulation used in the search stage where only some attributes factor into the utility function, all attributes contribute to the purchasing utility. Additionally, since the objective in this stage is to choose the one utility maximizing option, attribute variety (D) is not considered.

$$V(j) = \sum_{k=1}^{K} \beta_k \cdot x_{jk} \tag{11}$$

Moe (2006) applied this model to clickstream data pertaining to two separate product categories at an online retailer. Empirical results indicated that a smaller set of product attributes are considered in stage one (that is, search stage) of the model than in stage two (that is, purchasing stage). However, this finding should not be surprising given the extant research on two-staged decision processes. Instead, the model provides a tool for online retailers interested in micro-targeting individuals based on their search criteria and attribute preferences. For example, an individual interested in searching across a wide variety of price points may respond more positively to ads that feature products of varying prices than to ads that feature only products within a single price tier. Additionally, such a model would also allow marketers to better design promotional ads that feature the consumer's preferred product based on estimated attribute preferences in order to encourage a purchase.

While a web retailer has abundant customer data on search and purchasing behavior at their site, this data provides only a partial view of an individual's overall online shopping. Shopper behaviors at competing retail sites or third-party information sites are not available to the web retailer. Furthermore, analysis of within-site data can only inform targeting decisions involving shoppers who have already visited the site. Advertising to prospective visitors requires different data and different methodologies, which we discuss next.

3.3.2 Behavioral targeting across an ad network

Content providers across the Internet sell ad space on their webpages in order to support their ability to provide free content. Ad networks purchase an inventory of ad space from a wide variety of content providers and resell it to advertisers. This allows the ad network to create both an inventory of websites that will host ads as well as an inventory of varied advertisements to serve. The resulting network of ads and ad space is what enables behavioral targeting across the Internet by: (1) providing the ability to observe behavior across websites; and (2) providing the opportunity to present targeted ads based on the visitor's observed behavior.

One common approach to behavioral targeting is to differentiate between users according to their online navigational clickstream and advertise only to those whose behavioral history indicates an interest in the advertised product (Ha, 2004). Figure 9.2 provides a simple illustration of such a process and highlights the role that ad networks have in enabling this process. Technologically, when an individual visits a website on

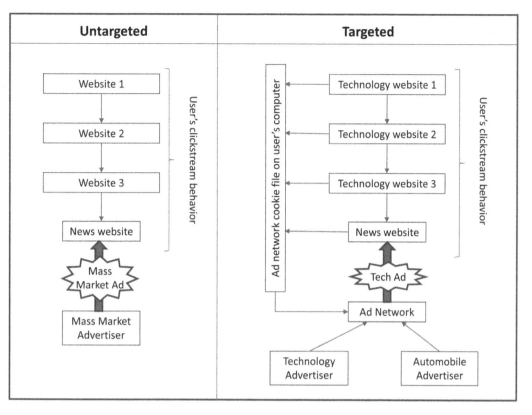

Figure 9.2   Illustration of clickstream-based behavioral targeting across an ad network

which an ad network has purchased space, the ad network saves a cookie file on the individual's computer. On this cookie, they record an interest category based on the content available on the page. For example, an individual who visits a technology review site is assumed to be interested in technology. If an ad network has purchased space on this site, they will then record this interest on a cookie stored on the user's computer. Later, when the same computer visits a news site on which the ad network has also purchased space, the ad network will read the cookie and show the user a targeted ad that features a technology brand (rather than an auto brand, for example). In the absence of an ad network, a mass market (untargeted) ad would be served instead.

While the above illustration highlights the use of observed clickstream behavior to identify individuals to target, other behaviors can also be tracked and leveraged using similar cookie technologies and analysis methods. For example, Yan et al. (2009) examine the value of using browsing/clickstream, search query, and click-through histories for targeting purposes. The key question they address is whether or not these behavioral histories can actually improve advertising effectiveness. First, they compared the behavior of users who clicked on an ad to those who did not. They represented each individual with a large-scale matrix that indicates either the pages they have viewed or the words they have searched. Using these matrices, they computed classical cosine similarity measures between individuals. On average, those who clicked on an ad were similar to each other but notably different from those who did not click, in terms of their page view and search behavior. Then, to quantify the potential benefits of behavioral targeting, they cluster analyzed individuals using only their browsing or search behavior and compared CTRs across the resulting segments. They found that an ad's CTR can vary greatly across segments, highlighting the potential benefits of matching ads to appropriately targeted user segments. Further examination of potential segmentation schemes showed that short behavioral histories (one day) are more effective than long histories (seven days) and search queries are more effective than page view histories in identifying the variance in CTR across segments. Overall, Yan et al. (2009) demonstrate how short click-through histories can be used to target individuals based on what pages they have viewed or what words they have searched to increase future advertising CTR.

In a later study of how behavioral history can inform ad targeting, Chen et al. (2009) propose a linear Poisson regression model to examine how various types of behaviors can predict ad clicks. Let y = the number of ad clicks, w = a weighting vector, and x = behavioral covariates:

$$P(y) = \frac{\lambda^y \exp\{-\lambda\}}{y!} \text{ where } \lambda = w^\mathsf{T} x \tag{12}$$

In their model, six types of covariates that described an individual's behavioral history were considered: ad clicks, ad views, pageviews, search queries, algorithmic search result clicks, and sponsored search result clicks. Their approach provided a parsimonious and highly efficient method for identifying individuals for targeting purposes. In a set of large-scale experiments using Yahoo's behavioral data, the authors document a 20 percent lift in CTR using their approach.

As both computing and analytical technologies develop, advertisers are increasingly incorporating more information into their targeting models and integrating multiple targeting approaches. For example, Kazienko and Adamski (2007) propose a system that they named AdROSA. This system utilizes behavioral history (that is, clickstream and click-through) and webpage content to personalize advertisements for specific individuals and to match the advertisements to the webpage on which it is offered.

Finally, while most of the extant behavioral targeting research focuses on leveraging behavioral data related to pageviews, ad clicks, and search queries, there are opportunities to further refine behavioral targeting algorithms by bringing in ad impression histories (for example, Braun and Moe 2011). Consider an individual with an interest in buying a new computer. Figure 9.3 illustrates how repeated exposure to the same ad creative affects advertising goodwill in the presence of wear-out effects. For comparison purposes, Figure 9.3 also illustrates how exposures to two unique ad creatives affect advertising goodwill. The figure highlights that in the presence of advertising wear-out effects, repeated exposures to the same computer ad will decrease the effectiveness of that ad and may be an inefficient use of advertising resources, even when the alternative ad is of lower (baseline) quality. Consequently, it can be beneficial for an ad network to introduce some variety, either in terms of the creative copy presented or in advertising another product category for which the user has also exhibited an interest, in order to optimize the value of that advertising opportunity.

The model proposed by Braun and Moe (2011) provides a measure of how effective an ad will be given an individual's ad impression history. For example, consider a campaign

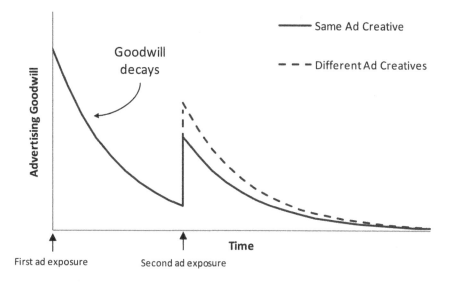

Figure 9.3   Illustration of how ad exposures affect advertising goodwill

consisting of three ads (A, B, and E) where A is the ad with the most effective creative content and B and E have similar but less effective content. Based on a simulation, Tables 9.4 and 9.5 show how the next ad (served in week 5) will affect visits and purchase conversions for various individuals (each with a unique ad impression history) depending on the ad's creative content. Notice that while ad A can be considered a more effective ad (sans wear-out and restoration effects), there are instances where the advertiser would be better off serving ads B or E. For example, impression histories 1, 3, and 5 consist exclusively of ad A in the first 4 weeks. As a result, ad A is less effective in week 5 due to ad wear-out and ads B and E would be more effective. Impression histories 2, 4, and 6 lead to a worn-out ad B (in addition to ad A). For individuals with those histories, ad E would be more effective as the week 5 ad.

While Tables 9.4 and 9.5 provide stylized examples to illustrate the role of impression histories, the model provided by Braun and Moe (2011) can be applied to any impression

Table 9.4   Expected visits for various ad impression histories

	Wk 1	Wk 2	Wk 3	Wk 4	Week 5 ad		
					A	B	E
Impression History 1	A	A	A	A	.820	**.921**	**.922**
Impression History 2	A	B	A	B	1.049	1.014	**1.117**
Impression History 3	AA		AA		.977	**1.058**	**1.067**
Impression History 4	AB		AB		1.253	1.242	**1.306**
Impression History 5	AAAA				1.390	**1.479**	**1.471**
Impression History 6	ABAB				2.305	2.237	**2.425**

Table 9.5 Expected conversion for various ad impression histories

	Wk 1	Wk 2	Wk 3	Wk 4	Week 5 ad A	B	E
Impression History 1	A	A	A	A	.308	**.345**	**.341**
Impression History 2	A	B	A	B	.397	.383	**.427**
Impression History 3	AA		AA		.364	**.407**	**.400**
Impression History 4	AB		AB		.477	.467	**.499**
Impression History 5	AAAA				.524	**.567**	**.562**
Impression History 6	ABAB				.898	.838	**.937**

history observed in the data. This allows the advertiser to determine which ad to serve next given the individual being targeted. Overall, the research and its findings suggest that advertisers should consider impression histories (and include this information in their cookies to inform future ad impressions), in addition to behavioral histories, to design more effective targeting policies.

4 Risks of Targeting Display Ads

The targeting of display ads has greatly improved the ROI of online display advertising. However, this practice is not without its risks. These risks range from those associated with ignoring sentiment to missed cross-selling opportunities to privacy concerns.

In December 2006, Reuters.com ran a story with the headline, "Over 250 sick after eating at Indiana Olive Garden." On the left side of the page was a contextually targeted ad that read, "Free Dinner for Two at Olive Garden" (Aker, 2008). While the targeting algorithm correctly identified the topic featured on the webpage, the sentiment in the content was ignored. Often times the text analysis conducted to categorize webpage content focuses exclusively on identifying the interest category without any consideration of the sentiment expressed in the content. This can lead to inappropriate, distasteful, and sometimes comical results that may draw unwanted attention to the advertiser.

Additionally, efforts expended in matching advertising content with an individual's past browsing behavior tends to overlook cross-selling opportunities. For example, an Amazon shopper who has a long history of purchasing books would likely be targeted with book-related promotions and ads. However, there is an opportunity cost. Using the advertising opportunities to deepen the interest in books does so at the expense of potentially cross-selling another product category and broadening the overall relationship with the retailer.

Finally, many consumer advocates have been very concerned with the privacy implications of online targeting. While many consumers prefer targeted ads which they consider to be more relevant to them individually, some are concerned about personal privacy. This issue is particularly salient for behaviorally targeted advertising practices that rely on tracking individual's web browsing behavior across the Internet. Data that tracks strictly behavioral data is anonymous, that is no personally identifiable information (PII) is recorded. However, it is possible to collect PII or infer sensitive user characteristics from one's behavioral data. Currently, these practices are self-regulated which leaves the onus of protecting consumers' identities and data on the ad networks.

5 Future Research

The current state of research has documented effects of display ads, identified a number of performance metrics, explored the effects of various forms of targeting, and considered privacy concerns. However, there are still several questions that remain unanswered.

First, research in academia and practice has favored CTR as a measure of ad performance. Some recent research has begun to examine non-immediate effects of ads on future behavior. However, there is still a need to better understanding how online ads affect ROI and the overall brand. Additionally, consumers are increasingly engaged in multi-channel and mobile commerce. Future research on the effects of advertising across platforms is also needed.

Second, behavioral targeting across websites is a relatively nascent practice. Further research is needed to better understand what works and what doesn't. While computer scientists at ad networks have been diligently data mining and refining adaptive algorithms, marketers have little understanding as to the theoretical mechanisms that are driving the consumer's response to behavioral targeting. This is a critical gap in our knowledge that needs to be filled if we want to improve how we design our advertising campaigns, identify target consumers, and structure targeting policies. Critical in this pursuit is a careful study of how to measure advertising ROI, especially in the presence of behavioral targeting. When advertisers pursue behavioral targeting measures, the causal effect of the ad impression must be carefully separated from the elevated CTR and purchasing conversion rate associated with the targeted consumer, who should theoretically be more likely than the average consumer to click-through and purchase.

In assessing the value of behavioral targeting, the practice should be compared to simpler targeting methods based on user characteristics. While some ad networks employ algorithms that consider both behavior and inferred user characteristics, the value of each in terms of how it might improve advertising ROI is unclear. Additionally, a significant risk is associated with attempts to identify user characteristics. Consumers typically view their behavior online as anonymous. Efforts to associate an identity to these consumers may raise privacy concerns (Angwin, 2010).

Overall, as behavioral targeting becomes increasingly popular and the profiling of website visitors becomes more accurate, privacy issues begin to concern consumer advocates. Many have advocated government regulation of the industry. Researchers need to begin considering how possible regulation would affect online advertising. In the absence of regulation, advertisers need to be mindful of the ethical responsibility of securing consumer data, masking individual consumer identities, and protecting consumer privacy. Therefore, we encourage additional research into how advertising practices affects these responsibilities.

References

Aker, J.B. (2008). How to avoid contextual tragedies. *iMedia Connection*, December 9 2008. Available at: http://www.imediaconnection.com/article_full.aspx?id=21333 [accessed 2 November, 2011].

Angwin, J. (2010), The Web's New Gold Mine: Your Secrets, *The Wall Street Journal*, July 30.

Ansari, A., Mela, C. and Neslin, S. (2008). Customer channel migration. *Journal of Marketing Research, 45*(1), 60–76.

Beales, H. (2010). The value of behavioral targeting. Available at: http://www.networkadvertising.org/pdfs/Beales_NAI_Study.pdf [accessed 16 October 2012].

Bettman, J.R., Johnson, E.J. and Payne, J.W. (1990). A componential analysis of cognitive effort in choice. *Organizational Behavior and Human Decision Processes, 45*(1), 111–39.

Blattberg, R.C., Kim, B.-D. and Neslin, S.A. (2008). *Database Marketing: Analyzing and Managing Customers*. New York, NY: Springer Science+Business Media LLC.

Braun, M. and Moe, W.W. (2011). Online advertising response models: Incorporating multiple creatives and impression histories. Available at: http://ssrn.com/abstract=1896486 [accessed 16 October 2012].

Chatterjee, P., Hoffman, D.L. and Novak, T.P. (2003). Modeling the clickstream: Implications for web-based advertising efforts. *Marketing Science*, 22(4), 520–41.

Chen, Y., Pavlov, D. and Canny, J.F. (2009). Large-Scale Behavioral Targeting, *Proceedings of the 15th ACM SIGKDD International Conference on Knowledge Discovery and Data Mining*, Paris, France.

Cho, C-H. and Cheon, H.J. (2004). Why do people avoid advertising on the Internet. *Journal of Advertising, 33*(4), 89–97.

De Bock, K.W. and Van den Poel, D. (2010). Predicting website audience demographics for web advertising targeting using multi-website clickstream data. *Fundamenta Informaticae, 98*(1), 49–67.

Dinner, I.M., Heerde, H.J. van and Neslin, S.A. (2011). Driving Online and Offline Sales: The Cross-Channel Effects of Digital versus Traditional Advertising, Working Paper.

Drèze, X. and Hussherr, F-X. (2003). Internet advertising: Is anybody watching? *Journal of Interactive Marketing*, 17(4), 8–23.

Edwards, S.M., Li, H. and Less, J.-H. (2002). Forced exposure and psychological reactance: Antecedents and consequences of the perceived intrusiveness of pop-up ads. *Journal of Advertising, 31*(3), 83–95.

Fader, P.S. and McAlister, L. (1990). An elimination by aspects model of consumer response to promotion calibrated on UPC scanner data. *Journal of Marketing Research, 27*(3), 322–32.

Gensch, D.H. (1987). A two stage disaggregate attribute choice model. *Marketing Science, 6*(Summer), 223–31.

Gilbride, T.J. and Allenby, G.M. (2004). A choice model with conjunctive, disjunctive, and compensatory screening rules. *Marketing Science, 23*(3), 391–406.

Goldfarb, A. and Tucker, C. (2011). Online display adsvertising: Targeting and obtrusiveness. *Marketing Science, 30*(3), 389–404.

Ha, S.H. (2004). An intelligent system for personalized advertising on the Internet. In K. Bauknecht, M. Bichler and B. Proll (Eds) *Proceedings of the 5th International Conference on E-Commerce and Web Technology*, LNCS 3182. Berlin/Heidelberg: Springer-Verlag, 21–30.

Inman, J.J., Shankar, V. and Ferraro, R. (2004). The roles of channel-category associations and geodemographics in channel patronage. *Journal of Marketing, 68*(April), 51–71.

Interactive Advertising Bureau (2004), IAD Internet Advertising Revenue Report (April). Available at: http://www.iab.net/media/file/resources_adrevenue_pdf_IAB_PwC_2004full.pdf [accessed 16 October 2012].

Interactive Advertising Bureau. (2006). IAD Internet Advertising Revenue Report (May). Available at: http://www.iab.net/media/file/resources_adrevenue_pdf_IAB_PwC_2006_Final.pdf [accessed 16 October 2012].

Interactive Advertising Bureau. (2008). IAD Internet Advertising Revenue Report (March). Available at: http://www.iab.net/media/file/IAB_PwC_2008_full_year.pdf [accessed 16 October 2012].

Interactive Advertising Bureau. (2010). IAD Internet Advertising Revenue Report (April). Available at: http://www.iab.net/media/file/IAB_Full_year_2010_0413_Final.pdf [accessed 16 October 2012].

Kazienko, P. and Adamski, M. (2007). AdROSA – adaptive personalization of web advertising. *Information Sciences, 177*(11), 2269–95.

Li, Ha., Edwards, S.M. and Lee, J.-H. (2002). Measuring the intrusiveness of advertisements: Scale development and validation. *Journal of Advertising, 31*(2), 37–47.

Manchanda, P., Dube, J.P., Goh, K.Y. and Chintagunta, P.K. (2006). The effect of banner advertising on Internet purchasing. *Journal of Marketing Research, 43*(1), 98–108.

Moe, W. (2006). An empirical two-stage choice model with decision rules applied to internet clickstream data. *Journal of Marketing Research, 43*(4), 680–92.

Moore, R.S., Stammerjohan, C.A. and Coulter, R.A. (2005). Banner advertiser–web site context congruity and color effects on attention and attitudes. *Journal of Advertising, 34*(2), 71–84.

Naik, P.A., Mantrala, M.K. and Sawyer, A.G. (1998). Planning media schedules in the presence of dynamic advertising quality. *Marketing Science, 17*(3), 214–35.

Nerlove, M. and Arrow, K.J. (1962). Optimal advertising policy under dynamic conditions. *Economica, 29*(114), 129–42.

Neslin, S.A. and Shankar, V. (2009). Key issues in multichannel customer management: Current knowledge and future directions. *Journal of Interactive Marketing, 23*(1), 70–81.

Rutz, O.J. and Bucklin, R.E. (2011). From generic to branded: A model of spillover in paid search advertising. *Journal of Marketing Research, 48*(1), 87–102.

Shamdasani, P.N., Stanaland, A.J.S. and Tan, J. (2001). Location, location, location: Insights for advertising placement on the web. *Journal of Advertising Research, 41*(4), 7–21.

Sherman, L. and Deighton, J. (2001). Banner advertising: Measuring effectiveness and optimizing placement. *Journal of Interactive Marketing, 15*(2), 60–64.

Yan, J., Liu, N., Wang, G., Zhang, W., Jiang, Y. and Chen, Z. (2009). How Much Can Behavioral Targeting Help Online Advertising. *Proceedings of the 18th international conference on World Wide Web*, Madrid, Spain.

10 *Paid Search Advertising*

OLIVER J. RUTZ AND RANDOLPH E. BUCKLIN

1 Introduction

The rise of the Internet – and with it the rise of Internet search engines such as Google, Yahoo! and Bing – has revolutionized the way information can be accessed by consumers. In the wake of this seismic shift in information search comes a new tool that allows marketers to intercept and target consumers during their search process – search engine marketing (SEM). SEM breaks down into two key parts, search engine optimization (SEO) and paid search advertising (paid search). The goal of SEO is to optimize a firm's position in the so-called organic listings provided by search engines, that is, the search results based on the algorithms search engines use. On the other hand, paid search allows firms to buy a placement in the so-called sponsored or paid listings of the search engine results page (SERP). The purpose of this chapter is to discuss how paid search functions as an advertising vehicle and to show how firms can use data and analysis to better leverage their spending on it.

Why is this topic important? Internet advertising has been growing rapidly with a compound annual growth rate (CAGR) of 20 percent over the past ten years in the United States. Total spending amounted to $31.7 billion in 2011 (PriceWaterhouseCoopers 2012). Of this overall spending on Internet advertising, 47 percent is now related to SEM, followed by display (or banner) advertising with 22 percent. It's noteworthy that search's share of the total has grown to its current 47 percent from 15 percent in 2002. Thus, not only has the total size of the online advertising market grown dramatically, but SEM has been able to triple its share.

Our discussion begins with a brief overview of the history of paid search which is important for understanding the underpinnings of how the serving of paid search ads works and how costs and positions are determined. After describing the data that are typically provided to advertisers by the search engines, we turn to its analysis. We consider this in two stages (please see Figure 10.1). First, we examine the productivity of paid search advertising using a short-run or direct marketing perspective. This is based on the notion that the advertising data on impressions, clicks, costs, and conversions can be used to assess – and at least partially optimize – a paid search campaign. Second, we examine the issues involved in assessing the long-run or indirect effects of paid search. This requires a broader perspective on the impact of paid search advertising and typically requires the analyst to conduct additional analysis and/or to gather additional information on customer behaviors and link that to the paid search campaign. The indirect effects of paid search include such factors as spillover to future searches, spillover to organic search, spillover to bookmarking and direct type-in of URLs, and spillover to future purchasing.

DIRECT VS. INDIRECT VIEW

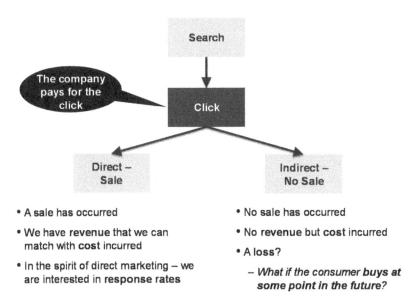

Figure 10.1 Direct versus indirect effects of paid search

Our chapter closes with a look at emerging developments in the paid search analysis and then concludes.

1.1   SEARCH ENGINE OPTIMIZATION (SEO) VERSUS PAID SEARCH

Since this chapter will focus on paid search advertising, we provide just a brief overview of SEO before returning to paid search. SEO is based on understanding the ranking algorithms used by search engines and on adapting a firm's website so that it is classified as relevant and therefore listed high up on the organic portion of the SERP. SEO can be conceptualized as similar to a firm's brand equity, but taken from the perspective of the search engines versus end consumers (as with traditional brand equity). Firms with high "search equity" are deemed relevant for certain queries by the search engines and will be displayed high in the organic rankings. However, as is true with a firm's brand equity, managing SEO is a long-run process and search engines actively discourage short-term gamesmanship. These so-called "black-hat" strategies can lead to the (at least temporary) removal of the offender's website from search engine listings. For example, both BMW and J.C. Penney suffered from this after they attempted to bolster organic rankings using link farms. (Link farms artificially inflate the number of sites which link to the firm's site, thereby making the site appear more relevant to the search engine.) From our perspective, managing SEO is not a topic yet suited for database marketing analysis. Nonetheless, we note that efforts devoted to improving a firm's organic search results can be seen as a complementary endeavor to paid search and one which often competes with it for scarce marketing resources.

Paid search advertising allows firms to appear on SERPs without the need to first be found relevant by a search algorithm. This means that firms with undeveloped SEO (for example, firms new to the web) or unsuccessful SEO to date can still obtain listings and exposure in response to certain user search queries, enabling them to reach this audience. Paid search ads are not displayed in the organic listings but in specifically marked sections on the SERP, for example, Google marks this section as "Ads." Placement and labeling have changed over recent years, for example, Google formerly called its paid search section "Sponsored Results" and used to place paid search ads only to the right of the organic ads.

1.2 A BRIEF HISTORY

We start our discussion of how paid search works with a short history (without any claim to completeness). In 2000, Google started its Adwords program, although smaller, now defunct search engines, offered paid search programs as early as 1995. Initially, advertisers were billed by impressions, that is, the number of searches. Next, the more appealing pay-per-click concept was introduced, where advertisers paid only for clicks on their search ads. In traditional advertising, available advertising space is limited and the value of the space can be easily assessed, for example the cost of a one-page ad in the New York Times. In paid search, each search provides the opportunity to place advertising, so the effective ad space is unbounded. This makes it hard from the search engine's perspective to correctly price a click based on the search query alone – some searches are much more valuable from an advertiser's perspective than others. The problem was solved with the use of real-time second-price auctions to determine the cost-per-click (CPC). In a second price auction, a firm pays slightly above the bid of the firm below and firms bid their willingness-to-pay.

For search engines, however, the second price auction by itself did not provide the optimal way to price its online real estate. The most valuable spot a search engine has to sell is the first position in the paid listings. A second price auction only ensures that the ad displayed in the first position has the highest CPC. Assuming different bidder valuations, in a second price auction the winner pays the second highest bid plus a small delta. In the case of paid search, this is one cent more than the second highest bid. For the search engine, revenue also depends on the number of clicks a paid search ad generates. One of Google's most successful business decisions was to abandon the pure second price auction mechanism and introduce an enhanced auction that takes into account the past performance of the paid search ad to determine its future ranking. Google uses a so-called quality score to represent the past performance and other ad-related differences, such as campaign performance and fit of the ad to the search (for more details please see Google's own description of quality score). In this enhanced auction, the first position goes to the ad which will, in expectation, provide Google with the most revenue based on the number of clicks and the CPC. All major search engines followed Google's lead and switched to using an enhanced auction mechanism to determine the rankings of paid search ads. Unfortunately for advertisers these mechanisms have become a black-box, as search engines keep their auction algorithms secret and provide descriptions in vague terms. (Based on our conversations with search engine managers, it seems highly unlikely that more information on these proprietary algorithms will be provided to advertisers anytime soon.) This limited information poses a challenge not only to managers but also to researchers who are seeking to understand the nature and effectiveness of paid search advertising (Yao and Mela, 2009).

Though advertisers are not privy to the "black-box" which determines their ad placement and exact CPC, the search engines have nonetheless made it relatively easy to set up a paid search advertising campaign. First, the advertiser selects a set of relevant keywords, that is, search terms, which seem likely to be used by consumers interested in or shopping for the firm's product or service. Search engines also provide tools to aid advertisers in developing a set of keywords or what is also called a campaign. Second, bids (or the willingness-to-pay for clicks from searches involving a given keyword) are set, along with budgets for daily and monthly spending ceilings. Third, text ads – a headline, two lines of body, and a URL – are created. Fourth, the landing pages that are to be linked with the text ad via the URL are created or specified. Paid search allows keywords to be linked with customized ad copy and a customized landing page. However, most firms use similar ad copy and/or landing pages for groups of keywords. Naturally, all these decisions should be driven by profit implications. While it is easy to set up a campaign, it is not as straightforward to determine which keywords will perform well, how much to bid, what ad copy to use, and what landing page design to implement. Fortunately, these questions can be addressed to a large extent through database analysis.

1.3   WHAT DATA ARE AVAILABLE FOR ANALYSIS?

Google and the other major search engines provide an extensive amount of data to their advertisers. These data are standardized and aggregated to the keyword-ad level. For each keyword-ad combination, the search engines provide daily information on the number of impressions (that is, number of searches), the number of clicks, the average position of the ad, and the cost incurred. (Advertisers can also obtain more detailed hourly information in some cases if desired.) Additionally, an advertiser can track, by itself or by using a third-party provider, whether a paid search visitor to its site goes on to make a purchase on the site or take some other desired action. Thus, data available on keywords are aggregated across customers, but allow targeting customers by keyword and ad copy.

On the other hand, advertisers are not able to easily (if at all) collect additional data on the process that occurs before a searcher arrives at their site. Indeed, Google discourages backtracking of searches and efforts to scrape its SERP by threatening to suspend the offending advertiser's paid search campaign. Citing privacy concerns, search engines also do not provide searcher-level data to advertisers. And, unlike in consumer packaged goods where marketing research firms like Nielsen collect and share competitive data across firms, search engines do not provide information on competitive advertising. For example, firms cannot even obtain information on which other firms are listed on the SERP along with their own, nor do they see competitor bids or rankings.

2   A Short-term Perspective – Paid Search as a Direct Marketing Tool

Taking a short-term perspective, paid search can be conceptualized as a direct marketing tool. Traditionally, direct marketing focuses on eliciting a direct response using a targeted marketing action. The goal of direct marketing is to determine which marketing offers generate response and who should be targeted, that is, which consumers are more likely to respond. An example of a traditional direct marketing campaign would be a special offer sent to a subset of customers. First, the firm has to determine what the offer should be, for example, a special holiday item. Second, the firm has to determine to which of its existing customers the offer should be extended. In general, extending an offer is costly, for example, the firm incurs mailing costs to send the offer, and as such the offer should only be extended to consumers who are likely to buy. Whether a consumer might respond to the offer is generally evaluated based on a test mailing, the customers' demographics or the customers' past response to other, similar, offers. Applying this direct marketing perspective to paid search, the performance of a paid search campaign can be evaluated based on click-through and conversion performance. Profit generated directly by paid search can be derived based on:

$$Profit = Impressions \times CTR \times (CVR \times M - CPC) \tag{1}$$

where CTR is click-through rate, CVR is conversion rate, M is margin and CPC is cost-per-click.

In the short-term (or direct) view the focus is on whether a consumer who has clicked on a paid search ad buys directly following this click. Recall that paid search is a pay-per-click model: the firm has to pay for each click on its paid search ads and thus incurs costs. A direct view asks whether the resulting revenues that can be directly tied to these clicks, that is, occurring in the session that was started by the click, outweigh the costs incurred for these clicks. Thus, measuring this direct performance is relatively simple given the data provided by the search engines. Potentially, a paid search click could be a starting point of a buying process and a consumer might come back several times after a paid search click before buying or buy through another channel, for example, via phone. As such, the direct view only provides a partial perspective on the success of a paid search campaign and can function as a lower bound. As we will discuss in the next section, taking an indirect (or long-run) perspective requires a different modeling approach and additional information on behavior (that is, additional data need to be collected) or insights into the firm's business model. Models to help evaluate the direct effect can be seen as a one-size-fits-all approach that can be easily implemented across different firms and industries. Models to investigate indirect effects, on the other hand, are far more customized and cannot as easily transferred across domains.

Direct evaluation can be done either at a campaign-level or at more granular units such as individual keywords. To illustrate the development of a direct approach we first introduce a real-world paid search dataset for an anonymous national US hotel chain. For discussion, we use data from April 2004 and we note that Google still reports data to advertisers using the same format (Table 10.1). The campaign used 301 keywords, spent $5,106.74 on paid search and generated 14,302 clicks and 518 sales (in the case of the hotel chain, reservations for rooms). Taking a direct view at the campaign-level, the CTR is 0.6 percent and the conversion rate 3.6 percent (click-to-sales ratio). From a direct marketing perspective, a conversion rate of 3.6 percent is very good. The average cost-per-sale is $9.86, which is well below expected revenue. Thus, from a campaign perspective, paid search appears to be profitable. However, the chain is spending money on 301 different keywords. Using an overall campaign evaluation, that is, average cost-per-sale of $9.86, we do not know whether performance is also profitable for all of the keywords.

Table 10.1 Sample statistics for a hotel campaign on Google

April 2004 – Google	
Keywords (in campaign)	301
Position (daily average)	6.0
Impressions (total)	2,281,023
Clicks (total)	14,302
Reservations (total)	518
Cost (total)	$5,106.74
Click-through-rate	0.6%
Conversion Rate	3.6%
Cost/Impression	$0.002
Cost-per-Click	$0.36
Cost-per-Reservation	$9.86

Because paid search data are reported at a keyword-level, it should possible to repeat this basic data analysis, that is, calculating performance ratios such as CTR and conversion rate for specific keywords. However, for most campaigns, this is not trivial to do. While some keywords generate many searches, clicks, and sales, most keywords do not. In the case of the hotel chain, 217 keywords (out of 301) did not generate any sales in April 2004, but did generate clicks for which the firm was charged by Google. If we were to rely on the same simple ratios as above, we would conclude that these 217 keywords are money losers – costs for clicks are incurred, but no sales have been generated. Additionally, many of the 84 keywords that generated sales had very few searches and very few clicks. From a statistical perspective, making reliable statements with regards to their performance is problematic due to the sparse number of observations. For example, keyword #181 (we cannot reveal the actual keywords) generated eight clicks and zero sales, while keyword #221 generated eight clicks and one sale. Relying on simple ratios, one would erroneously conclude that keyword #221 is a very good keyword with a conversion rate of 12.5 percent, while keyword #181 is unprofitable. From a statistical perspective, a reliable estimate of conversion rate for these two keywords cannot be calculated. It is also not possible to conclude that the conversion rate of keywords #181 and #221 is significantly different. Firms need a way to handle the data problems driven by the inherent sparseness present in paid search data on a keyword-level. In addition, advertisers might also be interested in learning what drives differences in keyword performance. This is difficult to assess using the simple ratios of CTR or conversion rate alone.

Taking a modeling approach to the analysis of paid search data permits analysts to address the sparseness problem and to assess the drivers of keyword-level performance. One potential driver of performance is the position in which the paid search ad is served. For example, ads in higher positions could be signaling a better fit of the firm's offering to the searcher's need. Also, the nature of the keyword itself could play a role. Shorter, more general search terms such as "hotels CA" may be more likely to be used earlier in the search process while longer, narrower keywords such as "hotels CA Anaheim Disneyworld" might be used later in the search. Keywords used later in the search might convert at higher rates because consumers are closer to the end of the purchase funnel. We now briefly describe a simple modeling approach which can be used to assess the drivers of keyword performance, such as position and keyword characteristics, while also providing better estimates of conversion in the presence of sparse data. The latter, of course, could be particularly helpful to firms pursuing a "long-tail" strategy in their paid search campaigns. Additionally, if ad-level covariates are available, they can be included in the analysis. Recall that search engines use a keyword-ad level to set up the data. We will discuss the use of ad-level information and the resulting complexities later.

One way to model paid search performance is to begin by casting consumer decisions here in a binary (that is, 0/1) framework. Following a search and the serving of ad impressions, we might assume that a consumer clicks on a firm's paid search ad if the utility provided by the ad exceeds a certain threshold. Based on standard paid search data, a keyword-level click-through model can be formulated as:

$$u_{kt}^{click} = X_{kt}^{click}\beta_k + \varepsilon_{kt} \qquad (2)$$

where u_{kt}^{click} represents the utility for a consumer using keyword k at time t, X_{kt}^{click} are keyword-specific covariates such as position or broad vs. narrow for keyword k at time t, β_k is the response sensitivity of consumers using keyword k and ε_{kt} is a logit error. Based on the assumption of an extreme value error, the probability of a click p_{kt}^{click} conditional on a search using keyword k at time t is given by:

$$p_{kt}^{click} = \frac{exp\left(u_{kt}^{click}\right)}{1 + exp\left(u_{kt}^{click}\right)} \qquad (3)$$

The model in Equation (3) is keyword-centric and assumes that consumer response is homogeneous within keywords, that is, all consumers using a certain keyword in their search will respond equally to, for example, the position of the ad. While a consumer-level model would be more appealing, paid search data does not contain consumer-level information to build such a model. Similar to the click-model given by (1) and (2), a model for the probability of conversion $p_{kt}^{conversion}$ conditional on a click on keyword k at time t can be specified. More details on how to estimate an integrated click and conversion model is provided, for example, in Ghose and Yang (2009) or in Rutz et al. (2012). In paid search, care has to be taken with respect to position as a covariate, as managerial feedback, missing competitive information, and measurement error (search engines only report aggregate data) can bias the estimation of the effect of position. Ghose and Yang (2009), Rutz et al. (2012), and Narayanan and Kalyanam (2011) provide different approaches to address this potential bias.

A key finding from the estimation of keyword-level models on various data sets is that CTR and conversion rates do differ significantly across keywords. This means that advertisers who manage paid search at the campaign level are likely to miss substantial opportunities to improve performance. For example, Rutz et al. (2012) show how estimated conversion rates can be used to determine precisely which keywords are profitable or not. Based on the ability to calculate profitability at the keyword-level, they show in a hold-out sample that a new selection of keywords determined by the model can outperform a campaign-level evaluation. The model also performs better than using simple analytical strategies based on observed ratios and CTRs.

A second key finding from models is that keyword-level measures such as position and semantic keyword characteristics improve the assessment of CTR and conversion rates. Position is a particularly important and interesting measure. An ongoing debate among paid search practitioners involves the extent to which conversion rates vary by keyword position, if they vary at all. In a 2009 blog post, Google chief economist Hal Varian argued that conversion rates do not vary much by position (Friedman, 2009). While some evidence from the practitioner community suggests higher positions raise conversion rates (Brooks, 2004), other evidence supports Varian's contention (Ballard, 2011; van Wagner, 2010). The empirical evidence is also mixed from the academic marketing literature, based on papers that have measured the effect of position on conversion. Ghose and Yang (2009) and Rutz et al. (2012) find that higher position yields higher conversion rates. Narayanan and Kalyanam (2011) report that the first position usually performs better than others, but their findings are mixed for lower positions. The argument for higher position to yield higher conversion rates stems from a potential association between position and "quality" or "trust" perceptions (Ghose and Yang, 2009).

Agarwal et al. (2011) take a different approach to the study of position effects and use data from a field experiment with randomized bidding. They focus on the top seven positions and find conversion rates increase at lower positions. Their argument for higher position to yield lower conversion rates stems from the notion that buyers higher up the purchase funnel often click on ads in higher positions without purchasing while buyers lower down the purchase funnel are more likely to visit lower positions. Another perspective on top positions is given by Jerath et al. (2011). Taking a game-theoretic approach, the authors find that a position paradox can exist where a superior firm may bid lower than an inferior firm and will obtain a position below, but still obtain more clicks. This is a profitable strategy for the superior firm if it can receive only slightly fewer clicks at the lower ranked position, but at a greatly reduced cost. Thus, position is an important element of paid search performance, but at this point it remains unclear whether a generalizable effect exists or whether the effect of position will depend on the product category, competition, and/or other factors.

Lastly, modeling results also show that keyword semantics are important. For example, inclusion of a brand name (either the firm's own brand or brands of products the firms sells) increases both click-through and conversion rate. Inclusion of other keywords semantics, for example, a certain phrase, say "hotel," or other measures related to keywords, for example, keyword length or keyword count, helps to improve estimates of click-through and conversion rates on a keyword-level. However, the effect of these semantic characteristics is highly situational and based on the currently available research no empirical generalizations have yet emerged. For example, including the firm's brand could potentially lead to cannibalization if the firm's SEO presence is very strong.

3   A Long-term Perspective – Indirect Effects of Paid Search

Using the direct or short-term perspective discussed above, every click that does not result in a sale for the firm would be categorized as a loss. A direct marketing analogy is that a catalog which fails to generate an order in a certain timeframe after it was mailed is seen as ineffective. This approach to measuring the performance of mail-order catalogs ignores the potential advertising value of the catalog itself. Thus, it might lead to suboptimal targeting if this indirect effect is not considered (Simester, et al., 2006). A similar problem arises in paid search. First, a consumer could very well decide not to purchase during the visit triggered by the paid search click, but return to the site at a later point in time. On the return visit(s), opportunities exist to generate revenue for the firm. These revenues could include sales, but could also involve other sources such as advertising revenue from displaying banner ads on the site. Second, a consumer could decide to purchase using another channel, for example, via phone or visiting a brick-and-mortar store. A critical question is how to attribute this indirect revenue back to the paid search click. As noted above, a standard model for the direct effect can be set up, but evaluating the indirect effect of paid search is a highly situational task which from our perspective requires a customized approach. We will discuss three case studies in how to define an indirect effect of interest to the advertiser and how this indirect effect can be captured by using a model-based approach.

3.1 SPILLOVER FROM GENERIC KEYWORDS TO BRANDED KEYWORDS

The first case study brings us back to the US hotel chain we discussed above. A prominent feature of the data is that certain categories of keywords show very different performance. One categorization scheme that shows a striking difference is branded versus generic keywords. A branded keyword includes the brand name of the advertiser, while a generic keyword does not. From a performance perspective, branded keywords seem to perform significantly better than generic keywords on all dimensions: CTR (13.68 percent vs. 0.26 percent), conversion rates (6.03 percent vs. 1.05 percent), CPC ($0.18 vs. $0.55), and cost-per-reservation ($2.94 vs. $55).

The performance of branded keywords seems "too good to be true." Indeed, some consumers may use paid search ads as a short cut to get to the website – as "white pages" so to speak. Thus, these consumers would not have been acquired by paid search in a direct marketing sense. To our knowledge, this issue has not yet been researched and may require survey-based data in conjunction with paid search data to investigate.

On the other hand, is the performance of the generic keywords truly as bad as it appears? Potentially, a generic search could generate awareness for the brand and lead to subsequent branded search. If this is the case, then some branded search volume might be attributable to generic search activity. Looking at the data over time one can observe patterns of modest spikes in generic activity followed by increases in branded search. Industry studies also have advanced the notion of "generic first, branded second." According to one study, 70 percent of searches begin with a generic keyword and, as the search process continues, it tends to become increasingly specific (Search Engine Watch, 2006). For example, consider a consumer searching for a cruise vacation (Enquiro, 2006). A user starts his search using the keyword "cruise," a generic keyword that returns a broad number of results. His next search narrows down the destination, as he searches for "Caribbean cruise." In the early stage, as the consumer can explore the space of options available to him, conversion rates are low. As the searches become more narrow, the consumer researches options in more detail. This particular consumer narrowed his search by reading third-party reviews on Panama cruises. After reading the reviews, his final search included a brand name, "Princess Panama cruise." This type of highly-targeted search had a much higher conversion rate, possibly 30 percent-40 percent according to the study.

Typical paid search data do not include the search history of individual consumers. This makes it impossible to examine spillover from generic to branded or effects relating to the search funnel at the consumer level. Fortunately, a test for spillover at the aggregate level can be performed, as demonstrated by Rutz and Bucklin (2011). In their approach, awareness of the relevance of the brand for the search purpose is conceptualized as an unmeasured, latent construct following the leaky-bucket (or ad stock) formulation of Nerlove and Arrow (1962). This construct permits past generic search activity to be linked with current branded search activity in a regression-type model. Exposure to brand-related information due to generic search raises awareness and, in turn, greater awareness raises subsequent branded search activity. From the model estimates of this process, adjustments to the value of generic search can be made (for details on the model, estimation, and findings, please see Rutz and Bucklin 2011).

3.2 SPILLOVER TO FUTURE SITE VISITS

In our second example, we focus on a source of firm revenue that does not stem from selling products, but from hosting advertising on its website. Next to selling products and services, many firms also host banner advertising on their sites. Unlike the pay-per-click model in paid search, banner advertising revenue is typically based on impressions, that is, the number of times the advertisement is viewed. To increase the number of impressions served, firms can drive new users to the site and/or increase the number of page views for each visitor. In this situation, the productivity of paid search could be affected by the extent to which those users acquired through search return to the site for future visits and the extent to which they browse the site.

The company providing the data for this study is in the automotive business, selling new cars and trucks by linking buyers with local car dealerships. The firm also generates substantial advertising revenue by displaying ads from major car manufacturers on its website. Due in part to the long search process for new cars and the large number of keywords in the company's list (more than 15,000), trying to determine which keywords attract visitors who will ultimately buy was prone to significant error. On the other hand, because buying a car is a lengthy process, the company knew that some consumers visit the site many times following their initial visit via paid search. If there are differences across keywords in the propensity to attract such repeat visitors, this could be factored into keyword selection.

Visitors can access a website either by typing in the URL or using a saved bookmark (direct) or by clicking on either an organic or a paid search result (indirect). (Access via click on a banner ad is also possible; the firm in question was not using banner ads on other sites). The firm tracked daily counts of how many visitors were sourced directly versus indirectly (through either paid or organic search). This enables one to set up a model in which current direct visits are modeled as a function of past direct and indirect visits. The idea is to use the model to gauge the proportion of direct traffic that is related to past paid search activity, thus determining aggregate spillover. But the firm also has visits recorded at the keyword level. Can the model be extended to link subsequent direct visits to paid search visits by keyword? Doing so poses the challenge of the so-called "small n, large p" problem: a limited time series (in this study example, 60 days), but many thousands of predictors (keywords).

Rutz et al., (2011) show how to address this modeling issue and report a series of findings from the automotive website study. The results show that paid search visitors do return to the site, generating additional advertising revenue over and above that from the initial paid search visit. They also find that keywords differ in their ability to generate such return traffic. For the keywords which are significant in generating return visits (599 out of 3,186 examined), the average number of return visits is 3.3 per click. Moreover, the authors also find that semantic characteristics of the keywords can be used to shed light on these differences. The best keywords for generating repeat visitors include the firm's brand name, car brand names, general terms relating to search (for example, "search," "information," comparison"), and general terms related to web use (for example, "online," "web"). Keywords that are very specific ("BMW 325i sports package"), or include general terms related to price and general terms related to used cars, have a lower propensity to generate return visits. In sum, the findings indicate that broad keywords appear to be better than narrow keywords for capturing consumers who will come back to the site.

3.3 PAID SEARCH AND CUSTOMER LIFETIME VALUE

Our third example takes another view on paid search – how does paid search affect customer lifetime value (CLV)? So far, we have looked at the direct effect and specific indirect effects in scenarios where consumers purchase from the firm on a one-shot basis. For firms that strive to achieve a relationship with their customers over time it is of interest to evaluate the performance of paid search from a CLV perspective. Chan et al. (2011) investigate this for a small US B-2-B firm in the biomedical and chemical lab supplies business. The firm sells both online and through offline channels. While traditional word-of-mouth was historically used to reach new customers, the firm had recently started to use paid search to acquire new customers. The authors assembled a dataset that allows lifetime tracking of customers that were acquired by paid search, that is, the customers' initial visits to the firm's website came via paid search. The key question is whether lifetime customer profits exceed the initial acquisition cost. Note that the acquisition cost in paid search is not only the CPC that was spent on the customer's click but also money spent on paid search that did not result in sales. For example, out of 100 paid search visitors (100 clicks), only one visitor becomes a customer by purchasing. If CPC is $0.50, acquisition cost for this customer is $50, not $0.50 as one could erroneously conclude.

In their study, Chan et al. find that customers acquired through Google have a higher lifetime value than customers acquired through other channels (CLV $1,332 versus CLV $1,028). They also find that it is important to take into account offline purchases as customers who purchased offline after finding the company through paid search have a higher CLV ($1,637 versus 1,226) when compared to customers who only bought online after a paid search click. In other words, for this firm, the "Google" customer dominates the "non-Google" customer from a CLV perspective. The authors also look at the value of customer acquisition, that is, how does CLV compare when adjusted by customer acquisition cost? Correctly accounting for offline purchases as well as taking the customer lifetime perspective, each customer acquired from Google nets the company $1,280 on a lifetime basis. Thus, using paid search as a customer acquisition tool is highly profitable. In a final analysis, the authors consider the recent rise in CPC for paid search. They calculate a breakeven CPC of $13.56, significantly greater than the current CPC of $0.80.

4 Beyond Keywords

Up to this point our focus has been on approaches that use keyword-level covariates, such as position or keyword semantic characteristics, to investigate differences in keyword-level performance, either from a direct or an indirect perspective. However, while a consumer searches by keyword, he or she ultimately clicks on the firm's small text advertisement. These ads, unlike traditional ads used in most marketing campaigns, are entirely text – a paid search ad consists of a headline, two lines of text and a URL. Because the ads consist only of text, it may be possible to mine it to develop new predictors that could help understand paid search performance. These could be included in simple models such as the direct model given in Equations (1) and (2).

We discuss text mining in paid search following the approach developed by Rutz and Trusov (2011) for a dataset in the ringtone space. The approach begins by defining linguistic characteristics and design elements used in paid search advertising by firms competing in the ringtone space. A particular advertiser may have specific creative skills or favor certain approaches to ad design which could differ from others. Thus, they propose to analyze ads created by many different firms in the ringtone space. The question of how to collect these ads is addressed using a novel procedure which expands the list of possible competitors, and therefore improves the representativeness of the ads sampled. The procedure uses the Google API for Adwords Sandbox tool: for each keyword from the firm's campaign, for example, "ringtones," the Adwords Sandbox tool is used to produce a list of a certain number (in their example 100) of related terms which include, for example, "free ringtones," "poly ringtones," "sony ericsson ringtones," and "ringtones no subscription." Based on the resulting list of relevant keywords, Google is used to search for each of the identified keywords and collect the displayed paid search ads. The resulting unique ads (11,356 in this case) had 5,843 unique headers and 7,211 unique bodies. The longest ad contained 117 characters, the longest header was 35 characters long, and the longest body was 84 characters long. The longest body in their sample had 16 words: "Send System Of A Down Ringtones To Your Cell and Get 10 Bonus Tones Now!" and the shortest one had three: "Ultrasonic Ringtones Complimentary." The longest headers contained five words, for example, "Find Hot Hip Hop Ringers," while the shortest headers contained only one, for example, "Mosquitotone."

Although this descriptive exploration was done in a fully automated fashion, their proposed ad content analysis mainly relied on human intelligence. Based on unique headers and bodies, 11 distinct features could be identified. Some of the features occur relatively infrequently in the corpus. For example, Price and Discount/Promotion appear in less than one percent of headers (44 instances). On the upper end, approximately 64 percent (3726 instances) of headers contain the Tone Identifier feature or list a specific song or artist. A key difference between header and body is that it is typical to have just one, or, in some cases, two features listed in the ad header while the ad body typically includes multiple features. For example, the following ad body includes three features – Call for Action, Artist, and Promotion: "Send Metallica Ringtones To Your Cell and Get 10 Bonus Tones Now!"

Next, an Attention → Desire → Action framework was used to investigate how the different textual features can be combined to create a successful ad. When it comes to generating attention two types of stimuli on the SERP may attract the consumer's gaze. The first one is low-level stimuli, such as the ad location and visual characteristics (for example, Itti and Koch 2000; Pan, et al., 2007; Van der Lans, et al., 2008). The second one is high-level stimuli which include "higher order scene structure, semantics, context or task-related factors" (for example, Cerf, et al., 2008). Applying this framework to textual ads, candidates for measuring differences in low stimuli across ads are the density of an ad (number of words/characters in the rectangular area occupied by the ad) and the brightness of the ad (number of words/characters rendered using "Bold" font). Also, since a larger font is used for ad headers, the length of the header (measured in number of words or number characters) may have an additional effect on attracting attention.

While the main purpose of a headline is to capture attention and generate interest, the main function of the ad body is to create desire for the product and "to create real conviction in a product's superiority to competitors" (Vestergaard and Schroder, 1985). Google's recommendation is to "tell that audience exactly what you have to offer." After investigating thousands of ad copies, virtually no cases of superiority claims could be found in the ringtone space. Thus, it appears that most advertisers do follow Google's advice to stay very specific and to list product/service/phone/media-format features in the hopes that their ad will be seen by a customer with matching interests. As with the header, it can be expected that feature(s) match with a reader's interest revealed through a search query translates into higher likelihood of perceiving an ad as relevant to the reader.

With respect to action, Vestergaard and Schroder (1985) state that as much as "'Buy X' is the most direct exhortation one can think of, [but] it is rare." Indeed, out of 7,211 unique ad bodies, only five invite a reader to buy a product or a subscription. The rest of the advertisers use different expressions to get action from a potential customer. Overall, in a ringtone corpus a call-for-action appears only in 8.2 percent of cases. This seems particularly surprising given that Google explicitly recommends to "include a call-to-action in your copy that tells users what you expect them to do after clicking your ad." Given the very competitive market of ringtone advertisers, the low occurrence of a call-for-action in the ad body is unlikely to be an oversight, but perhaps reflects specificity of the product.

The authors use the textual feature in a model of click-through to test their predictions with regards to performance of different features. While many of the textual features have the predicted effects and help to explain differences in CTR across keywords, some features are not significant in explaining click-through behavior (for details, see Rutz and Trusov, 2011). However, the basic text mining framework proposed by Rutz and Trusov (2011) can be easily applied and is valid across categories.

5   Emerging Topics

In sections 1–4 we have covered the basics of paid search and set forth how to use modeling to investigate a paid search campaign's performance. In this final section we discuss emerging topics for which research is still in its infancy. We expect that more attention will be paid to these topics as the management of paid search advertising becomes better understood.

5.1   THE LONG TAIL IN PAID SEARCH

The idea of a long tail in paid search is straightforward. Frequently searched keywords are generally expensive, as many firms bid competitively in the auction, increasing CPC and thus lowering profits from a sale. But literally millions of keywords exist which are hardly searched at all. CPC on these long-tail keywords is lower due to less competition. If keywords can be identified which are cheap, but will result in clicks and conversions, they could be "diamonds in the rough." To investigate this, we have examined multiple paid search datasets. We find that across these datasets, about 20 percent of keywords account for roughly 80 percent of all impressions and clicks, while 20 percent of keywords account for 80–90 percent of the conversions. Thus, as discussed above, it is crucial to be able to manage the major keywords (the top 20 percent) correctly using data- and model-driven approaches.

Given this empirical regularity, is it worthwhile for firms to expend the effort needed to manage a long tail in a keyword list? Using the same three data sets, we have examined the relationship between sales revenue per ad dollar spent and the popularity of the keyword in the list. The analysis indicates that long-tail keywords actually show lower direct profitability than the popular keywords. We have also investigated how well long-tail keywords generate future website visits when compared to popular keywords and find that long-tail keywords underperform major keywords in this respect. Our findings are not conclusive (and could be driven by poor selection of long-tail keywords and/or not weeding out the ineffective ones). Nonetheless, caution should be used when focusing on the long tail, as early indications are that "diamonds in the rough" appear to be hard to find. Even when they can be found, it is important to note that they will be very low-volume keywords. Thus, managers will need to weigh the potential gains from high ROI but low-volume keywords against the costs of managing much larger keyword lists.

5.2   PAID SEARCH VERSUS ORGANIC SEARCH

The SERP displays two types of results – organic search results and paid search advertising. As discussed in the introduction, different factors drive the position of listings in the organic versus the paid search section of the results page. Because each organic listing is "free," it is of interest to consider whether organic search aids or hinders paid search and vice versa. Yang and Ghose (2010) investigate this relationship by modeling the effect of an organic listing on a paid listing. More specifically, they investigate whether the presence of an organic listing for the firm has a positive, negative, or neutral effect on a paid search ad that is shown on the same SERP. To do this, they use an integrated modeling approach that is again similar to Equations (1) and (2), that is, search volume, CTR, conversion rates, CPC, and position (see Yang and Ghose 2010 for details). They find that higher organic click-throughs lead to higher paid click-throughs and vice versa. However, the effect is asymmetric, with organic to paid about three to four times stronger than paid to organic. Based on their empirical findings, they estimate that the interdependence increases firm profits by roughly 5 percent. They also validate this finding in a controlled field experiment. These findings suggest that the commonly held perspective that paid search cannibalizes the free organic results might be incorrect. Rather than cannibalization, the evidence suggests that there are positive synergies.

6   Conclusion

The effective management of paid search advertising provides both new opportunities and poses new challenges for database marketers. The data provided by search engines to advertisers is extensive and detailed. In this chapter, we began by discussing how this permits paid search campaigns to be assessed and managed at a granular level by taking a direct or short-term perspective. For example, individual keywords within an advertiser's campaign can be assessed by their performance in producing clicks and conversions in a cost effective manner. In cases where keyword performance data are sparse (for example, for keywords in the long tail of a campaign's list), model-based analyses enable analysts to extend their evaluation to the entire list of keywords and improve results when compared to model-free approaches.

The effects of paid search advertising also extend beyond the direct effects that can be linked to a particular click-through. Data-based analyses can be developed to assess some of these indirect or longer term effects. For example, if generic keyword searches spillover to influence subsequent branded keyword searches, adjustments to the returns from both types of keywords can be made by regression-type modeling approaches. Paid search can also produce additional site visits in the future, over and above those due to the initial click-through as well as be responsible for higher levels of lifetime customer value. Model-based approaches can be used to estimate these effects, though they will typically need to be tailored to the company, category, and industry involved. Looking more broadly ahead, search advertising can also be tied to significant effects on offline sales channels, in addition to its strong effect on e-commerce sales (for example, Dinner, et al., 2011).

In addition to evaluating the profitability of individual keywords in both a direct and indirect manner, a series of additional opportunities await ambitious database marketers. For example, advertisers also can use paid search data and models to assess the effects of different text ad content. This capability enables advertisers to further optimize the effectiveness of the spending on paid search ad campaigns. Research is also ongoing into emerging topics such as the productivity of the long tail in paid search and the effect of paid search listings on the performance of organic listings. In sum, working in paid search provides a rich set of possibilities, some straightforward while others more nuanced, for database marketers to contribute to the productivity of online advertising in the years ahead.

References

Agarwal, A., Hosanagar, K. and Smith, M.D. (2011). Location, location, location: An analysis of profitability in position in online advertising markets. *Journal of Marketing Research, 48*(6), 1057–73.

Ballard, M. (2011). Paid Search Conversion by Position. Available at: http://www.rimmkaufman.com/blog/paid-search-conversion-by-position/30092011/ [accessed September 28, 2012].

Brooks, N. (2004). *The Atlas Rank Report II: How Search Engine Rank Impacts Conversions*. New York, NY: Atlas Institute.

Cerf, M., Frady, E. and Koch, C. (2008). Using Semantic Content as Cues for Better Scanpath Prediction. *Proceedings of the Symposium on Eye Tracking Research and Applications*.

Chan, T., Wu, C. and Xie, Y. (2011). Measuring the lifetime value of customers acquired from Google Search Advertising. *Marketing Science, 30*(5), 837–50.

Dhar, V. and Ghose, A. (2010). Sponsored search and market efficiency. *Information Systems Research, 21*(4), 760–72.

Dinner, I., Heerde, H. van and Neslin, S. (2011). Driving Online and Offline Sales: The Cross-Channel Effects of Digital versus Traditional Advertising, Working Paper, Tuck School of Business, Dartmouth College, Hanover, NH.

Enquiro (2006). Inside the Searcher's Mind. Available at: www.enquiro.com [accessed October 16, 2012].

Friedman, D. (2009). Conversion Rates Don't Vary Much by Ad Position. Available at: http://ad words.blogspot.com/2009/08/conversion-rates-dont-vary-much-with-ad.html [accessed October 16, 2012].

Ghose, A. and Yang, S. (2009). An empirical analysis of sponsored search in online advertising. *Management Science, 55*(10), 1605–22.

Goldfarb, A. and Tucker, C. (2011). Search engine advertising: Channel substitution when pricing ads to context. *Management Science, 57*(3), 458–70.

Itti, L. and Koch, C. (2000). A saliency-based search mechanism for overt and covert shifts of visual attention. *Vision Research, 40* (10–12), 1489–506.

Jerath, K., Ma, L., Park, Y. and Srinivasan, K. (2011). A 'position paradox' in sponsored search auctions. *Marketing Science, 30*(4), 612–28.

Narayanan, S. and Kalyanam, K. (2011). Measuring Position Effects in Search Advertising: A Regression Discontinuity Approach, Working Paper, Stanford Graduate School of Business.

Nerlove, N. and Arrow, K. (1962). Optimal advertising policy under dynamic conditions. *Economica, 29*(114), 129–42.

Pan, B., Hembrooke, H., Joachims, T., Lorigo, L., Gay, G. and Granka, L. (2007). In Google we trust: Users' decisions on rank, position, and relevance. *Journal of Computer-Mediated Communication, 12*(3), 801–23.

PricewaterhouseCoopers. (2012). IAB Internet Advertising Revenue Report. Available at: http://www.iab.net/media/file/IAB_Internet_Advertising_Revenue_Report_FY_2011.pdf [accessed October 16, 2012].

Rutz, O.J. and Bucklin, R.E. (2011). From generic to branded: A model of spillover dynamics in paid search advertising. *Journal of Marketing Research, 48*(1), 87–102.

Rutz, O.J. and Trusov, M. (2011). Zooming in on paid search ads – an individual-level model calibrated on aggregated data. *Marketing Science, 30*(5), 789–800.

Rutz, O.J., Trusov, M. and Bucklin, R.E. (2011). Modeling indirect effects of paid search advertising: Which keywords lead to more future visits? *Marketing Science, 30*(4), 646–65.

Rutz, O.J., Bucklin, R.E. and Sonnier, G.P. (2012). A latent instrumental variables approach to modeling keyword conversion in paid search advertising. *Journal of Marketing Research, 49*(3), 306–19.

Search Engine Watch. (2006). Delving Deep Inside the Searcher's Mind, A Special Report from the Search Engine Strategies Conference, August 2–5, 2004, San Jose, CA.

Simester, D.I., Sun, P. and Tsitsiklis, J.N. (2006). Dynamic catalog mailing policies. *Management Science, 52*(5), 683–96.

Van der Lans, R., Pieters, R. and Wedel, M. (2008). Competitive brand salience. *Marketing Science, 27*(5), 922–31.

Van Wagner, M. (2010). PPC Mad Scientists Prove Google Right and Wrong. Available at: http://searchengineland.com/ppc-mad-scientists-prove-google-right%E2%80%A6-and-wrong-45236 [accessed October 16, 2012].

Vestergaard, T. and Schroder, K. (1985). *The Language of Advertising*. Oxford, New York: Basil Blackwell Ltd.

Yang, S. and Ghose, A. (2010). Analyzing the relationship between organic and sponsored search advertising: Positive, negative, or zero interdependence? *Marketing Science, 29*(4), 585–601.

Yao, S. and Mela, C. (2009). Sponsored search auctions: Research opportunities in marketing. *Foundations and Trends in Marketing 3*(2), 75–126.

Yao, S. and Mela, C. (2011). A dynamic model of sponsored search advertising. *Marketing Science, 30*(3), 447–68.

11 *Social Media Management*

DINA MAYZLIN

1 Introduction

Traditionally, firms have communicated with consumers through advertising. However, it has always been known that a large fraction of the information flow about products occurs between consumers. In the past decade, the growth of technologies (such as the Internet, smartphones, and so on) has allowed firms to play a more active role in these consumer-to-consumer conversations, or, more broadly, "social interactions." In Godes et al. (2005) we define "social interactions" as an action that a) is taken by an individual not actively engaged in selling the product or service and that b) impacts others' expected utility for the product or service. (We will refer to the person making the product recommendation as the "sender," and the person receiving the information as the "receiver.") That is, social interactions are broader than the traditional concept of word-of-mouth (WOM) since they encompass new types of communication such as email, blogging, and text-messaging.

In this chapter we will mostly focus on social interactions that take place online, commonly referred to as "social media." That is, our definition of social media is one where the communicator is the consumer, and the conversations take place on one of the online social platforms, such as Facebook, Twitter, YouTube, and so on. In particular, we examine how firms can manage social media. We discuss the three main roles that the firm can play in managing social interactions:[1]

1. Observer – the firm listens to conversations;
2. Influencer – the firm fosters and shapes social interactions; and
3. Participant – the firm plays a role in these interactions (see Figure 11.1).

This chapter is organized in the following manner. In Section 1, we start by discussing the building blocks of social interactions. First, we discuss research that relates to the sender's motivation to engage in WOM – the "why" of social media. Second, we discuss recent research that explores how product characteristics influence the volume of WOM about the product – the "what" of social media. In Section 2, we address the issue of data collection by discussing which social media metrics have been shown to be managerially relevant. In Section 3 we describe how these factors affect how the firm can effectively

---

1   This framework is a modified version of the one described in Godes et al. 2005.

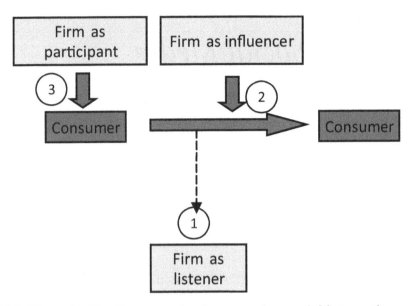

Figure 11.1 The roles the firm can play in managing social interactions

manage social media: that is, how the firm can listen, influence, and participate in social media.

One caveat that must be mentioned is that while in the past several years there has been an explosion of research on social media, due to space constraints we focus on a small subset of the literature. (*Marketing Science* devoted a special issue to the emergence and impact of user-generated content in May–June 2012, and *Information Systems Research* will soon publish a special issue on Social Media and Business Transformation). The upside of this narrow focus is that we are able to discuss research in greater detail.

2 The "Why" and "What?" of Social Media

To manage social media, the firm must first understand what drives consumer interactions. In this Section we review the latest findings on the effect of the following three factors on social interactions:

1. the sender's motivation – *why* do people talk about products?;
2. the effect of product characteristics on the diffusion of information – *what* products are more likely to be discussed.

2.1 WHY DO PEOPLE TALK ABOUT PRODUCTS?

The fact that consumers routinely recommend or advise against products implies that consumers enjoy making WOM recommendations. However, considering the importance of sender's motivation on the spread of WOM about a product, there has been relatively little academic research on the topic. Altruism (or the desire to help others) has been often suggested as another driver of social interactions (see Price, et al., 1995). Here we discuss recent research by Wojnicki and Godes (2012) and Moore (2012) that suggests that senders of WOM may also be driven by more selfish desires. Moreover, we show that these motivations have important implications for the firm's management of social interactions and social media.

Wojnicki and Godes (2012) examine how the desire to project a strong image to others (to "self-enhance") affects who engages in WOM as well as the valence (or sentiment) of the interactions. In particular, the authors hypothesize that a consumer is more motivated to share a positive product experience since a positive experience signals the sender's ability to make good choices. They present laboratory evidence that this is in fact the case, and that the desire to self-enhance is moderated by the extent to which the experience was attributable to the sender's expertise: while self-described experts were more likely to discuss a positive than a negative experience, no such difference was seen in novices. This study has several important implications for marketers. First, in terms of targeting consumers for participation in WOM campaigns, this suggests that the most motivated consumers will be ones for whom the information is most likely to enhance her self-image. That is, it is important to find consistency between target and the message that the company wants to disseminate: the nature of the message should depend on what is valued by the target group.

Moore (2012) suggests that WOM may serve as a form of psychotherapy. She shows (using laboratory and empirical data) that sharing a recommendation influences the sender's evaluation of the experience. In particular, she finds that the use of explaining language dampens the sender's evaluation of the hedonic experience. That is, the act of having a conversation about the product changes the consumer's positive experience to be less positive and changes the consumer's negative experience to be less negative. One implication of this research is that engaging in a conversation about a negative experience with a friend may make the experience less painful. This of course would imply that consumers may strategically choose to discuss very negative hedonic experiences, an important take-away for the firm.

Finally, since both of these theories deal with the incentives of consumers to share positive versus negative experiences, it is interesting to observe that empirically we observe that online WOM is largely positive. Godes and Mayzlin (2004) find that only 27 percent of online posts about TV shows are negative (22 percent of posts are mixed, and 51 percent are negative). Chevalier and Mayzlin (2006) find that an average book review rating on Amazon is 4.14/5 stars. Interestingly, Mayzlin et al. (2012) find that the average hotel review is slightly lower (3.95 on Expedia.com and 3.52 on Tripadvisor.com).

2.2 THE EFFECT OF PRODUCT CHARACTERISTICS ON SOCIAL INTERACTIONS

Firms and consumers have strong intuition that some categories of products (for example, movies, music, restaurants) easily lend themselves to discussion, others (for example, certain medications) do not. Until recently, however, there has been little academic research that examines factors that contribute to an increase in WOM activity for certain products.

Two recent papers use real-world data to examine this issue. Berger and Milkman (2012) examines what characteristics of NYTimes.com articles make them more likely to be emailed. In particular, the authors study how the emotional content of the article (whether the article is positive or negative, and whether it inspires anger, for example) affects the probability that it makes the most-emailed list at the newspaper's site. The authors find that the amount of emotional content influences the "virality" of the article. Specifically, they find that positivity, awe, anger, and anxiety all increase the probability that the article will be shared. Interestingly, the authors also find that sadness decreases the sharing rate.

Berger and Schwartz (2011) undertake a similar examination in a very different context. The authors analyze 300 campaigns conducted by the WOM agency BzzAgent. The company maintains a panel of "agents" that they activate on the behalf of a client. That is, the company recruits consumers (or "agents") to join their panel. At the beginning of a particular campaign, the company selects agents from the panel based on the fit between the agent and the product to generate WOM on behalf of the client's product. The agents are also asked to document all incidents of WOM about the client product. The campaign participants are awarded points (which can be exchanged for prizes) based on the company's evaluation of their reports. Interestingly, Godes and Mayzlin (2009) report that most agents never redeem their points. This implies that the incentive to generate WOM in these agents is largely intrinsic. The authors examine the effect of three product characteristics on the amount of WOM by the agents:

1. cues (how frequently will the surrounding environment remind the sender about the product);
2. the public visibility of the product; and
3. how interesting is the product.

The main findings are the following. First, the authors find that publicly visible products and products that are more interesting generate more immediate WOM about the product, where "immediate" WOM is defined as WOM within the first three weeks of the campaign. Second, the only predictors of the ongoing WOM are the environmental cues and the product's public visibility. Whether or not the product was interesting had no effect on ongoing WOM, which is defined as WOM that occurs in the period from the fourth week on. This surprising finding suggests that makers of more mundane products can expect as much ongoing WOM as their more interesting counterparts.

3   Social Media Metrics and Data Collection

The first two decisions that the firm must make when starting to collect data on conversations are: (1) the universe of sites from which to collect the data; and (2) the keywords (defined in more detail below) that will be used in data collection. Let's start with the first question: which platforms should the firm track? The answer depends on the goal behind the measurement. For example, suppose that the firm is engaged in real-time tracking for the purposes of reacting to customer comments. In this case, the firm must have a very broad coverage. On the other hand, suppose that the firm is not measuring for the purposes of crisis management, but instead is measuring to predict sales next period. In this case, it is not as crucial to cover every platform, and indeed may make sense to have a more narrow but in-depth view of a few platforms.

Collecting social media data requires the researcher to define search criteria or "keywords." The selection of keywords determines the quality as well the volume of data collected. The basic tradeoff that the firm faces is trading off accuracy versus recall.[2] For example, consider searching for a TV show called "Supernatural." If a firm searches for all tweets that contain the term "Supernatural," there will be many conversations (recall is high), but a lot of them will not relate to the show (the accuracy is low). Hence, a broad keyword has high recall but low accuracy. On the other hand, if a firm searches for conversations that contain a combination of terms "Supernatural and TV show and CW," most of the results will relate to the show (accuracy is high), but there will be fewer results (recall is low). In particular, there may be conversations that the firm will miss since they do not mention the name of the network, for example. Hence, a narrow keyword has low recall but high accuracy. The optimal trade-off depends on the resources available to the researcher. That is, if a lot of manual data processing is possible, recall may be the most important criterion. On the other hand, if the researcher is constrained in her processing capacity, high accuracy may be the more important criterion. We next discuss meaningful and managerially-relevant metrics.

It is important to point out that while a lot of the social media data is public (for example, Twitter, consumer reviews, many user forums are public), some important data sources (such as a large portion of Facebook) are not. Moreover, even if a user "likes" a brand on Facebook, the firm is not able to view that user's social graph (her friends) if that user has reasonably secure privacy settings. Many of the studies we discuss below bypass this problem by having very detailed data that would not ordinarily be available to the firm. However, the insights obtained from these studies can hopefully generalize to more realistic scenarios where only limited data is available to the company.

3.1 SOCIAL MEDIA METRICS: VOLUME, DISPERSION, VALENCE AND VARIANCE

Godes and Mayzlin (2004) collect measures of online WOM conversations and tied them to a firm's sales. Specifically, the authors collect posts about new TV shows in the 1999/2000 season on public Usenet forums as the measure of online conversations. The study examines two measures of WOM: the volume of conversations and the dispersion of conversations across communities. While the volume measure is quite intuitive, the dispersion measure is inspired by two influential sociological theories:

1. Granovetter's theory of weak ties (Granovetter 1973); and
2. Ron Burt's theory of structural holes (Burt 1995).

Granovetter's study showed that among men who found jobs through personal contacts, only 16.7 percent found them through strong ties (or friends). In other words, more than 80 percent of the men found jobs through acquaintances. The underlying mechanism behind this effect is that one's acquaintances are more likely to be exposed to different information compared to one's close friends. That is, by reaching out to more distant contacts, a person is more likely to be exposed to novel information. In a related concept, Burt defines a "structural hole" between two nodes as a lack of a connection between them. Similarly to Granovetter, Burt points out that if a person were seeking to maximize the value of information derived from her ties, she may benefit from having ties that

---

2   The "recall versus accuracy" terminology was coined by Nina Stratt Lerner, who was formerly at Nielsen.

have structural holes between them. Both of these theories have been shown to be very robust in empirical data (see Rapoport and Horvath, 1961; Podolny and Baron, 1997.

The two sociological theories above suggest that information that is more dispersed across the network spreads faster. Godes and Mayzlin (2004) apply this logic to the setting of online discussion forums. Specifically, let $n = 1$ to N index the relevant set of newsgroups, where the authors argue that each newsgroup is a proxy for a community of consumers. The authors define *Volume* of WOM as the number of posts in newsgroup n about show i between episodes t and $t+1$. So, the total volume of conversations about show i in this time period is:

$$Volume_{i,t} = \sum_{n=1}^{N} Post_{i,t}^{n} \tag{1}$$

The dispersion measure indicates the degree to which these conversations are confined to a few groups (low dispersion) or are spread out across many groups (high dispersion). Note that the dispersion measure was motivated by the sociological theories of Granovetter and Burt in the sense that information that is spread across different groups is more likely to reach more people in the future. That is, it is not just the volume of information that is important but also where the information resides in the network. To quantify dispersion, the authors use a measure developed in Information Theory and physics: entropy.

$$Entropy_{i,t} = -\sum_{n=1}^{N} \frac{Post_{i,t}^{n}}{Volume_{i,t}} \ln \left[\frac{Post_{i,t}^{n}}{Volume_{i,t}} \right] \tag{2}$$

To illustrate the measure, suppose that there are ten conversations that mention the show. The dispersion is maximized when there is exactly one conversation per group, and it is minimized when all the ten conversations are confined to a single group. Again, the idea is that in the former case many more people will be exposed to the conversation than in the latter case.

The paper estimates a model of next period's ratings as a function of previous ratings, WOM measures, and the show fixed effect. The simplest regression has the following form:

$$Ratings_{i,t+1} = \mu_i + \beta Ratings_{i,t} + \gamma Volume_{i,t} + \delta Entropy_{i,t} + \varepsilon_{i,t} \tag{3}$$

This study had several important results. The most important substantive finding is that early on more-dispersed WOM is associated with higher viewership in the next period – δ is positive. In later periods, the WOM measures are no longer significant. The authors speculate that this is due to the fact that there is less uncertainty later on, and hence other people's experiences are less impactful. In contrast, the paper shows that the information provided by the volume metric is already contained in the previous sales variable, and hence is not significant once we control for previous ratings – γ is not significant. More generally, the study shows that it is important to consider how information travels in a network when studying the effect of online conversations.

Given the study's results, it may appear surprising that in practice most companies have concentrated on obtaining volume-based metrics, such as the number of Facebook likes, the number of comments, the number of Twitter followers, and so on. We can speculate that there are several reasons for this. The first has to do with the fact that volume metrics are easily available. The second may have to do with the fact that while the task of calculating entropy is relatively easy on Usenet, where there are clear demarcations between communities, the same calculation is less obvious on a platform such as Facebook. Hence, obtaining dispersion measures on social media platforms such as Facebook and Twitter is a fertile area for future research.

3.2 SENTIMENT METRICS

While metrics such as volume or dispersion do not involve content analysis, information on the content (or sentiment) of the interactions should be useful. One natural setting where this can be tested is in consumer reviews since reviews often contain a star-rating based on the reviewer's experience with the product. Indeed, Chevalier and Mayzlin (2006) find a causal link between the users' ratings (the valence of the reviews) on Amazon and BN.com and the book's sales on these sites. Interestingly, that paper finds that the effect of review rating is asymmetric – an incremental negative review has a bigger relative impact on the book's sales than an incremental positive review.

While the review's rating provides a measure of sentiment, there are many contexts where a rating is not available. In fact, even in the context of reviews, processing the review text could in principle provide the researcher with richer information. A few recent papers have used sophisticated techniques to automatically process and analyze text data. For example, a recent paper by Archak et al. (2011) proposes a method for learning about the consumer's relative preference for different features by analyzing review text. Similarly, Netzer et al. (2012) use text-analytic techniques from computer science to infer the market structure.

Finally, Sun (2012) suggests that it is important to measure the variance of ratings as well as the average rating. In particular, she shows that conditional on having a low mean, the product is better off if the variance of rating is high since this suggests that there is a group of consumers who think highly of the product. In other words, this work suggests that it is important to measure the interaction between average rating and the variance of ratings.

4   The Firm's Management of Social Interactions (and Social Media)

In this Section we consider the three roles that the firm can play in managing social interactions, and, more specifically, social media:

1. observer;
2. influencer; and
3. participant.

We use this framework to describe recent relevant research in more detail.

4.1   FIRM AS OBSERVER

The effectiveness of any management strategy relies in part on the ability to measure. However, in the past, the lack of data availability on social interactions has implied that researchers have had two measurement techniques available to them: surveys (Reingen and Kernan, 1986) and inference (Bass, 1969). The growth of the Internet, and the subsequent growth of social media, has provided companies and researchers with the opportunity to track conversations in real-time. The primary challenge to measuring social interactions is establishing what aspects of conversations (highly unstructured data) should be measured and are managerially meaningful, an issue that was addressed in the previous section.

Once a relationship between social media metrics and relevant outcomes (such as sales) has been established, the fundamental question is whether social interactions have a direct impact on sales, the alternative hypothesis being that both reviews and sales are associated with a common unobservable variable such as product quality. That is, if it is simply the case that product quality drives both better WOM and higher sales, the implications for firm's management of social media are very different compared to the case where conversations affect sales directly.

4.1.1 The direction of causality

Chevalier and Mayzlin (2006) examine the effect of Amazon.com and BarnesandNoble.com reviews on book sales. While both Godes and Mayzlin (2004) and Chevalier and Mayzlin (2006) deal with measures of social interactions and tie them to sales, the latter is able to address the issue of causality more directly. Determining that WOM has a causal effect on sales and is not simply correlated with product success is especially important when one considers the firm's role in managing social interactions through a communication strategy.

As an illustration, suppose that a new cookbook is heavily promoted by the publisher. This may generate a lot of WOM for the book as well as elevated sales. In order to conclude that it is WOM that is driving sales and not another factor such as the underlying quality of the book or the offline advertising campaign (that may be correlated with both WOM and sales), the paper utilizes a difference-in-differences approach: the authors examine the effect of user reviews across BarnesandNoble.com and Amazon.com and across time. That is, the study examines whether a scathing review of a Julia Child cookbook on Amazon results in the book's lower popularity on Amazon relative to BN.com. The study also rules out that the difference is driven by differences in preferences across sites by differencing across time. That is, suppose that:

$$\ln(\text{rank}^A_i) = \mu_i^A + v_i + \alpha^A \ln(P^A_i) + \gamma^A \ln(P^B_i) + X\Gamma^A + S\Pi^A + \varepsilon^A_i \qquad (4)$$
$$\ln(\text{rank}^B_i) = \mu_i^B + v_i + \alpha^B \ln(P^B_i) + \gamma^B \ln(P^A_i) + X\Gamma^B + S\Pi^B + \varepsilon^B_i \qquad (5)$$

where A stands for Amazon, and B stands for BN.com. That is, the $\ln(\text{rank})$ book i on the site k is a function of the book-site fixed effect (μ_i^k), the book fixed effect (v_i), the prices (P^A_i and P^B_i), the vector of review variables on both sites (X), and other controls related to shipping times on the site for that book on the site (S). First, note that the book fixed effect is decomposed into the following two components:

1. an effect (μ_i^k) that may vary across sites due to differences in preferences, for example; and

2. an effect (v_i) that is book specific and site-invariant.

Also note that the specification allows both sites' reviews (X) to influence each other's' sales ranks.

By differencing the equations across sites and across time, the authors eliminate the site-book fixed effect which in principle could be correlated with review variables. Hence, the authors estimate:

$$\Delta[\ln(rank^A_i) - \ln(rank^B_i)] = \beta^A \, \Delta\ln(P^A_i) + \beta^B \, \Delta \ln(P^B_i) + \Delta X\Gamma + \Delta S\Pi + \varepsilon_i \qquad (6)$$

That is, the change over time in the difference in sales rank between the two sites is related to temporal changes in prices, reviews, and other controls such as shipping. This method allows the authors to interpret the effect of reviews as causal.

An alternative approach to the difference-in-difference method described above is to employ exogenous instruments for WOM variables. Consider Chintagunta et al. (2010) as an example of this approach. This paper examines the effect of online reviews on movie box office performance. In particular, the authors examine the effect of online user reviews on the opening gross performance for movie i in market j as a function of reviews at the time that the movie is released in market j (X_{ij}), as well as other controls (C_{ij}), which include among others the amount of competition.

$$\log(OPENINGGROSS_{ij}) = \alpha + X_{ij}\Gamma + C_{ij}\Pi + e_{ij} \qquad (7)$$

Movies are often released sequentially in different markets. For example, a movie may first open in New York and Los Angeles, to be followed by openings in Boston and Chicago, and a wide release later on. The source of possible concern about endogeneity here is that the studios may release the movies strategically. That is, a movie will be released in market j only if the studio thinks that the movie will do well there, which may induce a correlation between ε_{ij} and X_{ij} (the average and volume of ratings). In order to deal with this endogeneity issue, the authors use competitive variables in previous markets to instrument for the endogenous WOM variables. That is, for example, if the movie i were competing against a popular movie in the previous market, its ratings would be lower for reasons other than its intrinsic quality, which of course implies that these instruments are orthogonal to ε_{ij}.

These papers demonstrate two different approaches to dealing with the issue of causality. Chevalier and Mayzlin (2006) utilize a variation in reviews across different sites and across time, while Chintagunta et al. (2010) use instrumental variables to deal with the issue of endogeneity.

4.2   FIRM AS INFLUENCER: EXOGENOUSLY-CREATED WORD-OF-MOUTH

The firm may choose to take a yet more active role in influencing interactions by encouraging consumers to engage in WOM. Godes and Mayzlin (2009) implemented a field study within the context of a "buzz" campaign conducted by a BzzAgent on behalf of a national restaurant chain. Unlike previous work that dealt with "endogenous" or naturally-occurring WOM, this paper tested empirically whether a firm can create "exogenous" WOM that impacts sales.

The authors find that the firm is able to generate WOM that increases sales. (As we described in Section 1, BzzAgent created WOM by encouraging the agents to talk about the product offline and online. The promoters are incentivized to report instances where product-related conversations took place). Interestingly, they also find that it is the less loyal customers whose incremental WOM leads to higher sales since their friends and acquaintances have not been previously exposed to information about the product. In order to more-precisely demonstrate the underlying mechanism, the authors replicate their results in a laboratory setting as well. This study implies that the firm may optimally choose to concentrate on its new customers in spreading WOM as part of a viral campaign as opposed to the very loyal customers whose networks have already been saturated with WOM.

Interestingly, Iyengar et al. (2011), which we discuss in more detail below, find that in the case of prescription drugs, doctors who prescribe a drug heavily have more of an influence on their peers. This of course seems to imply that heavy users should be targeted for spreading WOM. The authors reconcile their results with Godes and Mayzlin (2009) by pointing out that in situations where a significant amount of risk is involved, which is the case for prescription drugs, heavier users may be more influential. That is, when awareness is the most important consideration (which is the case when the risk is low, for example), the firm should choose to target less loyal customers (or light users) for its WOM campaign. On the other hand, when persuasiveness is more important (which would be the case for high-risk categories), the firm may choose to target its more loyal (or heavy) users.

These two papers imply that a customer impacts the firm's bottom line in two ways. First, she generates a direct benefit and a cost to the company through her own consumption. Second, indirectly, she influences the company's bottom line by generating WOM to her peers. Indeed, there is a growing literature in the area of customer relationship management that concerns itself with including this indirect WOM (or "referral") effect into the calculations of the customer's value to the company. For example, Kumar et al. (2010) propose that the firm should calculate two distinct measures:

a) the customer's lifetime value to the firm (CLV); as well as
b) the customer's referral value (CRV), which is calculated as follows:

$$CRV_i = \sum_{t=1}^{T} \left(\sum_{y=1}^{n1} \left(\frac{A_{ty} - a_{ty} - M_{ty} + ACQ1_{ty}}{(1+r)^t} \right) + \left(\sum_{y=n1+1}^{n2} \left(\frac{ACQ2_{ty}}{(1+r)^t} \right) \right) \right) \tag{8}$$

Where:

T	= number of periods predicted into the future.
A_{ty}	= the gross margin contributed by customer y who otherwise would not have bought the product.
a_{ty}	= cost of referral.
$n1$	= number of customers who would not buy without a referral.
$n1-n2$	= the number of customers who would have bought anyway.
M_{ty}	= marketing costs needed to retain the referred customers.
$ACQ1_{ty}$	= the savings in acquisition costs from customers who would not join without a referral.

$ACQ1_{ty}$ = the savings in acquisition costs from customers who would have joined anyway.
r = discount rate.

Note that in order to differentiate between customers who would have joined anyway and those for whom a referral was necessary, the firm asked each newly-acquired customer the likelihood that she would have joined in the next 12 months without a referral.

The authors show using field experiments that this measure yields substantial results in helping the firm target what customers to select in its referral campaigns. That is, the authors find that the CRV and the CLV measures allow the firm to categorize each customer as being low or high on each measure. They also find that targeting customers that are low on CLV with campaigns to increase own purchase behavior and targeting customers that are low on CRV to increase WOM is effective compared to a control group. Moreover, the authors find that the two suggested measures, CRV and CLV, are distinct. That is, it is clearly not enough for a company to only measure CLV, but it is important to measure both.

Kumar et al. (forthcoming demonstrate that customer's "referral value" can be calculated in social network settings such as Facebook and Twitter. While the methodology used is quite different, the principles behind the concepts – that different customers exert a different degree of influence and that a firm can use this information to target a campaign – are the same.

4.2.1   The role of opinion leaders

How should the firm go about virally spreading the message about its product? That is, who should it target as the initial seeds for its WOM campaigns? In particular, what is the role of opinion leaders in spreading information in a network.

Before we can answer this question, it is important to define what exactly we mean by "opinion leader" or, more generally, by an "influential" consumer. Iyengar et al. (2011) discuss three methods of identifying opinion leaders:

1. survey methods where responders are asked to answer a series of questions about their influence on their peers;
2. sociometric techniques where interactions among peers or the network structure is observed; and
3. key informant techniques where respondents are asked to identify the influentials among their peers.

It is not a priori clear which method is more valid, or whether a combination of methods should be used.

We start by discussing Godes and Mayzlin (2009), who used a survey to identify opinion leadership through self-reports. The authors find that that while opinion leaders are more likely to spread information about a product to which they are loyal, they are no more likely than other consumers to spread information about the product to which they are less loyal. Since the paper finds that non-loyal consumers are especially effective at increasing product sales, this finding implies an important limitation of using opinion leadership as a screening criterion to selecting "buzzers" for a campaign. That is, while opinion leaders are willing to promote a product that they love, they are less likely to promote one to which they are less loyal.

Next, we turn to studies that used sociometric techniques to identify influentials. First, Hinz et al. (2011) conduct a series of experiments that focus on optimal seeding strategies. In particular, they compare three different seeding strategies:

1. seeding hubs (those consumers who occupy a central role in the network);
2. seeding fringes; or
3. seeding bridges (consumers who connect different groups of consumers).

The participants on the study were students who shared their friendship information on a Facebook-like site with the experimenters. The authors in turn activated the students (the hubs, the seeds, or the bridges) based on this social network data. The experimenters asked the participants to share experimenter-generated information with their friends, and the experimental set-up allowed the authors to trace the diffusion of the information on the network. The authors find that seeding hubs and bridges outperforms seeding fringes.

Iyengar et al. (2011) investigate the differences in the information obtained by sociometric measures and survey measures. They study the diffusion of a new prescription drug with uncertainty on its efficacy and side-effects. Through a mail survey, the authors collected data on:

1. physicians' social network: the doctors were asked to name the physicians with whom she feels comfortable discussing patient issues (discussion ties) and the physicians to whom she feels comfortable referring patients (referral ties);
2. the doctors' personal characteristics such as patient volume; and
3. self-reported measures of opinion leadership.

The authors also collected adoption data on an individual physician level. The authors find that doctors with higher sociometric measures on opinion leadership adopt earlier, and physicians with high reported opinion leadership measures have a higher intrinsic tendency to adopt early, but are less sensitive to contagion from peers. Hence, the authors find that self-reported opinion leadership measures and sociometric measures are distinct: they are weakly correlated and play different roles in adoption and peer influence. Finally, the authors also find that adoption is affected by peers' usage volume.

Finally, Trusov et al. (2010) propose a novel method to identify influentials on a social networking site. They treat the number of log-ins per day as an indicator of higher usage, and the authors observe whether an increase in activity level by a user results in an increase in activity level by her friends. Consequently, the authors identify those people who influence the usage level of their friends as influential. The authors find that only about 20 percent of a person's friends influence his behavior, which is consistent with psychological theories that posit a great level of heterogeneity on the interpersonal influence attribute between people. Under what circumstances would a company have access to such detailed data on user's own activity as well as her friends' activity? First, the social network itself (such as Facebook) can observe this level of detail and can in principle sell some form of this information (after performing some anonymization) to advertisers. Second, some social networks (such as Twitter) are open-access in the sense that advertiser can observe the entire stream of user activity.

4.2.2   Surreptitiously manipulating word of mouth – promotional chat

Another option for firms to influence consumer conversations is to manipulate conversations surreptitiously by exploiting the anonymity afforded by online communities. (Note that we consider this under the "influencer" role since we define the "participant" role as one where the firm speaks publicly under its own identity. Here the firm hides its identity and instead tried to affect consumer conversations surreptitiously). This approach raises some fundamental questions regarding the viability of online WOM since a large amount of this kind of promotion would undermine the credibility and, thus, usefulness of online conversations.

Mayzlin (2006) was the first paper to study this blurring of the lines between advertising and WOM. In this paper, I develop a game theoretic model where two products are differentiated in their value to the consumer. Unlike the firms, the consumers are uncertain about the products' quality. Firms have the option of posting anonymous, positive reviews about their product. One question that immediately arises is whether – given this anonymity and given the firms' obvious self-interest – consumers would be influenced by online reviews? Broadly speaking, as more and more consumer purchases are being influenced by reviews posted by anonymous others and as the incentive grows for firms to surreptitiously manipulate these reviews, should consumers in equilibrium continue to place faith in them? In a unique equilibrium where online WOM is persuasive, I conclude that the answer is yes. In this equilibrium, firms spend more resources promoting inferior products: the firm with the better product optimally free-rides on unbiased WOM. The intuition behind this result is the following: the high-quality firm has lower costs of promotion since its product receives many positive (and free from the firm's perspective) reviews from real consumers. The low-quality firm, on the other hand, has to pay for every single one of its reviews. That is why the high-quality firm ends up having more positive reviews and ends up engaging in less manipulation on its own.

Dellarocas (2006) studies a similar problem – the strategic manipulation of Internet opinion forums. He finds that depending on the extent to which manipulation is a function of the firm's quality, strategic manipulation may increase or decrease the information value of forums to consumers. In particular, in the case when manipulation increases in the firm's quality, the consumer actually benefits from strategic manipulation. The author also points out that manipulation can be decreased as firms develop filtering technologies that differentiate real from manufactured WOM.

While both of the papers above have explored the concept of promotional reviews (or strategic manipulation) from an analytical perspective, there has been little work addressing the issue empirically. The primary challenge behind empirical work in this area is that in principle a well-manufactured review is impossible to tell apart from a real review. Hence, any strategy that relies on classifying any one particular review as either real or fake is extremely difficult (if not impossible) to implement. Mayzlin et al. 2012 undertake an empirical analysis of the extent to which manipulation occurs and the market conditions that encourage or discourage this activity. Specifically, the paper examines hotel reviews, exploiting the organizational differences between two travel websites: Expedia.com and TripAdvisor.com. Anyone with an email address can post a review on Tripadvisor. In contrast, Expedia.com is a website through which travel is booked; consumers are also encouraged to post reviews on the site, but, a consumer can only post a review if the consumer actually booked at least one night at the hotel through the website in the six months prior to the review post. Thus, the cost of posting a fake review on Expedia.com is quite high relative to the cost of posting a fake review on Tripadvisor. Further, since the reviewer had to undertake a credit card transaction on Expedia.com, the reviewer is not anonymous to the website host and thus, the potential for detection might also be higher. Thus, the cost of posting a fake review on Expedia.com is quite high relative to the cost of posting a fake review on TripAdvisor.com.

The paper shows that the differences in the distribution of reviews for a given hotel between TripAdvisor.com and Expedia.com are affected by the firm's incentives to manipulate. In particular, we show that a branded chain hotel that is owned by a multi-unit owner engages in the least amount of manipulation (both positive manipulation for own site and negative manipulation for competitor). In contrast, an independent hotel that is owned by a single-unit owner engages in the greatest amount of manipulation. The methodology proposed in this paper avoids the challenge of classifying individual reviews as fake and, instead, uses differences between sites to infer manipulation.

4.3 FIRM AS PARTICIPANT

The most active role that the firm can play in managing social interactions is to actually participate in consumer conversations. For example, the firm can post its views on a corporate blog, inviting and responding to comments and feedback. One key question here is how the firm's posting behavior affects the size of its audience. Mayzlin and Yoganarasimhan (2012) start to address this issue by analyzing the role of links to other blogs as signal of blog quality.

Mayzlin and Yoganarasimhan (2012) model bloggers as producers, and readers as consumers, of information (or "breaking news"). We model bloggers as differing along two dimensions:

1. the ability to post news-breaking content; and
2. the ability to find news in other blogs.

By linking, a blog signals to the reader that it will be able to direct her to news in other blogs in the future. The downside of a link is that it is a positive signal about the rival's news-breaking ability. Hence, one action (a link) sends multiple signals to the reader: a positive signal about the quality of a focal blog as well as a positive signal about the quality of a potential rival. We show that linking will be an equilibrium outcome when the heterogeneity on the ability to break news is low relative to the heterogeneity on the ability to find news in other blogs. One implication of the linking mechanism is that blogs that are high on news-breaking ability are more likely to gain readers. Hence, despite the fact that bloggers link for purely selfish reasons, the macro effects of this activity is that readers' learning is enhanced. While the setting of the model is blogs, the mechanism outlined here could be used to explain other instances of referrals in the absence of an explicit referral payment structure. That is, a Nordstrom salesperson who refers a customer seeking a particular brand of handbag to Lord and Taylor may benefit by appearing well-informed to the customer. This is the first paper to address the issue of referrals in the absence of explicit incentives.

Arguably, the participant role of social interaction management has been the least-studied area academically. Below we discuss some interesting issues that have not been answered so far:

1. The value of engagement:
   Consider a Facebook page for a brand that is maintained by the brand itself or an agency that has been hired by the firm. The Facebook page (or a platform such as Twitter) allows the brand to interact with consumers directly. While it is generally assumed that the firm must engage in these kinds of conversations, it is less clear what effect these conversations have on perceptions or sales. In other words, what is the value of customer engagement with the brand to the firm? Do customers who visit the Facebook page regularly (or follow the Twitter feed) develop more loyalty for the product? The difficulty inherent in addressing this issue is in disentangling the direction of causality. That is, suppose a loyal customer is more likely to "like" a brand's page or to follow the brand's Twitter feed. Hence, the fact that Twitter followers are more loyal and engaged is not by itself sufficient to conclude that social media participation results in more loyalty and engagement.

2. Crisis management:
   Companies have been using social media in order to communicate with consumers about product-related issues. One interesting managerial question that has not been addressed is when the firm should react to consumer comments as opposed to ignore them. This is a particularly important issue when it comes to early crisis management. That is, suppose that the firm sees a few negative comments about its product. When should the firm react to the comments? When would the firm's involvement validate the rumor or the complaint versus mitigate the problem? This also relates to the issue of influence. That is, presumably the firm would not want to respond to negative comments posted by a consumer with little influence. On the other hand, the firm probably does need to respond promptly to more influential consumers. Future research needs to address how to obtain these optimal thresholds – (1) what constitutes a large enough volume of comments that warrants a response; and (2) what is the minimum amount of influence that necessitates a response.

3. Optimal loss of control:
   Any interaction that the firm has with consumers on social media is by definition public. For example, consider the question of whether a firm should enable user comments on its Facebook page, and suppose that the firm does not moderate the comments very heavily. That is, the firm allows negative (as well as positive) comments to be posted. In the case of negative comments posted by consumers, the firm is amplifying potentially damaging content. The positive aspect of allowing relatively unmoderated user comments is that it lends credibility to the content. That is, by allowing users to post unmoderated comments the firm is signaling to the consumer that it is confident that the comments posted will be mostly positive. In general, this suggests that there may be an optimal loss of control in social media. By ceding control of the content to the consumers the firm signals confidence. On the other hand, ceding too much control may result in too much risk for the firm. Hence, the optimal loss of control is an interesting topic for future research.

References

Archak, N., Ghose, A. and Ipeirotis, P. (2011). Deriving the pricing power of product features by mining consumer reviews. *Management Science, 57*(8), 1485–509.

Bass, E.M. (1969). A new product growth for model consumer durables. *Management Science, 15*(5) 215–27.

Berger, J. and Milkman, K. (2012). What makes online content viral? *Journal of Marketing Research, 49*(2), 192–205.

Berger, J. and Schwartz, E. (2011). What drives immediate and ongoing word-of-mouth? *Journal of Marketing Research, 48*(5), 869–80.

Burt, R.S. (1995). *Structural Holes: The Social Structure of Competition.* Cambridge, MA: Harvard University Press.

Chevalier, J. and Mayzlin, D. (2006). The effect of word of mouth on sales: Online book reviews. *Journal of Marketing Research, 43*(3), 345–54.

Chintagunta, P.K., Shyam, G. and Sriram, V. (2010). The effects of online user reviews on movie box office performance: Accounting for sequential rollout and aggregation across local markets. *Marketing Science, 29*(5), 944–57.

Dellarocas, C. (2006). Strategic manipulation of internet opinion forums: Implications for consumers and firms. *Management Science, 52*(10), 1577–93.

Godes, D. and Mayzlin, D. (2004). Using online conversations to measure word of mouth communication. *Marketing Science, 23*(4), 545–60.

Godes, D. and Mayzlin, D. (2009). Firm-created word of mouth communication: Evidence from a field test. *Marketing Science, 28*(4), 721–39.

Godes, D., Mayzlin, D., Chen, Y., Das, S., Dellarocas, C., Pfeiffer, B., Libai, B., Sen, S., Shi, M. and Verlegh, P. (2005). The firm's management of social interactions. *Marketing Letters, 16*(3/4), 415–28.

Granovetter, M. (1973). The strength of weak ties. *American Journal of Sociology, 78*(6), 1360–80.

Hinz, O., Skiera, B., Barrot, C. and Becker, J.U. (2011) Seeding strategies for viral marketing: An empirical investigation. *Journal of Marketing, 75*(6), 55–71.

Iyengar, R., Van den Bulte, C. and Valente, T. (2011). Opinion leadership and social contagion in new product diffusion. *Marketing Science, 30*(2), 195–212.

Kumar, V., Bhaskaran, V., Mirchandani, R., and Shah, M. (forthcoming). Creating a measurable social media strategy for hokey pokey: Increasing the value and ROI of tangibles and intangibles. *Marketing Science.*

Kumar, V., Petersen, J.A. and Leone, R.P. (2010). Driving profitability by encouraging customer referrals: Who, when, and how. *Journal of Marketing, 74*(September), 1–17.

Mayzlin, D. (2006). Promotional chat on the internet. *Marketing Science, 25*(2), 155–63.

Mayzlin, D., Dover, Y. and Chevalier, J. (2012). Promotional Reviews: An Empirical Investigation of Online Review Manipulation Promotional Reviews, Yale Working Paper.

Mayzlin, D. and Yoganarasimhan, H. (forthcoming). Link to success: How blogs build an audience by promoting rivals. *Management Science.*

Moore, S.G. (2012). Some things are better left unsaid: How word of mouth influences the storyteller. *Journal of Consumer Research, 38*(6), 1140–54.

Netzer, O., Feldman, R., Goldenberg, J. and Fresko, M. (2012). Mine your own business: Market-structure surveillance through text mining. *Marketing Science, 31*(3), Special Issue, 521–43.

Podolny, J.M. and Baron, J.N. (1997). Resources and relationships: Social networks and mobility in the workplace. *American Sociological Review, 62*, 673–93.

Price, L.L., Feick, L.F. and Guskey-Federouch, A. (1995). Everyday market helping behavior. *Journal of Public Policy and Marketing, 14*(2), 255–66.

Rapoport, A. and Horvath, W.J. (1961). A study of a large sociogram. *Behavioral Science,* 6 October, 279–91

Reingen, P.H. and Kernan, J.B. (1986). Analysis of referral networks in marketing: Methods and illustration. *Journal of Marketing Research, 23*(4), 370–78.

Sun, M. (2012). How does the variance of product ratings matter? *Management Science, 58*(4), 696–707.

Trusov, M., Bodapati, A. and Bucklin, R. (2010). Determining influential users in internet social networks. *Journal of Marketing Research, 47*(4), 643–58.

Van den Bulte, C. (2000). New product diffusion acceleration: Measurement and analysis. *Marketing Science, 19*(4), 366–80.

Wojnicki, A. and Godes, D. (2012). Word-of-mouth as self-enhancement, University of Maryland Business School Working Paper.

CHAPTER 17

12 *Dynamic Customer Optimization Models*

SCOTT A. NESLIN

1 Introduction

Dynamic customer optimization is the development of decision rules that specify what marketing to target to which customers at what times in order to maximize the lifetime value of the customer (CLV). The managerial relevance and methodological challenge of dynamic customer optimization has generated a burgeoning literature over the last decade. The theme of these efforts is that CLV is something to be managed, not only measured. Traditional applications treat CLV as a marketing metric – for valuing customers, deciding which customers to acquire and invest in, and for valuing the firm (Gupta, et al., 2004). CLV was seen as a static customer characteristic. In contrast, the dynamic customer optimization *movement* asks "what actions can we take to increase, that is, optimize, CLV?"

We first discuss the impetus for dynamic customer optimization – what are the "dynamics" and why is it important to take them into account? Next we review the elements of dynamic customer optimization. Our purpose is not to provide a complete textbook, but to present the framework underlying dynamic customer optimization and introduce the methods that comprise the framework. We then review the development of this field, observing important trends. Next we discuss a few exemplars of dynamic customer optimization. We close with a discussion of key challenges and future research.

2 The Impetus for Dynamic Customer Optimization

2.1 THE DYNAMICS OF CUSTOMER LIFETIME VALUE AND THEIR ROLE IN CUSTOMER DECISION MAKING

Two key forces underlie the *raison d'être* for dynamic customer optimization models:

1. the dynamics of CLV; and
2. the role these dynamics play in customer decision making.

CLV is the present value of the customer to the firm. It is the discounted sum of the customer's profit contribution starting from the current period onward. It therefore innately has a time dimension to it. CLV is a *dynamic* concept.

The dynamic nature of CLV by itself does not imply that CLV can or should be managed over time. There are several models of CLV (Berger and Nasr, 1998; Schmittlein, et al., 1987; Fader, et al., 2005; Bemmaor and Glady, 2012) that find ample application without managing CLV over time (Blattberg, et al., 2008). However, the fact that the dynamics driving CLV are influenced by marketing presents an opportunity for managing CLV over time. That is the domain of dynamic customer optimization models.

Consider the classic recency/frequency/monetary value (RFM) characterization of the customer. Recency, the time since the previous purchase, changes over time by definition. Several studies show that the customer's probability of purchasing is influenced by recency (Blattberg, et al., 2008). Marketing actions induce purchase, which resets recency to zero. This means that marketing actions influence the recency "state" of the customer, and this influences the customer's chance of purchasing over time. We need to take this into account to optimize customer lifetime value dynamically.

RFM is usually defined with respect to historical customer purchasing. However, RFM can also be defined with respect to historical marketing activity, for example, the number of times the customer was contacted in the past year. So we have $RFM_{purchase}$ and $RFM_{marketing}$, both of which change over time, influence the customer's decision, and are determined by marketing.

Three phenomena related to $RFM_{marketing}$ are especially important: wear-in, wear-out, and forgetting (Blattberg, et al., 2008). Consider the case of an email campaign implemented each week over two months. Figure 12.1 shows wear-in, wear-out, and forgetting. The campaign takes a few weeks to reach peak effectiveness. Once the campaign reaches peak effectiveness, it begins to wear-out. Customers get tired of seeing

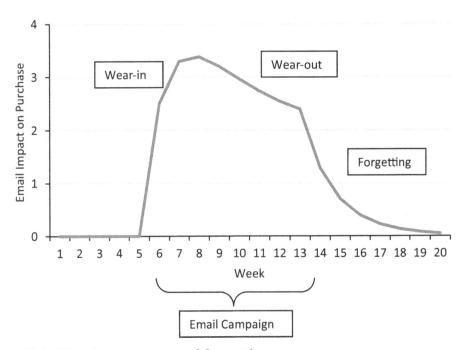

Figure 12.1 Wear-in, wear-out, and forgetting

the email. Finally, after the campaign ends, the customer remembers the message for a few more weeks before memory trace vanishes and the campaign has fully run its course.

The key insight is that customer response to a campaign changes over time. Perhaps there is a way to "pulse" the email so that effectiveness is maintained at peak level, avoiding wear-out. This suggests the potential for dynamic customer optimization.

2.2 AN ILLUSTRATION OF WHY DYNAMICS MATTER

Figure 12.2 illustrates how dynamics influence optimal customer management. Assume a customer is described by whether he or she had received ("State 1") or not received

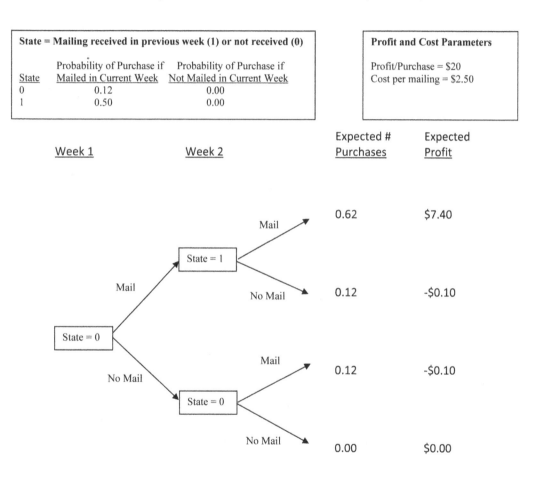

State = Mailing received in previous week (1) or not received (0)			Profit and Cost Parameters	
State	Probability of Purchase if Mailed in Current Week	Probability of Purchase if Not Mailed in Current Week	Profit/Purchase = $20 Cost per mailing = $2.50	
0	0.12	0.00		
1	0.50	0.00		

Profit in Week 1:

If Mail	0.12×$20 - $2.50 = -$0.10
If No Mail	0.00×$20 - $0.00 = $0.00

Figure 12.2 The need for dynamic customer optimization – optimal mailing in the presence of wear-in

("State 0") a mailing in the previous week. The top-left box of Figure 12.2 shows wear-in. The customer has a 0.12 chance of purchasing if he or she had not received a mailing in the previous week and is mailed in the current week, but a 0.50 chance if he or she had received a previous mailing. The top-right box shows the profit and cost parameters – profit contribution per purchase is $20, and the cost for each mailing is $2.50.

The firm must decide whether to mail to this customer in Weeks 1 and 2. If the firm is myopic, it will not mail in Week 1. The profit of mailing (0.12×$20 – $2.50 = -$0.10) is lower than that of not mailing ($0.00). The customer will remain in State 0 so there will be no mailing in Week 2 either. However, if the firm takes into account the dynamics of wear-in, the tree diagram becomes the basis for the decision. This shows that the best action is to mail in Weeks 1 *and* 2. The reason is intuitive – by mailing two periods in a row, the firm takes advantage of wear-in and pushes the customer to peak responsiveness. Total expected profit is $7.40, compared to $0.00 if the firm behaves myopically and doesn't mail in either period.

The key lesson is that the dynamics of customer response to marketing require the firm to be forward looking, to consider not only the current period but the impact of their actions on future periods. This is the fundamental intuition behind dynamic customer management and dynamic programming, the method used to derive optimal customer management policies.

3   The Elements of Dynamic Customer Optimization

Figure 12.3 shows the key elements of dynamic customer optimization – (1) the customer response model; (2) the dynamic optimization; and (3) the application – and examples of these elements. We now focus on the first two elements, and emphasize applications in the rest of the chapter.

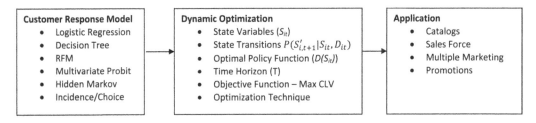

Customer Response Model	Dynamic Optimization	Application
• Logistic Regression • Decision Tree • RFM • Multivariate Probit • Hidden Markov • Incidence/Choice	• State Variables (S_{it}) • State Transitions $P(S'_{i,t+1}\|S_{it}, D_{it})$ • Optimal Policy Function $(D(S_{it}))$ • Time Horizon (T) • Objective Function – Max CLV • Optimization Technique	• Catalogs • Sales Force • Multiple Marketing • Promotions

Figure 12.3 The three components of dynamic customer optimization

3.1   CUSTOMER RESPONSE MODEL

The basis for any dynamic customer optimization is the customer response model, that is, how marketing and other factors influence customer behavior. Behavior includes purchase, brand choice, revenues, web navigation, and call-center contact. Current and historical marketing activity, customer characteristics, and historical purchase history determine behavior. The key determinants are those that vary over time: RFM$_{behavior}$,

RFM$_{marketing}$, wear-in, wear-out, and forgetting. These are the dynamics that will drive the optimization.

Several types of customer response models have become part of the database marketer's toolkit. These range from simple RFM, decision tree, regression and logistic regression models to complex multivariate probit, incidence/choice/quantity, incidence/expenditure, or hidden Markov models. The choice of response model involves tradeoffs among simplicity, predictive accuracy, insights, and what elements of CLV need to be predicted as a function of marketing. For example, incidence/choice/quantity models are used when the application calls for predicting whether the customer purchases, if so what brand, and if so, how much bought (Zhang and Krishnamurthi, 2004). Incidence/expenditure models might combine a probit model of whether the customer purchases with a regression model of how much is spent, given the customer purchases (Khan, et al., 2009).

The dynamic optimization, while focused on time-varying effects, must also take into account factors that do not vary over time. Consider the following logistic regression model for the probability customer i purchases in period t:

$$ProbPurchase_{it} = \frac{1}{1 + e^{Z_{it}}} \tag{1}$$

$$Z_{it} = \beta_{0i} + \beta_{1i} Recency_{email,it} + \beta_2 Gender_i \tag{2}$$

The key dynamic is $Recency_{email,it}$. How recently the customer has received an email describes the state of the customer and must be considered in the optimization. However, the customer-specific β's and the *Gender* variable also describe the customer and must also be considered in the optimization. One way to do this is to derive an optimal policy for each customer. Another way is to consider the customer-specific but time-invariant variables as state variables and derive a policy in one big optimization that considers not only *Recency* but these other variables as well.

3.2 DYNAMIC OPTIMIZATION

Dynamic optimization is a well-developed field (Judd, 1998), although continues to see important advances such as optimizing partially observable Markov decision processes (Littman, 2009) and using explore/exploit schemes for mutli-armed bandit problems (Agarwal, et al., 2009). The key preliminary concepts are:

- *State Variables:* The customer is described in each period by several variables. The resulting "state" of the customer is denoted S_{it}. S_{it} might include RFM as well as non-time varying descriptors such as demographics.
- *State Transitions:* The optimization must account for how S_{it} changes depending on what the firm does and what the customer does. For example, consider $Recency_{purchase}$, so that $S_{it} = \{1, 2, 3, ...\}$ depending on when the customer previously purchased. Assume the customer has a 0.20 probability of purchasing if the customer has not purchased in five weeks and is contacted in period t. Then if the customer is contacted, $S_{i,t+1} = 1$ with probability 0.20 and 5+1 = 6 with probability 0.80. In general, the state transitions can be denoted as $Prob(S_{i,t+1}' \mid S_{it}, D)$, the probability the customer

transitions to state S' in period $t+1$ given the customer is currently in state S and the firm takes action D.

- *Optimal Policy Function:* This is the key output of the dynamic customization optimization. It expresses what action the firm should take depending on the state of the customer. We use $D(S_{it})$ to denote what decision the firm should make if customer i is in state S in period t.

- *Time Horizon:* Time horizon refers to how far ahead the firm considers. A fundamental distinction is between infinite and finite horizon optimization. In Figure 12.2, we merely looked one period ahead. Ideally we would look an infinite number of periods ahead, because CLV is defined over an infinite horizon.

Now we develop the objective function for dynamic customer optimization. We first quantify CLV. Let:

π_{it} = Profit contribution from customer i in period t.

δ = Discount factor.

CLV is the present value of the customer's profit stream:

$$CLV = \sum_{t=0}^{\infty} \pi_{it} \delta^t \qquad (3)$$

The objective is to maximize *CLV*. Let:

S_{it} = State of customer i in period t.

$D(S_{it})$ = Decision firm makes if customer i is in state S in period t.

T = Time horizon.

Then the objective function is:

$$\max_{D(S_{it})} \sum_{t=0}^{T} \pi_{it}\left(S_{it}, D(S_{it})\right)\delta^t \qquad (4)$$

Equation (4) is a "dynamic program." The objective is to find the decision rule that specifies the action to take if customer i is in state S at time t and we want to maximize the present value of the customer's profit stream.[1] The value of T can be a finite number or infinity. The distinction between Equations (3) and (4) is crucial. Equation (3) views CLV as a static number. Equation (4) views CLV as customer performance *determined by the firm's actions*.[2]

---

1   For infinite horizon problems, we find the "steady state" solution so the optimal decision depends on the state but not the time period. In finite horizon problems, the solution will depend on t. $D(S_{it})$ is therefore the most general notation for the decision rule, but we will use $D(S)$ when referring to infinite horizon problems.

2   Note the problem as stated is unconstrained – there is no budget or other constraint that would require us to balance the profitability of one customer versus another. Constraints can be added for finite horizon problems (Neslin, et al., 2009; Khan, et al,. 2009) but are difficult to incorporate in infinite horizon problems.

There are many ways to find the optimal decision rule $D(S_{it})$, but they all are based on the "principle of optimality" enunciated by Bellman (1957). This is expressed in the "Bellman equation." Let:

$V_{it}(S_{it})$ = The maximum net present value profit we can expect to generate from customer i starting in period t given that customer is in state S at the beginning of that period. This is called the value function.

The principle of optimality states that $V_{it}(S_{it})$ depends on a decision rule that maximizes current profit *plus* what we can expect to achieve in the future because of the state transitions that result from that decision rule:

$$V_{it}\left(S_{it}\right) = \max_{D(S_{it})}\left\{E\left[\pi_{it}\left(S_{it}, D(S_{it})\right)\right] + \delta E\left[V_{i,t+1}(S'_{i,t+1})\right]\right\} \qquad (5)$$

The first term in brackets is the current period profits; the second is what we can expect in the future once the customer progresses to state S' in the next period because of our decision. The Bellman equation expresses what we did in Figure 12.2. Myopic optimization considered just the first term in Equation (5). However, once we took into account that mailing in Week 1 would transition the customer to a more responsive state S' in Week 2, we realized that the correct decision was to mail to the customer when $S=0$ as well as when $S=1$.

The key is to derive the optimal decision rule $D(S_{it})$. Methods for doing so include value iteration, policy iteration, linear programming, and backward induction (see Judd, 1998; Ross, 1983). Also available are approximation techniques for complex problems (Bitran and Mondschein, 1996; Keane and Wolpin, 1994). Another approach is "multi-armed bandit" methods (Hauser, et al., 2009; Scott, 2010; Agarwal, et al., 2009).

One approximation technique, rolling horizon, has been applied in operations management and more recently in marketing (Zhang and Krishnamurthi, 2004; Zhang and Wedel, 2009; Neslin, et al., 2009). The concept is simple: adopt a finite horizon, say five weeks, and optimize over those five weeks. After the results for the first of those weeks are observed and the new state of the customer is known with certainty, optimize over the next five weeks, and so on. The benefit of the rolling horizon approach is that it partially alleviates uncertainty by considering the situation anew each period, *knowing* the customer's state in that period.

Another approach is used when the state of the customer is never observed, but modeled as a latent trait. This is a partially observed Markov decision process (POMDP). The solution to the POMDP might require value iteration and interpolation (Montoya, et al., 2010).

4   The Development of the Dynamic Customer Optimization Field

Table 12.1 depicts the research that has developed the dynamic customer optimization field. The table shows the type of response model and three key characteristics of the optimization: the time horizon, method of solution, and state variables. It also shows the domain in marketing where the model has been applied.

Table 12.1 Examples of dynamic customer optimization model

Reference	Response Model	Horizon	Method	State Variables*	Decision Variables
		Optimization Method			**Application**
Bitran and Mondschein (1996)	RFM	Infinite	Approximation	RFM	Catalogs
Gönül and Shi (1998)	Dynamic Structural Probit	Infinite	Value Iteration	RF	Catalogs
Campbell et al. (2001)	Regression	Finite	Linear Programs	Previous catalogs	Catalogs
Elsner et al. (2003; 2004)	Regression, Decision Tree	Finite	Direct Calculation	RFM	Catalogs
Ching et al. (2004)	Bernoulli	Infinite, Finite	Linear Program	M	Promotions
Zhang and Krishnamurthi (2004)	Incidence/Choice/Quantity	Rolling	Direct Calculation	Purchase history	Price Promotions
Li et al. (2005)	Dynamic Structural Probit	Infinite	Value Iteration	RF	Communication, Price
Lewis (2005)	Logistic Regression	Infinite	Value Iteration	Customer tenure	Price
Simester et al. (2006)	Average Profit per State	Infinite	Policy Iteration	Purchase/response history	Catalogs
Zhang and Wedel (2009)	Incidence/Choice/Quantity	Rolling	Simplex Algorithm	State dependence	Price Promotions
Neslin et al. (2009)	Decision Tree	Rolling	Linear Program	R of invite, last response	Online Panel Response
Hauser et al. (2009)	Bernoulli	Infinite	Gittins Indices	Preference estimate	Website Design
Khan et al. (2009)	Incidence/Expenditure	Finite	Backward Induction	RFM	Coupons, Free Shipping
Montoya et al. (2010)	Hidden Markov	Infinite	Approximation	Frequency	Detailing, Sampling
Li et al. (2011)	Multivariate Probit	Finite	Backward Induction	Financial state	Direct Mail, Email
Sun and Li (2011)	Incidence/Duration/ Retention	Infinite	Backward Induction	Probability of contacting call-center	Call center assignment
Neslin et al. (2013)	Logistic Regression	Infinite	Value Iteration	Recency, previous marketing	Direct Mail, Email

Note: * Sampling of state variables; some papers have additional state variables. R=Recency; F=Frequency; M=Monetary Value.

4.1 PIONEERING WORK

The roots of dynamic customer optimization lie in the field of sales force management, where the objective was to schedule sales force customer visits to maximize profitability (Zoltners and Sinha, 1980; Montgomery, et al., 1971; Lodish, 1971). These models often considered dynamics such as carryover effects of sales force visits. Examples of the modern application of these ideas to managing customer lifetime value are shown in Table 12.1. The pioneering work by Bitran and Mondschein (1996) contained real-world complexities rarely seen in subsequent work. Bitran and Mondschein consider not only customer profits and costs, but inventory costs as well. This results in a complex mathematical programming optimization that they can solve only by approximation. Another pioneering paper was Gönül and Shi (1998). This work contained the interesting notion that not only is the firm forward looking, but the customer is as well. We will summarize this paper in more detail later on.

4.2 KEY TRENDS

Table 12.1 suggests several important trends. First is the application beyond catalogs to other elements of marketing, including emailing, promotions, and sales force visits. This progression is natural. Catalogers pioneered the field of direct marketing, since they regularly collect the required data and management of their customer list is the lifeblood of these companies. Campbell et al. (2001) and Elsner, et al., (2003; 2004) describe sophisticated dynamic customer optimization systems for catalog mailings. More recently, a broad array of companies can collect data through loyalty programs, data services, and online cookies, so more applications emerge. For example, Neslin et al. (2013) examine an online meal service provider and the targeting of direct mail and email. Montoya et al. (2010) examine a pharmaceutical company and the targeting of sales force visits ("detailing") and product sampling.

A second important trend is the movement from considering single to multiple marketing instruments. Whereas early applications focused on catalogs only or promotions only, later applications consider multiple instruments, such as direct mail and email (Li, et al., 2011; Neslin, et al., 2013), detailing and sampling (Montoya, et al., 2010), and coupons, free shipping, and reward programs (Khan, et al., 2009). Considering multiple instruments is not difficult given the dynamic programming machinery summarized earlier. However, more states are now needed to describe the customer. With a single marketing instrument, say catalogs, a state variable might be how recently the catalog was mailed to the customer. This variable might be quantified to equal 1, 2, 3, ..., ≥ 10, for example, defining ten possible states for each customer. With two instruments, say catalogs and email, we have the ten catalog recency states, and *for each of these*, ten email recency states. That yields a total of $10 \times 10 = 100$ states. This means that the solution algorithm needs to consider more states and this can drastically increase computation time. This is called the "curse of dimensionality." Advances in state space interpolation (Keane and Wolpin, 1994; Lovejoy, 1991) and computing speed enable one to handle many states. However, as companies see the need to optimize multiple marketing instruments, the curse of dimensionality becomes a concern.

Another trend is the use of "unobserved" states to describe the customer. This is most evidenced by the use of hidden Markov models (HMMs) where the customer is assumed to be in a state of readiness to buy that is not directly observable (Montoya, et al., 2010; Li, et al., 2011). Other examples include Hauser et al. (2009) and Sun and Li (2011). These models are quite realistic – consumers are in latent states that we cannot observe. The consideration of unobserved states does however add complexity to the modeling effort (see the above references).

5   Applications

In this section we review a sampling of the applications depicted in Table 12.1. This allows the reader to see how the issues we have been discussing play out in actual work.

5.1   OPTIMIZING AND FIELD TESTING A CATALOG MAILING MODEL (SIMESTER, ET AL., 2006)

Problem Context: Simester et al. (2006) tackle the problem of which of a set of pre-scheduled catalogs should be mailed to each customer. The mail dates are not decision variables (see Campbell et al. 2001 for a relaxation of this). Still, this is a very realistic problem. Often companies know they will be mailing catalogs at pre-specified dates, determined by seasonality, departmental goals, and so on. The question is who should get which catalog.

Response Model: Simester et al.'s response model is simple. Once the customer states are determined, the authors use historical data to calculate the expected profit ("reward" in the parlance of the paper) directly. That is, the authors find all customers in state s and calculate the average profit among customers who were mailed a catalog when in that state.

Optimization: The key innovation in this paper is the derivation of the states. A common approach simply is to place customers in RFM states (Bitran and Mondschein, 1996). The authors aim to improve upon this by ensuring that customers within a state are likely to be equally responsive to a given policy – the "homogeneity" criterion. In addition, they want to create states so that customers within a given state are similar to each other in terms of a set of predictor variables – the "representative" criterion. To create the states, the authors first calculate the profit for each customer during a previous period. Next, they run a regression where historical profit is the dependent variable and the predictors include RFM and other measures. They portray this process as passing the hyperplane defined by the regression through the data, and separating the data at the "line" where the regression passes through. This creates two segments (states) that each responded similarly to the historical policy (homogeneity) and have similar predictor variables (representative). The process proceeds iteratively. In their application, the authors define 500 states in this manner.

Once the states are defined, the authors calculate directly the average reward across all customers in a given state who were mailed a catalog. That is the response model. The authors then calculate the state transitions directly as well, by noting the probability customers in state S progressed to state S' if mailed a catalog.

The optimization is infinite horizon where the "time periods" can be of unequal length due to the different actual times between catalogs in the pre-determined catalog mailing schedule. The optimization is solved using policy iteration.

Application: The authors apply their model in a six-month field test involving 60,000 customers and 12 catalog mailings. The authors divide customers into low, moderate, and high-value segments. They then use the historical policy for half the customers and the proposed policy for the other half. The results were as follows:

- Low-value customers earned lower profits using the proposed policy versus the historical policy during the test period but ended the test in higher-value states.
- Moderate-value customers earned equal profits (proposed versus historical) during the test but also ended the test in higher-value states.
- High-value customers earned lower profits (proposed versus historical) during the test and ended the test in *lower*-value states.

The lack of profits during the test may have been due to the "turnpike property" (Kopalle, et al., 1992; McKenzie 1976). Optimal solutions for infinite horizon problems apply to a system in "steady state," yet the authors applied their optimal policy to customers who were not yet in steady state. The finding that the low- and moderate-value customers ended up in higher-value states suggests that customers were evolving to steady state. The high-value results were of most concern, because not only were profits lower during the test, but the customers were left in *lower*-value states. The authors show that in fact performance was improving for the high-value customers, and that the "error" was in under-mailing to this group. The authors note that since the company was mailing to the high-value customers 85 percent of the time, there wasn't enough data to accurately measure the reward and transition quantities.

There are two important lessons to be learned from this field test. First, it may be necessary to sacrifice short-term profits for the long term in implementing a dynamic customer optimization model. Second, it may be difficult to derive optimal policies if there are not enough data for each state. A good solution would be to run a test first where decisions are varied systematically among customers so that there is ample data on customer response for all states.

5.2 CONSIDERING CUSTOMER AS WELL AS FIRM OBJECTIVES (GÖNÜL AND SHI, 1998)

Problem Context: Gönül and Shi's (1998) key insight is that the firm and the customer each maximize their long-term benefits. The customer is maximizing long-term utility, while the firm is maximizing long-term profits. Most of the literature does not incorporate this dual maximization. However, there is a large literature that customers are forward looking (see Kopalle et al. 2012 and the references in that paper). Gönül and Shi consider the case of catalog mailing, where in considering whether to purchase in the current time period, the customer considers the future catalog mailings he or she might receive as a result of purchasing. Li et al. (2005) follow up on this approach in the context of a grocery store is optimizing customer-level pricing and messaging (email, text, and so on).

Response Model: The important foundation of the response model is the customer is maximizing expected long-term utility, that is:

$$E\left(\sum_{t=1}^{\infty}\delta_c^{t-1}u_{it}d_{it}\right) \qquad (6)$$

where $d_{it} = 1$ if customer i purchases in period t; 0 otherwise, u_{it} is the utility customer i obtains if he or she purchases in period t, and δ_c is the customer's discount factor. Utility is a function of catalogs received, recency, and frequency, so the customer decides whether to purchase in period t taking into account the impact that decision will have on future utility. For example, the customer realizes that if he or she does not need to purchase now, he or she will move to a higher recency state, which might induce the firm to mail another catalog. It is clear that the customer and firm are "playing" a stochastic game.

The authors formulate the utility function with a normal error term, so the result is a probit incidence model that takes into account current as well as subsequent utility, that is:

$$Prob_{it}\left(d_{it} = 1 | S_{it}, m_{it}\right) = \Phi[\bar{u}_{it} + \delta_c(V^c_{i,t+1}\left(S'_{i,t+1} | d_{it} = 1\right) - V^c_{i,t+1}\left(S'_{i,t+1} | d_{it} = 0\right)] \qquad (7)$$

where $\bar{u}_{it}$ is the customer's current expected utility based on the state variables recency and frequency S_{it}, and whether he or she receives a catalog (m_{it}). $V^c_{i,t+1}$ is the customer's value function, the maximum utility the customer can expect in the future depending on whether he or she purchases in period t.

Optimization: The state space for a given customer is $S_{it} = \{Recency_{it}, Frequency_{it}\}$. The probability of transitions between states is calculated using the probabilities of purchase derived from Equation 7. For example, recency re-sets to zero with $Prob(d_{it}=1)$ and increases by one with probability $1 - Prob(d_{it}=1)$. The firm's decision variable is whether to send a catalog to customer i in period t (m_{it}). Analogous to Equation (4), the objective function for the firm is:

$$\max_{m_{it}} \sum_{t=1}^{\infty} \pi_{it}\left(Recency_{it}, Frequency_{it}.m_{it}\right) \qquad (8)$$

Analogous to Equation (5), the value function can be expressed as:

$$V^f_{it}(S_{it}) = \max_{m_{it}}\{\pi_{it}\left(S_{it}, m_{it}\right) + \delta_f[V^f_{i,t+1}\left(S'_{i,t+1} | d_{it} = 1\right) \times Prob_{it}(d_{it} = 1 | S_{it}, m_{it}) + V^f_{i,t+1}\left(S'_{i,t+1} | d_{it} = 0\right) \times Prob_{it}(d_{it} = 0 | S_{it}, m_{it})]\} \qquad (9)$$

where δ_f is the firm's discount factor and $S_{it}=\{Recency_{it}, Frequnency_{it}\}$. Equation (9) shows that the maximum expected profit we can obtain from customer i is the catalog decision that maximizes expected immediate profits π_{it} plus what we can expect in the future assuming we pursue optimal catalog mailing thereafter. This future expectation depends on whether or not the customer purchases in period t, because the customer's state in period t (that is, recency and frequency), signified by $S'_{i,t+1}$ depends on whether the customer purchases.

Equations 6–9 clearly show the stochastic game being played between customer and firm. The customer has his or her value function, V^c_{it} that figures into his or her probability of purchase; the firm has its value function, V^f_{it}, that figures into its derivation of the optimal decision. The key methodological challenge is to jointly estimate the parameters of the utility function, both the customer and firm value functions, and the optimal policy. The authors embed the parameter estimation into a value iteration optimization procedure. They assume a starting value for the parameters, derive the implied value functions, then iterate to a new set of parameters, re-derive the implied value functions, and so on.

Application: The authors apply their model to a catalog mailing firm. They show that the forward-looking customer model outperforms a myopic model, suggesting that indeed in this application the customer is forward looking. They find for example the firm should not mail as often to low-frequency as to high-frequency customers. This makes sense in that high-frequency customers probably will buy often even if not mailed a catalog in the current period. The authors calculate that the company could increase profits by 16 percent if the optimal catalog mailing policy were used rather than the current policy.

5.3 USING A MOVING WINDOW LINEAR PROGRAMMING APPROACH TO OPTIMIZE ONLINE PANEL SURVEY RESPONSE RATES (NESLIN, ET AL., 2009)

Problem Context: Neslin et al. (2009) develop and apply an optimal contact model to increase response rates for an online survey panel. Online panels have become a common form for gathering survey data. These panels are created and maintained by polling or market research companies. The panel manager has a set of surveys to field in chronological order, and must decide which panelists to solicit for which surveys. High response rate is the key objective for the panel manager.

Response Model: Data were available for 38,212 panelist invitations. The authors use a decision tree to model whether or not the panelist responds to a given invitation. They find four variables predict response:

1. days between last invite and current study (a larger number of days was associated with decreasing response, perhaps due to a loss of interest on the part of the panelist);
2. response to previous invitation (a positive response was associated with higher response rate for the current invitation);
3. response to an email confirmation request (an affirmative confirmation was associated with higher response rate, perhaps indicating high panelist involvement), and gender (females were generally more likely to respond).

Optimization: The decision tree model split the variables as follows: days since last invite was divided into two categories (0–61 days and 61+ days). Completion of the previous invite was divided into yes, no, and has not received a previous invite. Response to the email confirmation request was divided into "OK,", "Not OK," or not asked. Gender was male or female. This generates $2 \times 3 \times 3 \times 2 = 36$ states. Transition between states depended on the probability of response indicated by the decision tree model. Assume the probability that a panelist in state "62+, No, OK, Male" responds to a request is 0.30. If that panelist is invited to participate in the current study, the customer would transition to "0-61, Yes, OK, Male" with probability 0.30, and "0-61, No, OK, Male" with probability 1-0.30 = 0.70. The decision tree thus created the states, the probability of response given the state, and the transition probabilities between states.

A challenge was to handle the sample size and composition requirements for each study. For example, a study might require 200 males and 100 females. To address this, the authors formulated a linear program version of a finite horizon model, but used a "rolling horizon" to address the concerns with finite horizon. The authors chose a horizon of four studies. They first optimized over studies 1 through 4 and used the model's prescriptions to invite panelists to the first study. After the first study was completed, actual responses were observed and panelist state status was updated. Then the authors optimized for studies 2 through 5, and so on. The linear program enabled the authors to incorporate constraints demanded by each study, yet take advantage of the known response to the previous study to update the placement of customers into states for the beginning of the second study. This means that there is no steady state policy function $D(S)$. The policy is derived on a rolling horizon basis as the model is re-run given the current distribution of customers in states.

Let S equal the number of studies considered in the rolling horizon. Let X_{js} be the number of panelists from state j invited to participate in study s. Let N be the number of states. Let A_{js} be the number of panelists in state j available to participate in study s. Let p_{jk} equal the probability an invited panelist transitions from state j to k. Let q_{jk} equal the probability a non-invited panelist transitions from state j to k. Assume there are G demographic groups and Q_{sg} equals the number of respondents from demographic group g desired for study s. Finally, let r_j be the response rate for panelists in state j if invited to participate in a study. Then the optimization is:

$$\min_X \sum_{s=1}^{S} \sum_{j=1}^{N} X_{js} \tag{10}$$

subject to:

$$X_{js} \le A_{js} \quad j = 1,\ldots,N; s = 1,,S \tag{10a}$$

$$\sum_{j=1}^{N} r_j X_{js} \ge Q_{sg} \quad g = 1,,G; s = 1,,S \tag{10b}$$

$$A_{ks} = \sum_{j=1}^{N} p_{jk} X_{j,s-1} + \sum_{j=1}^{N} q_{jk}\left(A_{j,s-1} - X_{j,s-1}\right) + R_{ks} \quad k = 1,,N; s = 2,,S \tag{10c}$$

The objective (Equation 10) is to minimize the number of invites over the study horizon. This is equivalent to maximizing response rate. Constraint 10a ensures no more are invited from a given state than is available at the time of study s. Constraint 10b stipulates the number of responses required for each study, from each demographic group. Note "rX" is the expected number of responses. Constraint 10c keeps track of how many panelists will be available in each state for each study.

Application: The authors field-tested their model with 33,000 panelists. Each panelist was randomly assigned either to a model-managed, management-heuristic, or random-invitation group. Over the course of four studies, the response rates for the model-managed group were 26 percent, 45 percent, 50 percent, and 51 percent, versus 23 percent, 22 percent, 28 percent, and 27 percent for the management-heuristic group. The random invitation group had response rates of 11 percent, 11 percent, 15 percent, and 14 percent. Clearly the model improved over current management practice.

The authors used simulation to compare their model to a greedy algorithm that was myopic and invited panelists in order of their likelihood of responding. The authors found that the greedy algorithm would have slightly outperformed their model. The required sample size was 400 for each of the four studies used in the field test. The greedy algorithm therefore did not have to "worry" about preparing for high requirements for the fourth study. The authors found that for a series of studies requiring 150, 200, 200, and 400 respondents, their model was superior to the greedy algorithm. For a series of studies requiring 1,000, 1,000, 1,000, and 1,324 respondents, the greedy algorithm could not generate feasible solutions in 69 percent of the simulations. This is because the greedy algorithm did not generate enough panelists in high response states to produce the required 1,324 respondents. The authors' model did not run into this problem because it was "aware" of the high requirements for the last study, and planned to have the right number of panelists in each state so that this demand could be achieved. Overall, greedy algorithms are worthwhile strong tests of dynamic customer optimization models. If the problem context does not require looking ahead, myopic algorithms can do quite well. If however dynamics are important or if future requirements are high, greedy algorithms can do rather poorly.

5.4 CUSTOMIZING PROMOTIONS ACCOUNTING FOR DYNAMICS AND HETEROGENEITY (KHAN, ET AL., 2009)

Problem Context: Khan et al. (2009) investigate optimal customer promotion strategies for an online retailer. The firm could target coupons, free shipping offers, and reward program offers. The question was which customers should receive which offers at what time. A key contribution of this paper is to compare the gains in profits from one-to-one customization versus segment-level customization.

Response Model: The authors consider effects of cross-customer heterogeneity and dynamics, in particular recency, on response to promotions. The model consists of a probit purchase incidence model coupled with an expenditures model. The purchase incidence model is:

$$
\begin{aligned}
U_{it}^* = &\beta_{0i} + \beta_{1i}\tau_{it} + \beta_{2i}ln(\tau_{it}) + \beta_{3i}Coupon_{it} + \beta_{4i}\left(Coupon_{it}\ln\left(\tau_{it}\right)\right) + \\
&\beta_{5i}\left(Coupon_{it}Frequency_i\right) + \beta_{6i}Freeship_{it} + \beta_{7i}\left(Freeship_{it}\ln\left(\tau_{it}\right)\right) + \\
&\beta_{8i}\left(Freeship_{it}Frequency_i\right) + \beta_{9i}Reward_{it} + \beta_{10i}\left(Reward_{it}\ln(\tau_{it})\right) + \\
&\beta_{11i}\left(Reward_{it}Frequency_{it}\right) + \beta_{12i}Price_t + \beta_{13i}ln(Previous\,Spend_{it}) + \beta_{14i}Banner_t + \varepsilon_{it}
\end{aligned}
\tag{11a}
$$

$$
U_{it}^* > 0 => Purchases\ made\ by\ customer\ i\ in\ week\ t
\tag{11b}
$$

All parameters are customer-specific (indexed by i). For example, customer A may react differently to coupons than customer B ($\beta_{3A} \neq \beta_{3B}$). Recency is captured by τ_{it}, which equals the number of weeks since customer i last purchased. The parameters β_{1i} and β_{2i} capture baseline recency effects, that is, how recency affects the probability of purchasing apart from promotion effects. The linear and log terms allow for flexible impact. The estimated parameters suggested that baseline incidence likelihood followed an inverse-U impact – incidence likelihood peaked roughly three weeks after the previous purchase, then slowly declining.

The interactions between the three promotional variables and recency (β_{4i}, β_{7i}, and β_{i10}) allow customer response to change depending on recency. For example, the authors found that customers on average were less likely to respond to coupons if it had been a long time since they had purchased ($\beta_{4i} < 0$). As can be seen in Equation (11a), the model also includes interactions between promotions and customer frequency, and includes important covariates such as price, the amount of expenditure on the previous purchase occasion, and the presence of banner ads.

The expenditure model used the log of expenditures as the dependent variable, which is set equal to zero if the customer does not purchase. If the customer does purchase, the model is:

$$\ln\left(Expenditure_{it}\right) = \delta_{0i} + \delta_{1i} \ln\left(\tau_{it}\right) + \delta_{2i} Coupon_{it} + \delta_{3i} Freeship_{it} + \delta_{4i} Reward_{it} +$$
$$\delta_{5i} \ln\left(previous\, spend\right) + \delta_{6i} Price_t + \delta_{7i} Banner_t + \mu_{it} \quad (12)$$

The authors find that expenditures increase with recency ($\delta_{1i} > 0$ on average). They also find that coupons, free shipping, and reward on average do not have a strong effect on expenditures, but there is considerable heterogeneity in these δ's.

Optimization: The state variables included recency, expenditure on previous purchase, the quantities needed to calculate frequency (number of orders and time in database), and cumulative spending (needed to determine if the customer was eligible for a reward program offer). The authors also kept track of the number of promotions the customer had received as of a given time. The authors imposed the restriction that the customer could not receive more than two promotions over an eight-week period.

State transitions were calculated using the estimated response model. For example, the authors use Equations 11a–11b to calculate the probability of purchasing in time *t*, given the state of the customer at time *t*. This determined the probability the customer would transition to a different state in time *t*+1.

The objective was to determine the policy function $D(S_{it})$ to maximize firm profits over an eight-week finite horizon, which allowed the authors to solve the dynamic program for each customer using backwards recursion. The decision variables were whether to offer a coupon, a free shipping promotion, or reward program bonus points, subject to the constraint that each customer could receive more than two promotions over the eight-week period. Another way to include this constraint implicitly would be to incorporate wear-out in the utility function (see Gönül, et al., 2000; Neslin, et al., 2013).

Application: The authors investigated the gain in profits from customizing at the individual versus segment level, and the gain from incorporating dynamic changes in customer response. The authors found that including dynamics increased profits by 7.8 percent versus a benchmark of no customization. Adding cross-sectional heterogeneity increased profits still further, by a total of 13.2 percent. So including dynamics and cross-customer heterogeneity is important for optimal contact policies.

To investigate segmentation, the authors clustered customers based on their response parameters and then optimized for each segment. The authors derived four segments and found that profits from this method increased 10.9 percent over the baseline. Compared to the 13.2 percent gain from customer-level optimization, the authors conclude "the value of the 2 percent improvement over segment-level customization must be traded off against the effort needed to develop individual-level policies." Note however that the segment-level analysis clustered individual-level estimated parameters, so the effort saved was not in response model estimation but in not having to solve a separate dynamic program for each customer. Nevertheless, the research suggests that in practical applications, segment-level optimal contact policies may perform quite well (see Zhang and Wedel, 2009).

5.5 OPTIMAL CONTACT USING A HIDDEN MARKOV MODEL (MONTOYA, ET AL., 2010)

Problem Context: This application involves the targeting of pharmaceutical detailing (sales calls) and sampling to physicians. Detailing and sampling are major marketing expenditures for pharmaceutical companies. The unique aspect of this research is the use of a HMM for the response function, and a POMDP to solve the optimization.

Response model: The HMM posits that at any given time, physicians are in a state related to their prescription behavior but not directly observed by the researcher. With a standard RFM model, RFM can be calculated directly for each physician and that defines the state. The advantage of HMMs is the potential for better predictive validity and insights on how marketing influences physician behavior within a given state (short-term effects) and how marketing influences the transition to other states (long-term effects). The authors use a Binomial model for the number of prescriptions written by physician i in time t. The parameters of this distribution are W_{it} and p_{ist}, where W_{it} is the number of prescriptions written in the product category by physician i in time t (assumed not influenced by marketing), and p_{ist} is the fraction of prescriptions physician i writes for the focal drug in time t, given the physician is in state s. p_{ist} is a logistic function of baseline preference for physicians in state s ($\hat{a}^0_s$) and marketing, that is, detailing and sampling.

Optimization: The states are not directly observed, but the authors partially determine their characteristics by correlating prescription frequency with state number. That is, the authors assume that if there are three states, the states are ordered so that the baselines follow $\hat{a}^0_1 < \hat{a}^0_2 < \hat{a}^0_3$. This enables the states to be identified statistically.

Transition between states is governed by an ordered logit model, $q_{is'st} = P(X_{it}=s|X_{it-1}=s, z_{it-1})$, where q is the probability the physician transitions from state s' to s in time t, given marketing effort in time t-1(z_{it-1}). The ordered logit follows from the stipulation that higher states correspond to higher levels of intrinsic preference for the drug.

The infinite horizon objective function is:

$$\max_{z_{it}} E\left\{\sum_{\tau=t}^{\infty}\delta^{\tau-1}R_{i\tau}\right\} \tag{13}$$

where d is the discount factor, z_{it} is a vector representing the amount of detailing and sampling to use for physician i in time t, and R_{it} is the profit generated by physician i in period t. Profit is a random variable whose expected value is:

$$E[R_{it}] = \sum_{s=1}^{S}b_{it}(s)r_{ist} \tag{14}$$

where r_{ist} is the expected profit given physician i is in state t at time t, contingent on marketing targeted at the physician and calculated through the logistic response function, and $b_{it}(s)$ is the researcher's belief physician i is in state s at time t. The beliefs are updated each period using Bayes rule and based on the marketing expended in the period and the response (p) and transition models (q). For example, if a physician is targeted with heavy detailing in period t, and detailing is associated with a high likelihood of prescribing (p)

and transitioning to a higher state (q), the beliefs will be updated so that it is likely the physician is in a higher state at the end of period t.

Equation (13) accompanied by the HMM that drives response is a POMDP and is solved for the optimal decision rule $D(s)$ using a combination of value iteration and value function interpolation.

Application: The application is for a new drug. The data consist of 300 physicians observed over 24 months. Current firm policy is for the average physician to receive nine samples and two detail visits per month. This is a high level of marketing expenditure. The estimated model finds three states, "inactive," "infrequent," and "frequent" and provides insights on the impact of marketing both in the short term (within a given month) and the long term (transitioning physicians to higher states). In particular:

1. marketing is generally more effective in transitioning physicians to higher states than creating a sale in the current month;
2. detailing is particularly effective at transitioning physicians out of the inactive state;
3. sampling is particularly effective at keeping physicians in the frequent state.

The authors estimate the optimal policy would increase prescriptions by 62 percent, generating an additional \$412 in profits per physician per month.[3] These gains are achieved by cutting spending by 20 percent but allocating those expenditures toward physicians who are most receptive, and by using detailing for physicians in the active state but curtailing it for physicians in the infrequent or frequent states. That is, detailing is used to invest in the long term, moving physicians to higher states.

Overall, Montoya et al. show the potential for HMMs of response and state transition to add insights as well as profits through optimal contact. See Li et al. (2011) for an application of HMMs in the financial services industry.

5.6   KEY INSIGHTS FROM APPLICATIONS

The above discussion reveals several insights about the application of dynamic customer optimization models. These include:

- *Field tests are crucial*: As demonstrated by the Simester et al. (2006) and Neslin et al. (2009) papers, field tests are very valuable for the lessons learned as well as for establishing the external validity of dynamic customer management models.
- *The "optimal" policy is only as good as the data*: This is illustrated most vividly by Simester et al. (2006). The general lesson is that optimization can prescribe solutions that are out of the range of the data. In fact, that is what one would expect. But too much out of the range and the prescribed policies can be suboptimal.
- *Dynamic customer management models promise higher performance*: Montoya et al. (2010), Khan et al. (2009), and Neslin et al. (2009) all report higher profits or performance using dynamic customer management models. However, we need more field tests to clearly establish that actual experience fulfills the promise.

---

3   The authors note this estimate may be biased upwards, but estimate the extent of potential bias and find it to be about 10.2 percent. So even if the bias is that high, the optimal policy still generates substantial additional profits.

- *Fit the method to the problem*: There are several customer response models and optimization methods. One should start with the problem and find the right method, rather than start with the method and find a problem. For example, Khan et al. (2009) realized they needed to incorporate constraints regarding promotion frequency and using a finite horizon was the easiest way to do this.

6 Summary, Key Challenges, and Future Research

The design of a dynamic customer optimization model starts with a problem context, which defines the decision variables, the data requirements, and the nature of the model to be formulated. The model consists of a response model, that is, a model that predicts customer response to marketing actions depending on the "state" the customer is in, and an optimization model. The optimization requires a definition of the customer states, an objective to be optimized, and a solution approach for generating the marketing actions to be taken depending on what state the customer is in. The applications reviewed in this chapter and cataloged in Table 12.1 show the diversity of approaches available.

Our overall conclusion is that optimal contact models have high promise for prescribing which customers should be targeted with which marketing at what time. We have seen field tests that demonstrate their value, and non-field evidence that these models improve over current management practice.

However, there are several challenges ahead for this field. First is scalability. Ideally one would estimate individual-level response model parameters and incorporate them in the optimization. However, firms are concerned with 100,000s or even millions of customers. How can one derive a reliable set of response parameters for each customer? For example, estimating a Bayesian model of customer heterogeneity for 1,000,000 customers would require exorbitant computational time. Even then, it isn't clear how precise these estimates would be. An alternative would be to estimate a hierarchical Bayes model on a subset of customers and use that to predict the response parameters for the rest of the population. But it isn't clear how accurate that would be. Another approach would be just to incorporate observed sources of heterogeneity, for example, interact demographics and marketing. A final approach would be to estimate segment-level models for a subset of the population, into which the rest could be accurately classified. In any case, how individualized to make the response model, and how to derive individualized response parameters for millions of customers, is a significant challenge.

A second challenge is to find solution mechanisms for complex dynamic programs. Real-world applications often have constraints. For example, management may be planning a catalog mailing in January, March, and May, and requires a minimum and maximum number of catalogs to be mailed for each campaign. This can be accommodated in a finite horizon model, although finite horizons have their limitations due to end-game and initialization problems. The challenge is to include cross-customer constraints in infinite horizon models.

A third challenge is to optimize recently developed methods of measuring CLV. A good example of this is Motoyal et al.'s (2010) work using a hidden Markov model of CLV. However, particularly fertile ground for future research would be to optimize using stochastic models of CLV (Schmittlein, et al., 1987; Fader, et al., 2005; Abe, 2009; Bemmaor and Glady, 2012) An additional area for future research is to utilize sophisticated customer response models such as those based on ensemble learning, neural networks, support vector machines, or Bayesian Networks. One would need to incorporate marketing in these models and develop methods for optimization.

A fourth challenge is how to deal with an over-abundance of states. As noted earlier real-world problems can generate 100,000s of states. For example, consider a response model utilizing $RFM_{behavior}$ and $RFM_{marketing}$. If we have ten states for each of these six variables, we have $10^6 = 1,000,000$ states. Standard methods of dynamic programming would require huge computing power to optimize over this many states. The current solution here is to use interpolation methods as in Montoya et al. (2010). These methods are approximations but may be preferred in some circumstances. The point is, the number of states must be addressed in any optimal contact model application.

A fifth challenge is when to update the response function. The optimal decision policy is only as good as its response model. To the extent that response parameters change over time for reasons not addressed in the model (for example, recession or fundamental changes in the competitive environment), the decision rules become less accurate. A promising method for addressing this is to continually learn the response function (Sun, et al., 2006). Another interesting approach would be to use a dynamic linear model.

A final challenge is deciding between finite and infinite horizons. Finite horizons suffer from starting point and end game effects. Infinite horizons assume steady state transitions yet applying a steady state solution to a system not in steady state may run into the turnpike property and not be the optimal way to take that system to steady state. Perhaps rolling horizons offer a suitable compromise between finite and infinite horizons.

While there is no shortage of challenges, the opportunities and accomplishments to date of the growing field of optimal contact models are most encouraging. The previous ten years has witnessed very important advances; the next ten years promise to be exciting ones for this field.

References

Abe, M. (2009). "'Counting your customers' one by one: A hierarchical Bayes extension to the Pareto/NBD Model. *Marketing Science, 28*(3), 541–53.

Agarwal, D., Chen, B.-C. and Elango, P. (2009). Explore/Exploit Schemes for Web Content Optimization, 2009 Ninth IEEE Conference on Data Mining.

Bellman, R. (1957). *Dynamic Programming*. Princeton, NJ: Princeton University Press.

Bemmaor, A.C. and Glady, N. (2012). Modeling purchasing behavior with sudden 'death': A flexible customer lifetime model. *Management Science, 58*(5), 1012–21.

Berger, P.D. and Nasr, N.I. (1998). Customer lifetime value: Marketing models and applications. *Journal of Interactive Marketing, 12*(1), 17–30.

Bitran, G.R. and Mondschein, S.V. (1996). Mailing fecisions in the catalog sales industry. *Management Science, 42*(9), 1364–81.

Blattberg, R.C., Kim, B.-D. and Neslin, S.A. (2008). *Database Marketing: Analyzing and Managing Customers*. New York, NY: Springer.

Campbell, D., Erdahl, R., Johnson, D., Bibelnieks, E., Haydock, M., Bulluck, M. and Crowder, H. (2001). Optimizing customer mail streams at fingerhut. *Interfaces, 31*(1), 77–90.

Ching, W-K, Ng, M.K., Wong, K.-K. and Altman, E. (2004). Customer lifetime value: Stochastic optimization approach. *Journal of the Operational Research Society, 55*(8), 860–68.

Elsner, R., Krafft, M. and Huchzermeier, A. (2003). Optimizing Rhenania's mail-order business through dynamic multilevel modeling (DMLM). *Interfaces, 33*(1), 50–66.

Elsner, R., Krafft, M. and Huchzermeier, A. (2004). Optimizing Rhenania's direct marketing business through dynamic multilevel modeling (DMLM) in a multicatalog-brand environment. *Marketing Science, 23*(2), 192–206.

Fader, P.S., Hardie, B.G.S. and Lee, K.L. (2005). Counting your customers the easy way: An alternative to the Pareto/NBD Model. *Marketing Science, 24*(2), 275–84.

Gönül, F. and Shi, M. Z. (1998). Optimal mailings of catalogs: A new methodology using estimable structural dynamic programming models. *Management Science, 44*(9), 1249–62.

Gönül, F., Kim, B.-D. and Shi, M. (2000). Mailing smarter to catalog customers. *Journal of Interactive Marketing, 14*(2), 2–16.

Gupta, S., Lehmann, D.R. and Stuart, J.A. (2004). Valuing customers. *Journal of Marketing Research, 41*(1), 7–18.

Hauser, J.R., Urban, G.L., Liberali, G. and Braun, M. (2009). Website morphing. *Marketing Science, 28*(2), 202–23.

Judd, K.L. (1998). *Numerical Methods in Economics*. Cambridge, MA: Massachusetts Institute of Technology.

Keane, M.P., and Wolpin, K.I. (1994). The solution and estimation of discrete choice programming models by simulation and interpolation. *The Review of Economics and Statistics, 76*(4), 648–72.

Khan, R., Lewis, M. and Singh, V. (2009). Dynamic customer management and the value of one-to-one marketing. *Marketing Science, 28*(6), 1063–79.

Kopalle, P.K., Assunção, J.L. and Lehmann, D.R. (1992). A Numerical Approach to Solve Finite Horizon Optimal Control Problems Exhibiting the Turnpike Property. *Proceedings of the 31st Conference on Decision and Control*, Tuscon, Arizona, December 1992.

Lewis, M. (2005). A dynamic programming approach to customer relationship pricing. *Management Science, 51*(6), 986–94.

Li, C., Xu, Y. and Li, H. (2005). An empirical study of dynamic customer relationship management. *Journal of Retailing and Consumer Services, 12*(6), 431–41.

Li, S., Sun, B. and Montgomery, A.L. (2011). Cross-selling the right product to the right customer at the right time. *Journal of Marketing Research, 48*(4), 683–700.

Littman, M.L. (2009). A tutorial on partially observable Markov decision processes. *Journal of Mathematical Psychology, 53*(3), 119–25.

Lodish, L.M. (1971). CALLPLAN: An interactive salesman's call planning system. *Management Science, 16*(4), Application Series Part 2, P25–P40.

Lovejoy, W.S. (1991). A survey of algorithmic methods for partially observed Markov decision processes. *Annals of Operations Research, 28*(1–4), 47–65.

McKenzie, L.W. (1976). Turnpike theory. *Econometrica, 44*(5), 841–65.

Montgomery, D.B., Silk, A.J. and Zaragoza, C.E. (1971). A multiple-product sales force allocation model. *Management Science, 18*(4), Application Series Part 2, P3–P24.

Montoya, R., Netzer, O. and Jedidi, K. (2010). Dynamic allocation of pharmaceutical detailing and sampling for long-term profitability. *Marketing Science, 29*(5), 909–24.

Neslin, S.A., Novak, T.P., Baker, K.R. and Hoffman, D.L. (2009). An optimal contact model for maximizing online panel response rates. *Management Science, 55*(5), 727–37.

Neslin, S.A., Taylor, G.A., Grantham, K.D. and McNeil, K.R. (2013). Overcoming the 'recency trap'. *Journal of the Academy of Marketing Science*, forthcoming.

Ross, S. (1983). *Introduction to Stochastic Dynamic Programming*. New York, NY: Academic Press.

Schmittlein, D.C., Morrison, D.G. and Colombo, R. (1987). Counting your customer: Who are they and what will they do next. *Management Science, 33*(1), 1–24.

Scott, S.L. (2010). A modern Bayesian look at the multi-armed bandit. *Applied Stochastic Models in Business and Industry, 26*(6), 639–58.

Simester, D.I., Sun, P. and Tsitsiklis, J.N. (2006). Dynamic catalog mailing policies. *Management Science, 52*(5), 683–96.

Sun, B. and Li, S. (2011). Learning and acting on customer information: A dimulation-based demonstration on service allocations with offshore centers. *Journal of Marketing Research, 48*(1), 72–86.

Sun, B., Li, S. and Zhou, C. (2006). 'Adaptive' learning and 'proactive' customer relationship management. *Journal of Interactive Marketing, 20*(3/4), 82–96.

Zhang, J. and Krishnamurthi, L. (2004). Customizing promotions in online stores. *Marketing Science, 23*(4), 561–78.

Zhang, J. and Wedel, M. (2009). The effectiveness of customized promotions in online and offline stores. *Journal of Marketing Research, 46*(2), 190–206.

Zoltners, A.A. and Sinha, P. (1980). Integer programming models for sales resource allocation. *Management Science, 26*(3), 242–60.

13 *Direct Marketing in the Non-profit Sector*

GRIET VERHAERT

1   Introduction

Traditionally, one makes a distinction between the private, public, and non-profit sector. All of them are important in human society since each has a specific role to accomplish in the satisfaction of human need (Sargeant, 2009). Since most business cases come from the private sector, less is known from the non-profit sector. In this chapter, we focus on the non-profit sector. This sector is interesting to study for every manager because these three main sectors increasingly interact with each other (for example, increased joint ventures between corporations and non-profits). Consequently, it can be relevant for managers in all three sectors to understand how marketing is used in the non-profit environment (Andreasen and Kotler, 2008).

A non-profit organization, or not-for-profit organization, is an organization who does not pursue profit and who tries to finance their production of general purpose goods by other means than selling at a price covering production. From a technical point of view, the private sector differs from the non-profit sector in terms of resources. More specific, in the private sector, the price should cover the production costs. In contrast, in the non-profit sector, it is not the revenue on sales but other resources that are important like individual and corporate donations, government support, and so on. Notwithstanding the term, non-profit involves a substantial amount of money. In 2010 in the US alone, individuals gave $211.77 billion (National Center for Charitable Statistics, 2012, see http://nccs.urban.org/). The majority of the funds are raised from private donors. Therefore, we will concentrate on the resources coming from individual "donors." In addition it is relevant to identify the similarities as well as dissimilarities between the "donor" in the non-profit sector and the "consumer" in the private market. The best known example of a non-profit organization is a charity. Consequently, in this chapter, we will focus on fundraising for charities from private donors.

The practice of direct marketing in the profit sector is a well-known area. However, the practice of direct marketing in the non-profit sector is less known compared to the private sector. Nevertheless, direct marketing, and direct mail in particular, is crucial for the non-profit sector and is becoming more and more advanced and highly professionalized (cfr., DMA Nonprofit Federation). In practice, there are a lot of similarities in both sectors but there exist some remarkable specific practices for non-profit marketers as well. In this chapter, we provide an overview of some important trends of direct marketing in the non-profit sector by focusing on database marketing in private donor fundraising. In the next part, we start with discussing the different stages in the donor lifecycle, that is, acquisition, retention, and reactivation. In the third section, we elaborate on the diverse channels at the disposal of the non-profit organization and stress the relevance of an integrated multichannel marketing strategy. Next, we consider the database of a non-profit organization and identify some strategies to optimize the target selection as well as the content of the campaigns. This will bring us to the campaign evaluation section. Finally, we end by discussing challenges and opportunities for the future. Beside this, through this chapter, based on three previous studies (Verhaert, 2010), we will have a closer look at three specific cases that are relevant to illustrate some important trends of database marketing in direct mail fundraising.

2 Different Aspects of the Donor Lifecycle

Charities usually distinguish between three principal stages in the donor lifecycle: acquisition, retention, and reactivation (Sargeant and Shang, 2010). In this section, we will explain each stage and focus on the aspects which are different for a non-profit/ fundraising setting compared to a more traditional setting, like retail, banking, and so on.

The graph below (Figure 13.1) summarizes the different steps of the lifecycle together with the specific actions a non-profit marketer could take.

2.1 ACQUISITION

The first stage is called the acquisition stage and is meant to attract new donors by sending the appeal to people who have never donated to the charity before. For this, like in business, charities often rely on list brokers to rent prospect addresses from newspapers, magazines, or mail order companies. Some charities even exchange their household lists with other charities because of the low costs as well as because of better campaign results. This approach is very specific for the non-profit setting since "competitors" in the private sector are very unlikely to swap the household list of their clients with each other.

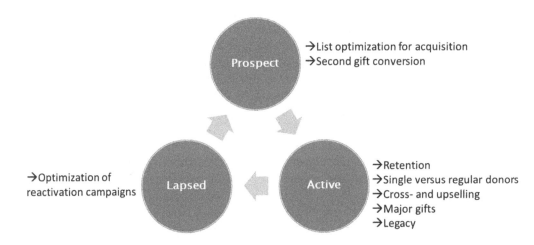

Figure 13.1 The donor lifecycle with marketing actions

CASE STUDY 1

To investigate whether exchanging an address/donor could also hurt the loyalty of the donor with the initial existing mother charity, we (Verhaert, 2010; Verhaert, et al., 2010) investigated this issue of list exchange in more depth by designing a large-scaled field experiment in which we controlled the competition between 24 European charities during ten months at an individual level. We operationalized competition through manipulating the exchange of household lists. Hence, the experimental manipulation consists of sending a number of experimental acquisition mailings in addition to the charities' regular retention campaigns. We systematically varied the number of sent acquisition campaigns, going from a very low intensity (that is, zero campaigns) to very high mailing pressure (that is, 22 to 24 acquisition campaigns). Because we want to know whether active donors choose to remain loyal toward their mother charity or not, we estimate a logistic regression. This analysis results in a maximum likelihood function that is maximized to achieve appropriate fit to the data (Allison, 1999). We modeled individual i's {i=1,2,...,N} loyalty decision for each mother charity m {m=1,2,...,M}. Let y_{im} be a binary variable reflecting whether the donor i remains loyal or not toward the mother charity m during the experimental period. More specifically, as soon as the donor donates to the mother charity, we consider this individual as a loyal donor. The probability to remain loyal to the mother charity is estimated as follows:

$$P(y_{im} = 1|\mathbf{x}) = \frac{1}{1 + exp^{-(w_0 + \mathbf{w}\ \mathbf{x})}} \tag{1}$$

with $\mathbf{x}$ as an n-dimensional input vector reflecting the independent variables, $\mathbf{w}$ the parameter vector and w_0 the intercept. Regarding the independent variables, direct mail response behavior is traditionally modeled as a function of RFM-variables by considering the distinction between solicitation and purchase history. Solicitation history involves the communication initiatives toward the individuals taken from the company/charity, and purchase history involves past behavior of individuals receiving direct mail campaigns (Elsner, et al., 2004). Consequently, the explanatory variables involved past donation behavior toward the mother charity, mother mailing pressure during the experimental period and external mailing pressure. In general, the analysis reveals that all mother charities are hurt by acquisition campaigns of other charities. This negative effect of competition confirms the results of most of the studies on competitive advertising interference (for example, Unnava and Sirdeshmukh, 1994; D'Souza and Rao, 1995; Burke and Srull, 1988; Keller, 1991; Bagozzi and Silk, 1983). However, the impact of being solicited from external charities differs across charities and it seems that some charities are better protected against new entries on the market than others. More specifically, we demonstrated that stronger, well-established brands with a higher brand equity are better protected from competition than brands with a lower brand equity. In addition, the results also show that, although there is some decrease in share of wallet, increased competition involves an increase in size of the donor's wallet. Increased competition leads thus to a growth in the market rather than splitting up the pie.

The findings offer practical implications for fundraising management on exchanging their household list. The good news is that the total sum of both streams of giving and receiving is positive. This means that the exchange of addresses increases total funds for the mother charity. Although the total sum is positive, this does not imply that the mother charity only gains. More specifically, we identified business stealing effects when competition, and thus exchange, increases. It is therefore important that fundraising managers bear in mind the harmful effect of the external mailing pressure on the loyalty of their existing donors. However, not all charities are equally affected. For big, well-known charities the threat is of a lower extent than for recently introduced charities with rather low brand equity. Therefore, fundraisers of these smaller charities could be advised to better protect their donor list until they established a strong brand. An important remark here is that small charities have a lower number of donors and therefore a lower number of addresses to exchange. To obtain plenty of new donors, simply exchanging is not sufficient for these charities. These organizations still need to acquire new addresses by renting rather than by exchanging.

In sum, acquisition reflects the first stage in the donor lifecycle and these potential donors are called prospects. After the first donation, it is crucial that the donor donates a second time. Some charities even speak about "hot prospects" after the first donation indicating that one is considered as a real donor as soon as he/she made a second donation. The follow-up period, after the first gift, or honeymoon, or welcome stage, is important to convert the donor to the second gift. After this, the retention program can start working.

2.2 RETENTION

Retention campaigns are the second category in which the charity tries to preserve the current donors and to upgrade their donation behavior. This segment involves active donors. In this second stage, charities have a broad range of specific actions at their disposal to cultivate their relationship with existing donors. Examples of these programs are regular giving, upselling, cross-selling, membership, major donor, and legacy. We will discuss each of them below.

Single versus regular donors – It is important to take into account the distinction between the single and regular donors. Single donors are donors who only give once after the donation request and for whom the charity needs to ask again for a next gift. In contrast, regular donors are committed to give a fixed amount on a regular base like every month or every year. In the stage of retention it is important to inspire donors to donate frequently and to convert them as soon as possible to a regular/monthly donor through a permanent order. This type of donating is comparable with contractual settings in the for-profit world (that is, insurance products in banking). Regular donors are more preferable than single donors because it implicates a kind of certainty (that is, the charity might anticipate on future incomes of the specific donor) and it is quite cost-efficient (that is, there is no need to send an appeal every month meaning that the number of solicitations can be reduced). To convert single donors to regular donors it is important to talk about the long-term work (that is, "the problem is not solved immediately") and to create a long-term commitment in the mind of the donor. Child sponsorship (for example, Plan International) or adopting an animal (for example, WWF) are examples of these long-term commitments.

Cross- and upselling – As in other settings, cross- and upselling are also applicable to fundraising. An example of upselling can be found in an attempt to increase the amount of the monthly donation. Cross-selling is not always possible for a charity. However, if we compare this with a traditional setting, the different projects of a charity can reflect the different products in a retail context. The Red Cross, for example, can ask their blood-donors to make a monetary contribution.

Major gifts – Identifying and following donors that can make a major donation is often a separate division in a charity. The term "major" is relative and its definition depends on the organization. For some this starts from a contribution of at least €250. Others assign a donation to a major gift starting from €1,000. The marketing strategy applicable for this segment is completely different than that for the traditional private donors. It is important that the charity tries to know as much as possible about the major donor prospect which makes this preparation time consuming. Some very individual contacts are key to transform the personal relation to the major gift.

Legacy – The death of the donor not necessarily mean the end of the relationship. Legacy fundraising becomes more and more developed during the last years. The legacy fundraising guru Richard Radcliffe investigated potential bequest supporters through focus groups. The following characteristics are seen to describe legacy donors: monthly donors, high length of relationship (that is, multi-year donors), high frequency, low recency, and no children. It is not the size of previous gifts but rather the frequency that determines whether a donor will put the charity is his/her will or not. As with major donors, the marketing strategy concerning legacy donors is based on a personal approach. It is clear that the evaluation of these efforts, takes time.

2.3 REACTIVATION

Finally, the third stage is the reactivation of (almost) lapsed donors. This involves reactivation campaigns, meant to reactivate donors who had dropped out and who have not given for extended periods of time. It is clear that is much more profitable to reactivate lapsed donors than to acquire completely new donors. Therefore, charities, especially those with a large donor base of inactive donors, need to organize special campaigns to reactivate lapsed donors. Optimizing these kinds of campaigns, by selecting only the donors who are most likely to respond on a reactivation campaign, can be effective. The definition of a lapsed donor can differ across charities. In addition, it depends on the setting as well. Concerning single donors, it is less clear when a donor ends the relationship. There, a lapsed donor can be defined as someone who did not respond to any mailing received during the last two years. In contrast, for regular donors, like in a contractual setting, once the donor stops his/her monthly payment, the donor can be defined as a churner.

3 Multi-channel Approach

On the one hand, non-profit organizations communicate through the traditional above-the-line mass media channels like television, radio, magazines, newspaper, cinema, and so on. On the other hand, below-the-line promotion has becoming increasingly important in the communication mix of charities over the last decades. Nowadays, a successful strategy is "through the line" involving both above and below-the-line communications. It is common for customers to use different channels at different stages of their decision process. This strategic approach allows the charitable brand to engage with a donor at multiple points. For example, the donor will see the television commercial, hear the radio advert, and can be addressed by a volunteer on the street. Non-profit organizations need to adapt their marketing strategy to reach such multichannel donors by multichannel marketing. An example here is a prospect using the charities' website to obtain information about a specific charity but making a donation offline through a traditional banking transfer document obtained by direct mail. All elements of the communication program should be integrated. This enables an integrated communications approach where consistent messaging across multiple media create the perception of the customer. Because of the importance of direct marketing for the non-profit sector, in this section, we will elaborate on the most important direct marketing communication channels. We will provide an overview of the range of channels including usage, advantages, disadvantages, and costs based on Sargeant (2009) and Andreasen and Kotler (2008).

Direct mail – This medium (that is, letters sent through postal services) is highly used in fundraising along the donor lifecycle. In general, it is quite expensive but also effective. The outside characteristics of the envelope need to stimulate the opening rate. On the inside, a good fundraising letter contains one emotional story. Although direct mail remains the most successful medium to raise individual donations (Direct Marketing Association, 2010), non-profit organizations increasingly use other channels next to this traditional medium.

Telemarketing – Telemarketing is a confidential, personal, and interactive medium. However, the cost can be high and it is sometimes perceived as intrusive. An effective message on the phone should be short and motivating, containing a concrete ask and story. The terminology is important as well. This channel can be used for example in campaigns toward (almost) lapsed donors or to upgrade the amount that is given by regular donors.

Face-to-face – Face-to-face (that is, direct dialogue, or street fundraising as well as door to door) is frequently used to acquire regular/monthly donors via signing a direct debit contract. Trained staff, standing in the street or in private sites, approach passers-by to sign up to support a charity with a regular gift. On the other hand, the trained staff can go from door to door in specific neighborhoods to find regular donors or to collect cash donations (that is, collection box).

Mobile – Mobile phones become more and more a payment device. Concerning text messaging, there are two possibilities. On the one hand, the charity can send a text message to their mobile contacts asking for a donation through text messaging. On the other hand, potential donors can respond on poster or billboard campaigns with a text message. Once someone responds, the charity has a new contact that can also be contacted by outbound telemarketing. The effectiveness of mobile in case of emergency is proven by the American Red Cross on the occasion of the earthquake in Haïti (2010). For the first time, mobile donation contributed meaningfully to cause with 16 percent of total donations. In a one-hour period, it peaked at $500,000. It is important to take into account that the gift size of mobile donation is rather small. In addition, games for smartphones become important as well since recently, some charities even created specific aps designed for smartphones.

Online and DRTV – Although, the majority of the funds are raised from other channels than the online channels, charities are increasingly developing their online strategy. Email, website, social media, and direct response television become important channels to communicate with (potential) donors.

Consequently, one of the major challenges is to integrate all these channels and to follow one individual across different channels. It is clear that, in terms of evaluation, the situation becomes increasingly more difficult (cfr., Infra).

4   Database and Methods to Optimize Direct Marketing in Fundraising

Understanding charitable giving is a crucial element in attracting and retaining private donors. Past behavior and socio-demographics form traditional predictor sets of charitable giving. In general, the core of the database of a charity basically consists of the complete solicitation history as well as the detailed donation history per individual donor. This historical information enables charities not only to build predictive models to optimize the selection of donors ("who to target") but also to optimize or even personalize the content of the campaign ("which offer"). In this section, we will elaborate on obtaining a more effective target selection as well as on improving the content of appeals based on information stored in the database.

4.1   TARGET SELECTION: PREDICTIVE MODELING AND DATA AUGMENTATION

Target selection is traditionally approached by RFM models (that is, recency, frequency and monetary value) aimed at predicting response behavior to determine whom to mail. Consequently, predictive models are often used to optimize the household list in direct mail campaigns. As we mentioned above, next to the name and address, the database of the charity consists of the solicitation history as well as the donation history of each contact in the database. Solicitation history involves the communication initiatives toward the individuals taken from the charity, and donation history involves past behavior (that is, responses) of individuals receiving charitable campaigns (Elsner, et al., 2004). Direct marketing, and direct mail fundraising in particular, generally considers past response behavior as the best predictor for future response. On the basis of the transactional data, past donation behavior is then traditionally conceptualized as (r)ecency, (f)requency, and (m)onetary value. In a charitable context, recency commonly involves the number of days since the last donation. Frequency usually reflects the number of donations over a period of time. Finally, monetary value implicates the total amount donated by a particular individual (Bitran and Mondschein, 1996). Prior studies show that past donation behavior is an important driver of both donation decision and generosity (for example, Bult, et al., 1997; Jonker, et al., 2004). From a practical point of view, the computation of RFM variables is relatively easy because this information is stored in the database of the charity and consequently this set does not require an additional data collection. However, an important remark here is that the calculation of RFM variables is based on previous donations by considering one charity.

Despite overwhelming evidence that RFM variables are an important predictor set, different studies (for example, Van Slyke and Brooks, 2005; Bekkers, 2006) investigate the effect of including other predictors as well. For example, by considering the name and address of the donor, one is able to extract some socio-demographical information of the donor like gender. However, most of these other predictors, such as socio-demographic variables, often require an additional data collection. Consequently, charities can augment their database with additional characteristics to ameliorate their relationship with the donor and approve their communication with the donor. This can be based on questionnaires as well as on data enrichment through purchase from external data providers. Examples of these characteristics are age, family composition, income indicators, media preferences, and features of the district where the donor lives.

In line with prior research findings, it seems that age will positively affect charitable giving (for example, Van Slyke and Brooks, 2005). This prediction is also in line with current practices in fundraising because charities are more likely to target older people. Bekkers (2006) finds that financial capital promotes traditional philanthropy (that is, monetary donations). Starting from the integrated theory of volunteer work (Wilson and Musick, 1997), Bekkers states that, the availability of resources in the form of financial capital reduces the cost of charitable giving. More specifically, for individuals with higher income, a $100 donation to a charitable organization is less costly than for those earning lower incomes. Therefore, income could be an important driver of generosity. Beside these sets, it can also be useful to include donation intentions. Starting from the Theory of Planned Behavior (Ajzen, 1991), De Cannière et al. (2009) found that behavioral intentions predict purchase behavior, even in combination with actual past behavior. Although these authors investigated purchase behavior rather than charitable giving, they conclude that intentions might capture unique variance in the purchase decision that past behavior does not capture. Next to these above predictor sets, some psychological information (for example, personality traits like empathic concern and personal distress) can be collected as well. Certain studies (for example, Batson, 1991; Bendapudi, et al., 1996) on charitable giving investigate personality traits to have a better understanding of underlying motivations and reasons of charitable giving. Therefore, it can be relevant to examine whether it is useful to collect information about psychological measures and store this information in the charity's database. The following section will elaborate on this by discussing a study (Verhaert and Van den Poel, 2011a) investigating whether certain personality traits capture unique variance in predicting donation behavior that is not captured by RFM, intentions, nor socio-demographics.

CASE STUDY 2

Recently, we conducted a study to examine whether and how psychological measures of empathy can be relevant information to augment the database of a charity. More specifically, the focus lied on the personality traits empathic concern and personal distress measured by a 7-point Likert Scale. According to Davis (1983), both constructs involve emotional dimensions of empathy and reflect distinctive feelings toward unfortunate others or oneself. Empathic concern is other oriented and personal distress is self-oriented. Whereas previous research (for example, Batson, 1991; Bendapudi, et al., 1996) often proposes empathy as an explanation for helping behavior, this study looks at the predictive power of both personality measures on top of past behavior, intentions, and socio-demographics.

The results indicate that past behavior, intentions, socio-demographics as well as psychological measures of empathy are all important in predicting charitable giving. Consequently, this study confirms previous findings regarding traditional predictor sets of monetary donations in fundraising. The key contribution is that this study extends previous findings by demonstrating the added value of important psychological measures of empathic concern and personal distress on top of traditional independent measures. More specifically, both emotional dimensions of empathy have a differential influence on the donation decision and generosity decision toward the charity of interest. On the one hand, empathic concern positively affects the donation decision. This finding makes sense, given that donors with a high level of empathic concern focus on alleviating their negative mood toward the unfortunate others which could be accomplished by making a donation. However, personal distress does not influence the decision to donate. An explanation is that in the context of this study, the ease of escape was higher than what was assumed. On the other hand, both measures of empathy could negatively affect the donor's generosity toward the individual charity. For empathic concern, this unexpected result leads to a second study. This additional data collection points out that donors high on empathic concern are individuals who donate toward different charities. These people have a higher breadth and are thus more likely to comply with donation requests of diverse charities. An explanation is that they are rather other oriented and feel compassionate with others. Hence, they want to repair their negative feelings toward the people in need by dividing their money across many different initiatives. Interestingly, looking only at generosity toward one charity could lead to wrong interpretations because, by summarizing the donations across all charities, people high on empathic concern are more generous in general. Individuals high on personal distress are less generous toward one charity as well as toward all other charities together. These egoistically motivated individuals are rather self-oriented and the fact that the main concern of individuals high on personal distress is likely to repair the negative mood toward themselves may explain this negative effect on generosity. A mere decision to donate may repair this negative mood. Apparently, making a high contribution is not necessary for individuals high on personal distress, given that merely making a contribution itself may already satisfy their main motivation. Personal distress is not related to the breadth of the donor. Hence, this study demonstrates similarities as well as dissimilarities between both measures of empathy. Because of the positive direct effects of empathy on the decision to donate, we conclude that individuals high on empathic concern or high on personal distress are more likely to respond to charitable direct mails. In contrast, when charities want to maximize the gift size, it is better to target individuals low on empathic concern or low on personal distress.

The findings also offer practical implications for fundraisers improving their direct mail marketing strategy. From a managerial point of view, the database of a charity is a crucial source of information and highly important in predicting charitable giving. Data augmentation through data collection about individuals' socio-demographics and psychological measures, could improve predictions of donation behavior. Therefore, the most important practical implication is that it might be relevant for addressing providers to collect information about empathic concern as well as about personal distress. When such a provider sells a household list to a charity, the addressing provider can use personality information to come up with a more effective household list. However, the distinction between the decision to donate and the donation amount is crucial. More specifically, people with a high score on empathic concern are more likely to make a donation in the next period but this does not imply that these people will be more generous toward the charity of interest.

Besides this, surveys can also be an interesting tool for fundraisers in augmenting their database and learning more about their donors. For example, when a charity wants to set up a legacy campaign, it can be relevant to focus only on the oldest donors without children. On the basis on a survey, a charity can collect these kinds of information. However, one should take into account that only a fraction of the donors respond to the survey so that there exists only certainty amongst a subsample of the donor population. Evidently, there exists some methods to extrapolate the characteristics to the whole donor database. When a charity wants to conduct a survey amongst their donors, it can be wise not only to send the questionnaire per direct mail but also to provide the ability to complete the survey online because this decreases the input costs afterwards. In addition, to increase the response on a survey, one can send a reminder after a certain period of time.

4.2 CONTENT

Studying content is useful to determine what message to communicate to potential donors. There is an extensive part in literature investigating the content of direct mail campaigns. Some studies focused on outside characteristics (for example, envelope type) to increase opening behavior (for example, De Wulf, et al., 2000) while other studies investigated the inside characteristics of a direct mail campaign. Related to these latter studies, we might refer to Das et al. (2008) investigating message framing or Obermiller (1995) investigating sick versus well baby appeals. However, because we focus on how database marketing can improve the content of fundraising appeals, we will discuss how personalized elements, extracted from the database, can make fundraising campaigns more effective by taking into account the different donor segments across the lifecycle. Moreover, based on the database of the charity, it is possible to distinguish the less loyal donors from the more loyal donors based on the RFM-values.

There are different levels related to the content of a direct mail campaign. It is important to choose each aspect carefully in order to maximize the results of the campaign. First of all, there are the outside characteristics. The looks of the envelope are extremely important to influence the opening rate. First, there are a lot of possibilities concerning the format of the envelope. Most common formats are US, A4, and A5. In addition, the material of the envelope may differ as well: absence/presence of a window, slim box, box, and so on. The address might be handwritten or printed on the envelope or printed on the letter. The identification of the sender can be the name of the non-profit organization, simply the address, the name of the president, or even omitted. This can be on the front or backside, while changing the headline, use of pictures, colors, In sum, a lot of possibilities to create the outside of a direct mail exist. Once a potential donor has decided to open the envelope, another range of elements must be chosen. All of them influence the success of a campaign. First of all, there is the story. In addition, the length of the letter and use, position, and type of pictures are important as well. One should keep in mind that preferences might differ across donors. For example, there are donors who like the inclusion of a premium and for which adding a premium will definitely increase the results of the campaign. For other donors, however, the enclosure of the premium would have counterproductive effects. Therefore, it is essential to take this into account by segmenting the database and to adapt the communication based on the implicit or explicit preferences of the donor.

On the one hand, the database can be used to explicitly (hyper)personalize the content of the campaign. Traditionally, most of the campaigns are personalized concerning salutation, if possible. However, more advanced personalized elements are probable. An example is a personalized image including the name of the donor. A Personalized URL (PURL) is an online example. In addition, proximity can play an important role as well. Legarson (2011) investigated this issue by testing whether a match between the city of the donor as well as the city of the advertised victim positively influences donation behavior. The results indicated that proximity positively affects the donor's decision to donate. In other words, if a donor receives an appeal concerning a victim living in his/her city, the donor will be more likely to help.

On the other hand, the database can be relevant to adapt the communication based on preferences of the donor. These preferences may differ on many aspects. For example, there are donors who abominate enclosed premiums. For them, the charity can omit the premium in the campaigns. In addition, for charities with different projects in different countries, based on previous campaigns, one is able to know for which projects/countries the donor is more/less likely to respond. Therefore, it can be wise to create and send different appeals (for example, in terms of project/country) based on previous response behavior. In the next section we will elaborate on "personalized suggested donation amounts" as another example of personalizing the content of direct mail appeals. This is based on a recent field study (Verhaert and Van den Poel, 2011b) examining the suggested personalized donation amount in combination with donor segment and social comparison.

CASE STUDY 3

Requesting a specific donation amount is frequently used in professional fundraising since a solicitation letter often proposes a specific donation amount, commonly an identical amount for all potential donors (for example 40 euro to save an African child). However, this approach ignores that each individual may have different ask-preferences as well as decision criteria based on individual characteristics and previous experience. For example, some donors tend to give rather smaller amounts while others give higher amounts. Consequently, it seems that one should take into account the donor's zone of acceptable prices. Therefore, a differentiated donation request, based on one's previous donations, can often be more appropriate than asking for the same amount to all donors. Moreover, with very low additional costs, personalized donation suggestions are relatively easy to calculate as historical transactional data are stored in the database. Although it is relatively easy to calculate a personalized donation amount, the question remains which amount one should propose: the average, recent, or maximum donation amount? In addition, the suggested donation amount could also be complemented with social comparison: referring to other donors who are donating this personalized suggested donation amount as well. The study indicates that for acquiring and reactivating donors, the use of a recently suggested donation amount is most effective, whereas for retaining donors, it is preferred to use an average amount. In addition, the results demonstrate that social comparison is an excellent acquisition strategy, but that it could be harmful when reactivating lapsed donors. Social comparison was not found to have an effect on the donation behavior of current donors. This indicates that, in order to optimize fundraising campaigns, it is extremely important to take into account the differences among different donor segments along the lifecycle as well as the individual preferences. Therefore, the database of the non-profit organization is extremely important.

Measurability is one of the major advantages of direct marketing. Consequently, fundraisers are involved in a procedure of constant testing, learning, and optimizing. Experimenting the content of the appeals across different channels has proven to be key in improving direct marketing fundraising. The benefit in the context of direct marketing is that it is relatively easy to test in the field instead of in a laboratory. This contributes to the validity of the results. Moreover, we speak about a controlled experiment since one is able to randomly assign each individual to one of the experimental conditions. Moreover, in experimenting, it is of crucial importance that the version of the communication only differs on the factors that one wants to test. For example, if one wants to test three pictures in the appeal, one needs to make sure that the format and position of all three pictures are identical. The sample size is also important and depends on the significance/confidence level adopted as well as on the desired precision/power. Experimenting in non-profit marketing ranges from simple AB-testing and full-factorial designs to more advanced experimental designs like fractional-factorial and Plackett-Burman designs (Bell, et al., 2006). We refer to specialized handbooks for these specific methods on experimental design. In addition, one needs to take into account that for analyzing the gift size afterwards, one could only rely on the responders. For example, suppose that the size of two experimental groups is 10,000 each and that you obtain 1 percent in the first version and 2 percent in the second version, the gift size will be analyzed on sample sizes of 100 and 200 respectively. In general, charities are implementing between-subjects designs to identify the best version of the campaign. The number of factors that one would test can vary from one to several. Suppose that a charity wants to test two factors (the type of gadget: pen versus key chain versus greeting cards as well as two pictures), one needs to create six versions of the campaign to implement the 3x2 between subjects design. The sample size of each of the experimental groups needs to be sufficiently large. Consequently, the use of factorial experiments instead of the one-factor-at-a-time is efficient at evaluating the effects and possible interactions of several factors (for example, picture as well as gadget). However, if one is sure that the two factors are independent from each other, one can reduce the sample size because in the analyses afterwards, one would consider only one factor at the time.

5   Campaign Evaluation

To investigate the impact of any technique aimed at improving direct marketing fundraising campaigns, one needs to evaluate the campaign success rate. An appropriate evaluation of fundraising campaigns is extremely important in order to take future decisions. Traditionally, the campaign success rate is primary defined in terms of revenue, response rate, and gift size. Below, we will focus on evaluation criteria in direct mail fundraising campaigns.

Revenue – Regarding revenue, we consider revenue per appeal that was sent instead of overall revenue. Campaign revenues are driven by two aspects: the decision to donate and generosity.

Response rate – A potential donor needs to decide whether or not to donate. The decision of each potential donor is reflected in the response rate of a particular campaign. In this context, it is important to take into account that the response rate differs among the donor segments. Evidently, the response is highest for campaigns toward a warm household list of active and most loyal donors (for example, 12 percent on a direct mail campaign). The response is lowest in acquisition (for example, 2 percent on a direct mail campaign) since this kind of appeal is sent to a cold household list of prospects who did not donate to the charity before. Obviously, the response rate also depends on other elements like the brand equity of the charity, the country of the campaign, characteristics of the target audience, and so on.

Gift size – Once a donor decides to respond to the direct mail, (s)he needs to decide how much to donate. This is reflected in the average gift size (conditional on donating) of the campaign. This is reflected in the average gift size (conditional on donating) of the campaign which is calculated as the total revenue divided by the number of respondents. In general, the appeal refers to a specific donation amount. However, the donor can freely choose the size of his/her gift. It is important to note that one extreme high gift can bias the interpretation of this parameter. Therefore, it can be wise to calculate the average gift size on the 95 percent central values by removing the outliers.

For fundraising management, these three parameters (that is, revenue, response rate, and gift size) are considered to achieve maximum effect for the specific campaign objective. While, some of the previous studies on charitable giving only considered one of the three parameters (for example, Shang and Croson, 2007), we encourage focusing on all three parameters. However, depending on the stage in the donor lifecycle and thus the campaign objective, one of the parameters of campaign success rate (cfr. supra) may become more or less crucial as the focus of acquisition campaigns is to maximize response rate rather than to obtain a high average donation. For retention purposes, overall revenue is of relevance. Finally, as in acquisition, response rate is also of prime importance in reactivation campaigns.

Cost – Next to these the traditional parameters concerning response rate, average gift size as well as revenue per solicitation, other elements are important as well in the campaign evaluation. First, it is extremely important to take into account the cost of the campaign. By incorporating the costs, one is able to evaluate based on the net revenue. For example, the cost in direct mail generally consists of three elements: production costs, postal services costs, and address renting costs (only for acquisition campaigns). In general, acquisition campaigns are the most expensive ones because of the address costs as well as the higher production costs (for example, the frequently use of premiums). In contrast, as we saw that the response, and consequently the revenue per solicitation, is lowest for acquisition, the evaluation in terms of net profit, (often loss) is crucial here. In addition, by incorporating the cost, one is able to calculate the cost per new donor recruited.

Long term – In addition, charities more and more evaluate their direct marketing campaigns in the long term by parameters like "second gift conversion rate" and "lifetime value." This means that the evaluation period becomes larger. This implicates that fundraisers do not only take into account the results on one campaign but that they consider results on the subsequent campaigns as well. On the other hand, especially for recruiting new donors, where it is difficult to recruit with a positive net income, it is of relevance to know at which term the initial investment becomes profitable. In addition, the second gift conversion is important here. This means knowing at which term a new donor changes from hot prospect to a real active donor. Moreover, the second gift conversion rate indicates the percentage of hot prospects that became real active donors.

Multi-channel – In this section, we elaborated on direct mail because this remains one of the most important fundraising channels. However, other channels are important as well. If we speak about integrated marketing communication campaigns across different channels, it becomes very difficult to evaluate each specific channel since it becomes unclear which channels were more/less important in the donation decision.

6   Conclusion, Challenges, and Opportunities for the Future

Although "multichannel" and "integration" seem to be key in effective fundraising, there are a lot of challenges and opportunities here to implement this in reality since most of the charities still have separate departments, working next to each other, depending on the channel. However, a crucial condition to follow one individual donor across multiple channels is an advanced integrated database.

Charities generally store detailed information regarding donation and solicitation history of each individual donor. This wealth of data is stored in the charity's database. Charities can use this information to develop an individual relationship with their donors. Database marketing can not only be used to improve the target selection but also to optimize the content of the appeal. In this context, the direct marketing strategy will evolve toward sending different appeals through different channels based on the characteristics of the donor.

In addition, the blurring of traditional sector boundaries is a current issue in non-profit marketing. Finally, an important challenge for fundraisers and direct marketers in general is the evolving legislation concerning the protecting and privacy of donors/consumers.

We encourage further researchers to include the different segments along the donor lifecycle in one study to increase the scope of their findings. Moreover, it would be interesting to investigate whether previous findings hold for fundraising campaigns that use other channels than direct mail like fundraising online, by phone, or face-to-face. In addition, it is important to examine different evaluation parameters simultaneously rather than focusing on one aspect of campaign success rate. Finally, we encourage researchers to investigate all these issues in the field.

References

Ajzen, I. (1991). The theory of planned behavior. *Organizational Behavior and Human Decision Processes, 50*(2), 179–211.

Allison, P.D. (1999). *Logistic Regression Using the SAS System: Theory and Application*. Cary, NC: SAS Institute Inc.

Andreasen, A.R. and Kotler, P. (2008). *Strategic Marketing for Nonprofit Organizations*. Upper Saddle River, NJ: Pearson Prentice Hall.

Bagozzi, R.P. and Silk, A.J. (1983). Recall, recognition and the measurement of memory for print advertisements. *Marketing Science, 2*(3), 95–134.

Batson, C.D. (1991). *The Altruism Question: Toward a Social-psychological Answer*. Hillsdale, NJ: Lawrence Erlbaum Associates.

Bekkers, R. (2006). Traditional and health-related philanthropy: The role of resources and personality. *Social Psychology Quarterly, 69*(4), 349–66.

Bell, G.H., Ledolter, J. and Swersey, A.J. (2006), Experimental design on the front lines of marketing: Testing new ideas to increase direct mail sales. *International Journal of Research in Marketing, 23*(3), 309–19.

Bendapudi, N., Singh, S.N. and Bendapudi, V. (1996). Enhancing helping behavior: An integrative framework for promotion planning. *Journal of Marketing, 60*(3), 33–49.

Bitran, G.R. and Mondschein, S.V. (1996). Mailing decisions in the catalog sales industry. *Management Science, 42*(9), 1364–81.

Bult, J.R., van der Scheer, H. and Wansbeek, T. (1997). Interaction between target and mailing characteristics in direct marketing with an application to health care fund raising. *International Journal of Research in Marketing, 14*(4), 301–8.

Burke, R.R. and Srull, T.K. (1988). Competitive interference and consumer memory for advertising. *Journal of Consumer Research, 15*(June), 55–68.

Das, E., Kerkhof, P. and Kuiper, J. (2008). Improving the effectiveness of fundraising messages: The impact of charity goal attainment, message framing, and evidence on persuasion. *Journal of Applied Communication Research, 36*(2), 161–75.

Davis, M.H. (1983). Measuring individual differences in empathy: Evidence for a multidimensional approach. *Journal of Personality and Social Psychology, 44*(1), 113–26.

De Cannière, M. H., Pelsmacker, P. De and Geuens, M. (2009). Relationship quality and the theory of planned behavior models of behavioral intentions and purchase behavior. *Journal of Business Research, 62*(1), 82–92.

De Wulf, K., Hoekstra, J.C. and Commandeur, H.R. (2000). The opening and reading behavior of business-to-business direct mail. *Industrial Marketing Management, 29*(2), 133–45.

Direct Marketing Association. (2010). *DMA 2010 Statistical Fact Book.* New York, NY: Direct Marketing Association.

D'Souza, G. and Rao, R.C. (1995). Can repeating an advertisement more frequently than the competition affect brand preference in a mature market? *Journal of Marketing, 59*(April), 32–42.

Elsner, R., Krafft, M. and Huchzermeier, A. (2004). The 2003 ISMS Practice Prize Winner: Optimizing Rhenania's direct marketing business through dynamic multilevel modeling (DMLM) in a multicatalog-brand environment. *Marketing Science, 23*(2), 192–206.

Jonker, J.-J., Piersma, N. and Van den Poel, D. (2004). Joint optimization of customer segmentation and marketing policy to maximize long-term profitability. *Expert Systems with Applications, 27*(2), 159–68.

Keller, K.L. (1991). Memory and evaluation effects in competitive advertising environments. *Journal of Consumer Research, 17*(4), 463–76.

Legarson, F. (2012), *Issues on the Identification Effect in Fundraising.* Master Thesis. IESEG School of Management.

National Center for Charitable Statistics. (2012). Quick Facts about nonprofits. Available at: http://nccs.urban.org/statistics/quickfacts.cfm [accessed October 16, 2012].

Obermiller, C. (1995). The baby is sick/the baby is well: A test of environmental communication appeals. *Journal of Advertising, 14*(2), 55–70.

Sargeant, A. (2009). *Marketing Management for Nonprofit Organizations.* New York, NY: Oxford University Press.

Sargeant, A., and Shang, J. (2010). *Fundraising Principles and Practice.* San Francisco, CA: Wiley.

Shang, J. and Croson, R. (2007). Field Experiments in Charitable Donation: The Impact of Social Influence on the Voluntary Provision of Public Goods, Working Paper, University of Texas at Dallas.

Unnava, H.R. and Sirdeshmukh, D. (1994). Reducing competitive ad interference. *Journal of Marketing Research, 31*(August), 403–411.

Van Slyke, D.M. and Brooks, A.C. (2005). Why do people give? New evidence and strategies for nonprofit managers. *American Review of Public Administration, 35*(3), 199–222.

Verhaert, G. (2010). *The Role of Database Marketing in Improving Direct Mail Fundraising,* Phd Thesis, Ghent University.

Verhaert, G., De Bruyn, A. and Van den Poel, D. (2010). Assessing the Negative Impact of Competition in Direct Mail Fundraising, in Proceedings of the 2010 Direct/Interactive Marketing Research Summit, San Francisco: Direct Marketing Education Foundation.

Verhaert, G. and Van den Poel, D. (2011a). Empathy as added value in predicting donation behavior. *Journal of Business Research, 64*(12), 1288–95

Verhaert, G. and Van den Poel, D. (2011b). Improving campaign success rate by tailoring donation requests along the donor lifecycle. *Journal of Interactive Marketing, 25*(1), 51–63.

Wilson, J. and Musick, M. (1997). Who cares? Toward an integrative theory of volunteer work. *American Sociological Review, 62*(5), 694–713.

Index

accountability 1, 2
accuracy 134, 135, 136, 137, 145, 147, 161, 251
    of non-neural networks 149
acquaintances 251, 256
actions 1, 241, 266, 270
ad impression measures 210
ad networks 220–24
ad space 220, 221
ada boosting 83
AdaBoost 120, 122, 127–8, 130, 132, 133, 139
AdaCost 132, 133
Adipat, B. et al. 200
Adomavicius, G. et al. 180
Adomavicius, G. and Tuzhilin, A. 167, 180, 181
AdRosa 222
advertisers 195, 210, 222, 231, 232, 240
advertising 289
    on mobile apps 190, 193, 194, 195
    revenue 237, 242
    web 194–5, 209–10ff., 231
    see also display ads; paid search ads
advertising campaigns 2, 68, 82, 92, 254, 274
    exposure to 213
    online 232, 233
advertising goodwill 212–13, 214, 215, 222
Adwords 231, 240
affix removal stemmers 46
Agarwal, A. et al. 195, 200, 236, 269, 271
Agarwal, D. and Chen, B.-C. 177, 181, 183
age 294, 295
agents 250
aggregation 104
    and ensemble learners 121–3, 124
Agresti, A. 71
Ajzen, I. 294
Albuqquerque, P. et al. 191

algorithms 12, 17, 68, 146, 147, 151, 157, 229, 230, 273, 279
    ALS 53, 54
    behavioural targeting 222, 225
    EBN 84
    ensemble learners 118ff., 124–31
    estimation 182
    genetic 67
    HEA 68, 81–2
    HMM 46
    induction 21
    learning 27
    MCMC 102, 103
    NMF 52
    SEM 68, 81
    SGS 71
    stemming 46
        mixed 46
    YASS 46
Allison, P.D. 289
alternating least squares (ALS) 53, 54, 182
Amazon.com 167, 197, 219, 249, 253
Anderson, D.R. et al. 15
Anderson, E. et al. 198
Andreasen, A.R. and Kotler, P. 287
Andreassen, S. et al. 67
Andrews, R. et al. 146
Angry Birds 193
Angwin, J. 225
anonymity 259, 260
ANOVA 31, 34, 35
Ansari, A. and Mela, C. 177, 184, 200
Ansari, A. et al. 172, 175, 177, 181, 182, 215
API 58
Apple 192
applications 4, 5, 7, 26, 33, 57, 114, 122, 133ff., 167, 183, 189ff., 265, 268, 273, 274ff., 283

real-world 67, 69, 80
approximation techniques 271, 273
APRI 79
Aral, S. 196
Aral, S. et al. 195
Aral, S. and Van Alstyne, M. 197
Arauzo-Azofra, A. et al. 28
Archak, N. et al. 197, 253
Asuncion, A. and Newman, D.J. 22, 29, 118
asymmetric Laplace densities (ALD) 100, 101, 102, 103
asymmetry 109, 178, 253
attributes 12, 14, 15, 75ff., 83, 168, 169
AUC 117, 135, 137, 145
augmentation 78, 79
Automatic Interaction Detection (AID) 83
automatic relevance detection (ARD) 133
Autor, D. 200
awareness 179, 210, 212, 237, 256

Baesens et al. 34
bagging 118, 120
    ensemble learners 121, 122, 125, 132, 133
        diversity in 134, 135
    software 139
bag-of-words model 42–3
Balasubramanian, S. 198, 201
Ballard, M. 236
banks 110–11, 132, 134
banner ads 2, 5, 194, 202, 209, 218, 229, 237, 238
Banslaben, J. 12
Barakat, N. and Diederich, D. 157
BarnesandNoble.com 254
base learners 119, 121, 126, 130
Bassett, G. and Koenker, R. 97, 98
Basu, C. et al. 171
Batista, G. and Monard, M. 17
Batista, G. et al. 26
Batson, C.D. 294
Bauer, C.L. 11
Bauer, E. and Kohavi, R. 117, 125, 128
Baye, M. et al. 200
Bayes classifiers 75–6, 170
Bayes decision rule 75, 281
Bayesian estimation methods 182
Bayesian Information Criterion (BIC) 67

Bayesian multiple imputation 80
Bayesian networks 67–92, 133
    classifiers 76–80
        augmented 78
        naive 76–9, 85
            ensemble learners 121
            tree-augmented 79–80
        selective 78
    and direct marketing model 68–9, 83–4ff.
    and incomplete records 68, 80–81
    inference on 73–4
    learning 70ff., 80ff.
    missing values 67, 68, 80–82, 92
    neural (BNN) 85
    parameter values 67, 68
    results 69, 82, 87
    scoring 67, 72–3
    search problem 73
    selective 78
    uses of 73
Bayesian quantile regression 98, 100–101, 103, 112, 113, 114
bayesQR package 114
Bayesware Discoverer 84, 86, 87
Beales, H. 212, 215
beam-search method 158
Beaumont, G.P. and Knowles, J.D. 71
Becker, G.S. 191, 200
Becker, S. 200
behavioural histories 221ff.
behavioural targeting 218–24, 293ff.
    see also display ads
Bekkers, R. 293, 294
beliefs 281
Belk, R.W. 180
Bell, C. and Jones, K.P. 46
Bell, G.H. et al. 298
Bellman, R. 271
'below-the-line' promotion 291
Bemmaor, A.C. 196
Bemmaor, A.C. and Glady, N. 11, 266, 283
Ben-Akiva, M. and Lerman, S. 177
Bendapudi, N. et al. 294
Benoit, D.F. et al. 114
Benoit, D.F. and Van den Poel, D. 102, 106, 110
Berger, J. and Milkman, K. 249

Berger, J. and Schwartz, E. 250
Berger, P.D. and Nasr, N.I. 104, 266
Berry, Leonard 1
Berry. M.J.A. and Linoff, G. 12, 14, 17, 22
Berry, M.W. et al. 53
Berry, M.W. and Kogan, J. 53, 54
Berry, S. et al. 193
best rule learning 153
Bettman, J.R. et al. 219
BFGS method 151
Bhattacharyya, S. 83, 84
bias 196
Bilias, Y. et al. 101
binary dependent variables 101–3
binary quantile regression 112
binary values 14, 18
binomial log-likelihood 128
bins 23, 24, 29
Bishop, C. 148, 149
Bitran, G.R. and Mondschein, S.V. 271, 272,
    273, 274, 293
black-box models 136, 137, 145–6
    and rule extraction 148ff.
        decision tables 159
        pedagogical algorithms 156ff.
        SVM model 153
Blattberg, R.C. et al. 1, 215, 266
bloggers 247
    as producers 260
blogging 247, 260
Blum, B. and Goldfarb, A. 199
Bodapati, A. 177, 178, 179, 180, 183
body ads 232, 240
book sales 253
boosting 121, 127, 131, 132, 133, 139
bootstrap 75, 100, 102, 124, 125, 137
Bose, I. and Chen, X. 132
Bose, I. and Xi, C. 11
Bottou, L. 182
Bouckaert, R.R. 72
Bound-and-Collapse (BC) 68
Boutsidis, C. and Gallopoulos, E. 53
Boyd, D. et al. 197
Bradford, R.B. 56
Bragging 125
brain 148

brand equity 195, 212, 215, 230, 289, 290,
    298
brand names 57, 230, 236, 237, 239
brands 212, 261, 269, 289
    and mobile apps 189–90, 193
Braun, M. and Moe, W.W. 213, 214, 215,
    222, 223
Breese, J. et al. 170
Breiman, L. 27, 125, 126, 127, 136
Brill, E. 44
Brimicombe, A. and Li, Y. 199
Brooks, N. 236
Brown, G. et al. 120
Brown, I. and Mues, C. 126
Brown, J. and Goolsbee, A. 200
browsing paths 212
Bryll, R. et al. 125
Brynjolfsson, E. and Smith, M. 200
Brynjolfsson, E. et al. 200
Buchinsky, M. 105
Buckinx, W. and Van den Poel, D. 132, 133,
    136
Bühlmann, P. 125
Bult, J.R. et al. 293
Burez, J. and Van den Poel, D. 26, 132, 133
Burke, R. 171
Burt, R.S. 197, 251, 252
BzzAgent 250, 255, 256

Cabena, P. et al. 82
Cairncross, F. 198
call centers 57
Campbell, D. et al. 272, 273, 274
Carney, D.R. and Banaji, M.R. 200
Carroll, J.D. 176
CART 118, 121, 124, 125, 130, 131, 137
case studies 12, 29ff., 103ff., 160ff., 233,
    238, 239, 289ff.
catalog mailing model 274–5, 277
categorical attributes 15, 18–21, 28, 29, 33
    empirical results 31
Catlett, J. 24
causality 254–5
Centola, D. and Macy, M. 197
Cerf, M. et al. 241
Cerquides, J. and Màntaras, R.L. 24

certainty factor 83
C4.5 classifier 83, 121, 149, 151, 156–7
C5.0 classifier 131
Chae, M. and Kim, J. 200
CHAID 83, 121
Chan, T. et al. 239
channels 195, 198, 201, 202, 237, 291–2
    display ads 214–15
charities 288ff.
    databases 293–8
        content 296–8
        predictive models 293–6
    and donor acquisition 288–90
    long-term approach 299
    multi-channel approach 291–2
    and testing 298
Chatterjee, P. et al. 211, 215
Chawla, N.V. et al. 26
Cheeseman, P. et al. 67
Chen, C. et al. 26, 67, 70, 71
Chen, Y. et al. 222
Cheng, J. and Greiner, R. 80
Cheng, J. et al. 70
Cheng, Z. and Nault, B.R. 201
Chevalier, J. and Mayzlin, D. 249, 253, 254, 255
Chickering, D.M. et al. 73
ChiMerge 151
Ching, W-K. et al. 272
Chi-square tests 109
Chi2 algorithm 151
Cho, C-H. and Cheon, H.J. 212
choice 2, 12, 19, 33, 56, 104, 105, 121ff., 132, 140, 177, 182, 200, 219, 249, 268, 269, 272
Chow, C.K. and Liu, C.N. 79
Chung, T.S. et al. 181, 184
churn 11, 26, 57
    and ensemble learners ,118, 131ff.
    modeling tournaments 117–18
    prediction 4, 5, 57, 58, 110ff., 119ff., 131, 13304, 136, 140, 159, 160ff.
    and quantile regression 110–14
    and rule extraction 160–62
    UCI data 135, 138
circular city model 201
Clarabridge 58

class imbalance 133, 134
class predictions 122
classification 15, 17, 33, 52, 145, 153
    and Bayesian networks 67, 75ff.
    and direct marketing problem 83
    and ensemble learners 117–18, 119, 123–4
    imbalances 25–6
    models 31, 74, 160
    problem 74–5, 117
        neural networks 150
    trees 17
classifiers 74, 83, 123
    Bayesian 75–81
        naive 76–9, 83
        network 76ff.
    evaluation of 75
cleaning 13
Clearforest 58
clickstream behaviour 216, 221–2
    data 220
click-through rates (CTR) 210, 211–12, 218, 222
    histories 221
    paid search ads 233, 234, 236, 237, 241, 242
client/company interaction 41
clusters 155, 170, 218, 222, 280
cold-start problem 171, 174
Coleman, J.S. 197
Colgate, M.R. and Danalier, P.J. 111
collaborative filtering 167, 170–71, 176
    content boosted 171
combined approaches 118, 120, 121, 122
communication 41
competition 288, 289
complexity 18, 68, 72, 73, 79, 97, 100, 136, 140, 146, 171, 283
    reduced 118, 121
comprehensibility 25, 27, 136, 145
    and rule extraction 146, 147, 161
computer 58, 119, 167, 221, 222
computer science 41, 42, 57, 167
computing 2, 5, 17, 20, 21, 26ff., 54, 67, 71, 73, 75, 70, 80ff., 98, 102, 105, 109, 114, 121, 124, 138, 140, 148, 149, 156, 169, 170, 171, 182, 183, 284, 293
concepts 1, 4, 49, 50, 52, 56, 147, 269

loading 50, 52, 54
concept-term similarity matrix 50
conditional independence (CI) 70, 71, 72, 81, 182
conditional mean function 97, 98
conditional median (CLV) 107, 114
conditional probability table (CBT) 69
conditional quantile function, linear 100
Coney, K. 200
confusion matrices 113
consumers 41, 224, 225
   and display ads 210, 212
   future behaviour 3, 11
   learning 181, 191, 192
   and mobile apps 191–2, 194ff.
      demand for 192–4
      local behaviour 199
      product discussions 249–50
      reviews 253
   see also user preferences
content 176, 217, 220, 222
   and charity databases 296–8
   free 209
   mobile apps
      generation 191, 192, 197–8
      usage 191, 192ff.
   recommender models 169–70, 171, 176
contests 118, 119, 171
context 177, 178, 183, 196
   display ad targeting 216, 217–18
      risks 224
   models 180–81
context congruity 217, 218
conversation 249–50
   data collection on 250–53
conversion 213, 214, 233, 235, 236, 237, 242, 299
Cook, R.D. and Nachtsheim, C.J. 184
cookies 221, 273
Cooper, G.F. and Herskovits, E.H. 67, 73
Copernic Summarizer 58
cosine similarity measures 221
cost-per-click (CPC) 231, 232, 233, 237, 239, 242
cost-per-reservation 237
costs 27, 73, 104, 194, 195, 199, 201, 229, 232, 268, 273, 287

direct marketing 299
display ads 209, 218, 224
   mobile 199–201
   paid search ads 229, 237
coupons 273, 279, 280
Coussement, K. et al. 12, 136
Coussement, K. and De Bock, K.W. 133, 134
Coussement, K. and Van den Poel, D. 12, 42, 45, 48, 57, 58, 117, 132, 133
covariates 97, 99, 106, 107, 108, 172ff., 214, 222, 235
CPM model 210–11
Craven, M.W. and Shavlik, J.W. 157
credit ratings 18
crisis management 250, 261
Cristianini, N. and Shawe-Taylor, J. 153
Crone, S.F. et al. 12, 18, 22, 33
cross-channel effects 214–15
cross-selling 224, 290
cross-validation 75, 87, 124
Croux, C. et al. 125
cube 180
Cui, G. et al. 11
Cui, G. and Curry, D. 12
cumulative lift 87, 92
Cunningham, H. et al.
CUR decomposition 49
Curry, B. and Mouthino, L. 12
customer acquisition 1, 6, 119, 239
customer behaviour 41, 57, 111, 135, 181, 256, 268
   across ad networks 220–21
   influence of 256–7
customer comments 250, 261
customer complaints 145, 250
customer counts 215
customer development 1
customer lifetime value (CLV) 1, 11, 104–5
   and display ads 212
      paid search 239
   ensemble learners 133
   management of 265, 266
   measurement 283
   models of 266–7
   quantile regression case study 103–10
      concept 103–4
      data 105–6

results 106–10
and WOM 256–7
customer objectives 275
customer referral value (CRV) 256–7
customer relationship management (CRM)
    1, 201, 256
    churn prediction, and quantile
      regression 110ff.
customer response models 268, 269, 283
customer retention 1, 110
cycle prevention method 82

Das, E. et al. 296
Dasgupta, K.R. et al. 195
Dash, D. and Druzdzel, M.J. 72
data 1, 105–6, 111, 146, 196
    augmentation 295
    implicit preferences 178–80
    insights from 1, 2
    and optimization 275, 282
    ordinal preferences 177, 178
    paid search ads 232, 233ff., 237
      sharing 232
    projection 14, 18ff.
    recommender systems 168–9, 172
    reduction 14, 25–9
    selection 13
    training 75
    unstructured 42
    variety of 1
data collection 12, 177, 293
    and social media 250–53
data mining 13–14ff., 67, 168
    contests, and ensemble learners 119
    software 58
    standard table 14–15
data preprocessing 3, 33–4
    objectives 12, 27
    and predictive models 12
    software 12, 28–9
database marketing
    criticism of 2
    definitions 1, 2
    and ensemble learners 118, 131–4
    origins of 1
    see also charities; non-profit sector
databases 42, 44, 67, 68, 84

charity 293–8
complete 68
incomplete 68
recommender 168, 169
Davis, M.H. 294
Davison, H. and Wickens, C. 200
De Bock, K.W. and Van den Poel, D. 12, 122,
    131, 133, 134, 137, 216
De Bock, K.W. et al. 121, 126, 131
de Campos, L.M. and Heute, J.F. 72
De Cannière, M.H. et al. 294
De Wulf, K. et al. 296
Dean, M. 200
decile analysis 86, 87
decision tables (DT) 158–60
decision rules 219, 271
    optimal 271
decision templates 122, 123
decision trees 17, 20, 75, 117, 277
    and Bayesian classifier 78
    ensemble learners 118, 121, 125
      interpretability 136
    multiple 118, 125
    and rule extraction 157
decisions, customer 266
Decker, R. and Trusov, M. 57
decomposition 49ff., 67, 146
decompositional rule extraction
    from neural networks 148–53
    from SVM 153–6
Deerwester, S. et al. 49, 57
Deichmann, J. et al. 12
Dellarocas, C. 259
demographic information 11, 14, 15, 82,
    105, 111, 168, 170, 171, 173, 175,
    216, 233, 269, 278, 283, 293ff.
Dempster, A.P. et al. 16, 81
dependency analysis approach 67, 70, 71–2
    problems of 72
dependent variables 11, 12, 83, 97, 98, 99,
    106, 111, 124, 155, 274, 280
    binary 114
depth-of-file 83, 86, 87
DeSarbo, W. et al. 176, 180
designs 298
Desrosiers, C. and Karypis, G. 170
detailing 273, 281, 282

Dietterich, T.G. 117, 119, 123
dimension reduction 48–52
dimensionality, curse of 273
Dinner, I.M. et al. 215
direct mail 287, 292
    campaigns 296
    evaluation 298
    fundraising 293ff.
    likelihood of response to 11
direct marketing 1, 3, 4, 7, 27, 273
    and Bayesian networks 68–9, 83–4ff.
    campaigns
        costs 299
        evaluation of 298–9
        long-term factors 299
        response rates 298, 299
        revenue 298, 299
    modeling problem 82–4
    multi-channel approach 291–2
    and non-profit sector 287–300
        predictive models 293–4
    and paid search ads 232–6
    standard data mining table 14–15
    testing 297–8
    see also charities; direct mail
Dirichlet Process Priors 100
discretization 23–4, 150
display ads 209–25
    ad networks 220–24
    creative content 222, 223
    cross-channel effects 214–15
    definition of 209
    expenditure 209, 218
    and future research 225
    immediate effects 211, 215
    and impressions 213, 222–4
    intrusiveness 217, 218
    matching 218
    metrics 210–16, 218
        behavioural 210, 211, 212
        browsing paths 212
        exposure 211, 212–13
        long-term effects 212, 215
        pricing 210, 211
        revenue models 212–14
    targeting strategies 216–24
        behavioural 216, 218–24

        and future research 225
        contextual 216, 217–18, 224
        geotargeting 216–17
        risks 224–5
        user-based 216–17
distance 198–9
distance computations 21
Distimo 192
distortion 120
diversity 119, 120, 121, 130, 134–5, 183
documents 52
    text mining 42ff.
    vector aggregation 48
    weighted-term vectors 47
donations 289ff., 299, 300
    amounts 297
    major 291
    see also private donors
Doncaster, C.P. and Davey, A.J.H. 31
Donkers, B. et al. 104, 109
Dougherty, J. et al. 24
Drèze, X. and Hussherr, F-X. 211, 212, 215
Drèze, X. and Zufryden, F. 200
DRTV 292
Drummond, C. and Holte, R.C. 26
dtSearch 58
Du, R.Y. et al. 11
Duda, R.O. and Hart, P.E. 75
Duin, R. and Tax, D. 121
Duke University 117, 119
dummy-encoding 19, 29, 31, 32, 33, 108,
    150
Dunson, D.B. et al. 100
dynamic customer optimization 266, 267,
    269–74
    applications 275–83
    and data 275, 282
    field tests, 279ff., 282
    future research 283
    models 268ff., 274ff., 283
    problems 283, 284

economic behaviour 191, 197ff.
economic value 197, 198, 199
economics 2, 98, 114, 177, 198
Edwards, S.M. et al. 217
Efron, B. et al. 28

Ekstrand, M. et al. 167

Eliashberg, J. et al. 57

Ellison, G. and Ellison, S.F. 200

Elsner, R. et al. 272, 273, 289, 293

email 2, 41, 48, 57, 167, 169, 184, 218, 247
    marketing campaigns 266–7, 273
        charity donations 292

emotions 249–50, 294, 295

empathy 294–5

empirical studies 12, 17, 29, 31, 78, 83, 139,
        157, 168, 169, 198, 214, 215, 220,
        236, 242, 249, 255, 259

endogeneity 255

engagement 261

enhanced auctions 231

Enquiro 237

ensemble classifiers 120, 123
    rotation-based 130–31

ensemble fusion 123

ensemble learners 117–140
    algorithms 118, 119, 120, 121, 124–31
    and database marketing 118, 131–4
    diversity in 119ff., 130, 134–5
    framework 119–20
    fusion rules 121–3
    and interpretability 136–8
    literature 131–3
    performance 117–18ff., 123–4, 130ff.
    rationale of 117, 123
    software 139
    strategies 118
    terminology 119

ensemble members 119, 120, 121

entropy 252

envelopes 296

equilibrium 201, 259, 260

errors 13, 15–16, 54, 56, 75, 99, 108, 126,
        134, 135, 151, 178, 276
    training 112

estimation 16, 80, 81, 98, 104, 193
    adaptive conjoint 184
    and recommender systems 182–3

estimators
    median 99
    quantile 99
    uncertainty 182

evaluation 75, 83, 112, 137, 147, 184, 298–9

evolutionary algorithms 67, 73, 84

Evolutionary Bayesian Network (EBN) 84ff.,
    87, 92

exogenous WOM 255–6

Expectation Maximum (EM) 68, 80–81, 84

Expedia.com 249, 260

experience 249

experimental design 298

experts 160
    learning from 70

external data 27

eye-tracking technology 212

Ezawa, K.J. and Norton, S.W. 79

Facebook 58, 192, 198, 216, 247, 251, 253,
    257, 258, 261

face-to-face 292

factor analysis 25, 31, 49, 56

factorial experiments 298

Fader, P.S. et al. 105, 106, 266, 283

Fader, P.S. and McAllister, L. 219

false negative rate 112, 114

Farquhar, P.F. and Rao, V.R. 184

Fayyad, U.M. and Irani, K.B. 24, 150

Fayyad, U.M. et al. 13, 14

feature 74, 123, 154
    extraction 120, 130
    selection 26–7, 78, 121

Federov algorithm 184

feedback 198

Feinerer, I. 64

Feldman, R. and Sanger, J. 42, 45, 46

fidelity 147

field tests 194, 275ff., 282

filters 27, 28, 180, 181

financial services companies 110, 111, 131,
    133

financial capital 294

finite horizon 277, 283, 284

firms 232, 247, 270
    and long-term benefits 275
    and mobile apps 190ff.
    and social media 247, 248
        as influencer 255–7, 259
        as observer 253–4
        as participant 259, 260–61
    responses by 250, 261

forecasting speed 27
forgetting 266
Forman, C. et al. 195, 198
Forrester Research 198
free content 209, 220
free shipping 273, 279
frequency 1, 24–5, 119, 122, 158, 197, 212,
    214, 215, 272, 276ff., 282, 283
  and donors 291, 293
frequentist model 98–100, 102
  logit 112
Freund, Y. and Schapire, R.E. 83, 127
Friedman, D. 236
Friedman, J.H. 27, 129, 130
Friedman, J.H. et al. 127
Friedman, J.H, and Popescu, B.E. 122
Friedman, N. 68, 81
Friedman, N. et al. 77, 78, 79ff.
Friedman, T. 198
friends 251, 256, 258
Fung, G. et al. 156
Fung, R.M. and Crawford, S.L. 71
fusion rules 121–3
future benefits 275
future customer behaviour 11, 275, 276, 277
future research 5, 19, 20, 34, 140, 191, 192,
    194ff., 198, 200ff., 225, 253, 261,
    265, 283, 300
fuzzy rules 147, 151, 152, 153

gains table 86
GAMens 121, 122, 131, 133, 134, 137, 139
GAMensPlus 134
games, internet 189
GAMs 121, 126, 134
game-theoretic approach 236, 259
Ganesh, J. et al. 110, 111, 117
Gartner 194
GATE 58
Gauss 99, 125, 152
Geman, S. and Geman, D. 80
generality 147
generalization 145
  error 126
generalized additive models (GAMs) 117
generation 84
genetic algorithms (GA) 67, 83

genetic programming (GP) 83, 158
Gensch, D.H. 219
geography 5, 6, 196, 198–9, 217
geotargeting 216–17
Gheyas, I.A. and Smith, L.S. 17
Ghose, A. et al. 194, 195, 196, 197, 199
Ghose, A. and Han, S. 191, 192, 193, 195,
    199
Ghose, A. and Ipeirotis, P.G. 57
Ghose, A. and Yang, S. 195, 200, 235, 236
Ghosh, A. 12
Gibbs algorithm 102
Gibbs sampling (GS) 68, 80, 81, 103, 182
gift size 292, 298, 299 see also donations;
    private donors
Gilbride, T.J. and Allenby, G.M. 219
Gini coefficient 28
Glady, N. et al. 11, 132, 133
Godes, D. and Mayzlin, D. 196, 197, 249,
    250, 251, 252, 254, 255, 256, 257
Godes, D. et al. 241
Goldfarb, A. and Tucker, C. 195, 217, 218
Gönül, F. and Shi, M.Z. 272, 273, 275–7
Gönül, F. et al. 280
Google 218, 231, 232, 233, 234, 240
GPUs 183
gradient boosting 27
Granovetter, M.S. 196–7, 251, 252
granular data 189, 192
GraphLab 183
greedy algorithms 278–9
Green, P.E. and Rao, V.R. 180
Greenacre, M.J. 176
G-REX 158
Gu, Q. et al. 28
Gupta, S. et al. 104, 105, 106
Guyon, N. and Elisseeff, A. 27, 28
Guyon, I. et al. 25, 27

Ha, K. et al. 132
Ha, S.H. 220
Haddawy, P. 73
Haley, D.T. et al. 56
Hall, M.A. 28
Hampton, K. and Wellman, B. 199
Hanchuan, P. et al. 28
Hansotia, B. and Rukstales, B. 105

Hastie, T. et al. 12, 15, 19, 20, 25, 26, 27, 28, 31, 138
Hauser, J.R. et al. 271, 272, 274
Haykin, S.S. 22, 25
He, X. et al. 28
headline ads 232, 240
Heckerman, D. 67, 68, 80
Heckerman, D. and Wellman, M.P. 73
Heckman, J. 178
Herlocker, J. et al. 170, 178
heterogeneity 167, 172, 214, 258, 279, 283
    cross-sectional 280
    item 174–5
    unobserved 196
    user 172, 173–4, 175
heteroskedasticity 97, 99
Hewson, P. and Yu, K. 100
hidden Markov models (HMMs) 273–4, 281–2
hierarchical models 172ff., 178, 181, 182, 283
high-value customers 275
Hinz, O. et al. 258
historical data 3, 266, 268, 274, 275, 293, 297
Ho, T.K. 32, 125
Hoff, P.D. 177, 180
Hoffman, D.L. and Franke, G. 176
homogeneity 274
homophily 196
homoskedasticity 105
hosting 238
hotel reviews 43–6, 59ff, 233, 234, 237, 249, 259, 260
Hotelling, H. 201
household data 105–6, 289
household lists 288, 289, 293, 298
Hsu, C.-W. et al. 21
Hu, X.H. 121, 131, 132
Huan, L. and Lei, Y. 28
Huang, J. and Ling, C.X. 135
Hulse, J.V. and Khoshgoftaar, T. 26
Hulse, J.V. et al. 26
human/computer interaction 167
Hwang, H. et al. 104
hybrid ensembles 119, 121
Hybrid Evolutionary Algorithm (HEA) 68, 81, 84, 86

hybrid recommender systems 171–2
    latent factor models 172–7
        extensions 177–82
hypercubes 156
hypothesis 124
    testing 71

IBM SPSS Modeler 28, 58, 139
implementation 1, 2, 21, 34
implicit preferences data 178–80
impressions 210ff., 222, 235
Improved Balanced Random Forests (IBRF) 132, 134
imputation 15, 16, 17, 18
incentives 111, 145, 249, 250, 259ff.
incidence 269
incomplete records
    and Bayesian networks 68, 80–81
incomprehensibility 146, 148, 153
independence 78
independent component analysis (ICA) 49, 52
    ensemble learners 133
independent variables 11, 12, 82, 83, 98, 105, 137
individuals 81, 104, 105, 158, 169, 280, 283
    and behavioural targeting 218
    display ad responses 211–12
        and exposure 213–14
    influence of 258
    mobile behaviour 189, 196–7, 199
inference 67, 73–4, 80
infinite horizon models 283, 284
InfiniteInsight 29
influencer 247, 255–7, 259
information 168, 169, 222
    semi-structured 41
    social network 196–7
    unstructured 42
    see also data
Information Systems Research 248
initialization 53
Inman, J.J. et al. 214
instance 74
instance reweighting 120
instantiation 74
intentions 180, 201, 217, 218, 294

interactions data 169, 170, 176
Interactive Advertising Bureau (IAB) 211
internet 1–2, 57, 167, 292
    price rankings 200
    search ads 195
    see also email; mobile internet; paid
    search ads
interpersonal connections 196, 258
interpolation 271, 273, 282, 284
interpretation 14, 25, 136, 147
interval scaling 33
IP address 216–17
iPhone 192
item ranking 200
item selection model 183–4
Iterated Conditional Mode (ICM) 183
iterations 54, 57, 68, 86, 182, 274, 276
Itti, L. and Koch, C. 241
Iyengar, R. et al. 195, 256, 257, 258

Jacoby, J. et al. 191
Japkowicz, N. and Stephen, S. 25–6
Java, A. et al. 197
Javalgi, R.G. and Dion, P. 108
Jensen, F.V. 67
Jerath, K. et al. 236
Ji, S. and Carin, L. 27
Jiang, B. and Yao, X. 199
Jo, T. and Japkowicz, N. 26
Johansson, U. et al. 158
John, G.H. et al. 27
joint probability distribution 70
Joliffe, I.T. 56
Jones, M. et al. 200
Jonker, J.-J. et al. 293
journals 41, 57, 131
Judd, K.L. 269, 271
justifiability 145, 170, 182

Kalman filtering 181
kappa-error diagram 134–5
Kazienko, P. and Adamski, M. 222
KDD-Cup 21, 119
KEA 58
Keane, M.P. and Wolpin, K.I. 271, 273
Keogh, E.J. and Pazzani, M.J. 80
key informant methods 257, 258

keywords 195, 232ff.
    semantics 236, 239
    spillovers 237–8
    see also paid search ads
Khan, R. et al. 269, 272, 273, 279–80, 282, 283
Kim, H.S. and Yoon, C.H. 136
Kim, J. and Pollard, D. 102
Kim, J. et al. 200
Kim, Y.S. 133
Kim, Y.S. et al. 12, 25, 80, 106,
k-means 17
k-nearest neighbors 121, 125
k-rank 50, 56, 57
knowledge 42, 46, 58, 159
knowledge discovery from databases (KDD) 13–14
    see also data mining
knowledge engineering 70
Koenker, R. 98, 99
Koenker, R. and Machado, J.A.F. 100
Kohavi, R. and John, G.H. 28
Koller, D. and Murphy, K. 74
Kolmogorov-Smirnov test 28
Kononenko, I. 78
Kopalle, P.K. et al. 275
Koren, Y. et al. 170, 176
Koren, Y. and Bell, R. 171, 176, 181
Kottas, A. and Gelfand, A.E. 100
Kotz, S. et al. 100
Kraaij, W. and Pohlmann, R. 46
Kumar, V. et al. 11, 256, 257
Kuncheva, L.I. 122
Kuncheva, L.I. and Rodriguez, J.J. 130
Kuncheva, L.I. and Whitaker, C.J. 134
Kuncheva, L.I. et al. 126

Lagrange multipliers 154
Lai, C. et al. 126
Lakshminarayan, K. et al. 16, 80
Lam, W. and Bacchus, F. 67, 72, 73
Langley, P. and Sage, S. 77, 78
Langville, A.N. et al. 53
Laplace 99, 100, 102
Larivière, B. and Van den Poel, D. 132
Larrañaga, P. et al. 67, 73
latent factor models 170, 171, 172–7

latent semantic indexing (LSI) 49
latent states 274
latent trait 271
Lauritzen, S.L. 81
Le Blanc, M. and Tibshirani, R. 171
'leaky-bucket' method 238
learning 74, 184, 200
    Bayesian network 70, 80ff.
    consumer 181, 191, 192
    rule-based 145–6
        see also rule extraction
learning method 27, 79
learning set 74
least squares regression 106, 107
Lee, D.D. and Seung, H.S. 52, 53, 54
Lee, Ha et al. 218
Lee, J. et al. 171
Lee, T.Y. and Bradlow, E.T. 57
legacies 291, 295
legal incentives 145
Legarson, F. 296
lemmatization 46
Lemmens, A. and Croux, C. 12, 18, 26, 112,
    133
Lessmann and Voss 27, 28, 34
letters 41, 292, 296
Lewis, M. 272
Li, C. et al. 272, 274, 282, 275
Li, S. et al. 110
LibB 84, 87
lifetime value 104, 299 see also customer
    lifetime value (CLV)
lift 31, 32, 34, 87, 113, 122, 137
    top-decile 117
likelihood function 98
Likert scales 177, 294
Lima, E. et al. 160
linear city model 201
linear discriminant analysis 124
linear model 97, 99
linear regression 106, 108, 109, 121
linear response model 83
linear scaling 22
Ling, C.X. and Li, C. 26, 31, 83
link farms 230
linking 260
list 82, 83, 86

literature 56, 57, 83, 108, 131–3, 149, 167,
    177, 182, 184, 190ff., 236, 256, 275,
    296
Little, R.J. and Rubin, D.B. 16
Littman, M.L. 269
Liu, H. and Tan, S.T. 151
Liu, H. et al. 23, 24
loading 50, 52, 54
location-based services 190, 198–9, 217
Lodish, L.M. 273
logarithm 22, 47
logarithmic transformation 106
logistic regression (LR) model 83, 85, 86,
    112, 113, 117, 128, 133
logit models 12, 18, 83, 219, 220
    binary 29, 32, 112
    empirical results 31, 32
LogitBoost 128, 132
log-transformation 22, 23, 33, 138
long-term benefits 275
loopy-belief propagation 74
Lops, P. et al. 170
loss function 100, 121, 183
Lovejoy, W.S. 273
Lovins, J. 46
low-value customers 275
Lynch, J.G. and Ariely, D. 200

McCall, J. 201
McFadden, D. 177
machine learning 70, 80, 182, 183
McKenzie, L.W. 275
mail-order catalogs 68, 83, 86, 236–7, 273ff.,
    283
majority voting 122, 123, 124
Malthouse, E.C. 12
Malthouse, E.C. and Blattberg, R.C. 105, 106,
    109
management 2
Manchandar, P. et al. 212, 215
Maniar, N. et al. 200
Manski, C.F. 101–2, 196
Margineantu, D.D. and Dietterich, T.G. 134
marketers 6, 42, 43, 210, 229, 242, 243, 249,
    287
marketing 273, 282
    customer optimization 265–6ff.

expenditures 282
historical 266, 267ff.
and mobile apps 189ff.
multiple approaches 273
and non-profit sector 287ff.
see also direct marketing
marketing analysis 57
Marketing Science 248
Markov Chain Monte Carlo (MCMC) 102, 103, 182, 183
Markov models, and dynamic optimixation 269, 271
Martens, D. et al. 20, 136, 145, 146, 153
Masand, B. et al. 136
mathematics 18, 24, 148, 149, 273
matrix 221
    concept-term similarity 50
    high-dimensional 42, 45, 48–9
    maximum margin 171
    non-negative 52ff., 171
    probabilistic 171
    term-by-document 43, 48
matrix factorization methods 170–71, 181, 182
    and bilinear component 176–7
Maudes, J. et al. 120, 121
Maximum A Posteriori (MAP) 182, 183
Maximum Score Estimator 101–2
Mayzlin, D. 259
Mayzlin, D. et al. 249, 259
Mayzlin, D. and Yoganarasimhan, H. 260
mean absolute deviation (MAD) 108
mean combination 122
mean regression 110
mean squared error 108
mean values 16–17, 80, 97, 98, 99, 253
mean/mode replacement 17
measurement 18, 30, 74, 215, 235, 250, 254
median 97, 99, 100, 109, 114
Melville, P. et al. 171
memory-based methods 170
Mercer theorem 154
merge operators 82
Merler, S. et al. 127
message framing 296
meta model 123
methodologies 1, 2, 3

methods 117, 120, 170–71, 182, 283
metrics 250ff. *see also* measurement
Metropolis-Hastings scheme 102–103, 182
microblogs 197
Mierswa, I. et al. 58
Miller, G.A. and Newman, E.B. 45
Miller, J. and Krosnick, J. 200
minimization problem 100
Minimum Description Length (MDL) 67, 68, 72, 73
missing data 177–8
missing values 15–18, 29, 86
    and Bayesian networks 67, 68, 80–82, 86, 92
    evolutionary (EBN) 84
Mitchell, P.M. et al. 44
Miyahara, K. and Pazzani, M. 170
mobile internet 189–202
    apps 189–90
        advertising 190, 194, 195
            and web 194–5, 201, 202
        charging 192–3
        consumer behaviour 189, 191–2, 196–7
        consumer demand for 192–4
        free 192, 193
        peer influence 195–6
    channels 201–2
    portal sites 191
    user-generated content 191, 192, 197–8
mobile operators 191
mobile phones, and charity donations 292
mode 74
modeling 3, 14, 15
moderate-value customers 275
Moe, W. 219, 220
M-of-N rules 147, 158
Mokbel, M.F. and Levandoski, J.J. 180
monetary value 97, 293
Monte Carlo Expectation Maximization (MCEM) 183
Montgomery, D.B. et al. 273
Monti, S. and Cooper, G.F. 80
Montoya, R. et al. 272, 273, 274, 281, 282, 283, 284
Moore, R.S. et al. 217
Moore, S.G. 249

Mortensen, D. 201
Mosteller, F. and Tukey, J.W. 98
Mountain, D. et al. 199
movie rating prediction 119
movie recommendations 167, 172ff.
   data 168, 172
   online user reviews 255
   ratings matrix 169
movie scripts 57
Mozer, M.C. et al. 117, 131, 132
'multi-armed bandit' method 269, 271
MultiBoost 128, 130, 132
multichannel fundraising 299, 300
multichannel retailing 201
   display ads 214–15
Multilayer Perceptron (MLP) neural network
   148
multiple classifier systems 117, 118, 119
   see also ensemble learners
multiple regression analysis 83
multiple targeting methods 222, 273
multiplicative update (MU) 53–4
multivariate approach 17, 19, 24
music apps 189, 192
music recommendations 119, 167
mutation operators 82
Myers, J.W. et al. 68
myopic optimization 268, 271, 277, 278, 279

Naik, P.A. et al. 213
Nair, H. et al. 195
naive models 109, 113
   Bayesian 76–9, 80, 85
      ensemble learner 121
Nam, S. et al. 195
Narayanan, S. and Kalyanam, K. 235, 236
National Advertising Initiative 218
Nauck, D. 151, 153
Nefclass 149, 151–3
negative comments 253, 261
negative experience 249, 295
negative manipulation 260
negative values 85, 100, 106
neighbourhood-based methods 170
Nerlove, M. and Arrow, K.J. 212, 238
Neslin, S.A. et al. 11, 12, 34, 117, 131, 136,
   271, 272, 273, 277–9, 282

Neslin, S.A. and Shankar, V. 214
Netflix 167, 171, 176, 181
   dataset estimation 182, 183
network density 197
network structure changes 67, 68
Netzer, O. et al. 253
neural networks 12, 18, 22n., 31, 32, 75, 83,
   160
   Bayesian (BNN) 85, 86
   decompositional rule extraction from
      146, 148–53
      decision tables 158–60
   ensemble learners 121, 125, 132, 133
neurons 148, 149, 150, 151
neurorule 149, 150–51
new customers 111, 256
new items 171, 175
new products/services 193–4, 195
new users 171, 174, 175
New York Times 231, 249
news 260
newsgroups 252
N-gram stemming 46
Niculescu-Mizil, A. et al. 21
nominal attributes 18
non-hybrid ensembles 121, 133
non-linear relationships 22n., 23, 53, 124,
   138, 149, 153
non-negative double singular value
      decomposition (NNDSVD) 53
non-negative matrix factorization (NMF)
   52–6
non-parametric discriminant analysis
      (NDA) 130
non-profit sector 287–300
   mult-channel approach 291–2
non-purchases 178, 179
NP-hard 73, 74
numeric attributes 15, 21–4, 28, 29, 33
   empirical results 31
Nunamaker, J.F. et al. 200
Nuñez, H. et al. 155

Obermiller, C. 296
O'Brien, T.V. 11
observer 247, 253–4
offline advertising 195, 212, 215

display ads 213
offline purchases 198
O'Hara, K. et al. 199
online advertising 195
    and offline sales 215
    see also mobile internet
online communities 216, 251ff.
online customer reviews 57
online data 2, 41
online discussion forums 252
online learning 181, 182, 200
online purchases 198-9
online revenues 215
online reviews 253, 255
online survey panel 277
open-source software 58, 139
opinion leaders 257-9
optimal contact models 277ff., 283
optimal dimension selection 56-7
optimal policy function 270
optimality principle 271
optimization 81, 83, 184, 271
    problem 154
oracle 123, 146, 161
Orange 29
ordering-based measure 109
ordinal preferences data 177, 178
ordinary least squares (OLS) 97, 98, 99, 108
organic search 6, 195, 229ff., 238, 242
Orsenigo, C. and Vercellis, C. 27
orthogonal transformation 22, 25
outliers 15-16, 97
outputs
    continuous 122
    label 122
outside characteristics 296
overfitting 183
oversampling 26

Paatero, P. and Tapper, U. 52
pageviews 213, 219, 222
paid search ads 195, 229-43
    auctions 231
    and CLV 239
    data 232, 233ff., 237
    and direct marketing 232-6
    keywords 232, 233

    branded 195, 237, 238
    data analysis 234ff.
    generic 237, 238, 239
    long-tail 241-2
    text mining model 240-41
long-term approach 233, 236-9
models 234-6, 240-41
and organic search 242
placement 231, 234, 236
and return visits 239
and spillover 229, 238-9
Palmisano, C. et al. 180
Pan, X. et al. 201, 241
parallel programming 183
parameter learning 68, 80
parameter values 67, 81, 276-7
parametric choice models 105, 121
Pareto-optimal solutions 83
partial dependence plots 137-8
partially observed Markov decision process
    (POMDP) 271, 281, 282
participant 247, 250, 253, 258, 259, 260-61
particle filtering 181
part-of-speech tagging 43, 44-5
past behaviour 26, 105, 111, 224, 238, 289,
    293, 294
past observations 12, 70, 231, 233
past purchases 11, 14
Payne, J.W. et al. 180
pay-per-click 231, 233 *see also* cost-per-click
    (CPC)
pedagogical rule extraction 146, 147, 156ff.
peer influence 195-6
Peña et al. 68
Penn TreeBank1 44
percentage of correctly classified test
    instances (PCC) 145, 160
percentage variance 56
performance 282
    and ensemble learners 117-18ff., 123-4,
    139-40
    and rule extraction 153
permutation accuracy importance 136
personal distress 295
personality traits 294-5
personalization 222, 296-8
personally identifiable information (PII) 225

persuasiveness 256
Petrison, L.A. et al. 81, 82, 83
philanthropy 294
photos 191, 198
physicians 256, 258, 281–2
pictures 296, 298
Planned Behaviour Theory 294
platforms 201, 202, 250
Podolny, J.M. and Baron, J.N. 252
Poisson model 213–14, 222
Porter, M.F. 46
position (of paid search ads) 231, 234, 236
positive experience 249
positive partition test 155
posterior density 102, 103
posterior distribution 182
posterior probability 122
predictions 122, 131, 293ff.
    of CLV 105, 108–9
    of SVM 153
predictive models 1, 3, 11, 14, 15, 175
    accuracy 27
    alternative methods 16
        empirical results 31
    and charity donors 293–6
    ensemble learners 131, 133
    and preprocessing 12
preferences *see* user preferences
    see also private donors
premium 296, 297
premium mobile services 192
preprocessing *see* data preprocessing
prescription drugs 256, 258, 281–2
Price, L.L. et al. 248
prices 200, 210, 211
primacy effects 200
principal component analysis (PCA) 24–5,
        49, 52
    ensemble classifiers 130, 134
Prinzie, A. and Van den Poel, D. 132
privacy 192, 232
private donors 287
    acquisition of 288–90, 298
    legacy 291, 295
    major 290, 291
    preferences of 296
    psychological traits of 294–5

reactivation of 291
regular 290, 292
response rate 298, 299
retention of 290–91, 299
single 290, 291
target selection 293–6
private sector 287, 288
probability 67, 75, 86, 104, 122, 135
    churn 111, 112
    purchase 179, 266, 269, 276, 277ff.
probit models 18, 112, 276
problem context 283
product attributes 57
product characteristics 259
    public visibility 250
    and social media interactions 249–50
product choices 104, 105
product data 178
profits 104, 105, 111, 184, 192, 232, 233,
        235, 239, 268, 270, 271, 280, 285
promotion strategies 279–80, 283
promotional chat 259
promotional offers 219
propositional rules 147, 150
prospects 290
prototype vectors 155
proximity 296
pruning 21, 118, 121, 134, 150, 151, 153
psychological data 180, 258, 294, 295
purchase 266, 269, 276
    behaviour 212ff., 294
    frequency 212
    intentions 217
    multi-channel 214–15
    and search ads 195, 210
purchase data 169, 178, 183, 219
Pyle, D. 19, 22, 23

Qi, J.Y. et al. 136
QR decomposition 49
quadratic programming (QP) 155
quantile regression 97–114
    advantages of 97, 114
    Bayesian method 98, 100–101, 103, 112,
        114
    binary dependent variables 101–3
    case studies 103–14

churn prediction 103–14
  CLV model 103–10
  frequentist method 98–100, 102
  research 98
  software 114
quantitative models 11, 12
  text mining 41, 42ff.
quantity 269
questionnaires 293, 296
Quinlan, J.R. 151, 156, 157, 158

Radcliffe, Richard 291
Ramoni, M. and Sebastinani, P. 68, 81
random coefficient 193
random effects 174, 175, 176, 181
Random Forest model 17, 27, 29, 30, 31, 32,
    120, 216
  ensemble learners 121, 122, 126–7
    in database marketing 132ff.
      variables 136–7
  software 139
random initializations 53
random instance weighting 125
random missing data 16
random projections (RP) 130
random sampling 25, 74, 120, 136
random search 124
Random Subspace Method (RSM) 118, 122,
    125–6, 134, 135
random utility discrete choice models 177
random values 81, 84, 85, 86
random variables 3, 67, 68, 69, 73, 120
rankings 83, 86, 135, 200, 230, 231
RapidMiner 29, 58, 139
Rapoport, A. and Horvath, W.J. 252
ratings 169, 170, 253
  data 172
Ratner, B. 28
raw data 18, 22
raw text
  cleaning 43, 44
  tokenization 43, 44
real time 1, 2, 5, 189, 196, 198ff., 231, 250,
    254
recall 251
receiver 247
receiver operating curve (ROC) 145

recency 1, 266, 276, 293
recency-frequency-monetary model (RFM)
    1, 2, 11, 33, 82, 111, 266, 268ff., 272,
    274, 281, 284, 293ff.
  and donor prediction 293
  variables 33, 289
recoding 18, 31, 33
recommendations 2, 6, 18, 119, 167ff.
recommender systems 167–85
  and active learning 184
  components 168
  and context 177, 178, 183
  data 168–9
  hybrid 171ff.
  literature 167, 169
  methods 170–71
  purpose of 167–8
  user models 167, 169ff.
    collaborative filtering 170–71, 176
    content-based 169–70, 176
    general model 175–7ff.
    hierarchical multilinear 181
    latent factor models 172–7
records 3, 4, 17, 67ff., 80, 84, 86, 197
  see also incomplete records
Red Cross, American 290, 292
referrals 256, 257, 260–61
regression 2, 13, 15, 33, 80, 98, 105, 173, 178,
    252, 274
  hierarchical 172
  linear 27
  logistic 83, 85, 86
  and missing values 17
  model 269
  see also quantile regression
regulation 225
Reichheld, F.F. 110
Reichheld, F.F. and Sasser, W.E. 111
Reichheld, F.F. et al. 11
Reinartz, W.J. and Kumar, V. 108
Reingen, P.H. and Kernan, J.B. 254
relationship marketing 1, 224, 239
Rennie, J. and Srebro, N. 171
resampling 56–7, 75, 120
research 12, 17, 34, 41, 42, 58, 98, 104, 108,
    181, 190, 193ff., 212, 215, 219, 241,
    248, 271

see also future research; literature
researchers 41, 97, 105, 167, 213, 232, 251
response models 82–3, 86, 87, 210, 213, 274, 275, 277, 279, 284
response rates, and charity donors 298, 299
response variables 97, 99, 113
restaurant reviews 255–6
results 13ff., 31ff., 44, 45, 67, 72, 78, 81, 84, 87, 92, 106ff., 112ff., 118, 121, 131, 133, 159, 231, 256ff., 271, 275, 296, 299
retailers 199, 201, 219ff., 279
return on investment (ROI) 210, 211, 219, 225
Reuters 224
revenue 298, 299
reward programs 273, 279, 280
Ricci, F. et al. 167
ringtone paid ads 240–41
risk 183, 224–5, 256
Rissanen, J. 72
Risselada, H. et al. 132
Rodriguez, J.J. et al. 130, 135
Rokach, L. 134
rolling horizon 271, 277–8, 284
Ross, S. 271
Rosset, S. et al. 11
Rossi, P.E. et al. 98, 106
Rotation Forest 118, 120, 122, 130
    in database marketing 132, 133ff.
    and diversity 134, 135
rotation-based ensemble classifiers 130–31, 133
RotBoost 120, 130, 133
Rubens, N. et al. 184
Rubin, D.B. 16, 80
Rud, O.P. 86
rule extraction 146–62
    case study 160–62
    decision tables 158–60
    decompositional 146, 147, 148ff., 153ff.
    pedagogical 146, 147, 156ff.
rules 5, 21, 46, 71, 75, 80, 83, 122, 136, 146, 147, 219
Rutz, O.J. and Bucklin, R.E. 195, 212, 215, 238
Rutz, O.J. and Trusov, M. 57, 240
Rutz, O.J. et al. 235, 236, 239

Salakhutdinov, R. and Mnih, A. 171, 182, 183
sales 97, 190, 210, 215, 237, 254, 256
sales force management 273
Salford Systems' Predictive Modeling Suite 28–9, 139
Salop, S.C. 201
Salton, G. 42, 47
Salton, G. and Buckley, C. 47
sampling 14, 25–6, 120, 273, 281, 282
Sanders, J. and Kandrot, E. 183
Sargeant, A. 287
Sargeant, A. and Shang, J. 288
Sarwar, B. et al. 170
SAS Enterprise Miner 28, 139
SAS Text Miner 58
scalability 147, 170, 171, 182, 283
Schafer, J.L. and Graham, J.W. 68, 80
Schmid, C.H. et al. 17
Schmittlein, D.C. et al. 266, 283
Schwenk, H. and Bengio, Y. 121
score-and-search approach 67, 70, 72–3
scoring 67, 72–3, 83, 136, 231
Scott, S.L. 271
scree plot approach 56
screen sizes 200
search ads 57, 195, 200
    see also paid search ads
search behaviour, mobile 200–201
search costs, mobile 199–201
search decisions, online 220
search engine marketing (SEM) 229
search engine optimization (SEO) 229, 230–31
search engine results page (SERP) 229, 230, 231, 232, 242
Search Engine Watch 237
search engines 195 *see also* paid search ads
search methods 67, 68, 81, 82, 158
search problem 73
search queries 119, 221, 222, 237–8ff.
    branded 237, 238
    generic 237ff.
search results 222
'second gift conversion rate' 299
second-price auctions 231
seeding strategies 258

Seemingly Unrelated Regression (SUR) 173, 178
segmentation 13, 109, 222, 280, 281, 296
self-enhancement 249
self-initiated purchases 179
semantics 236, 239
sender 247, 248, 249, 250, 296
sensitivity 145
sentiments 224
sequential member training 121
sequential tests 56
Setiono, R. 151
Setiono, R. and Liu, H. 150
Setiono, R. et al. 136, 151
Shamdasani, P.N. et al. 217
Shang, J. and Croson, R. 299
Shankar, V. and Balasubramanian, S. 201
Shankar, V. et al. 200, 201
Shaw, M.J. et al. 136
Sherman, L. and Deighton, J. 218
Shim, J.P. et al. 199
Shin, H. and Cho, S. 31
Shmueli, G. and Koppius, O.R. 26
Sill, J. et al. 171
Simester, D.I. et al. 237, 272, 274, 282
similarity 170, 196, 221
simplicity 78, 170, 269
simulation 182, 278
simultaneity 196
Singh, M. and Provan 78
singly-connected network 73
singular value decomposition (SVD) 49–52, 80, 170
Sinisalo, J. 201
skewness 25, 30, 31, 33
Skurichina, M. and Duin, R.P.W. 126
Slater, P. 176
smartphones 194, 197, 201
Smith, K.A. et al. 117
SMS 191, 194, 197, 292
Snowball framework 46
social class 107, 108
social contagion 196, 197
social interactions 196, 247, 248
    management of 253–61
    and product characteristics 249–50
social media 190ff., 247–62, 292

and causality 254–5
data collection 250–53
definition of 247
and loss of control 261
metrics 250ff., 253–4
social interactions 247, 248–9
    management of 253ff.
    see also social networks
social networks 2, 41, 58, 189, 190, 252
    and consumer behaviour 191ff., 196–7
    peer influence 195–6
sociodemographic data 293, 294, 295
sociological theories 251–2
sociometric techniques 257, 258
software 12, 28–9, 42, 58, 114, 139, 167, 183
song recommendations 183, 184
Sparck Jones, K. 47
sparse random projections (SRP) 130
Spatz, C. and Johnston, J.O. 71
special offers 233
specificity 145
spillover effects 195, 229, 238–9
Spirtes, P. et al. 67, 71, 72
SPSS Modeler 139
stability 170
stacking 171
standard deviations 87, 92
states 269–71, 274ff., 284
    multiple instruments 273
    RFM 274
    transitions 269, 280, 282
    variables 269, 271, 273
state-space models 181
statistical analysis approach 83
statistical hypothesis tests 28
statistical stemmers 46
statistical models 2, 15, 81, 168, 170
steady state 275, 284
stemming 46
Stephen, A. et al. 197
Stigler, G. 201
stochastic gradient boosting 119, 129–30, 132, 182
    software 139
stochastic models 276, 283
stochastic search 67, 82
stochastic variables 99, 276

stopwords 45
strategic manipulation 259–60
Strobl, C. et al. 136, 137
structural approximation 74
Structural Expectation-Maximization (SEM) 68, 81
structural holes 251
structure learning 68
structured data 42
Su, X. and Koshgoftaar, T.M. 167
Su, X. et al. 171
subsampling 102
subsets 120, 283
Sultan, F. et al. 201
Sun, B. and Li, S. 272, 273
Sun, B. et al. 284
Sun, M. 253
supervised learning 11–12, 15, 24, 117
support vector machines (SVM) 117
    and rule extraction 146
        decompositional 153–6
        plus prototype 155
surfing behaviour 199
surveys 210, 216, 254, 257–8, 277–8, 295, 296
Susarla, a. et al. 195
Suzuki, J. 72
switching methods 171
symbolic learning algorithm 157
symbolic rules 146, 149
symbols 24

TAN learning 79–80, 85, 86
Tan, K.C. et al. 136
Tanner, M. and Wong, W.H. 102
target variables 12, 15, 20, 24, 27
targeting 190, 293ff.
task definition 13
TBT 31, 32, 33
telemarketing 292
TEMIS 58
temporal factors 181, 191 see also time
Teradata Center 117, 119
term filtering 45–6
term vector weighting 47–8
test documents 52
testing, and donor campaigns 298
testing set 75

text ads 232, 240
text messaging 191, 194, 197, 292
text mining 41, 42–57
    applications 57
    paid search ads 240–41
    and text preprocessing 42–3
textual customer data 41–63, 253
    analysis 42ff.
        unpopularity of 42
    literature on 57
    research 41
    software 42, 58
thermometer encoding 150
Thomas, L.C. et al. 20
three-way analysis 180
'through-the-line' campaigns 291
ties 197, 251–2
time 181, 191, 196, 212, 213, 236, 238, 274
    and CLV 265, 266ff.
time horizon 270
tokenization 44
tracking 250, 254
trade-off 251, 269
Train, K. 177
trained neural network 146, 150
training data, and ensemble learners 120, 121, 122
training document 52, 57
training set 74, 75, 77, 87, 105, 111
    ensemble learners 124, 136
translucency 146
transportation costs 201
travel behaviour 199
tree-augmented structures 79, 80
tree-based methods 12, 20–21, 32, 80, 157, 160
    pruning 21, 118
TreeBoost 130
Trepan 157–8, 160, 161
trimming 125
Tripadvisor.com 249, 260
Trusov, M. et al. 191
Tucker, C. 195
Tucker, L.R. 176
'turnpike property' 275, 284
Twitter 192, 196, 198, 216, 247, 251, 253, 257, 258

UCI Machine Learning Repository 22, 118, 131, 135, 136, 137, 138
unary data 169, 178–9
undersampling 26
United States 229, 287
univariate approach 16, 20–21, 23, 24
unstructured data 42
unsupervised methods 24, 117
upselling 119, 290
URLs 229, 232, 238, 240
    personalized 296
US Census 29ff., 33
Usenet 253
user characteristics, and display ads 216–17
user forums 251
user model 167, 169–70
    mobile apps 192, 193
user preferences 167, 168, 169, 170
    contextual modeling 180–81
    and display ads 219
    evolution of 181–2
    item selection model 183–4
utility function 169, 219, 276

validation set 105, 111, 159
Van den Bulte, C. and Lilien, G. 196
Van den Poel, D. and Larivière, B. 111
Van der Lans, R. et al. 241
Van Slyke, D.M. and Brooks, A.C. 293, 294
Van Wagner, M. 236
van Wezel, M. and Potharst, R. 132
Vanthienen, J. and Wets, G. 159, 160
Vanthienen, J. et al. 159
Vapnik, V.N. 153
variable importance measures 136–7
variables 12, 18, 24, 33, 68, 70, 83, 97, 99, 111, 126, 136–7, 150, 255, 269ff., 279ff.
    dyad-specific 172, 173ff.
    item-specific 172, 174, 175
    latent 176, 182
    observed 172, 176
    unobserved 172, 173
vectors 175, 193
    aggregation 48
    quantization 49
    test 52

    training 52
    weighting 47–8
vector-space approach 42, 43
Venkatesan, R. and Kumar, V. 104
Venkatesan, R. et al. 104
Verbeke, D. et al. 11, 19, 26, 28, 34, 160
Verhaert, G. 288, 289
Verhaert, G. and Van den Poel, D. 297
Verhaert, G. et al. 289
Verhoef, P. and Donkers, B. 104
verification 159
Veropoulos, K. et al. 26
Vestergaard, T. and Schroder, K. 241
viral campaign 256
volume-based metrics 252

Wagging 125, 128
WAP 194
Watts, D. and Strogatz, S. 197
weak ties 197, 251
wear-in 266, 267ff.
wear-out 213, 214, 222, 223, 266ff., 280
web advertising 194–5, 200, 217
    and mobile apps 194, 195
    targeting 219–20ff.
    see also internet
Webb, G.I. 128
websites 167, 191, 201–2
    behaviour targeting in 219–20
    target 218
    visitor metrics 210
    see also web advertising
weight of evidence (WOE) 20, 29, 31, 32, 33
weighting 47–8, 171
    augmented normalized 47
    binary frequency 47
    ensemble learners 122
    logarithmic 47
Weiss, G.M. 26
Weiss, S.M. and Kulikowski, C.A. 74, 75, 76
WEKA 29, 58, 139
West, P.M. et al. 12
white box models 145
Wild, S. et al. 53
Wilson, J. and Musick, M. 294
Wojnicki, A. and Godes, D. 249
Wong, M.L. et al. 67, 73

Wong, M.L. and Leung, K.S. 67, 81
word of mouth (WOM) 192, 247, 248
  and causality 254–5
  manipulation of 259–60
  metrics 250ff.
  and product characteristics 249–50
  and sales 255–6
  variables 255
Wordnet 44
WordStat 58
words 42ff., 221
wrappers 27–8

Xie, Y.Y. et al. 132, 134
Xue, G.-R. et al. 170

Yahoo 183, 201, 222, 229
Yan, J. et al. 221, 222
Yang, S. and Ghose, A. 195, 200, 242
Yao, S. and Mela, C. 195, 200, 232

Yelp 198
Ying, Y. et al. 177, 178, 182
Yu, K. and Moyeed, R. 100, 102, 103
Yu, K. and Stander, J. 100
Yu, K. and Zhang, J. 100, 103
Yu, K. et al. 171

Zahavi, J. and Levin, N. 83
Zeithaml, V.A. et al. 104, 105, 108, 109
Zellner, A. 173
Zhang, C.X. and Zhang, J.S. 127, 130
Zhang, J. and Krishnamurthi, L. 269, 271, 272
Zhang, J. and Wedel, M. 271, 272, 281
Zhang, X. 198
Zheng, S. 112
Zio, M.D. et al. 80
Zipf, G.K. 45
Zoltners, A.A. and Sinha, P. 273
z-scores 22, 33